Factor Analysis and Related Techniques

INTERNATIONAL HANDBOOKS OF QUANTITATIVE APPLICATIONS IN THE SOCIAL SCIENCES

Including selected volumes originally published as Quantitative Applications in the Social Sciences (QASS)—a Sage University Papers series

Series Editor: **Michael S. Lewis-Beck,** *University of Iowa*

Factor Analysis and Related Techniques

Michael S. Lewis-Beck
editor

International Handbooks of Quantitative Applications
in the Social Sciences
Volume 5

SAGE Publications
Toppan Publishing

For information address:

SAGE Publications Ltd.
6 Bonhill Street
London EC2A 4PU
United Kingdom

SAGE Publications, Inc.
2455 Teller Road
Thousand Oaks, California 91320
United States

SAGE Publications India Pvt. Ltd.
M-32 Market
Greater Kailash I
New Delhi 110 048 India

Printed in Singapore

British Library Cataloguing in Publication Data

Main entry under title:

Factor Analysis and Related Techniques.—(International
Handbooks of Quantitative Applications in
the Social Sciences; Vol. 5)
   I. Lewis-Beck, Michael S. II. Series
   519.5
   ISBN 0-8039-5431-X

94   95   96   97   98   10   9   8   7   6   5   4   3   2   1

Sage Production Editor : Susan McElroy

CONTENTS

Editor's Introduction   viii
    by Michael S. Lewis-Beck

Part I: **Introduction to Factor Analysis:**
            What It Is and How to Do It
            by Jae-On Kim and Charles W. Mueller

    1. Introduction   1
    2. Logical Foundations of Factor Analysis   6
    3. Obtaining Factor Analysis Solutions   40
        Note   64
        Questions Pertaining to Books, Journals, and
            Computer Programs   65
        References   65
        Glossary   69

Part II: **Factor Analysis:**
            Statistical Methods and Practical Issues
            by Jae-On Kim and Charles W. Mueller

    1. Introduction   75
    2. Methods of Extracting Initial Factors   80
    3. Methods of Rotation   97
    4. Number of Factors Problem Revisited   109
    5. Introduction to Confirmatory Factor Analysis   114
    6. Construction of Factor Scales   128
    7. Brief Answers to Questions Frequently Asked   141
        References   146
        Glossary   150

Part III: Principal Components Analysis
by George H. Dunteman

1. Introduction   157
2. Basic Concepts of Principal Components Analysis   165
3. Geometrical Properties of Principal Components   173
4. Decomposition Properties of the Principal Components   192
5. Principal Components of Patterned Correlation Matrices   195
6. Rotation of Principal Components   198
7. Using Principal Components to Select a Subset of Variables   200
8. Principal Components Versus Factor Analysis   205
9. Uses of Principal Components in Regression Analysis   215
10. Using Principal Components to Detect Outlying and Influential Observations   225
11. Use of Principal Components in Cluster Analysis   228
12. Use of Principal Components Analysis in Conjunction with Other Multivariate Analysis Procedures   230
13. Other Techniques Related to Principal Components   237
14. Summary and Conclusions   242
    References   244

Part IV: Confirmatory Factor Analysis: A Preface to LISREL
by J. Scott Long

Notation   247
Preface   249
1. Introduction   251
2. Specification of the Confirmatory Factor Model   258
3. Identification of the Confirmatory Factor Model   274
4. Estimation of the Confirmatory Factor Model   296
5. Assessment of Fit in the Confirmatory Factor Model   301
6. Conclusions   319
    Appendix I: Correlations and Standard Deviations from Wheaton/Hennepin Sample   322
    Appendix II: Software to Estimate the Confirmatory Factor Model (CFM)   322
    Notes   323
    References   326

**Part V: Covariance Structure Models:
An Introduction to LISREL**
by J. Scott Long

Notation   329
Preface   331
1. Introduction   333
2. The Measurement Model   341
3. The Structural Equation Model   347
4. The Covariance Structure Model   377
5. Conclusion   405
Appendix: Covariance/Correlation Matrices for Examples
408
Notes   410
References   411

Index   415

About the Editor   422

About the Authors   423

EDITOR'S INTRODUCTION

Social science concepts usually have different parts, aspects, or facets. More formally, we may say that a concept is composed of dimensions, components, or factors. Take, for example, the concept of "democracy." A political scientist might suspect the concept can be separated into four factors: the Economic, the Social, the Cultural, the Political. Then, he or she may attempt to measure nations, according to the quantity of each factor they possess. Perhaps the available measures are indicators in various statistical yearbooks, and number in the hundreds. The difficulty becomes which measures to select, in order to represent empirically the factors under study. How to make sense of all these data, reducing it in order, reducing it in orderly fashion? Factor analysis is the solution most widely employed.

Consider now the hypothetical example of Grace Grey, an organizational psychologist studying Job Satisfaction. She gives a paper-and-pencil survey to 200 employees in a business office, including thirty-five closed-ended questions on different aspects of satisfaction in the workplace. The responses to these items provide a rather unwieldy set of thirty-five variables, whose patterns of relationship are difficult to discern from the covariance or correlation matrices. To reduce these observed variables to a smaller set of hypothetical (unobserved) variables, she applies an *exploratory factor analysis* (EFA), lucidly explicated in our first paper by Kim and Mueller.

Utilizing a *varimax orthogonal rotation* she extracts two *factors* (i.e., two have an *eigenvalue* greater than one). The first factor is dominated by items 6, 14, and 8, as indicated by their high *factor loadings*. Since these items each appear to measure, in some way, attitudes about financial reward, she labels the factor Material Satisfaction. The second factor is dominated by items 9, 17, 25, and 32, which all ask something about praise from superiors. She labels this factor Symbolic Satisfaction. Lastly, she creates a factor scale for each of these new (and unobserved) variables—Material Satisfaction and Symbolic Satisfaction.

In sum, Grey has reduced the data pile from thirty-five variables to two, and seemingly identified two distinct factors of job satisfaction. Did Grey make the right choices in executing this EFA? The answer depends on whether the logical and statistical requirements, which Kim and Mueller fully spell out in their second paper, are met. Among other things, EFA requires that observed variables are linear combinations of unobserved factors. Principal components analysis (PCA), in contrast, has no requirement of underlying, unobserved factors.

While PCA is often regarded as a type of factor analysis, there are differences. PCA aims to account for the total variation in the observed variables, while EFA aims to account only for the common variance. Still, both are common techniques for data reduction. If Grey applied a PCA to these data, the eigenvalues may show, again, that just the first two components have utility. In the third paper, Dunteman presents PCA in mathematical and geometric detail, sprinkling the text liberally with helpful examples. He also draws out the links between PCA and factor analysis, as well as the related data-reduction methods of cluster analysis, discriminant analysis, correspondence analysis, and canonical correlation.

While PCA is less demanding than EFA in terms of underlying causal assumptions, confirmatory factor analysis (CFA) is more so. CFA is guided by hypotheses, such as expectations about the number of factors, the magnitude of factor loadings, the correlation of certain error terms. In other words, CFA poses constraints on relationships within the models, then examines whether sample estimates *confirm* the constraints (hypotheses). For example, Grey may have initially hypothesized that there were three Job Satisfaction factors—Material, Symbolic, and Moral. She might also have had hypotheses about which items would load high on what factors, and which items might have common sources of error. If this were her initial orientation, CFA, which Long masterfully unfolds in the fourth paper, would have been the methodology preferred over EFA.

In CFA, the correlation between factors can be estimated. For instance, suppose Grey hypothesized a correlation between the factors of Material and Symbolic Satisfaction (but not between Material and Moral, or Symbolic and Moral). Even if the hypothesis is confirmed by a CFA, Grey may want to know more. In particular, she might wish to estimate the structural relationship between Material and Symbolic Satisfaction. What is the causal connection between the two? Does

Material Satisfaction determine Symbolic, or vice-versa? And what are the structural coefficient estimates? If these estimates are sought, what other variables or constraints need to be brought to the model in order to satisfy the requisite of *identification*?

Fortunately, the last paper, also by Long, deals fully with these issues. With *covariance structure models* one postulates a system of equations representing the causal relationship among a set of unobserved variables, following well-established traditions in econometrics. Moreover, the unobserved variables are built along CFA lines. This approach is known popularly as LISREL, after the name of the computer program developed by Jöreskog and his colleagues. LISREL achieves the highest level of sophistication for factor analysis, embedding within the techniques of structural equation modeling.

—Michael S. Lewis-Beck
Series Editor

INTRODUCTION TO FACTOR ANALYSIS
What It Is and How to Do It

PART I

JAE-ON KIM and CHARLES W. MUELLER

I. INTRODUCTION

Basic Orientation

In recent years, factor analysis has become accessible to a wider circle of researchers and students, primarily due to the development of high speed computers and the packaged computer programs (e.g., BMD, DATATEXT, OSIRIS, SAS AND SPSS). This has resulted in a large group of users who do not have enough mathematical training to follow standard texts on the subject (e.g., Harman, 1976; Horst, 1965; Lawley and Maxwell, 1971; Mulaik, 1972) but are nevertheless eager to explore and exploit the potentials of the method for their own research.

The audience we have in mind is this growing population of consumers of factor analysis who are willing to let the computers do the work and let the specialists worry about the statistical and computational problems, but who are willing to invest some effort to gain a firmer grasp of its conceptual foundations in order to apply the method correctly and creatively. In addition, because we anticipate our typical reader to be a nonspecialist, but a potentially active user of the method, we believe the numerous practical problems often encountered should be addressed.

Although this is an elementary introduction to factor analysis, it is not an ordinary introductory text. The assumption which guided our writing is that what is most obvious to an expert is often most obscure to a novice. Therefore, we have discussed in greater detail than usual the fundamental assumptions and logical foundations of factor analysis. It has been a challenge for us to attempt to cover the fundamentals in greater detail than usual and at the same time discuss the practical issues which users continually confront. It is possible in principle to propose such a book because the logical (mathematical) foundation of factor analysis can be separated from the statistical solutions, because the method's logical foundation is straightforward and easy to understand, *and* because an understanding of this foundation will be the basis for the intelligent use of the method. In short, we believe many of the statistical issues in factor analysis are truly subsidiary, and placing emphasis on them diverts attention away from the logical foundation and results in a confused and tentative potential user.

1

The difference between what we call logical and statistical may not be clear at this early stage; therefore, some comments are in order. Factor analysis assumes that the observed (measured) variables are linear combinations of some underlying source variables (or factors). That is, it assumes the existence of a system of underlying factors and a system of observed variables. There is a certain correspondence between these two systems and factor analysis "exploits" this correspondence to arrive at conclusions about the factors. For instance, the mathematical (logical) properties of the correspondence are such that one causal system of factors always leads to a unique correlation system of observed variables, but not vice versa. Therefore, only under very limited conditions can one unequivocally determine the underlying causal structure among the factors from the correlations among the observed variables. This fundamental indeterminancy in factor analysis is due to the indeterminancy inherent in making *inferences* about the causal structure from the correlational structure; it is a logical or mathematical indeterminancy. However, there also are problems of a different nature. As an example, in practice one has to contend with uncertainties introduced by sampling and measurement errors. How to estimate the underlying population parameters from the examination of samples under these uncertainties is a *statistical* problem. Our position is to let statisticians worry about providing us the most efficient ways of estimating population parameters as well as answers to other statistical problems. The logical issues we will address.

We do not and cannot promise not to rely on mathematics, but our use of mathematics will be limited primarily (but not entirely) to simple algebra, and we strongly recommend to the readers that they make an honest attempt to follow the algebra presented. In anticipation that some readers might be discouraged by the mere appearance of the word mathematical, we emphasize once again that our approach is not mathematically rigorous. We will try to explain such terms as "factors," and "variable," "linear combination of variables," and "linear causal systems" by way of illustration. With regard to the statistical background expected of the reader, we will assume some familiarity with correlation and regression analysis. We will rely on path analysis to aid in illustrating the factor models we refer to. Path diagrams readily allow for the visual portrayal of the underlying causal relationships among factors and observed variables. We will explain the essentials of path diagrams as we go along. The use of path diagrams as a means of expressing linear relationships and the requisite assumptions about them should not prove difficult to those who have had no previous exposure to path analysis. (For those wishing a more complete introduction we recommend the Asher [1976] volume in this series or one of the standard references; see Duncan, 1966; Land, 1969; Li, 1975).

What is Factor Analysis?

Factor analysis refers to a variety of statistical techniques whose common objective is to represent a set of variables in terms of a smaller number of hypothetical variables. To make our introductory discussion of factor analysis more concrete, suppose we have interviewed one thousand individuals who are randomly selected from the population, and have asked them many questions about their political opinions on taxation, labor laws, civil rights issues, and so on. The responses to these questions then constitute observed variables.

In general, the first step of the analysis involves an examination of the interrelationships among these variables. Suppose that we use the correlation coefficient as a measure of association and have prepared a table of correlations. Inspection of the correlation matrix may show that there are positive relationships among these variables, and that the relationships within some subsets of variables are higher than those between the subsets. A factor analytic approach may then be used to address whether these observed correlations can be explained by the existence of a small number of hypothetical variables. For instance, we might ask whether there is a liberal-conservative continuum which characterizes the general political outlook of the people. Or we might conjecture that there may be some subdivisions of liberalism-conservatism. For example, it is quite possible that economic issues may tap a somewhat different dimension than civil rights issues. We might then consider whether these potential subdivisions really do emerge from the data. These kinds of questions are best handled by factor analytic techniques.

At one extreme, the researcher may not have any idea as to how many underlying dimensions there are for the given data. Therefore, factor analysis may be used as an expedient way of ascertaining the minimum number of hypothetical factors that can account for the observed covariation, and as a means of exploring the data for possible data reduction. This form of use is *exploratory,* with probably the majority of the applications in the social sciences belonging to this category.

But the use of factor analysis need not be confined to exploring the underlying dimensions of the data. Depending upon the knowledge of the researcher, the method can be used as a means of testing specific hypotheses. For instance, the researcher may anticipate or hypothesize that there are two different underlying dimensions *and* that certain variables belong to one dimension while others belong to the second. If factor analysis is used to test this expectation, then it is used as a means of confirming a certain hypothesis, not as a means of exploring underlying dimensions. Thus, it is referred to as *confirmatory* factor analysis.

The division between the two uses is not always clearcut. For instance, it is possible that the researcher may specify that there will be, say, two factors but may not anticipate exactly what variables will represent each. Or to illustrate one of the numerous strategies that can be employed, the researcher may use one-half of the sample to explore the possible factor structure, and then use the other half of the sample to test the factorial hypothesis that was developed from the examination of the first half.

Factor analysis is used not only as a formal method of ascertaining underlying factor structure, but is also often used as a heuristic device. For example, assume the researcher is certain that on the basis of previous research or strong theory there are two separate dimensions of liberalism—one mainly concerned with the economic issues and the other with civil rights issues. This researcher is interested primarily in constructing a scale of economic liberalism (to be used as a variable in further analysis), but is uncertain whether the opinions about providing financial aid to unwed mothers reflect the dimension of economic liberalism, or is better subsumed under the civil rights dimension. Here factor analysis may be used as a means of checking out the meaning of a particular variable or variables. The researcher might find out through factor analysis that variables X_1, X_2, X_3, clearly reflect economic liberalism, and variables X_5 and X_6 reflect social liberalism, but that variable X_4 is related to both dimensions, and its meaning, given the immediate research objective of constructing the scale of economic liberalism, is ambiguous. Therefore, X_4 could be dropped from the index of economic liberalism.

Without going into the details of the method, it would not make much sense to elaborate further about its potential uses for research. We merely state for now that it can be used in a variety of research situations, and that proper use of factor analysis does not require mastering complex statistical techniques but rests primarily on an understanding of its conceptual and logical foundation.

Doing Factor Analysis

It is one thing to study and grasp the principles of factor analysis and it is another to apply it to actual data. Except for very unrealistic hypothetical data, it is impractical to do factor analysis without the help of modern computers. Because only a very small minority would have the expertise to write the appropriate program, it is almost imperative that one rely on some existing computer program. Fortunately, there are some well-known and widely used general purpose computer packages that contain factor analysis programs. Unfortunately, however, there are so many methods and variants of factor analysis that we cannot cover them here, nor will any single computer package include them all. Furthermore, there appears to be no end in sight regarding new modifications and improvements. Hence, the program available to the user may not be up-to-date or, if up-to-date, may seem too complicated to use. For most factor analysis problems, one does not have to use the most up-to-date version nor does one need to know all of the complexities in order to use the newest versions. We will show that it is possible to ignore most of these complications, especially at the early stages of learning, and obtain the desired results by preparing a minimum number of computer control statements.

It is our belief that being able to apply factor analysis to fairly complex and real problems right from the beginning not only helps the user to become acquainted with the technique quickly, but also diminishes the need for learning the actual algorithms that are involved. We do recommend and, therefore, will illustrate, the use of existing packaged computer programs. It is expected that the reader will attempt to use one of these programs as early as is possible. However, as much as we emphasize the fact that reliance on an existing computer program is a fact of life, we also expect that the user will consult this volume and the companion volume, *Factor Analysis: Statistical Methods and Practical Issues,* University Paper, 07-014, in order to develop a deeper understanding of factor analysis.

The general purpose programs to be illustrated are BMD, OSIRIS, SAS, and SPSS. It should be noted, however, that we have used these packages for illustrative purposes and it is not necessary that one has access to these particular ones. Any program can serve the purpose, but to be successful in learning factor analysis, one must be prepared to spend some time learning how to use at least one factor analysis computer program.

General Outline of Presentation

The discussion of factor analysis is presented in two volumes. In the first volume, coverage is confined to a description of the conceptual foundations of factor analysis, and the use of computer programs as a means of obtaining basic solutions. Discussion of various methods of extraction and rotation, as well as more advanced topics, is included in the companion volume.

More specifically, the first volume is organized into three main sections. The section following this introduction, Section II: Mathematical Foundations of Factor Analysis, deals with the logical foundations of the technique. In order to present this material in the simplest manner possible, we will assume that we are creating the world according to the factor analytic scheme. In this hypothetical world there will be no errors of sampling or measurement. Here we will introduce the basic concepts of variable and factor, variance and covariance, and linear causal system.

The properties of the linear system will be examined rather thoroughly by way of illustrations and mathematical derivations pertaining to the simplest possible situations. We will also examine the sources of logical uncertainties and ways of handling these uncertainties by adopting some fundamental postulates of factor analysis.

In Section III we provide a discussion of how factor analysis is actually conducted. We begin by describing the major steps involved in using the technique, and then illustrate these steps by analyzing error-free data. Descriptions of how to use four of the readily available packaged computer programs are presented. Finally, we describe briefly the complications introduced when real data are analyzed, leaving the treatment of specific and technical issues to the companion volume. Also included in this volume are (1) a brief introduction to the books, articles, and computer programs on factor analysis, (2) a glossary of difficult terms used in this volume, and (3) references to the basic literature.

In the second volume, *Factor Analysis: Statistical Methods and Practical Issues,* we shift our focus to the statistical issues. Building on the conceptual foundations presented in the first volume, we present in order, (1) several standard methods of extracting initial factors, (2) numerous methods of orthogonal and oblique rotations, (3) the rules for determining the number of common factors to retain and interpret, (4) introduction to confirmatory factor analysis, and (5) methods of constructing factor scales. In addition, several practical problems that most social scientists are likely to encounter are discussed in a question and answer format. A glossary and references appear at the end, as in the first volume.

II. LOGICAL FOUNDATIONS OF FACTOR ANALYSIS

Fundamental Concepts of Factor Analysis

FACTORS AND VARIABLES

Factor Analysis is based on the fundamental assumption that some underlying factors, which are smaller in number than the number of observed variables, are responsible for the covariation among the observed variables. To illustrate the model, let us examine the simplest case where one underlying common factor is responsible for the covariation between two observed variables. Such an assumption may be expressed in a path analytic causal diagram as follows:

This diagram implies that X_1 is a weighted sum of F and U_1, and X_2 is a weighted sum of F and U_2. Because F is common to both X_1 and X_2, it may be called a common factor; likewise, because U_1 and U_2 are unique

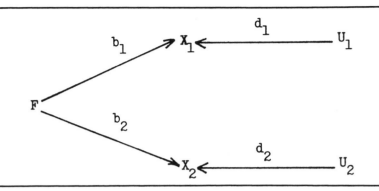

Figure 1: Path Model for a Two-Variable, One-Common Factor Model

to each observed variable, they may be referred to as unique factors. In algebraic form, the diagram implies the following two equations:

$$X_1 = b_1F + d_1U_1$$
$$X_2 = b_2F + d_2U_2$$

[1]

Furthermore, the diagram also indicates that there is no covariation between F and U_1, between F and U_2, or between U_1 and U_2. That is,

$$\text{cov}(F, U_1) = \text{cov}(F, U_2) = \text{cov}(U_1, U_2) = 0.$$

[2]

The preceding three equations, then, together describe a factor analytic linear system shown in Figure 1.

For those who might have trouble following the path diagram or imagining such an abstract system, we will present a concrete example. Assume that there are three source variables, F, U_1 and U_2, and eight cases (or entities) as in Table 1. Each source variable has two possible values, either 1 or -1, and they are uncorrelated with each other. Suppose now that you are asked to create variables from these source materials according to a set of rules. These specific rules are indicated by the causal diagram in Figure 2: these rules are to create X_1 by combining F and U_1 with weights of .8 and .6 respectively, and to create X_2 by combining F and U_2 with weights .6 and .8.

Such a set of operations can be summed up either by the following two equations:

$$X_1 = .8F + .6U_1$$
$$X_2 = .6F + .8U_2$$

or by the path diagram in Figure 2.

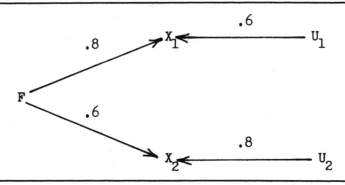

Figure 2: Path Model for a Two-Variable, One-Common Factor Model (consistent with Table 1 Data)

The path diagram actually contains more information than the two equations; in the diagram, the absence of direct or indirect connections between the source variables indicates no correlations among them, whereas the relationships among the source variables are left unspecified in the two equations. In order to indicate that variables X_1 and X_2 are created by the use of uncorrelated source variables, one must add the following conditions to the equations:

$$\text{cov}\ (F,\ U_i) = \text{cov}\ (U_i,\ U_j) = 0.$$

TABLE 1
Illustration of Factors and Variables:
Two-Variables, One-Common Factor

Cases	Source Variables[a]			Observed Variables	
	F	U_1	U_2	$X_1=.8F + .6U_1$	$X_2=.6F + .8U_2$
1	1	1	1	1.4	1.4
2	1	1	-1	1.4	-0.2
3	1	-1	1	0.2	1.4
4	1	-1	-1	0.2	-0.2
5	-1	1	1	-0.2	0.2
6	-1	1	-1	-0.2	-1.4
7	-1	-1	1	-1.4	0.2
8	-1	-1	-1	-1.4	-1.4

a. We use this unrealistic scoring of the source variables to simplify our computations on this basic factor model.

The variables created by applying these rules are presented in the fourth and fifth columns of Table 1.

If we treat X_1 and X_2 as observed variables, and F, U_1 and U_2 as unobserved variables, we have the simplest one common factor model.

Note that there are more factors (Fs and Us) than observed variables (Xs), but only the factor F is common to both X_1 and X_2 and, therefore, the number of common factors is smaller than the number of observed variables. Note also that in creating Xs we have used only certain types of mathematical operations: (1) multiplying the source variables by constants, and (2) adding these products. We did not multiply or divide one factor by the other. In technical language, we are using only linear operations and, hence are creating a linear system.

We will conclude this section by describing how the terms, variables and factors, are used and how they are related. A variable is a concept which has two or more values. In the example, F, U_1, and U_2 all have two values. We assume that these variables are given to us and we are not concerned with their sources. X_1 and X_2, created from the source variables through the linear operations, are also variables—each having four possible values. In order to indicate that the source variables are usually unobserved by the researcher and that the observed variables are created out of them, we call such source variables underlying *factors*. Since none of us really participates in the creation of real world variables by applying the kind of operations described above, we often call these source variables hypothetical constructs, hypothetical variables, or hypothetical factors. Of these factors, those that are involved in the creation of more than one observed variable are called common factors; those that are used in creating only one observed variable are called unique factors.

VARIANCE, COVARIANCE AND CORRELATION

There are two properties of a variable that play important roles in statistics: mean and variance. The mean (or expectation of a variable) indicates the central tendency of a variable, and the variance indicates the degree of dispersion (or variability). They are defined as:

$$\text{Mean} = \Sigma(X_i)/N \quad (i = 1, 2, \ldots, N)$$

$$= E(X) = \bar{X} \tag{3}$$

$$\text{Variance} = \Sigma[X_i - E(X)]^2/N \quad (i = 1, 2, \ldots, N)$$

$$= E[X - E(X)]^2 = V_x. \tag{4}$$

We will use the expectation notation E as an abbreviation for adding all the values and dividing that sum by the total number of cases.[1] If the variable is normally distributed, then these two statistics are sufficient to characterize the whole probability distribution of the variable.

The five variables in our example (F, U_1, U_2, X_1, and X_2) all have means of zero and variances of 1. Such variables are called *normed* variables or *standardized* variables. Any variable can be transformed into such a standardized variable by simply subtracting the mean from the observed values and dividing the resulting values by the square root of the variance. Therefore, we do not lose any generality by dealing with only standardized variables.

In characterizing linear relationships between variables, the concept of covariance plays a crucial role. Its definition is:

$$\text{cov}(X, Y) = \Sigma[(X_i - \bar{X})(Y_i - \bar{Y})]/N \quad (i = 1, 2, \ldots, N)$$

$$= E[(X - \bar{X})(Y - \bar{Y})] \tag{5}$$

Note that cases falling at the mean of each variable will not contribute to the magnitude of covariance; if a case has a higher value than the mean on one variable but a lower value on another, it will contribute a negative value to the covariance; if a case has either higher values or lower values on both variables, it will increase the covariance. Thus, covariance measures the extent to which values of one variable tend to covary with values of another variable. The *covariance* between standardized variables (with a mean of 0 and a variance of 1) has a special name: *correlation coefficient* or *product-moment* (*Pearson's*) *correlation coefficient*:

$$\text{cov}(X, Y) = E(XY) \tag{6}$$

if $\bar{X} = \bar{Y} = 0$;

$$= r_{xy}, \tag{7}$$

if $V_x = V_y = 1$.

If one variable can be expressed as a linear function of the other, as in $Y = a + bx$ (or as a linear combination of the other), the correlation coefficient will be either 1 or -1, and the coefficient of determination (R^2) will be 1. If the two variables are statistically independent, the magnitude of correlation will be zero. Otherwise, the magnitude of r will vary between $+1$ and -1. (If the distribution is bivariate normal, the means, the variances, and the correlation between the two completely specify the bivariate distribution.)

It is important to note that the notion of covariation is independent of the underlying causal structure; two variables can covary either because one variable is a cause of the other or both variables share at least one common cause, or both. In the linear system shown in Figure 1, there is covariation between X_1 and F because F is one of the source variables. However, there is covariation between X_1 and X_2 because both share a common source variable (F).

LINEAR COMBINATIONS AND DERIVATIONS
OF VARIANCE AND COVARIANCE

It is our belief that one of the main reasons why many people fail to grasp the mathematical foundation of factor analysis is lack of understanding of several basic characteristics of linear combinations of variables. Our task in this section is to aid in increasing that understanding. We will examine the mathematical basis of the covariance structure (or correlation structure) or linear systems (such as the one common factor model shown in Figures 1 and 2). We alert the reader in advance that this section will probably be one of the most difficult mathematically, but it is one that is crucial to understanding the mathematical basis for factor analysis. Do not despair prematurely; the algebra involved is actually not that difficult and, once mastered, the remainder of this paper will be much easier.

The derivation of the amount of variance in X_1 and the covariance between X_1 and F is possible due to the fact that X_1 is a linear combination of F and U_1 (i.e., $X_1 = b_1 F + d_1 U_1$). Since we assumed that F and the Us all have means of zero and variances of 1, these derivations can be simplified, without loss of generality. (In fact, the derivations would remain the same even if there is an additional constant as in $X_1 = a + b_1 F + d_1 U_1$.) The variance of X_1, Var (X_1), may be expressed as

$$\text{Var } (X_1) = E(X_1 - \overline{X}_1)^2$$

(which is given by the definition of variance, as in equation 4)

$$= E(X_1)^2$$

(which is obtained by assuming that the mean of X_1 is zero)

$$= E[b_1 F + d_1 U_1]^2.$$

(which is obtained by expressing X_1 in terms of the source variables) Through simple expansion this may be rewritten as

$$= E[b_1^2 F^2 + d_1^2 U_1^2 + 2b_1 d_1 F U_1],$$

and by knowing that the expectation of a constant is the constant, the constants may be factored out as follows,

$$= b_1^2 E[F^2] + d_1^2 E[U_1^2] + 2b_1 d_1 E[F U_1],$$

which allows us to recognize that the terms associated with the expectation notation have previously been defined as either variances or covariances. Hence, the variance of X_1 has been decomposed as follows

$$= b_1^2 \text{Var}(F) + d_1^2 \text{Var}(U_1) + 2b_1 d_1 \text{Cov}(F, U_1). \qquad [8]$$

Equation 8 is a general formula dealing with a case in which one variable is a linear combination of two source variables. In words, the resulting variance in X_1 is given by the sum of (1) the variance of F times the square of the weight associated with F, (2) the variance of U_1 times the square of the weight for U_1, and (3) two times the covariance between the source variables multiplied by the two respective weights. (If the preceding definitions and derivations are new to you, we recommend that you go over this material again. You must understand these basics if the following material is to be meaningful.)

Fortunately, equation 8 simplifies if the source variables are standardized and the covariance between the source variables is zero (as in our example above):

$$\text{Variance } (X_1) = b_1^2 \text{var}(F) + d_1^2 \text{var}(U_1), \qquad [9]$$

if cov $(F, U_1) = 0$.

Here the variance in X_1 is decomposed into only two parts: a component determined by the common factor F and a component determined by the unique factor U_1. The decomposition becomes even simpler if variables are all in standardized form:

$$\text{var } (X_1) = b_1^2 + d_1^2 = 1 \qquad [10]$$

if var (F) = var (U_1) = var (X_1) = 1 and cov (F, U_1) = 0.

Likewise, Var (X_2) can be decomposed as

$$\text{var } (X_2) = b_2^2 + d_2^2.$$

In our example, we have contrived data and coefficients (weights) in such a way that var (F) = var (U_i) = var (X_i) = 1 (that is, all the variables are in standardized form) and cov (F, U_j) = 0. Consequently,

$$\text{var } (X_1) = 1 = b_1^2 + d_1^2 = (.8)^2 + (.6)^2 = .64 + .36$$

$$\text{var } (X_2) = 1 = b_2^2 + d_2^2 = (.6)^2 + (.8)^2 = .36 + .64$$

Therefore, in our example, the proportion of variance in X_1 determined by the common factor is .64 while the proportion determined by the unique factor is .36.

In similar fashion the covariance between a factor and an observed variable may be derived:

$$\text{Cov}(F, X_1) = E[(F - \overline{F})(X_1 - \overline{X}_1)]$$

(from the basic definition of covariance, as given in equation 5)

$$= E[FX_1]$$

(which is possible because we have assumed $\overline{F} = \overline{X}_1 = 0$)

$$= E[(F)(b_1 F + d_1 U_1)]$$

(which is obtained by expressing X_1 in terms of its source variables)

$$= b_1 E[F^2] + d_1 E[FU_1]$$

(by recognizing that the constants may be factored out)

$$= b_1 \text{Var}(F) + d_1 \text{Cov}(FU_1) \qquad [11]$$

(which follows from the basic definitions of variance and covariance). Equation 11 is a general formula dealing with any situation in which a variable is a linear combination of two source variables. In words, the covariance between a source variable and the resulting variable is given by the sum of (1) the linear weight times the variance of the source variable, and (2) the linear weight of the other source variable times the covariance between the two source variables.

When the source variables are independent of each other, equation 11 simplifies to

$$\text{Cov}(F, X_1) = b_1 \text{Var}(F) \qquad [12]$$

and when the source variables have unit variances, it further simplifies to

$$\text{Cov}(F, X_1) = b_1. \qquad [13]$$

Furthermore, if the observed variable X_1 is also in standardized form, then

$$\text{Cov}(F, X_1) = r_{Fx_1} = b_1 = \beta_1. \qquad [14]$$

That is, the covariance is equivalent to the correlation and the linear weight b_1, which is equivalent to a standardized regression coefficient β_1. (Here the independent variable is the factor, and the dependent variable is the observed variable.) Likewise cov $(F, X_2) = r_{Fx_2} = b_2 = \beta_2$. Furthermore, the correlation between X_1 and the unique factor U_1, can be derived in exactly the same way: cov $(X_1, U_1) = r_{x_1u} = d_1$ = standardized regression coefficient.

We may now consider the relationships we have examined thus far in order to interpret the correlation coefficient in the context of factor analysis. In Figure 2 we may now identify the weights .8 and .6 as standardized regression coefficients. At the same time, we know that given the particular linear system in the example, they are also equivalent to correlations between the created variable and the source variables. The squares of these correlations (.64 and .36) correctly describe the proportion of the variance in X_1 and X_2, which is *determined* by the common factor. The square of the correlation coefficient is traditionally known as the *coefficient of determination*, a term which is apt if we have a causal system as shown in Figure 1. But it is used, in general, simply as a means of stating the degree of linear relationship without any reference to the underlying causal relationship. (At this point, we encourage the reader to calculate these coefficients using the data shown in Table 1. Such an exercise will provide an immediate check on whether the reader really understands how the concepts and definitions presented thus far are applied. As we said earlier these elementary concepts are essential to understanding the mathematical model underlying factor analysis. Some results of calculations are shown in Table 2 for those who wish to check their own computations.)

Finally, we derive the covariance between X_1 and X_2:

$$\text{Cov }(X_1, X_2) = E[X_1 - \bar{X}_1)(X_2 - \bar{X}_2)]$$

(from the definition of covariance as given in equation 5)

$$= E[b_1F + d_1U_1)(b_2F + d_2U_2)]$$

(because we have assumed the variables are standardized with means equal to zero, and by expressing the Xs in terms of source variables)

$$= E[b_1b_2F^2 + b_1d_2FU_2 + b_2d_1FU_1 + d_1d_2U_1U_2]$$

(by simple algebraic expansion)

$$= b_1b_2\text{var}(F) + b_1d_2\text{cov}(F_1U_2) + b_2d_1\text{cov}(F,U_1) \quad [15]$$

$$+ d_1d_2\text{cov}(U_1,U_2)$$

(by separating out the constants and recognizing that the remaining expected values are either variances or covariances).

Equation 15 is appropriate for the general case. However, it simplifies to the following if all the covariance terms vanish (as is the case for our hypothetical data):

$$\text{cov}(X_1, X_2) = b_1 b_2 \text{var}(F). \qquad [16]$$

And this simplifies further,

$$\text{cov}(X_1, X_2) = r_{X_1 X_2} = b_1 b_2 = \beta_1 \beta_2 \qquad [17]$$

if all the variables are standardized. In words, the covariance between two observed variables sharing one common factor is equivalent to the variance of the factor times the two respective linear weights involved. When all the variables are in standardized form, the correlation between two observed variables sharing one common factor is given by the multiplication of two standardized regression coefficients or two correlations between the observed variables and the common factor.

RECAPITULATION:
Factor Loadings, Correlations, and Causal Diagrams

Referring back to Figures 1 and 2, we will review the concepts and definitions examined thus far. If all the variables (both hypothetical and observed) are standardized to have unit variance, the linear weights, b_1 and b_2 in Figure 1, are known as *standardized regression coefficients* (in regression analysis), path coefficients (in causal analysis), or factor loadings (in factor analysis). Factor loadings are equivalent to correlations between factors and variables where only a single common factor is involved, or in the case where multiple common factors are orthogonal to each other.

The *communality* (h^2) of an observed variable is simply the square of the factor loadings for that variable (or the square of the correlation between that variable and the common factor), and the *uniqueness component* is simply $(1 - h^2)$.

The correlation between any two observed variables will be given by the multiplication of the two relevant factor loadings: $r_{ij} = (b_{iF})(b_{jF})$. This in turn implies that the residual correlation between X_i and X_j will be zero if the effect of the common factor is controlled: $r_{ij.F} = 0$.

Table 2 has been provided to illustrate the calculation of various coefficients, and to demonstrate the correspondence between theorems we have derived and the coefficients we actually calculated from the data. From this point on, we will assume that these theorems are self-evident and

TABLE 2
Illustration of Variance and Covariance:
Two-Variables, One-Common Factor

Source Variables			Observed Variables		Some Product Terms				
F	U_k	U_2	X_1	X_2	F^2	FU_1	FX_1	FX_2	X_1X_2
1	1	1	1.4	1.4	1	1	1.4	1.4	1.96
1	1	-1	1.4	-.2	1	1	1.4	-.2	-.28
1	-1	1	.2	1.4	1	-1	.2	1.4	.28
1	-1	-1	.2	-.2	1	-1	.2	-.2	-.04
-1	1	1	-.2	.2	1	-1	.2	-.2	-.04
-1	1	-1	-.2	-1.4	1	-1	.2	1.4	.28
-1	-1	1	-1.4	.2	1	1	1.4	-.2	-.28
-1	-1	-1	-1.4	-1.4	1	1	1.4	1.4	1.96
Sum					8	0	6.4	4.8	3.84
Expectation or Mean[a] =sum/N					1	0	0.8	0.6	0.48

a. The last row of numbers is equivalent, going from left to right, to var(F), cov(F,U$_1$), cov(F,X$_1$), cov(F,X$_2$), cov(X$_1$,X$_2$).
Furthermore, since all the variables are standardized, all the covariances are equivalent to correlations.

apply them in more complex situations without deriving them every time.

Finally, you should observe that a one-common factor model does not imply that the variation in an observed variable is completely determined by the common factor; the unique component may actually be much larger than the communality. But observe that the *covariation* between the observed variables is *completely* determined by the common factor; if the common factor is removed, there will be no correlation between X$_1$ and X$_2$.

In summary, the distinguishing characteristic of the factor analytic approach is the assumption that observed covariation is due to some underlying common factors. Although we normally do not attempt to factor analyze a bivariate relationship (for reasons to be made clearer in later discussions), one actually is applying the factor analytic model by considering the correlation between two observed variables to be a result of their sharing of common sources or factors, and not as a result of one being a direct cause of the other.

Correspondence Between Factor Models and Covariance Structures

In a typical factor analysis situation, the researcher is given a matrix of covariances for a set of variables obtained from a sample. The researcher must then attempt to make two distinct types of inferences. The first involves making inferences about the factor structures (causal structures) underlying the observed covariance structure; the second type involves generalizing the first type of inference based on a given sample. The first type of inference is a logical one while the second is a statistical one. It is our belief that statistical problems are subsidiary to logical ones, especially when attempting to present the basic factor model.

In this section we will address the nature of the logical uncertainties inherent to factor analytic approaches; we will examine the correspondence between various properties of the factor model, such as number of common factors and lack of orthogonality among factors; and the properties of the covariance matrix, such as the rank of an adjusted covariance matrix. (Unless otherwise indicated, we will use the terms "covariance" and "correlation" synonymously.)

DERIVATION OF COVARIANCE STRUCTURE FROM THE FACTOR STRUCTURE

1. One-Common Factor with Many Variables: Extension of the results derived from the examination of Figure 1 to a situation where there are many observed variables is simple and straightforward. Figure 3 shows an example of one-common factor model with m observed variables.

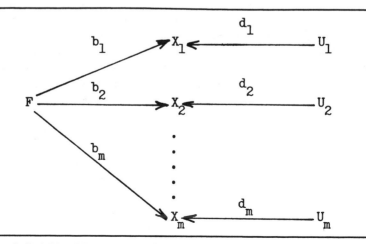

Figure 3: Path Model for a Multi-Variable, One-Common Factor Model

The diagram implies that cov(F, U_i) = 0, and cov(U_i, U_j) =0 and that the linear combinations involved are:

$$X_1 = b_1 F + d_1 U_1$$
$$X_2 = b_2 F + d_2 U_2$$
$$\dots \dots$$
$$X_m = b_m F + d_m U_m.$$

That is, we would arrive at the model shown in Figure 3 if we are given $m + 1$ source variables (F and Us) which are orthogonal to each other, and the m variables are created by linear operations. Since we assume that we know the factor model a priori, we have no problem in identifying b_1, b_2, ... b_m as factor loadings and b_1^2, b_2^2, ... b_m^2 as respective communalities. The correlations between the common factor and the variables are also equivalent to b_1, b_2, ... b_m, due to the assumptions that var(F) = var(U_i) = 1 and cov(F, U_i) and cov(U_i, U_j) = 0.

The resulting correlations between observed variables are from the theorems developed in Section II,

$$r_{12} = b_1 b_2, \; r_{13} = b_1 b_3 \dots r_{1m} = b_1 b_m, \text{ and so on.}$$

Finally, the residual correlations between any two variables are zero—
$r_{12.F} = r_{13.F} \dots r_{1m.F} = 0$.

In describing the one common factor model, it is useful to introduce two additional concepts: *factorial complexity* of a variable and the degree of *factorial determination* of variables. The factorial complexity refers to the number of factors having (significant) loadings on a given variable. In this example every variable loads only on a single common factor, therefore, the factorial complexity of every variable is one. But the fact that one-common factor accounts for the covariance structure does not tell us anything about the degree to which the observed variables are determined by the common factor. Therefore, it will be informative to have an index indicating the degree of such determination. For this purpose, we often use the *proportion of variance* explained by the common factor,

$$\Sigma b_i^2 / m. \tag{18}$$

(Remember that m stands for the number of observed variables.) This index measures the average proportion of variance of observed variables explained by the single common factor.

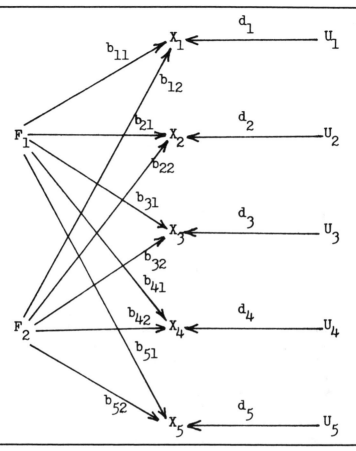

Figure 4: Path Model for Five-Variable, Two-Common Factor Model—The Orthogonal Case

2. *Two-Common Factors: The Orthogonal Case*: A one-common factor model, although useful in illustrating some of the basic properties, is too simple to demonstrate certain other properties of the factor model. We now describe a situation where the covariance in the observed variables is accounted for by two-common factors which are uncorrelated (orthogonal). We also use this opportunity to elaborate on more of the terminology encountered in factor analysis.

Now consider a situation in which you are given several source variables which are uncorrelated with each other. You are asked to create five variables by combining these sources variables linearly with the stipulation that two of these source variables may be used for the creation of every new variable, and one unique source variable should be used for each created variable (X_i).

We now have to complicate the subscripts of the path coefficients or factor loadings in order to specify the different factors in addition to the variables involved. As before, this diagram (Figure 4) implies the following assumptions and rules of linear combinations:

Assumptions: $\text{cov}(F_1, F_2) = \text{cov}(F_i, U_j) = \text{cov}(U_j, U_k) = 0.$

Linear Combinations:
$$X_1 = b_{11}F_1 + b_{12}F_2 + d_1 U_1$$
$$X_2 = b_{21}F_1 + b_{22}F_2 + d_2 U_2$$
$$X_3 = b_{31}F_1 + b_{32}F_2 + d_3 U_3$$
$$X_4 = b_{41}F_1 + b_{42}F_2 + d_4 U_4$$
$$X_5 = b_{51}F_1 + b_{52}F_2 + d_5 U_5.$$

By definition, F_1 and F_2 are common factors because they are shared by two or more variables, and $U_1 \ldots U_5$ are unique factors. When the linear weights associated with the two-common factors are arranged in a rectangular form, as shown below, they are jointly referred to as a factor *pattern matrix* or factor *structure matrix*, or simply as a matrix of factor loadings. In general, a pattern matrix is not equivalent to a structure matrix, for the pattern matrix consists of standardized linear weights (path coefficients), whereas the structure matrix contains respective correlation coefficients between the factors and the observed variables. However, where factors are uncorrelated with one another, a pattern matrix is equivalent to a structure matrix. The fact that the correlation ($r_{F_j X_i}$) between a common factor (F_j) and a variable (X_i) is equivalent to the linear weight (b_{ij}) is derived from a simple extension of equations 11 through 14.

The decomposition of the variance of X_i is given by:

$$\text{var}(X_i) = b_{i1}^2 + b_{i2}^2 + d_i^2. \qquad [19]$$

The proportion of variance of an observed variable (X_i) explained by the common factors—often referred to as the communality of variable i (h_i^2)—is given by:

$$h_i^2 = b_{i1}^2 + b_{i2}^2 \qquad [20]$$

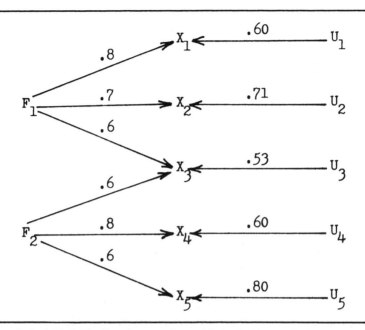

Figure 5: Path Model for Two-Common Factor Model Consistent with Data in Table 3

which is a simple extension of equations 8 through 10.

The covariance between any two observed variables (i and k) is likewise given by:

$$r_{ik} = b_{i1}b_{k1} + b_{i2}b_{k2} \qquad [21]$$

which is a simple extension of equations 15 and 16.

A specific example of a two factor model is presented in Figure 5. The matrix of factor loadings with appropriate statistics is presented in Table 3, following the usual format for reporting factor analytic results. The overall factorial determination is .570, indicating that 57 percent of the variance among the observed variables is determined by the two-common factors. The factor structure is very simple in that all the variables except X_3 have a factorial complexity of one. Of course, the factor loadings indicate both the causal weights as well as the correlations among given variables and factors.

The corresponding correlation matrix is presented in Table 4. Note the existence of zero correlations between the variables that do not share a common factor.

TABLE 3
Matrix of Factor Loadings for Figure 5

Variables	Common Factors		h_i^2	Uniqueness Component
	F_1	F_2		
X_1	.8	--	.64	.36
X_2	.7	--	.49	.51
X_3	.6	.6	.72	.28
X_4	--	.8	.64	.36
X_5	--	.6	.36	.64

3. *Two-Common Factors*: *The Oblique Case*: Now consider a situation in which five variables are created from seven source variables, as in the previous example, but with one additional complication. Two source variables are themselves correlated and these two are to be used as common factors. A general diagram depicting such a situation is presented in Figure 6.

TABLE 4
Correlation Matrix Corresponding to the
Factor Model Shown in Figure 5

	X_1	X_2	X_3	X_4	X_5
X_1	1.00	.56	.48	0	0
X_2		1.00	.56	0	0
X_3			1.00	.48	.36
X_4				1.00	.48
X_5					1.00

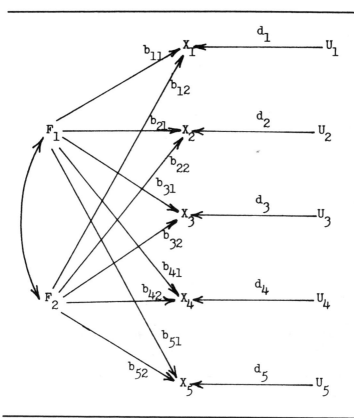

Figure 6: Path Model for a Five-Variable, Two Factor Model—The Oblique Case

The assumptions and rules of linear combinations for this model are the same as those for Figure 4, except that $\text{cov}(F_1, F_2) \neq 0$ in the oblique case. The rules for calculating the communalities and the various covariances are

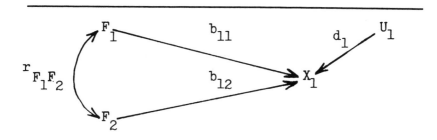

Figure 7: Path Model for One Segment of Figure 6

24

somewhat more complex than those for the orthogonal case. But we have already derived theorems covering a complex set in Section II. To illustrate, first consider only one segment for Figure 6.

By the simple extension of equations 8 and 9, the variance of X_1 can be decomposed as:

$$\text{var}(X_1) = (b_{11}^2 + b_{12}^2 + b_{11}b_{12}2r_{F_1F_2}) + d_1^2 \qquad [22]$$

$$= (\text{communality}) + d_1^2.$$

The variances of other variables can be similarly decomposed.

The correlation between one-common factor and a given variable now has two possible components—a direct connection and an indirect one:

$$r_{F_1X_1} = b_{11} + b_{12}r_{F_1F_2} \qquad [23]$$

which is an extension of equation 11. Therefore, as long as $(b_{12}r_{F_1F_2}) \neq 0$, b_{11} (the causal weight) will not be the same as the correlation $r_{F_1X_1}$. This is precisely why, in the oblique model, the factor structure is not the same as the factor pattern.

The correlation between two observed variables will have, in general, four components. Consider again a subdiagram involving X_1 and X_2:

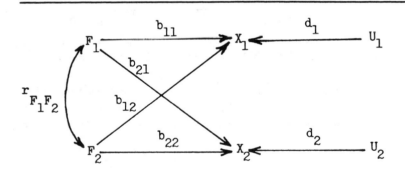

Figure 8: Path Model for One Segment of Figure 6

The correlation between X_1 and X_2 is expressed as:

$$r_{12} = b_{11}b_{21} + b_{12}b_{22} + b_{11}b_{22}r_{F_1F_2} + b_{21}b_{12}r_{F_1F_2} \qquad [24]$$

where the first component is due to the common sharing of F_1, the second component to the common sharing of F_2, the third and fourth components are due to the correlation between the factors. If $r_{F_1F_2} = 0$, equation 24 will be the same as equation 21. Equation 24 is also an extension of equation 11.

A concrete example of factorial causation that is similar to Figure 5, except for the correlation between the common factors and adjustment of weights for the unique factors, is presented in Figure 9. (The adjustments in the weights for the unique factors are made to make the resulting variables have unit variances.)

In this case, the pattern matrix will have the same elements as the orthogonal case but the structure matrix will contain different elements. Table 5 presents all the necessary statistics.

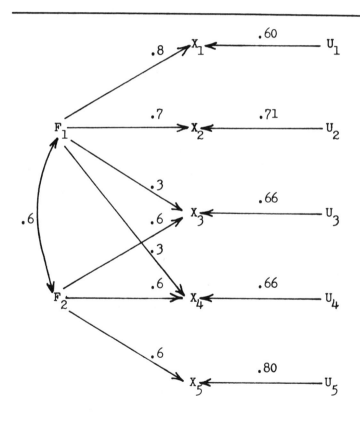

Figure 9: Path Model for an Oblique Two Factor Model Consistent with Data in Table 6

TABLE 5
An Oblique Two-Common Factor Model

Variables	Pattern Matrix F_1	Pattern Matrix F_2	h_i^2	Structure Matrix F_1	Structure Matrix F_2
X_1	.8	--	.64	.80	.48
X_2	.7	--	.49	.70	.42
X_3	.3	.6	.67	.66	.78
X_4	.3	.6	.67	.66	.78
X_5	--	.6	.36	.36	.60

Proportion of variance explained by the two common factors =

$$\Sigma h_i^2 / m = 2.82/5 = .564$$

Correlations Among Factors

	F_1	F_2
F_1	1.0	.6
F_2	.6	1.0

Note the differences between the pattern matrix and the structure matrix, especially the simpler structure of the pattern matrix in comparison to that of structure matrix. For example, although there is no direct causal connection between X_1 and F_2 (i.e., F_2 is not used in creating X_1), there is a substantial correlation between the two (.48) due to the indirect connection through F_1. Each matrix tells us about the different aspects of the relationship between factors and variables: the pattern matrix reflects the causal weights and structure matrix reflects the correlations.

NUMBER OF COMMON FACTORS AND
THE RANK OF THE ADJUSTED CORRELATION MATRIX

In the preceding section we illustrated with several examples the principle that *if the factor structure is known,* the corresponding co-

TABLE 6
The Resulting Correlations and Communalities
Expressed in Terms of Factor Loadings,
Given A Common Factor Model

	X_1	X_2	X_3	X_4
X_1	$b_1{}^2$	$b_1 b_2$	$b_1 b_3$	$b_1 b_4$
X_2	$b_1 b_2$	$b_2{}^2$	$b_2 b_3$	$b_2 b_4$
X_3	$b_1 b_3$	$b_2 b_3$	$b_3{}^2$	$b_3 b_4$
X_4	$b_1 b_4$	$b_2 b_4$	$b_3 b_4$	$b_4{}^2$

a. The single subscripts are used because there is only one factor.

variance structure can be derived without error. In practice, however, one rarely (if ever) knows a priori what the factor structure is. Thus, it is necessary to begin to examine the more realistic situation of deriving underlying factors from the known relationships among the observed variables. As will be shown, however, the strategy of making inferences about factors from known correlations has associated with it a number of indeterminacies. These will be identified in this section. We will begin by examining another type of correspondence between the structural properties of factors and correlations. The structural property of concern is the relationship between the number of common factors and the independent dimensions of the resulting correlation matrix after certain adjustments have been made to it. Before proceeding, however, a cautionary note is necessary. This section may be difficult for some, especially those with limited backgrounds in mathematics. Hopefully, however, our interpretive remarks should be sufficient to convey the intent and meaning of this section.

We refer again to the one-common factor model as presented in Figure 3. Given the factor loadings, we can reproduce the correlations among the observed variables without error. In Table 6, these correlations are expressed in terms of the underlying factor loadings, and the diagonal entries are replaced by the communalities (this is possible given several of the basic theorems derived previously).

All adjusted correlation matrices (those with the communalities in the main diagonal) produced by one-common factor share a fundamental structural characteristic—the rank of the matrix is one. Without providing the formal mathematical basis and definitions, we will say that the rank of a matrix refers to the degree of linear dependence in a set of vectors forming the matrix. We believe it is necessary to briefly describe this concept and indicate how it is related to the notion of number of factors. One way to verify that a matrix has a rank of K is to find out if the determinants of the submatrices with K + 1 or more variables are all zeroes, and if there is at least one submatrix of dimension K whose determinant is not zero.

If the dimension or rank of the matrix is one, then all of the determinants involving two or more variables should be zero. This property may be illustrated by examining Table 6. For example, the determinant for the matrix involving the first two variables is:

$$\det \begin{pmatrix} b_1^2 & b_1 b_2 \\ b_1 b_2 & b_2^2 \end{pmatrix}$$

$$= b_1^2 b_2^2 - (b_1 b_2)(b_1 b_2)$$

(by definition of a determinant, which in the 2x2 matrix tells one to subtract the product of the elements in the secondary diagonal from the product of the elements in the main diagonal)

$$= b_1^2 b_2^2 - b_1^2 b_2^2 = 0 \qquad [25]$$

(by multiplying and subtracting).

By acknowledging that the main diagonal elements are communality estimates and that in the one-common factor case, the b's are the same as the corresponding correlations between variables and factors, we may write:

$$\det \begin{pmatrix} h_1^2 & r_{12} \\ r_{12} & h_2^2 \end{pmatrix} = 0. \qquad [26]$$

Likewise, every possible square matrix containing two or more rows and columns has a zero determinant.

For example:

$$\det \begin{pmatrix} r_{12} & r_{13} \\ b_2^2 & r_{23} \end{pmatrix} = \det \begin{pmatrix} b_1 b_2 & b_1 b_3 \\ b_2^2 & b_2 b_3 \end{pmatrix} \qquad [27]$$

$$= (b_1 b_2)(b_2 b_3) - (b_1 b_3)(b_2^2) = 0.$$

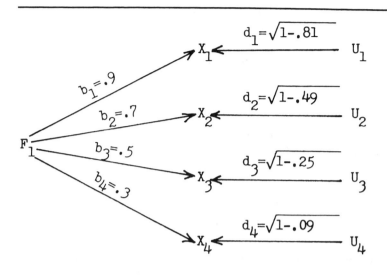

Figure 10: Path Model for Factor Model Consistent with Data in Table 7

As an empirical illustration, suppose that we are given a four variable correlation matrix which is based on the factor model depicted in Figure 10. The resulting correlation matrix without the main diagonal is presented in Table 7.

TABLE 7
Correlation Matrix Derived From the
Factor Model in Figure 10

	X_1	X_2	X_3	X_4
X_1	$b_1^{\,2}$	.63	.45	.27
X_2	.63	$b_2^{\,2}$	.35	.21
X_3	.45	.35	$b_3^{\,2}$	.15
X_4	.27	.21	.15	$b_4^{\,2}$

The rank-theorem implies that, given only one-common factor, the following relationships should hold:

$$r_{13}r_{24} - r_{14}r_{23} = 0 \qquad\qquad [28]$$

$$r_{12}r_{34} - r_{14}r_{23} = 0, \qquad\qquad [29]$$

$$r_{13}r_{24} - r_{12}r_{34} = 0, \qquad\qquad [30]$$

because, as shown in the preceding section, equations 28, 29, and 30, can be expressed equivalently in terms of factor loadings,

$$(b_1b_3)(b_2b_4) - (b_1b_4)(b_2b_3) = 0,$$

$$(b_1b_2)(b_3b_4) - (b_1b_4)(b_2b_3) = 0,$$

$$(b_1b_3)(b_2b_4) - (b_1b_2)(b_3b_4) = 0, \qquad\qquad [31]$$

inspection of which easily shows the equality because terms on either side of the minus sign amount to the same $(b_1b_2b_3b_4)$. Because the correlations in Table 7 meet this criterion,

$$(.45)(.21) - (.27)(.35) = 0,$$

$$(.63)(.15) - (.27)(.35) = 0,$$

$$(.45)(.21) - (.63)(.15) = 0,$$

we would confirm that one-common factor model fits the data.

Furthermore, continuing to use the theorem, we can ascertain the value of each communality and, therefore, the underlying factor loadings. For example, the rank-theorem also implies that

$$b_1{}^2 r_{23} - r_{13}r_{12} = b_1{}^2 r_{24} - r_{14}r_{12} - r_{14}r_{12} =$$
$$b_1{}^2 r_{34} - r_{14}r_{13} = 0 \qquad\qquad [32]$$

which in turn implies that,

$$b_1{}^2 = r_{13}r_{12}/r_{23} = r_{14}r_{12}/r_{24} = r_{14}r_{13}/r_{34}. \qquad\qquad [33]$$

In our example,

$$b_1{}^2 = (.45)(.63)/.35 = (.27)(.63)/.21 = (.27)(.45)/.15 = .81.$$

The square root of .81 is .9 which agrees with the factor loading shown in Figure 10.

When there are two-common factors, the rank of the adjusted correlation matrix will be two, not one. At least one determinant involving two columns and rows will not be zero, but those for three or more columns and rows will always be zero. The formal proof for this has not been included. Most standard texts (e.g., Harman, Mulaik) provide such proofs. Those with knowledge of matrix algebra may benefit by deriving the results by calculating determinants for submatrices of various dimensions. Those who have had some exposure to the discussion of multicolinearity in regression, may think of the rank problem in terms of complete determination in multiple regression—if the rank of the adjusted correlation matrix is one, it means that all the entries in one column can be predicted by the entries of another (without error); if the rank is two, the entries in any column can be determined completely by the linear combination of entries in any other two columns, and so on. Keep in mind, however, that we are evaluating the entries in a correlation matrix, and not the values in a standard data matrix.

To sum up, what we have attempted to demonstrate thus far with this discussion of matrices, ranks, determinants, and so on, is a basic principle about the correspondence between the number of common factors and the rank of the adjusted correlation matrix. The principle is: if the number of factors is known to be K, one may infer that the rank of the corresponding adjusted correlation matrix also is K. Such a correspondence suggests that the reverse of this inferential process is possible, that is, that the number of underlying common factors can be ascertained *from examination of the adjusted correlation matrix*. It was, in fact, the examination of such a correspondence that made factor analysis possible, at least, in its early development. As will be shown, however, inferences of this type are not as straightforward and unequivocal as when the factor structure is known. In particular, use of the rank theorem is restricted because of the following complications: (1) when there are two or more common factors, the exact configuration of loadings cannot be ascertained without additional assumptions; (2) the rank-theorem applies only when the causal operations (the rules for combining factors to create variables) meet a certain set of conditions; (3) the observed correlations are contaminated by the sampling and measurement errors; (4) the relationships in the real world even without sampling and measurement errors may not fit any factor model exactly.

Sampling and measurement problems will be addressed in a separate section, where various statistical issues are discussed. The remaining three problems are conceptual ones, arising from the inherent uncertainties in the relationship between the factor structure and covariance structure. Before the strategies of handling these problems are discussed, we will illustrate the main sources of these problems.

UNCERTAINTIES INHERENT TO
DERIVING FACTORS FROM COVARIANCE STRUCTURES

The properties of linear causal systems are simple and straightforward. Moreover, there is an unequivocal covariance structure associated with every linear causal system. That is, if the factor loadings are known, then correlations among the variables may be uniquely derived. But as already alluded to, the converse is not necessarily true. Knowledge of correlations among the observed variables does not lead to knowledge of the underlying causal structure, because the same covariance structure can be produced by many different causal structures. Thus, the main objective of factor analysis—to ascertain the underlying factorial structure from the examination of a covariance structure—is not as easily accomplished.

It is quite possible, however, that we may be able to eliminate the uncertainties to some extent if their nature is well understood. There are three basic types of problems which result in uncertainties about the relationship between the underlying causal structure and the resulting covariance structure: (1) a particular covariance structure can be produced by the same number of common factors but with a *different configuration* of factor loadings; (2) a particular covariance structure can be produced by factor models with *different numbers* of common factors; (3) a particular covariance structure can be produced by a factor analytic causal model as well as a non-factor analytic causal model. Before discussing implications of these three sources of uncertainty, some concrete examples of each type are presented.

(1)   *One Covariance Structure—Different Factor Loadings:* There are two versions of this type of uncertainty. Both of the causal structures in Figure 11 have two orthogonal factors but the factor loadings are different. Nevertheless, the resulting correlation matrices among the observed variables are identical except for rounding errors.

In general, there is an infinite number of such different configurations which can lead to the same correlation matrix. Therefore, determining the configuration of the linear weights actually operating in reality by examining the correlations among the observed variables is nothing more than guesswork (assuming no theory or past research findings).

A second example is illustrated in Figure 12 where one causal system is based on oblique factors while the other is based on orthogonal ones. Both produce the same correlation matrix for the observed variables.

In factor analytic literature, the type of uncertainty being illustrated here is often called the *problem of rotation*. The problems of rotation are dealt with in the companion volume.

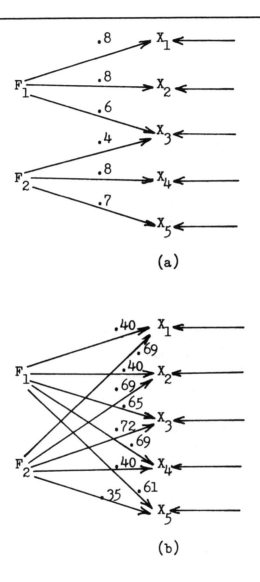

(a)

(b)

Figure 11: Path Models for Factor Models Consistent with a Single Correlation Matrix

(2) *One Covariance Structure—Varying Number of Factors:* **When** discussing the correspondence between the number of common factors **and** the rank of the adjusted correlation matrix of variables, we did not fully specify the conditions under which this correspondence exists. **Figure**

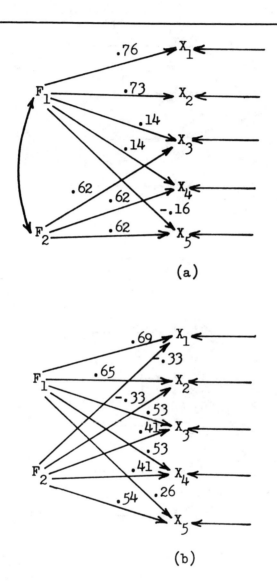

Figure 12: Path Models for Factor Models Consistent with a Single Correlation Matrix

13 shows two causal structures both leading to the same correlation matrix.

The important point to remember from this illustration is that one cannot infer the number of common factors responsible for the given

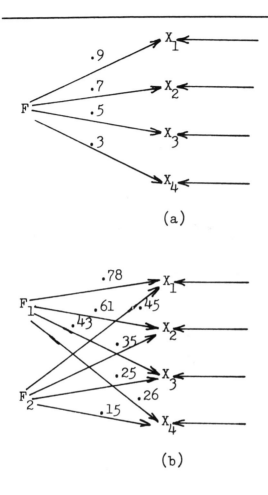

(a)

(b)

Figure 13: Path Models for Factor Models Consistent with a Single Correlation Matrix

correlation matrix; models with a greater number of common factors could have produced the same type of correlation matrix. It will be shown later that this uncertainty can be considered a special case of the general problem of *rotation*.

(3) *Competing Causal Structures:* Another fundamental uncertainty is that a variety of different causal relationships can lead to the same correlation structure. We mentioned at the beginning of Section II that the factor analytic approach typically assumes that the correlation be-

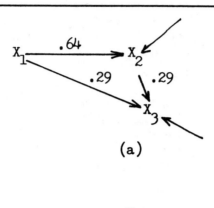

(a)

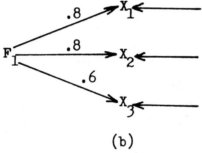

(b)

Resulting Correlations

	X_1	X_2	X_3
X_1	--	.64	.48
X_2		--	.48
X_3			--

Figure 14: Path Models Representing Two Causal Structures Which Result in the Same Correlations

tween two variables is due to their sharing of common factors. The correlation between two variables, X_1 and X_2, can be produced in several ways: (1) X_1 being the cause of X_2, (2) X_1 and X_2 sharing some common causes, or (3) by the combination of both.

Figure 14 gives two causal structures with three variables each, which result in the same correlational structure. One is a one-common factor model and the other is not a factor model.

The critical question then becomes whether it is possible to test empirically with the data whether the factor model is appropriate for the data. The answer is a simple "no." This type of indeterminacy is solved only by an imposition of the factor analytic structure purely on the basis of a theoretical argument, or the knowledge of the causal ordering among the variables based on previous research.

In a sense, problem 3 above is more serious than 2, and problem 2 is more serious than 1, because 3 implies that appropriateness of the factor analytic interpretation can never be proved, problem 2 implies that the number of common factors can never be proved, and 1 implies only that factor loadings may be different. These dilemmas may be resolved only by making assumptions.

Fundamental Postulates of Factor Analysis: Recapitulation

In the face of these seemingly insurmountable uncertainties inherent in examining the relationship between factorial structure and covariance structure, how does one apply factor analysis and have any assurance that the findings can be interpreted meaningfully? As with most other scientific methods, we try to minimize these uncertainties by relying on certain postulates. We use the term postulate to refer to basic assumptions or principles which must be adhered to by the users of factor analysis if the uncertainties are to be minimized. Some postulates may be more appropriate than the others for a given problem, but their ultimate validity is always subject to doubt.

The assumption one has to make even before attempting to use factor analysis may be called the *postulate of factorial causation*. Given relationships among variables, this postulate imposes a particular causal order on the data—that observed variables are linear combinations of some underlying causal variables. The researcher has to substantiate this postulate on the basis of other substantive knowledge about the data; the results of applying the factor analytic technique cannot be used to substantiate the validity of the postulate. The most that can be achieved is the conclusion that the structure of the observed data is not inconsistent with a particular factor model based on such a postulate. In other words, given these variables and covariation among them, it is the burden of the researcher to argue that the underlying causal structure is factorial as in Figure 14b instead of some other as in Figure 14a.

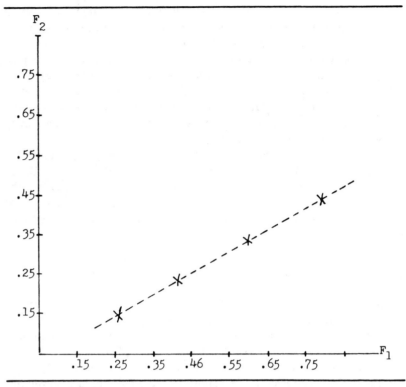

Figure 15: Cartesian Coordinate System for Factor Model in Figures 13a and 13b

The second indeterminacy (one covariance structure—varying number of factors) is resolved by adopting the *postulate of parsimony*. For example, given that both one-common factor and two-common factor models are consistent with the observed data, we accept on faith the more parsimonious model. Thus, given the two postulated models shown in Figure 13, we would choose (a) over (b). Such an assumption is not provable but is widely accepted in other fields of research.

One technical advantage of accepting this principle is that it often leads to a unique conclusion where such a conclusion is impossible otherwise. Again going back to Figure 13, there are infinite numbers of factor models that might have produced the observed correlation matrix, but there is only one particular configuration of factor loadings that is consistent with the one-common factor model. Here the rank-theorem on the correspondence between the number of common factors and the number of dimensions of the adjusted correlation matrix can be a useful tool. The hypothesis of interest is that there is a single common factor, which is the objective given the principle of parsimony. Application of the rank-theorem will alow one to "reject" or "not reject" this hypothesis. But failing to reject it does not prove that a single common factor accounts for the covariation among the variables. Stated another way, it is possible to determine if the data are consistent or inconsistent with a one-common factor model, but given that consistency is indicated, it is impossible to prove there is only one factor.

A reexamination of the two models in Figure 13 is informative at this point. In Figure 15 we represent the factor loadings of Figure 13b on a Cartesian coordinate system.

It is immediately clear that all these loadings line up on the dotted line. If we were to use the dotted line (which is 30 degrees from F_1 counter clockwise) as the new coordinate system, we will find the loadings on this new axis will be equivalent to the loadings shown in Figure 13a. In this sense, the *postulate of parsimony* is related to *rotation* (or data transformation) which is used more frequently in order to find a more "meaningful" or "interpretable" factorial structure.

As already indicated, the first indeterminacy (one covariance structure—different factor loadings) is often called the *problem of rotation*. Here the number of common factors is no longer an issue. A certain degree of parsimony is achieved by selecting the minimum number of common factors which could produce the observed covariance structure. But the question is how to choose between (a) and (b) of Figures 11 and 12.

Given the particular factor patterns in these models, it is relatively easy to argue that the "a" models display a greater degree of simplicity than their "b" counterparts in that some variables in the "a" models have factorial complexity of one, while all the variables in "b" have factorial complexity of two.

In actual factor analysis, where one has to deal with sampling and measurement errors, the choice may never be clear-cut. The final choice may be a matter of personal preference, because the appropriate rotation of axes (allowing obliqueness) can change one system to another without affecting the degree of fit between any of the rotated factorial systems and the given covariance structure. This is why the general problem of rotation is separated from the rotation leading to minimum factors. The latter is accepted as a fundamental guiding principle, but the former has not achieved such a general acceptance. A "simpler structure" for one researcher may not be a "simpler structure" for the other. The problem of rotation is covered in greater detail in University Paper 07-014, *Factor Analysis: Statistical Methods and Practical Issues*.

In summary, the factor analytic approach is possible only when the postulates of factorial causation and parsimony are accepted. We have illustrated why these postulates are necessary by showing the inherent indeterminacies in making inferences about the underlying causal structures from the observation of the covariance structure for the observed variables. These indeterminacies are logical, not statistical, in nature. We will treat factor analysis as a statistical tool and discuss its many variants in University Paper 07-014.

III. OBTAINING FACTOR ANALYSIS SOLUTIONS

In the remainder of this volume, we will describe the basic steps in doing factor analysis through the use of existing computer packages. It is our belief that it is essential that potential users be introduced to actual applications right from the beginning so they can relate more meaningfully to the varieties and complexities of actual factor analysis.

Major Steps in Actual Factor Analysis

In the preceding section, we examined the relationships between factors and variables assuming that the factor structure is known and that there are no measurement or sampling errors. We have identified basic uncertainties inherent in the process of making inferences about the underlying factor structure from the examination of covariance structures. We noted that these uncertainties are reduced only with the introduction of the postulates of factorial causation and parsimony. To be realistic, however, we must consider how these postulates are applied to the analysis of actual data which are subject to sampling and measurement errors. In this situation not only must one make inferences about the factorial structure from the examination of the covariance structure, but also make inferences about the population values from the examination of the sample statistics. Although this introduces a number of complexities, there are standard procedures for dealing with them. These are discussed fully in the companion volume, *Factor Analysis: Statistical Methods and Practical Issues.*

In this section we will provide an introduction to and illustration of how to obtain factor solutions by using existing packaged computer programs. This will provide enough information to allow a potential user to actually do factor analysis. Prior to presenting this, however, it is necessary to describe the major steps in applying exploratory factor analysis to actual data. There are four basic steps: (1) the data collection and preparation of the relevant covariance matrix, (2) the extraction of the initial factors, (3) the rotation to a terminal solution and interpretation, (4) construction of factor scales and their use in further analysis. Our discussion of each of these steps assumes that the reader will rely on computers for the data handling and analysis.

TABLE 8
Example of a Data Matrix

Entity	Variables			
	1	2	3 ....m	
1	5	20	9	52
2	3	18	10	48
3	2	31	11	21
4	1	15	8	63
.				.
.				.
.				.
.				.
.				.
.				.
i	9	22	14 21	

DATA COLLECTION AND PREPARATION
OF THE COVARIANCE MATRIX

The first step in factor analysis is collecting the relevant data for analysis and, as mentioned in the preceding sections, preparing a covariance matrix, the data used directly in the factor analysis. Many times the co-variance matrix is already available, but if not, the first step involves collecting information on a set of entities or objects for the variables of interest. For example, if one is interested in factor analyzing political attitudes of citizens, the objects (in this case, a given number of citizens) must be sampled and surveyed through interviews or other means regarding their views on various political issues. These basic data must then be arranged in a systematic way, usually called a data matrix. An example of such a matrix is given in Table 8.

Note that the data matrix has two modes (or dimensions): (1) the *entity mode* representing the objects or cases, which in the example is citizens, arranged as rows, and (2) the *variable mode* represented by different columns. The covariance matrix desired in ordinary factor analysis is for the relationships among variables (columns). We should mention in passing, however, that it also is possible to examine the "similarities" between objects (between rows) as defined in terms of their total profile on these variables. (See literature on cluster analysis and Q-factor analysis: Tryon and Bailey, 1970; Stephenson, 1953). Furthermore, it is possible to expand the data matrix by asking the same questions on the same subjects on different occasions. Then the data would contain three modes, not two, and such data can be analyzed by using three-mode factor analysis (See Tucker, 1966). But almost all factor analyses reported in the research literature deal with data in the basic two modes as shown in Table 8, and thus, our discussion is only in terms of this type.

Assuming that the basic covariance structure (matrix) of interest is for the variables, one could still make the choice between analyzing the *covariance* matrix or the *correlation* matrix. Because this issue requires a fairly lengthy discussion, we have delayed its presentation to our companion volume. Here we suggest that in exploratory factor analysis, one may rely on the use of a correlation matrix. Two practical advantages make this choice advisable: (1) many existing computer programs do not accept the covariance matrix as basic input data, and (2) almost all of the examples in the literature are based on correlation matrices—hence it will be easier for the reader to understand and compare results with others.

EXTRACTING INITIAL FACTORS

The second major step in factor analysis is to find the number of factors that can adequately explain the observed correlations (or covariances) among the observed variables. The typical approach at this stage is to input the relevant matrix into a factor analysis program and choose one of the many methods of obtaining the initial solution. There are several major alternatives: (1) maximum likelihood method (or canonical factoring), (2) least-squares method (variants are principal axis factoring with iterated communalities or Minres), (3) Alpha factoring, (4) Image factoring, and (5) principal components analysis. These alternatives are discussed in detail in the companion volume. Our advice is, that until a more complete understanding of the methods is gained, the researcher should use one of the first two methods, or the default option in the program.

At this stage of the analysis one should not be concerned with whether the underlying factors are orthogonal or oblique—all the initial solutions are based on the orthogonal solution. Nor should one be too concerned with whether the factors extracted are interpretable or meaningful. The chief concern is whether a smaller number of factors can account for the covariation among a much larger number of variables.

It also should be mentioned at this point that to obtain an initial solution the researcher must provide (1) either the number of common factors to be extracted, or (2) the criterion by which such a number can be determined. The reader should recall the rank-theorem in factor analysis which states that, in error-free data, the rank of the adjusted correlation matrix produced by k common factors is k. However, there are two reasons why this theorem is not used directly in factor analysis. First, the observed data are subject to many random errors, or, at the least, to sampling error, and therefore, an exact fit between the data and the model cannot be expected. Second, related to this first problem is the fact that one cannot ascertain the exact communalities.

The most commonly used procedure of determining the number of initial factors to be extracted is a rule-of-thumb—the rule known either as the Kaiser or eigenvalue criterion (eigenvalue greater than or equal to 1). Then the corresponding communalities are estimated iteratively, usually starting with some initial values (either specified by the researcher or more commonly in packaged programs, given by the multiple R-squared value between a given variable and the other variables) and ending with values to which successive reestimates or refinements converge. Some of the methods, such as the maximum likelihood solution, also provide large-sample statistical significance tests by which the adequacy of the initial guess (or the rule-of-thumb) can be evaluated. Several alternative means of determining the number of factors are more fully discussed in the companion volume. Until these are learned, we recommend that the user rely on the default options available with the particular computer program in use.

ROTATION TO A TERMINAL SOLUTION

To obtain the *initial* solution, certain restrictions typically are imposed. These restrictions are (1) there are k common factors, (2) underlying factors are orthogonal to each other, and (3) the first factor accounts for as much variance as possible, the second factor accounts for as much of the residual variance left unexplained by the first factor, the third factor accounts for as much of the residual variance left unexplained by the first two factors, and so on. The first restriction remains in effect throughout a given factor analysis, although its adequacy can be partially tested in certain methods of initial factoring and can be modified in subsequent factor analyses. The second and third restrictions are considered arbitrary, and one or both are removed in the rotation stage in order to obtain simpler and more readily interpretable results.

We remind the reader that no method of rotation improves the degree of fit between the data and the factor structure. Any rotated factor solution explains exactly as much covariation in the data as the initial solution. What is attempted through rotation is a possible "simplification." There exist different criteria of simplicity which lead to different methods of rotation. These various criteria of "simple structure" are discussed in the companion volume.

Our advice to the user is that one should not be unduly concerned about the choice of the particular rotation method. If identification of the basic structuring of variables into theoretically meaningful subdimensions is the primary concern of the researcher, as is often the case in an exploratory factor analysis, almost any readily available method of rotation will do the job. Even the issue of whether factors are correlated or not may not make much difference in the exploratory stages of analysis. It even can be argued that employing a method of orthogonal rotation (or maintaining the arbitrary imposition that the factors remain orthogonal) may be preferred over oblique rotation, if for no other reason than that the former is much simpler to understand and interpret. Nevertheless, the distinction between orghogonal and oblique rotations is important for a fuller understanding of the factor structure. We advise that beginners choose one of the commonly available methods of rotation, such as Varimax if orthogonal rotation is sought or Direct Oblimin if oblique rotation is sought. As the reader's understanding of factor analysis deepens, by becoming more acquainted with basic results of factor analysis, the variety of proposed criteria may be studied and "experimented" with.

CONSTRUCTION OF FACTOR SCALES
AND THEIR USE IN FURTHER ANALYSIS

With the exceptions of psychology and education, it is not misleading to argue that the main motivation behind the use of factor analysis is not in ascertaining the factor structure among a set of variables, but in achieving data reduction and obtaining factor scales which can be used as variables in a different study. Today it is not unusual to see factor scales being analyzed along with other variables, with no more fanfare than a brief note somewhere indicating that some of the variables are factor scales obtained through factor analysis.

Most factor analysis computer programs usually produce coefficients (or weights) with which to combine the observed variables to represent the underlying factor, and some even create such scales for the user. Therefore, creating factor scales from factor analysis is not a difficult task. But the user must be warned that factor scales so created, whichever method may have been selected, are not the same as the underlying factors. Not only are the correlations between the hypothetical factor and the corresponding scale likely to be much less than 1.0, but also the relationships among the scales are not likely to be the same as the relationships among the underlying factors. What we are emphasizing is that one should not forget the fact that factor scales are error-prone indicators of the underlying factors.

A more detailed discussion of various methods of constructing factor scales will appear in the companion volume. Here we merely note that factor scales for the underlying factors constructed by using different methods uusally correlate very highly with each other—in contrast to the fact that a given scale may not correlate as highly with the underlying hypothetical factor. This may relieve the anxiety on the part of the user who must choose one out of many options for constructing factor scales, or who may not have a choice and must rely on what is built into the program being used. It should also be noted that some analysis methods such as covariance-structure analysis and confirmatory factor analysis can handle both hypothetical variables such as factors and "raw" variables in the same analysis, which mitigates the need to rely on constructing "inadequate" factor scales. This point will be discussed more fully in the companion volume.

Illustration of Actual Analysis, as Applied to Known Error-Free Data

These major steps will be illustrated by applying factor analysis to a data set whose underlying factor structure is known, and where the observed data are free from sampling and measurement errors. We will then complicate the picture by introducing sampling and other practical problems.

For heuristic purposes suppose we know the underlying factor structure for a given set of variables. Let us consider a model that is somewhat more complex than the models examined in Section II, and thus a little more realistic. In partiçular, suppose there are two correlated factors underlying citizens' political attitudes, with a causal pattern as shown in Figure 16.

The first factor, F_1, is responsible for the covariation among the first three variables dealing with economic issues; the second factor, F_2, is responsible for the covariation among civil rights issues. There are also correlations between the first three and the last three variables because of the correlation between the two factors.

46

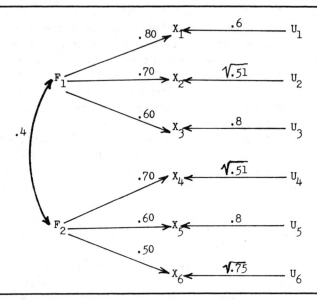

Figure 16: Path Model for Six-Variable, Two Oblique Factor Model Example, where the observed variables represent opinions on:

X_1 = whether government should spend more money on schools,
X_2 = whether government should spend more money to reduce unemployment,
X_3 = whether government should control big business,
X_4 = whether government should expedite desegregation, through busing,
X_5 = whether government sees to it that minorities get their respective quota in jobs,
X_6 = whether government should expand the headstart program.

In the population, such a factor pattern will produce a correlation matrix shown in Table 9. From Section II, it should be obvious that the basic data for factor analysis are a matrix of such correlations or covariances. (Unless otherwise noted, we will treat correlations and covariances as equivalent because we assume throughout most of our discussion that all the variables are standardized.)

Given such a matrix of correlations, one may directly proceed to examine the patterns of correlations and apply factor analysis. For example, we notice that there are two sets of clusters; the correlations among the first three variables and among the last three variables are in general higher than correlations between them, alerting the researcher to the possibility of finding two factors. However, in actual exploratory factor analysis the researcher may not have noticed such a patterning; it is fairly obvious in our example only because we have arranged the variables in a particular order.

TABLE 9
Correlation Matrix for Political Opinion Variables

	X_1	X_2	X_3	X_4	X_5	X_6
X_1	1.000	.560	.480	.224	.192	.160
X_2	.560	1.000	.420	.196	.168	.140
X_3	.480	.420	1.000	.168	.144	.120
X_4	.224	.196	.168	1.000	.420	.350
X_5	.192	.168	.144	.420	1.000	.300
X_6	.160	.140	.120	.350	.300	1.000

a. Variables are identified in Figure 16.

Suppose we decide to do an exploratory factor analysis for this correlation matrix and use some existing packaged computer program. Also, suppose we decide on the maximum likelihood solution, and, being a novice to factor analysis, simply do not know how many factors to extract and, therefore, decide to start with a one-common factor model.

The maximum likelihood solution finds the most likely population values that would have produced the given correlation matrix under the hypothesis (in this case) that a one-common factor model fits the data perfectly in the population and the joint distribution is multivariate normal. In this particular case, the hypothesis is wrong; we know that the correlation matrix is created by a two-common factor model. Nevertheless, it is heuristically useful to see what happens when we specify a smaller number of factors than there really are. Table 10 presents the major statistics produced by the solution (on the assumption that the sample size was 100).

The maximum likelihood solutions provide the pattern matrix (the loadings) and the estimated communalities, and a few additional statistics with which to evaluate the adequacy of the solution. In a one-common factor model communalities are no more than the squares of the respective factor loadings, and the total amount of variance explained is given by the sum of communalities. The most important question at this stage of initial factoring is whether or not the given factors adequately account for the observed correlations among the variables.

TABLE 10
Results of Fitting A One-Common Factor Model
to the Political Opinion Data in Table 9:
Maximum Likelihood Solution

Variables	F_1	Communalities	Communalities Implied by the Model
X_1	.774	.5995	.64
X_2	.696	.4842	.49
X_3	.598	.3573	.36
X_4	.345	.1193	.49
X_5	.306	.0939	.36
X_6	.263	.0690	.25

Amount of Variance Explained = 1.723

Percentage of Variance Explained = (1.723/6)100 = 28.7

χ^2- statistic with 9 degrees of freedom = 26.4

The expected correlations given the factor loadings in Table 10 are $r_{12} = (.774)(.696) = .5387$, $r_{13} = (.774)(.598) = .4529$, $r_{14} = (.774)(.345) = .2670$, and so on. The fit is not exact and there is substantial discrepancy when the relationships among the last three variables are considered (compare with Table 9). Since we know the true model that produced the observed correlations, we can also compare the estimated communalities with true communalities. We again notice (by comparing the last two columns of Table 10) that the discrepancy is substantial with respect to the last three variables. In real analysis, however, one does not know the true values and must rely on some other criterion, such as examining the fit between the observed correlations and those produced by a given factor model. The particular method we have selected provides an approximate large-sample χ^2-test to evaluate whether the data deviate significantly from the model, and in this case the deviation is statistically significant. We would, therefore, reject the adequacy of one-common factor model.

Having rejected the one-common factor model, it is logical to test the compatibility of a two-common factor model with the data. A solution (based on maximum likelihood procedures) is given in Table 11.

TABLE 11
Unrotated Factor Loadings (Pattern) for the Maximum Likelihood Canonical Solution: Political Opinion Example

Vars$_{(i)}$	Factors		Communalities
	F_1	F_2	
	b_{i1}	b_{i2}	
X_1	.766	-.232	.640
X_2	.670	-.203	.490
X_3	.574	-.174	.360
X_4	.454	.533	.490
X_5	.389	.457	.360
X_6	.324	.381	.250
Eigenvalues	1.827	.763	Sum = 2
Percent of Variance Explained	30.5	12.7	
Cumulative Percent of Variance Explained	30.5	43.2	

$\chi^2 = 0.$

We may check whether a two-common factor model is compatible with the data by comparing correlations with those expected, assuming the two-common factor model to be correct. The expected correlations (r_{ij}) due to the two hypothesized factors are given by

$$r_{ij} = b_{i1}b_{j1} + b_{i2}b_{j2}. \qquad [34]$$

For example, the expected correlation between X_1 and X_2 is

$$r_{12} = b_{12}b_{21} + b_{12}b_{22} = (.766)(.670) + (-.232)(-.203) = .56,$$

which is the observed correlation. Likewise, every other expected correlation (not presented here) is the same as the corresponding observed correlation. In addition, the χ^2- statistic indicates the adequacy of the model. Hence, we would accept that a two-common factor model is compatible with the observed correlation matrix. So far, then, we have accomplished what is usually known as the initial solution or initial extraction of factors.

We should note that the same result would have been obtained in a single step if we had specified from the beginning the criterion that the number of initial factors be equal to the number of roots (eigenvalues) of the unaltered correlation matrix that are greater than 1.0, or if we had set the limit of the maximum number of factors to be extracted at two (perhaps based on knowledge gained by examining the patterning of coefficients in the correlation matrix).

Before we consider the second major step, it is useful to comment on how the factor pattern given in Table 11 might be interpreted. The non-zero loadings on the first factor indicate that every variable in the set shares something in common. We might, therefore, call this first factor a general liberalism factor. It indicates that if a person holds a liberal opinion on one item that same person tends to hold a liberal opinion on another. This first factor might also be called a general conservatism factor or even a liberalism-conservatism factor. It is important to emphasize, however, that factor analysis does not tell the researcher what substantive labels or meaning to attach to the factors. This decision must be made by the researcher. Factor analysis is purely a statistical technique indicating which, and to what degree, variables relate to an underlying and undefined factor. The substantive meaning given to a factor is typically based on the researcher's careful examination of what the high loading variables measure. Put another way, the researcher must ask what these variables have in common. As will be discussed, certain factor solutions make this task easier.

Our examination of the factor pattern would also tell us that the second factor is bi-polar, i.e., it loads positively on some variables and negatively on others. Although such a bi-polar pattern indicates that there are two sets of variables which tap somewhat distinct dimensions, the interpretation of the bi-polar factor is not readily apparent; that is, we do not know what to call it. It is possible, however, to define this second factor with respect to the first; among those cases with a similar degree of overall liberalism (the same value on factor 1), those who have liberal opinions on the one set of variables tend to have conservative opinions on the other set. We must admit that such an interpretation is more complex than desirable, and we still want a factor solution that makes interpretation easier. (We remind the reader that in this case the model shown in Figure 16 is the true model, but in actual data analysis we would not have access to such information.)

Having found the minimum number of factors that can account for the observed correlations, the next step is to rotate the axis to get a simpler and/or more easily interpretable solution. At this stage, the researcher again has to make a few decisions: whether to use an orthogonal rotation (i.e., to assume that factors are uncorrelated), or an oblique rotation (i.e., to assume that factors may be correlated). In addition, one will have to choose which particular method to use. For heuristic purposes we will examine both an orthogonal rotation based on the Varimax criterion and an oblique solution, known as Direct Oblimin.

Before resorting to computer programs for rotation, let us examine a graphic presentation of the unrotated factor solution. Remember from Section II that it is possible to use a cartesian coordinate system to repre-

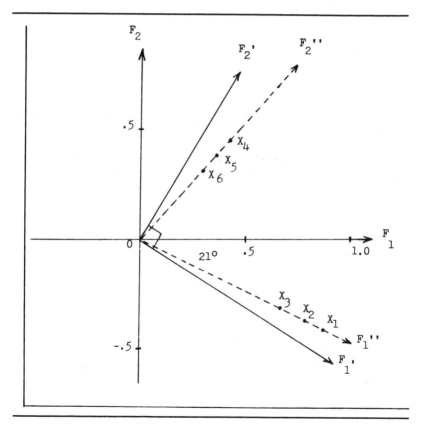

Figure 17: Factor Pattern Matrix for Table 11

Key:

F_1 and F_2: orthogonal factors (axes) before rotation;

F_1' and F_2': orthogonal factors after Varimax rotation;

F_1'' and F_2'': oblique factors after Direct Oblimin rotation. The angle between the two is 66.42°.

TABLE 12
Varimax Rotated Factor Pattern:
Political Opinion Example

Variables	F_1	F_2
X_1	.783	.163
X_2	.685	.143
X_3	.587	.123
X_4	.143	.685
X_5	.123	.587
X_6	.102	.489

a. The Initial Solution is given in Table 11.

sent the factor loadings of each variable on each factor—the coordinates for each variable indicate these factor loadings. Figure 17 presents a coordinate system representing the results of the factor analysis displayed in Table 11. Note that this geometric presentation clearly shows the clustering of variables.

Now consider rotating the axes (retaining the 90-degree angle) in a clockwise direction until they more closely intersect the two clusters of variables. The solid lines have been drawn to show the results of this procedure. As it turns out, one optimal rotation (according to a Varimax criterion) involves rotating these axes exactly 29.1 degrees clockwise. This particular rotation not only removes the negative factor loadings on the second factor, but also results in a simpler pattern. The results of the rotation are shown in Table 12.

The pattern shown in Table 12 is simpler than that shown in Table 11. The first factor loads high only on variables dealing with economic issues, and the second factor loads high only on variables dealing with civil rights issues. Thus, we have succeeded in identifying two-common factors with a relatively clear pattern; there is apparently one factor (an economic dimension) that is responsible for correlations among the first three variables, and another factor (a civil rights dimension) that is responsible for correlations among the last three variables.

TABLE 13
Factor Pattern and Factor Structure After Oblique
Rotation: Political Opinion Example

Variables	Pattern Matrix		Structure Matrix	
	F_1	F_2	F_1	F_2
X_1	.800	.000	.800	.320
X_2	.700	.000	.700	.280
X_3	.600	.000	.600	.240
X_4	.000	.700	.280	.700
X_5	.000	.600	.240	.600
X_6	.000	.500	.200	.500

a. The pattern matrix is an exact replica of loadings shown in Figure 16. The structure matrix shows the correlations between the factors and variables.

One could proceed further, however. A closer inspection of Figure 17 also shows that the clustering of two groups of variables forms an oblique angle (i.e., if the axes are placed directly through the two clusters, they no longer are at right angles). We should explore the possibility of an even simpler pattern by rotating each axis individually and, thereby, letting the two axes form an oblique angle. The result of applying an oblique rotation is given in Table 13, and the rotated axes are drawn in Figure 17. In a sense, the loadings in Table 13 are simpler than the loadings in Table 11, but at the "expense" of incorporating correlations between the two factors. In this case, the choice between the orthogonal and oblique factor models is relatively clear-cut, but it may not always be as clear in practice. Ultimately, one will have to make such a decision based on some theoretical expectations and extrastatistical knowledge about the nature of the data.

Let us recapitulate the steps we have followed in illustrating the application of factor analysis to error-free data. First, we selected a set of variables and prepared a matrix of correlation coefficients. Second, we tried to determine the minimum number of common factors that could have produced the observed correlations. Third, through rotation, we settled on the simplest solution among a potentially infinite number of solutions that are equally compatible with the observed correlations. We are now ready to address a few important issues the user confronts when dealing with actual data.

Obtaining Basic Factor Analysis Solutions
Through the Use of Computer Packages

When learning a complex subject such as factor analysis, it is good strategy to thoroughly acquaint oneself with the most simple methods before learning more subtle and involved aspects. It also is our belief that one of the best ways of accomplishing this is to apply it to actual data, and see the results. Therefore, it is essential that the reader begin by using existing computer programs to obtain some results as soon as possible.

Even if the reader does not yet have data to analyze, it is advisable to use some available computer program on hypothetical data, such as that shown in Table 9. Unfortunately, a problem in using existing programs is that they typically demand too many decisions for which the reader is not completely prepared. What we will demonstrate in this section is that there are many easy to use computer packages which are widely available, and that factor analysis programs included in these packages usually contain "default" options which require only a minimal number of decisions on the part of the user. As we have suggested several times, these default options are usually more than adequate, and, unless the user has a specific analysis problem that calls for a particular solution, it probably would be wise to rely on them.

The computer packages described and illustrated are limited to the following four widely available ones: BMD, OSIRIS, SAS, and SPSS. No endorsement of these packages over others is implied, and any program locally available can serve equally well. Before illustrating how these packaged programs can be used, it must be noted that each computer package has its own data handling system and set of control statements. We must assume that the potential user will study and learn these aspects of the system to be used. Therefore, what we show in these illustrations is not the entire set of control and specification statements, but only that portion which directly pertains to the factor analysis program.

ILLUSTRATION WITH SPSS

In using the factor analysis program, the user must specify: (1) the variables to be factor analyzed, (2) whether the data are in a raw form or in the form of a correlation or covariance matrix, (3) the number of common factors to be extracted or the criterion by which to determine such a number, (4) whether the diagonal elements of the correlation matrix are to be replaced by communality estimates and, if so, what type of estiates are to be used, (5) whether to employ orthogonal or oblique rotation, and (6) the particular type of rotation to be used.

We will first show how these choices are handled by the FACTOR program in SPSS. The simplest example of control cards in running factor analysis in which a minimum number of specifications are required of the user is as follows:

FACTOR   VARIABLES = VARA, VARC, VARF TO VARX/

STATISTICS ALL

The first statement specified (through implied default options) the following choices: (a) the variables to be included in the analysis are as listed in VARIABLES = list, (2) the input consists of raw data—that is, no correlation matrix has as yet been created, (3) the number of factors to be extracted is determined by the number of the roots (eigenvalues) of the correlation matrix which are greater than or equal to 1.0, (4) the communalities are estimated iteratively, (5) orthogonal rotation is to be used, and (6) the method of orthogonal rotation actually used is Varimax. The second statement will produce computer output consisting of the following items:

(1) means and standard deviations of all the variables included in the analysis;

(2) correlation matrix;

·(3) inverse and determinant of the correlation matrix;

(4) unrotated (orthogonal) initial-factor matrix;

(5) terminal orthogonal factor matrix, rotated by the Varimax method;

(6) factor-score coefficient matrix consisting of regression weights with which to construct factor scales;

(7) plot of rotated factors—a visual display of clustering of variables for each pair of factors.

If one wants to obtain a final solution based on an oblique rotation, the easiest specification would look as follows:

FACTOR   VARIABLES = VARA, VARC, VARF TO VARX/
           ROTATE = OBLIQUE/

STATISTICS ALL

The only additional specification is the inclusion of the ROTATE = OBLIQUE statement. This will produce a terminal solution based on a particular oblique rotation, Direct Oblimin (with DELTA value set at 0). The output from such an oblique rotation would contain in the place of point 5 above, an oblique pattern matrix, a structure matrix, and a matrix of correlations among the oblique factors. The plot (point 7 above) is not available for oblique rotations.

What should be obvious from the preceding illustration is that it is, indeed, easy (perhaps too easy for the purists to feel comfortable) to do factor analysis with an existing program. We wish to reiterate that for the beginner to successfully use an existing program, unnecessary complications associated with the many possible choices should be avoided. Most of the options not mentioned in our illustration are purely technical ones that do not bear on the basic properties of factor analysis.

ADDITIONAL ILLUSTRATIONS WITH SPSS, BMD, OSIRIS AND SAS

As in SPSS, the other popular computer packages, such as BMD, OSIRIS and SAS contain factor analysis programs that offer many standard default options. We will first illustrate for SPSS and BMD, the way to obtain the maximum likelihood solution with oblique rotation. In addition, we will assume that the input is a matrix of correlations. The user should have little trouble in generaliziang from this to other options.

The simplest way to obtain such a solution with SPSS is to specify the following:

```
FACTOR      VARIABLES = list/
            METHOD = RAO/
            ROTATE = OBLIQUE/
```

The current version of SPSS handles the maximum likelihood solution by way of Rao's cannonical factoring technique; the default oblique rotation specifies a Direct Oblimin (with Delta equal to zero). The fact that the input is a correlation matrix is handled through an OPTIONS card and modifications in Job Control Language statements (not explained here).

The same maximum likelihood solution with oblique rotation starting with the correlation matrix is obtained in BMD (BMDP4M) as follows:

```
PROB/
INPUT     VARIAB=6. FORMAT='(6F4.3)'. CASE=100. TYPE=CORR./
FACTOR    NUMBER=2. METHOD=MLFA./
ROTATE    METHOD=DOBLI./
END/
```

The first card is the problem card which can be used to name the run. The default option assumes that nothing is specified, but the card is required anyway. The slash indicates the end of the card. The input card specifies the number of variables, format of the correlation matrix, size of sample on which the matrix is based, and the nature of the data—in this case, a correlation matrix. By changing CORR to DATA one can input raw data, and by changing CORR to COVA, one can input a covariance matrix. The factor card specifies the number of factors requested and the method of extraction—the maximum likelihood solution. The rotate card indicates a Direct Oblimin (with default gamma value = 0). As is evident, specifying control cards for the factor analysis program in BMD is almost as easy as in SPSS.

As of this writing, OSIRIS and SAS do not contain a maximum likelihood solution, but they contain many other standard extraction methods and a variety of rotation methods. We will illustrate each program package to show the ease with which a simple specification is possible.

An example using the OSIRIS package is as follows:

```
$RUN    FACTAN
        AN ILLUSTRATION OF FACTOR ANALYSIS
        *
        SMR, ITER=20, OBLIMIN
        *
$MATRIX
        etc.
```

The first card specifies the program to be used; the second card is a label card—if deleted, the user has to insert a card containing *; the third card elects all the default specifications for the so-called global parameters— it indicates a matrix input form and what is referred to as the standard output; the fourth card specifies (a) that the number of variables analyzed is the same as the number of variables in the correlation matrix (by default), (b) the Kaiser criterion is used to determine the number of factors to be extracted (by default), (c) the initial estimates of communalities will be squared multiple Rs (by SMR), (d) these values will be iterated up to twenty cycles (by ITER = 20), (e) there will be no special output of factor scores or the pattern matrix (by default), and (f) the final solution will use (indirect) oblique rotation (by OBLIMIN). The next card with * on it specifies that all the default options in the oblique rotation will be chosen; for example, normalization of the factor matrix and use of the Biquartimin criterion. The last card, $MATRIX, specifies that information about the matrix follows. The "etc." means that the user must supply additional OSIRIS control cards for handling labels and input data.

An example of obtaining factor analysis through SAS is given below:

```
PROC   FACTOR   METHOD=PRINIT MINEIGEN=1   ROTATE=PROMAX
```

This statement specifies the choice of initial factoring based on principal axis factoring with iterations (PRINIT); the criterion of determining the number of factors is the Kaiser criterion; and the method of rotation is oblique PROMAX, which also implies that the initial rotation is done through Varimax. Data input and characteristics are described in other control cards which are not easy to describe without going into details of how SAS handles its input in general.

Complications in Analyzing Real Data

In the previous sections, we illustrated the application of factor analysis to error free data, and the general computer programs with which to obtain basic solutions. We concentrated on obtaining a solution while completely ignoring various complications that might arise. We must acknowledge, however, that the data one normally has will not fit the factor analysis model exactly. This is so because the data we usually analyze are not error free—they are subject to not only sampling and measurement errors but also to selection bias and disturbances created by minor factors not fully anticipated by the researcher. The computer programs we have introduced in the preceding section take these complications into account to a certain extent in obtaining a given solution, but some aspects of these complications are of an extra-statistical nature. For a fuller appreciation of factor analysis, the user must have at least a minimal degree of understanding of these complications. They are described below.

SAMPLING VARIABILITY

The correlation matrices we use as raw data for factor analysis are almost always based on sample data. Therefore, for any given sample, an observed correlation will never exactly reflect the underlying population correlation. The deviation from the underlying correlation matrix will be less as sample size increases, but even with a sample size, say 1,000, there can be substantial deviations for some correlations. One typical sample (to be precise, it is "typical" only in the sense that it happens to be the first random sample we have generated) of size 100 from the population model specified in Figure 16 and Table 9 is presented in the upper triangle of Table 14. Other sample results with the same size are presented in the lower triangle of Table 14.

By comparing these values with those shown in Table 9, and comparing the values in the upper triangle with the values in the lower triangle, you will notice that there is substantial variation from one table to another.

TABLE 14

**Correlations for Variables from two Samples of Size 100
from the Same Mother Population: The Upper Triangle Represents
a Different Sample from the Lower Triangle**

	x_1	x_2	x_3	x_4	x_5	x_6
x_1	--	.6008	.4984	.1920	.1959	.3466
x_2	.5461	--	.4749	.2196	.1912	.2979
x_3	.4734	.4284	--	.2079	.2010	.2445
x_4	.1119	.1625	.0673	--	.4334	.3197
x_5	.0387	.1348	.0275	.3804	--	.4207
x_6	.2639	.2070	.1597	.2817	.1543	--

a. The population correlations are given in Table 9.

Because factor analysis uses the correlation matrix as the data, we may infer that the result will be different when sample data are used and will vary across samples.

Because of this sampling variability one cannot rely completely on the rank-theorem presented in Section II. For instance, the rank-theorem that the reduced matrix will have a rank equal to the minimum of common factors compatible with the data will not hold exactly for any given sample. Likewise, there will be no way to replicate exactly the underlying communalities from the examination of a sample covariance matrix. Therefore, we will need either a general rule-of-thumb or some statistical test with which to test the adequacy of a particular solution based on sample data.

It can be said that almost all of the difficulties and complications in obtaining factor solutions are directly traceable to the computational difficulties in obtaining "good" estimates of underlying parameters by analyzing error-prone sample data. The logical problem of ascertaining the underlying causal (factor) structure from the examination of the covariance structure is more fundamental (as we have emphasized previously), but the resolution of that issue is handled by extra-statistical means and is not the major source of any computational complications. We will discuss the computational problems and their resolution more fully in the companion volume, when we describe various statistical methods of extracting factors.

We merely note at this point that with error free data (no sampling and measurement errors), a good factor analysis program should be able to

TABLE 15
Maximum Likelihood Two-Common Factor Solution Applied
to Data in the Upper Triangle of Table 14

Variables	Unrotated F$_1$	F$_2$	Communality	Rotated Using Direct Oblimin Criterion F$_1$	F$_2$
X$_1$	.747	-.300	.648	.817	-.027
X$_2$	.701	-.266	.562	.754	-.009
X$_3$	.599	-.176	.389	.602	.046
X$_4$	.428	.362	.314	.027	.547
X$_5$	.505	.605	.621	-.113	.833
X$_6$	.534	.248	.367	.202	.468
Sum of Squares[a]	2.132	.749		1.652	1.215
χ^2 with 4 degrees of freedom =	.825				

a. Sums of squares are equivalent to eigenvalues in the unrotated solution and this value divided by n gives the proportion of variance explained by that factor. In an obliquely rotated solution, they represent merely what might be called a "direct" contribution of each factor. The joint contribution (including that due to the correlation between the factors) is still equivalent to the sum of eigenvalues in the unrotated solution.

identify exactly the underlying simple factor structure. For instance, if we use the correlation matrix in Table 9, an extraction method based on either the maximum likelihood solution or the principal axis with iterated communalities solution, and final rotation based on the Direct Oblimin (with delta = 0), we should reproduce without error the known factor structure as shown in Figure 16. This cannot be expected when applied to sample data, however. To illustrate this, we have shown a terminal solution based on the maximum likelihood method and Direct Oblimin rotation as applied to the sample correlation matrix in the upper triangle of Table 14. (See Table 15.) This can be compared with Table 13.

SELECTION BIAS

In applying factor analysis, the most important decision is often made before the analysis, when the researcher selects variables to examine. Selection is invariably involved regardless of whether one designs a factor

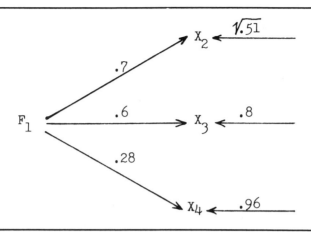

Figure 18: One Common-Factor Model Fit to a Subset of Variables from Table 9

analytic experiment or whether one takes a subset of variables from the existing survey. It will be difficult for any researcher to argue that a given set of items or variables constitutes the universe of all potential variables.

Once we admit that we always deal with a certain subset of items out of a potentially large universe of items, we must worry about the possible selection bias. Let us first examine some simple but dramatic examples. Consider a situation in which the researcher examines only three variables, say, X_2, X_3, and X_4, from the model shown in Figure 16. Suppose for heuristic purposes that there are no measurement or sampling errors; we would then get the correlation matrix in which $r_{23} = .420$, $r_{24} = .196$, and $r_{34} = .168$ (i.e., a submatrix out of Table 9).

The application of a one-common factor model to this matrix would result in the factor structure shown in Figure 18, which may be compared with Figure 16. Not only does the factor loading (and communality and uniqueness) for X_4 change, but also the fact that X_4 belongs to a different dimension than X_2 and X_3 is completely lost. This example is not adequate for illustrating this argument, however, because it capitalizes also on the fact that applying a factor model to a three variable matrix is not terribly informative. Many (but not all) arbitrary three variable correlation matrices will exactly fit a one-common factor model as long as the magnitude of one correlation is not less than the magnitude of the product of the remaining two correlations.

Let us therefore consider examining the first four variables from the model shown in Figure 16. If there is no sampling error, one-common factor will completely account for the observed correlations as before.

This is an invalid result when evaluated against the model presumed known, but in the absence of such knowledge it would have led us to believe that there is only one underlying common dimension. In general, the greater the ratio of the number of variables to the number of underlying factors, the more informative the factor analysis is. But what is crucial is not the overall ratio, but the number of variables for each factor. Some authors (Thurstone) recommend at least three variables for each factor for a good resolution of the dimensionality issue.

This leads us to an interesting dilemma. A good factor analysis requires that the researcher know a great deal about the factorial structure of variables, but many social scientists are attracted to the method because of its promise of bringing some order to a data matrix they consider to be complex and chaotic.

In general, deletion of variables from the universe of variables for a factor model *can* affect the identification of that model. For this reason, most factor analysis methods (except *image* analysis) assume that there is no sampling of variables. The implications of violating this assumption are more serious than it might first seem. In fact, anyone who uses factor analysis is likely to run into a problem of selecting variables (inclusion as well as deletion of variables). On the one hand, inclusion of "unrelated" variables is often scorned by a harsh statement such as "Garbage in, garbage out." On the other, deletion of variables in order to have a neat factorial structure can lead into an erroneous conclusion. What we want to emphasize here is that no researcher can avoid making a certain number of judgmental decisions. An awareness of the assumptions required to use factor analysis is one of the key ingredients leading to sounder decisions.

MEASUREMENT ERRORS

The data we obtain are also subject to measurement error. If the measuring instrument is systematically biased (the errors are correlated), there is no easy way to solve the problem. But factor analysis can accommodate random measurement errors without too much problem. When random measurement error is considered, it is often treated as part of the unique factors. For example, a simple three variable one-common factor model with random measurement error can be represented as in Figure 19. Note that the variance of an observed variable is now decomposed into three parts:

$$\text{Var}(X_i) = (\text{Variance}) + (\text{Variance due to specific factor } S_i) \quad [35]$$
$$\text{due to } F_1$$
$$+ (\text{Measurement Error } E_i) = b_i^2 + s_i^2 + e_i^2$$

The effect of random measurement error is to lower the expected magnitude of correlations among variables. Some factoring methods, principal axis factoring, and to some extent Alpha factoring, try to incorporate the random measurement error component.

When there is random measurement error, it is possible to factor a correlation matrix that is corrected for attenuation, provided the reliability of each variable is known. However, there are several complications to deal with. First, correcting for attentuation for each correlation coefficient may lead to a matrix that is not Gramian (i.e., some of the characteristic roots associated with such a matrix may be negative; see Bock and Petersen [1975] for a discussion of multivariate correlation of attenuation). Second, the estimates of reliabilities themselves are also subject to sampling variability. Third, usually, the estimates of reliabilities are not available. In short, correcting for attenuation should not be viewed as always appropriate.

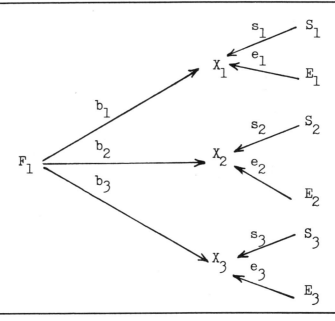

Figure 19: Simple One-Common Factor Model with Random Measurement Errors,

where $Var(X_1) = b_1^2 + s_1^2 + e_1^2$, F = common factor, S_i = specific factor, E_i = random error component. (Unique factor = $U_i = S_i + E_i$.)

64

MINOR FACTORS

The problem we wish to address here is different from a more fundamental problem that the factor analytic model may not fit the data at all. We assume at this point that the factor analytic model is, in general, applicable to the data at hand. What is at issue is that in addition to a few major factors there may be some minor factors which do not contribute *substantially* to the covariance structure among the observed variables but are *statistically significant* given a large enough sample size. Stated from a somewhat different perspective, the problem is that we may not be able to ascertain when a given minor deviation is really due to sampling variability or to the lack of exact fit.

To summarize this section, we wish to emphasize that contrary to the impressions a novice may obtain from glancing through seemingly complex statistical algorithms displayed in technical articles on factor analysis, there are numerous uncertainties which allow considerable judgmental discretion on the part of the user. Knowledge of this seemingly unguided freedom will undoubtedly leave the novice with an uncomfortable feeling. This is not unique to factor analysis, however; actual data analysis problems are almost always more complex than the well developed statistical procedures assume to be true. As a consequence, users of factor analysis often find that less well articulated "rules-of-thumb" that acknowledge the complexity may be relied on, instead of a well specified rule that is based on simple but formal and unrealistic models. A number of these rules-of-thumb will be addressed in the companion volume. The reader by now should be ready to appreciate the variety of factor solutions proposed in the literature, and to tolerate any lack of definitive solutions regarding some of the crucial questions.

The reader also should appreciate by now why another volume is needed in which various methods of extracting and rotating factors are introduced. While we encourage the reader to study the material introduced in the companion volume, we close this volume by paraphrasing Kaiser's dictum—that all the subtle variations in obtaining factor solutions do not really make that much difference (Kaiser, 1970). If the reader has grasped the logical foundations of the technique and the means of obtaining a basic solution, factor analysis will be found to serve as a valuable tool with many research applications.

NOTE

1. Mean and variance are defined here as descriptive statistics (they are not treated as estimates of underlying parameters) and only with respect to discrete distributions. This does not mean, however, that our discussion will be limited to discrete distributions. The expectation notation is not only more compact but has the advantage of being generalizable

to a continuous distribution. However, since it is not essential for the understanding of the subject, we will not repeat these definitions for a continuous distribution. Furthermore, it will be assumed throughout Section II that concepts are defined for the population, unless otherwise stated or implied in the context.

QUESTIONS PERTAINING TO BOOKS, JOURNALS, AND COMPUTER PROGRAMS

(a) *Are there any books or articles on factor analysis a novice can read and readily understand?*

Not really. Most require some technical background. However, the following are easier than the others: Rummel (1967); Schuessler (1971); Cattell (1952); Comrey (1973); Fruchter (1954).

(b) *What are the "next-level" books that the serious reader should consider examining?*

Harman (1976); Mulaik (1972); Lawley and Maxwell (1971).

(c) *What are the major journals which regularly publish articles on factor analysis?*

Psychometrika; British Journal of Mathematical and Statistical Psychology; Educational and Psychological Measurement.

(d) *What are some of the general purpose computer packages containing factor analysis programs?*

SPSS; OSIRIS; SAS; BMD.

(e) *What are the more specialized programs dealing with factor analysis that one should know about?*

Kaiser's—Little Jiffy, Mark IV; Sörbom & Jöreskog—COFAMM, LISREL

(f) *Where are the major simulation studies reported?*

Tucker, Koopman and Linn (1969); Browne (1968); Linn (1968); Hakstian (1971); Hakstian and Abell (1974).

(g) *Where can one find a good list of references?*

Each of the text books listed in question (b) above contain extensive references to the literature. For an even handier list, we have included in this volume all of the references cited in the companion volumes.

REFERENCES

ALWIN, D. F. (1973) "The use of factor analysis in the construction of linear composites in social research." Sociological Methods and Research 2:191-214.

ANDERSON, T. W. and H. RUBIN (1956) "Statistical inference in factor analysis." Proceedings of the Third Berkeley Symposium on Mathematical Statistics and Probability 5:111-150.

ASHER, H. (1976) Causal Modeling. Sage University Papers on Quantitative Applications in the Social Sciences, 07-003. Beverly Hills and London: Sage Pub.

BMDP-77: Biomedical Computer Programs (P-Series). W. J. Dixon, Series Editor, M. B. Brown, Editor 1977 edition. Los Angeles: Univ. of California Press, 1977.

BARGMANN, R. E. (1957) A Study of Independence and Dependence in Multivariate Normal Analysis. Mimeo Series No. 186. Chapel Hill, N.C.: Institute of Statistics.

BARTLETT, M. S. (1937) "The statistical conception of method factors." British Journal of Psychology 28:97-104.

BOCK, R. D. and R. E. BARGMANN (1966) "Analysis of covariance structure." Psychometrika 31:507-534.

BOCK, R. D. and M. LIEBERMAN (1970) "Fitting a response model for N dichotomously scored items." Psychometrika 26:347-372.

BOCK, R. D. and A. C. PETERSON (1975) "A multivariate correction for attenuation." Biometrika 62:673-678.

BROWNE, M. W. (1968) "A comparison of factor analytic techniques." Psychometrika 33:267-334.

COFAMM: Confirmatory Factory Analysis with Model Modification User's Guide. Sörbom, D. and Jöreskog, K. G. Chicago: National Educational Resources, Inc., 1976.

CARROLL, J. B. (1953) "Approximating simple structure in factor analysis." Psychometrika 18:23-38.

——— (1961) "The nature of data, or how to choose a correlation coefficient." Psychometrika 26:347-372.

CATTELL, R. B. (1952) Factor Analysis. New York: Harper and Bros.

——— (1965) "Factor analysis: an introduction to essentials. (I) the purpose and underlying models, (II) the role of factor analysis in research." Biometrics 21:190-215, 405-435.

——— (1966) Handbook of Multivariate Experimental Psychology. Chicago: Rand McNally.

——— and J. L. MUERLE (1960) "The 'maxplane' program for factor rotation to oblique simple structure." Educational and Psychological Measurement 20:269-290.

CHRISTOFFERSSON, A. (1975) "Factor analysis of dichotomized variables." Psychometrika 40:5-32.

COMREY, A. L. (1973) A First Course in Factor Analysis. New York: Academic Press.

CRONBACH, L. J. (1951) "Coefficient alpha and the internal structure of tests." Psychometrika 16: 297-334.

DUNCAN, O. D. (1966) "Path analysis: sociological examples." American Journal of Sociology 72:1-16.

EBER, H. W. (1966) "Toward oblique simple structure maxplane." Multivariate Behavioral Research 1:112-125.

FRUCHTER, B. (1954) Introduction to Factor Analysis. New York: Van Nostrand.

GREEN, B. F., Jr. (1976) "On the factor score controversy." Psychometrika 41:263-266.

GUILFORD, J. P. (1977) "The invariance problem in factor analysis." Educational and Psychological Measurement 37:11-19.

GUTTMAN, L. (1953) "Image theory for the structure of quantitative variates." Psychometrika 18:227-296.

——— (1954) "Some necessary conditions for common factor analysis." Psychometrika 19:149-161.

HAKSTIAN, A. R. (1971) "A comparative evaluation of several prominent methods of oblique factor transformation." Psychometrika 36:175-193.

——— and R. A. ABELL (1974) "A further comparison of oblique factor transformation methods." Psychometrika 39:429-444.

HARMAN, H. H. (1976) Modern Factor Analysis. Chicago: University of Chicago Press.
—— (in press) "Minres method of factor analysis," in K. Enstein, A. Ralston, and H. S. Wilf (eds.) Statistical Methods for Digital Computers. New York: John Wiley.
—— and W. H. JONES (1966) "Factor analysis by minimizing residuals (Minres)." Psychometrika 31:351-368.
HARMAN, H. H. and Y. FUKUDA (1966) "Resolution of the Heywood case in the Minres solution." Psychometrika 31:563-571.
HARRIS, C. W. (1962) "Some Rao-Guttman relationships." Psychometrika 27: 247-263.
—— (1967) "On factors and factor scores." Psychometrika 32: 363-379.
—— and H. F. KAISER (1964) "Oblique factor analytic solutions by orthogonal transformations." Psychometrika 29:347-362.
HENDRICKSON, A. E. and P. O. WHITE (1964) "Promax: A quick method for rotation to oblique simple structure." British Journal of Mathematical and Statistical Psychology 17:65-70.
HORN, J. L. (1965) "An empirical comparison of various methods for estimating common factor scores." Educational and Psychological Measurement 25:313-322.
HORST, P. (1965) Factor Analysis of Data Matrices. New York: Holt Rinehart and Winston.
HOTELLING, H. (1933) "Analysis of a complex of statistical variables into principal components." Journal of Education Psychology 24:417-441, 498-520.
HOWE, W. G. (1955) Some Contributions to Factor Analysis. Report No. ORNL-1919. Oak Ridge, Tenn.: Oak Ridge National Laboratory. Ph.D. dissertation, University of North Carolina.
JENNRICH, R. I. (1970) "Orthogonal Rotation Algorithms." Psychometrika 35:229-235.
—— (1974) "Simplified formulae in standard errors in maximum likelihood factor analysis." British Journal of Mathematical and Statistical Psychology 27:122-131.
JENNRICH, R. I. and P. F. SAMPSON (1966) "Rotation for simple loadings." Psychometrika 31:313-323.
JORESKOG, K. G. (1963) Statistical Estimation in Factor Analysis: A New Technique and Its Foundation. Stockholm: Almquist and Wiksell.
—— (1966) "Testing a simple structure hypothesis in factor analysis." Psychometrika 31:165-178.
—— (1967) "Some contributions to maximum likelihood factor analysis." Psychometrika 32:443-482.
—— (1969) "A general approach to confirmatory maximum likelihood factor analysis." Psychometrika 34:183-202.
—— (1970) "A general method for analysis of covariance structure." Biometrika 57:239-251.
—— (1976) Analyzing Psychological Data by Structural Analysis of Covariance Matrices. Research Report 76-9. University of Uppsala, Statistics Department.
JÖRESKOG, K. G. and D. N. LAWLEY (1968) "New methods in maximum likelihood factor analysis." British Journal of Mathematical and Statistical Psychology 21:85-96.
KAISER, H. F. (1958) "The varimax criterion for analytic rotation in factor analysis." Psychometrika 23:187-200.
—— (1963) "Image analysis," pp. 156-166 in C. W. Harris (ed.) Problems in Measuring Change. Madison: University of Wisconsin Press.
—— (1970) "A second-generation Little Jiffy." Psychometrika 35:401-415.
—— (1974) "Little Jiffy, Mark IV." Educational and Psychological Measurement 34: 111-117.
—— (1974) "An index of factorial simplicity." Psychometrika 39:31-36.
KAISER, H. F. and J. CAFFREY (1965) "Alpha factor analysis." Psychometrika 30:1-14.
KIM, J. O. (1975) "Multivariate analysis of ordinal variables." American Journal of Sociology 81:261-298.

68

——— and C. W. MUELLER (1976) "Standardized and unstandardized coefficients in causal analysis: An expository note." Sociological Methods and Research 4:423-438.

KIM, J. O., N. NIE and S. VERBA (1977) "A note on factor analyzing dichotomous variables: the case of political participation." Political Methodology 4:39-62.

KIRK, D. B. (1973) "On the numerical approximation of the bivariate normal (tetrachoric) correlation coefficient." Psychometrika 38:259-268.

LISREL III: Estimation of Linear Structural Equation Systems by Maximum Likelihood Methods. (User's Guide). Jöreskog, K. G. and Sörbom, D. Chicago: National Educational Resources, Inc., 1976.

LITTLE JIFFY, MARK IV. (See Kaiser, 1974)

LABOVITZ, S. (1967) "Some observations on measurement and statistics." Social Forces 46:151-160.

——— (1970) "The assignment of numbers to rank order categories." American Sociological Review 35:515-524.

LAND, K. O. (1969) "Principles of path analysis," pp. 3-37 in E. F. Borgatta (ed.) Sociological Methodology. San Francisco: Jossey-Bass.

LAWLEY, D. N. (1940) "The estimation of factor loading by the method of maximum likelihood." Proceedings of the Royal Society of Edinburgh 60:64-82.

——— and MAXWELL, A. E. (1971) Factor Analysis as a Statistical Method. London: Butterworth and Co.

LEVINE, M. S. (1977) Canonical Analysis and Factor Comparison. Sage University Papers on Quantitative Applications in the Social Sciences, 07-006. Beverly Hills and London: Sage Pub.

LI, C. C. (1975) Path Analysis—A Primer. Pacific Grove, Calif.: Boxwood Press.

LINN, R. L. (1968) "A Monte Carlo approach to the number of factors problems." Psychometrika 33:37-71.

LORD, F. M. and W. R. NOVICK (1968) Statistical Theories of Mental Test Scores. Reading, Mass.: Addison-Wesley.

MALINVAND, E. (1970) Statistical Methods of Econometrics. New York: Elsevier.

MAXWELL, A. E. (1972) "Thomson's sampling theory recalled." British Journal of Mathematical and Statistical Psychology 25:1-21.

McDONALD, R. P. (1970) "The theoretical foundations of principal factor analysis, canonical factor analysis, and alpha factor analysis." British Journal of Mathematical and Statistical Psychology 23:1-21.

——— (1974) "The measurement of factor indeterminacy." Psychometrika 39:203-221.

——— (1975) "Descriptive axioms for common factor theory, image theory and component theory." Psychometrika 40:137-152.

——— (1975) "A note on Rippe's test of significance in common factor analysis." Psychometrika 40:117-119.

——— and E. J. BURR (1967) "A comparison of four methods of constructing factor scores." Psychometrika 32:380-401.

MULAIK, S. A. (1972) The Foundations of Factor Analysis. New York: McGraw-Hill.

NEUHAUS, J. O. and C. WRIGLEY (1954) "The method: an analytic approach to orthogonal simple structure." British Journal of Mathematical and Statistical Psychology 7:81-91.

OSIRIS Manual. Ann Arbor, Mich.: Inter-University Consortium for Political Research, 1973.

RAO, C. R. (1955) "Estimation and test of significance in factor analysis." Psychometrika 20:93-111.

RUMMEL, R. J. (1967) "Understanding factor analysis." Conflict Resolution 11:444-480.

——— (1970) Applied Factor Analysis. Evanston: Northwestern University Press.

SAS: A User's Guide to SAS 76. Anthony J. Barr, James H. Goodnight, John P. Sall, and Jane T. Helwig. Raleigh, N.C.: SAS Institute, Inc., 1976.

SPSS: Statistical Package for the Social Sciences. Norman H. Nie, C. Hadlai Hull, Jean G. Jenkins, Karin Steinbrenner, and Dale Bent. New York: McGraw-Hill, 1975.

SAUNDERS, D. R. (1953) An Analytic Method for Rotation to Orthogonal Simple Structure. Research Bulletin 53-10. Princeton, N.J.: Educational Testing Service.

————— (1960) "A computer program to find the best-fitting orthogonal factors for a given hypothesis." Psychometrika 25:199-205.

SCHUESSLER, K. (1971) Analyzing Social Data. Boston: Houghton Mifflin.

SÖRBOM, D. and K. G. JÖRESKOG (1976) COFAMM: Confirmatory Factor Analysis with Model Modification User's Guide. Chicago: National Educational Resources, Inc.

STEPHENSON, W. (1953) The Study of Behavior. Chicago: The University of Chicago Press.

STEVENS, S. S. (1946) "On the theory of scales of measurement." Science 103:677-680.

STINCHCOMBE, A. L. (1971) "A heuristic procedure for interpreting factor analysis." American Sociological Review 36:1080-1084.

THOMPSON, G. H. (1934) "Hotelling's method modified to give Spearman's g." Journal of Educational Psychology 25:366-374.

THURSTONE, L. L. (1947) Multiple Factor Analysis. Chicago: University of Chicago Press.

TRYON, C. R. and BAILEY, D. E. (1970) Cluster Analysis. New York: McGraw-Hill.

TUCKER, L. R. (1966) "Some mathematical notes on three mode factor analysis." Psychometrika 31:279-311.

————— (1971) "Relations of factor score estimates to their use." Psychometrika 36:427-436.

—————, R. F. KOOPMAN, and R. L. LINN (1969) "Evaluation of factor analytic research procedures by means of simulated correlation matrices." Psychometrika 34:421-459.

TUCKER, L. R. and C. LEWIS (1973) "A reliability coefficient for maximum likelihood factor analysis." Psychometrika 38:1-8.

VELICER, W. F. (1975) "The relation between factor scores, image scores, and principal component scores." Educational and Psychological Measurement 36:149-159.

WAINER, H. (1976) "Estimating coefficients in linear models: it don't make no nevermind." Psychological Bulletin 83:213-217.

WANG, M. W. and J. C. STANLEY (1970) "Differential weighing: a review of methods and empirical studies." Review of Educational Research 40:663-705.

GLOSSARY

ALPHA FACTORING: a method of initial factoring in which the variables included in the analysis are considered samples from a universe of variables; see Kaiser and Caffrey in the references.

ADJUSTED CORRELATION MATRIX: the correlation matrix in which the diagonal elements are replaced by communalities; also used to refer to correlation or covariance matrices which are altered in a variety of ways before extracting factors.

BIQUARTIMIN CRITERION: a criterion applied in obtaining an indirect oblique rotation.

COMMUNALITY (h^2): the variance of an observed variable accounted for by the common factors; in an orthogonal factor model, it is equivalent to the sum of the squared factor loadings.

COMMON PART: that part of an observed variable accounted for by the common factors.

COMMON FACTOR: unmeasured (or hypothetical) underlying variable which is the source of variation in at least two observed variables under consideration.

CONFIRMATORY FACTOR ANALYSIS: factor analysis in which specific expectations concerning the number of factors and their loadings are tested on sample data.

CORRELATION: a measure of association between two variables; generally assumed to be the product-moment r (or Pearson's r); equivalent to the covariance between two standardized variables; also used as a general term for any type of linear association between variables.

COVARIATION: a crude measure of the degree to which two variables co-vary together; measured as the sum of cross-products of two variables which are expressed as deviations from their respective means; also used as a general term for describing the association between variables.

COVARIANCE: a measure of association between two variables; covariation divided by the number of cases involved; expected value of the sum of cross-products between two variables expressed as deviations from their respective means; the covariance between standardized variables is also known as the correlation.

COVARIANCE-STRUCTURE ANALYSIS: an analysis strategy (1) in which the observed covariance is expressed in terms of a very general model which can accommodate hypothetical factors as well as observed variables, and (2) in which the researcher then specifies appropriate parameters to evaluate the adequacy of the specification against the sample covariance structure.

COVARIMIN: a criterion for obtaining an oblique rotation; a variant of indirect oblimin rotation.

DETERMINANT: a mathematical property of a square matrix; discussed as a means of determining the rank (or the number of independent dimensions) of an adjusted correlation matrix.

DIRECT OBLIMIN: a method of oblique rotation in which rotation is performed without resorting to reference axes.

EIGENVALUE (or characteristic root): a mathematical property of a matrix; used in relation to the decomposition of a covariance matrix, both as a criterion of determining the number of factors to extract and a measure of variance accounted for by a given dimension.

EIGENVECTOR: a vector associated with its respective eigenvalue; obtained in the process of initial factoring; when these vectors are appropriately standardized, they become factor loadings.

EQUIMAX: a criterion for obtaining an orthogonal rotation; this criterion is a compromise between varimax and quartimax criteria.

ERROR-FREE DATA: contrived data where the underlying model is presumed known and there is an exact fit between data and model.

EXPECTATION: a mathematical operation through which the mean of a random variable is defined for both discrete and continuous distributions; an expected value is the property of a particular variable.

EXPLORATORY FACTOR ANALYSIS: factor analysis which is mainly used as a means of exploring the underlying factor structure *without* prior specification of number of factors and their loadings.

EXTRACTION OF FACTORS OR FACTOR EXTRACTION: the initial stage of factor analysis in which the covariance matrix is resolved into a smaller number of underlying factors or components.

ERROR COMPONENT: the part of the variance of an observed variable that is due to random measurement errors; constitutes a portion of the unique component.

FACTORS: hypothesized, unmeasured, and underlying variables which are presumed to be the sources of the observed variables; often divided into unique and common factors.

FACTOR LOADING: a general term referring to a coefficient in a factor pattern or structure matrix.

FACTOR PATTERN MATRIX: a matrix of coefficients where the columns usually refer to common factors and the rows to the observed variables; elements of the matrix represent regression weights for the common factors where an observed variable is assumed to be a linear combination of the factors; for an orthogonal solution, the pattern matrix is equivalent to correlations between factors and variables.

FACTOR SCORE: the estimate for a case on an underlying factor formed from a linear combination of observed variables; a by-product of the factor analysis.

FACTOR STRUCTURE MATRIX: a matrix of coefficients where the coefficients refer to the correlations between factors and variables; it is equivalent to a pattern matrix in the orthogonal case.

FACTORICAL COMPLEXITY: a characteristic of an observed variable; the number of common factors with (significant) loadings on that variable.

FACTORIAL DETERMINATION: the overall degree to which variations in observed variables are accounted by the common factors.

GRAMIAN: a square matrix is Gramian if it is symmetrical and all of the eigenvalues associated with the matrix are greater than or equal to zero; unadjusted correlation and covariance matrices are always Gramian.

IMAGE FACTORING: a method of obtaining initial factors; the observed variation is deomposed into (partial) images and anti-images, instead of into common parts and unique parts.

KAISER CRITERION: a criterion of determining the number of factors to extract; suggested by Guttman and popularized by Kaiser; also known as the "eigenvalue greater than one" criterion.

LINEAR COMBINATION: a combination in which variables are combined with only constant weights.

LINEAR SYSTEM: relationship among variables referred to as a whole, in which all the relationships are linear; factor analysis model in which all of the variables are assumed to be linear functions of underlying factors.

LEAST-SQUARES SOLUTION: in general, a solution which minimizes the squared deviations between the observed values and predicted values; a method of extracting initial factors, whose variants include principal axis factoring with iterated communalities and Minres.

MAXIMUM LIKELIHOOD SOLUTION: in general, a method of statistical estimation which seeks to identify the population parameters with a maximum likelihood of generating the observed sample distribution; a method of obtaining the initial factor solution; its variants include canonical factoring (RAO) and a method that maximizes the determinant of the residual partial correlation matrix.

MONTE CARLO EXPERIMENT: a strategy whereby various sample properties based on complex statistical models are simulated.

OBLIMAX: a criterion for obtaining an oblique rotation: it is equivalent to the quartimax criterion in orthogonal rotation.

OBLIMIN: a general criterion for obtaining an oblique rotation which tries to simplify the pattern matrix by way of reference axes; its variants include bi-quartimin, covarimin, and quartimin.

OBLIQUE FACTORS: factors that are correlated with each other; factors obtained through oblique rotation.

OBLIQUE ROTATION: the operation through which a simple structure is sought; factors are rotated without imposing the orthogonality condition and resulting terminal factors are in general correlated with each other.

ORTHOGONAL FACTORS: factors that are not correlated with each other; factors obtained through orthogonal rotation.

ORTHOGONAL ROTATION: the operation through which a simple structure is sought under the restriction that factors be orthogonal (or uncorrelated); factors obtained through this rotation are by definition uncorrelated.

PRINCIPAL AXIS FACTORING: a method of initial factoring in which the adjusted correlation matrix is decomposed hierarchically; a principal axis factor analysis with iterated communalities leads to a least-squares solution of initial factoring.

PRINCIPAL COMPONENTS: linear combinations of observed variables, possessing properties such as being orthogonal to each other, and the first principal component representing the largest amount of variance in the data, the second representing the second largest and so on; often considered variants of common factors, but more accurately they are contrasted with common factors which are hypothetical.

POSTULATE OF FACTORIAL CAUSATION: the assumption that the observed variables are linear combinations of underlying factors, and that the covariation between observed variables is solely due to their common sharing of one or more of the common factors.

POSTULATE OF PARSIMONY: this stipulates that, given two or more equally compatible models for the given data, the simpler model is believed to be true; in factor analysis, only the model involving the minimum number of common factors is considered appropriate.

QUARTIMAX: a criterion for obtaining an orthogonal rotation; the emphasis is on simplifying the rows of the factor pattern matrix.

QUARTIMIN: a criterion for obtaining an oblique rotation; the oblique counterpart of the quartimax rotation; requires the introduction of reference axes.

RANK OF A MATRIX: the number of linearly independent columns or rows of a matrix; the order of the largest square submatrix whose determinant is not zero.

REFERENCE AXES: these refer to axes that are orthogonal to the primary factors; they are introduced to simplify oblique rotation.

SCREE-TEST: a rule-of-thumb criterion for determining the number of significant factors to retain; it is based on the graph of roots (eigenvalues); claimed to be appropriate in handling disturbances due to minor (unarticulated) factors.

SIMPLE STRUCTURE: a special term referring to a factor structure with certain simple properties; some of these properties include that a variable has factor loadings on as few common factors as possible, and that each common factor has significant loadings on some variables and no loadings on others.

SPECIFIC COMPONENT: the part of the variance of an observed variable that is due to a factor which is specific to a given variable; used to designate the part of the unique component that is not due to random errors.

TARGET MATRIX: a matrix of coefficients used as a target in rotation; an initial factor solution may be rotated in such a way that the resulting factor loadings resemble the target matrix maximally.

VARIANCE: a measure of dispersion of a variable; defined as the sum of squared deviations from the mean divided by the number of cases or entities.

VARIATION: a measure of dispersion in a variable; loosely used as a general term for describing any type of dispersion around some central value; sum of squared deviations from the mean.

VARIMAX: a method of orthogonal rotation which simplifies the factor structure by maximizing the variance of a column of the pattern matrix.

UNIQUE COMPONENT: the part of the observed variance unaccounted for by the common factors; the proportion that is unique to each variable; it is often further decomposed into specific and error components.

UNIQUE FACTOR: the factor which is believed to affect only a single observed variable; often stands for all the independent factors (including the error component) that are unique to a variable.

74

AUTHORS' NOTE: *We wish to express our appreciation and thanks to the numerous people who helped make the completion of this manuscript possible. In particular, computer assistance was provided by James Meeks-Johnson, Chia Hsing Lu, and Gayle Scriven. David Kenney, James Rabjohn, Elaine Black, and James Duane offered advice and suggestions on an earlier draft of the manuscript. A special thanks should go to Eric Uslaner, Lawrence Mayer, and an anonymous reviewer for their useful comments and advice.*

FACTOR ANALYSIS PART II

Statistical Methods and Practical Issues

JAE-ON KIM

CHARLES W. MUELLER

I. INTRODUCTION

The conceptual foundation of factor analysis is simple and easy to learn. However, there are several reasons why mastering the method for practical application can be quite difficult. First, understanding the principles of statistical estimation in general requires more mathematical sophistication than is necessary for understanding the underlying conceptual model. Second, numerous methods of obtaining factor solutions have been suggested in the literature and even a relatively simple computer program is likely to provide many options at every stage of the analysis. Such complexities can be stupefying to the beginner and a source of uneasiness even to an expert. Third, the real research problem at hand is almost always more complex than the factor analysis model assumes to be true. For instance, (1) it may be that the level of measurement of some or all variables does not meet the measurement requirements of factor analysis, (2) some aspects of the model, such as independence of measurement error, may be unrealistic for one's data, or (3) one may have minor factors whose identification is not the primary concern but whose presence affects the identification of major common factors. The crux of the matter is that the researcher must in the end make some discretionary extrastatistical decisions. Fortunately, as will be shown, these difficulties can be overcome.

As we noted in the first volume, *Introduction to Factor Analysis: What It Is and How to Do It*, the researcher is more or less forced to rely

AUTHORS' NOTE: *We wish to express our appreciation and thanks to the numerous people who helped make the completion of this manuscript possible. In particular, computer assistance was provided by James Meeks-Johnson, Chia Hsing Lu, and Gayle Scriven. David Kenney, James Rabjohn, Elaine Black, and James Duane offered advice and suggestions on an earlier draft of the manuscript. A special thanks should go to Eric Uslaner, Lawrence Mayer, and an anonymous reviewer for their useful comments and advice.*

on existing computer programs for the actual solution, and these programs often provide standard default options that a user may depend on until some modification is felt to be necessary. Furthermore, as the researcher becomes acquainted with the variety of options in factor analysis, it will be evident that most variations are, to a large degree, superficial. In fact, there are several common threads underlying these variations. Even more important, the researcher will find that applying different methods and criteria to the same data will produce results that are equivalent for most practical purposes. In short, there is no need for the reader to learn and use all the options immediately. It is important, however, that the user *be aware of* the most important variations and options in obtaining factor analysis, and that this user appreciate right from the beginning the fact that there is no single definitive (or best) solution for most problems.

This volume assumes that the reader has a basic understanding of the conceptual foundation of factor analysis, such as that covered in the preceding volume. It is also expected that the reader is aware of the differences between the uncertainties inherent in inferring the underlying causal structure from an observed covariance structure (the logical problem), and the uncertainties inherent in making inferences about the population parameters from the examination of the sample statistics (statistical problem). Although these two problems are integrally intertwined in obtaining actual factor analysis solutions, it is important that the conceptual differences are kept clearly in mind. Before we discuss the statistical methods and practical issues, we believe it is useful to provide a brief recapitulation of the material covered in the first volume.

Review of Factor Analysis Basics

Factor analysis assumes that the observed variables are linear combinations of some underlying (hypothetical or unobservable) factors. Some of these factors are assumed to be common to two or more variables and some are assumed to be unique to each variable. The unique factors are then (at least in exploratory factory analysis) assumed to be orthogonal to each other. Hence, the unique factors do not contribute to the covariation between variables. In other words, only common factors (which are assumed much smaller in number than the number of observed variables) contribute to the covariation among the observed variables.

The linear system assumed in factor analysis is such that the user can identify the resulting covariance structure without error if the underlying factor loadings are known. However, ascertaining the underlying common factor structure from the observed covariance structure is always prob-

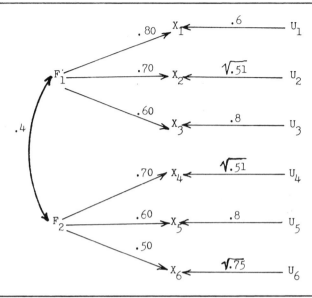

Figure 1: Path Model for Six-Variable, Two Oblique Factor Model Example, where the observed variables represent opinions on:

X_1 = whether government should spend more money on schools,

X_2 = whether government should spend more money to reduce unemployment,

X_3 = whether government should control big business,

X_4 = whether government should expedite desegregation, through busing,

X_5 = whether government sees to it that minorities get their respective quota in jobs,

X_6 = whether government should expand the headstart program.

lematic. These basic uncertainties have nothing to do with statistical estimation and must be resolved on the basis of extra-statistical postulates—the postulate of factorial causation and the postulate of parsimony.

Given these postulates and the properties of linear systems, it is possible to identify exactly the underlying factor pattern from the examination of the resulting covariance structure, provided that the underlying pattern is relatively simple and that it satisfies the requirements of simple factor structure. For example, it was shown in the previous volume that the two-common factor model illustrated in Figure 1 can be recovered from the error-free correlation matrix shown in the lower triangle of Table 1. (In that volume, we noted that an initial maximum likelihood factoring solution, followed by oblique rotation based on Direct Oblimin, produced exactly the same factor loadings as shown in Figure 1. It was also noted that any computer program, whatever algorithm it may rely on, ought to reproduce such a pattern reasonably well.[1])

TABLE 1

Correlations for the Population (in the lower triangle) and for a
Simulated Sample of 100 Cases (in the upper triangle), Pertaining to
the Two-Common Factor Model Represented in Figure 1[a]

	X_1	X_2	X_3	X_4	X_5	X_6
X_1	--	.6008	.4984	.1920	.1959	.3466
X_2	.560	--	.4749	.2196	.1912	.2979
X_3	.480	.420	--	.2079	.2010	.2445
X_4	.224	.196	.168	--	.4334	.3197
X_5	.192	.168	.144	.420	--	.4207
X_6	.160	.140	.120	.350	.300	--

a. Reproduced from Tables 8 and 13 in University Paper 07-013.

In practice, however, the covariance matrix one actually examines is
affected by a variety of random and non-random errors and will not be
the same as the covariance matrix implied by the factor pattern in the
population. For future reference, we have reproduced, in the upper
triangle of Table 1, a correlation matrix which is based on a sample of one
hundred cases from the theoretical universe defined by the factor pattern
in Figure 1 (or by the covariance matrix shown in the lower triangle of
Table 1). Note the discrepancies between the corresponding elements in
the upper and lower triangles, and the fact that every sample correlation
matrix from the same universe will be different to some extent from the
population covariance matrix *and* any other sample matrix. Therefore,
it is impossible in practice to recover the exact underlying factor pattern;
one merely tries to find estimates of the underlying values which meet
certain statistical and/or practical criteria.

There are three steps a researcher usually employs in obtaining solutions to exploratory factor analysis: (1) the preparation of an appropriate
covariance matrix; (2) extraction of initial (orthogonal) factors; and
(3) rotation to a terminal solution. Finally, we illustrated in the companion
volume the ways in which these steps are handled by several computer
packages and emphasized that it is relatively simple to obtain basic factor
analysis information.

Basic Strategies and Methods to be Covered

The uses of factor analysis are mainly *exploratory* or *confirmatory* depending on the major objectives of the researcher. In both applications, the three basic steps—of preparing the relevant covariance matrix, extracting initial factors, and rotating to a terminal solution—are implicitly involved. Although theses steps may not always be followed in obtaining the final solution (especially in testing specific hypotheses), it is convenient to discuss major variations in factor analysis with reference to these steps. Hence, the first part of this volume is organized around these steps.

We have noted in the previous volume that there is a crucial option in choosing the basic input data—whether to use ordinary covariances (correlations) among the variables or to use similarity profiles among the entities. We have so far confined our discussion to the former and will do so here also.

In the initial factoring step, we have the *common factor* model, which has served as our model of reference, and *principal components* analysis, where the underlying rationale is different from "common" factor analysis, except that both methods are effective, and widely used, means of exploring the "interdependence" among the variables. The basic difference between the two approaches is that the principal components are certain mathematical functions of the observed variables while common factors are not expressible by the combination of the observed variables. An alternative in initial factoring is image factoring. Image analysis is different from common factor analysis in that the observed variables are considered a sample from the potentially infinite universe of variables, in which the image factors are defined as linear combinations of the variables. The similarities and differences in these approaches will receive elaboration in this volume. In addition, there are many ways of actually extracting the initial factors when the common factor model is applied. The extraction methods to be described in this volume are (1) the maximum likelihood solution (which includes canonical factoring of Rao), (2) the least squares solution (which includes Minres and principal axis factoring with iterated communalities), and (3) Alpha factoring. Alpha factoring can be viewed either as a variant of the common factor model or as an alternative strategy.

The rotation step involves two major options—the orthogonal rotation and the oblique rotation. The oblique rotation can be further subdivided into those which are based on the direct simplification of loadings in the factor pattern matrix or the indirect simplification of the loadings on reference axes. Within each of these options there are many variants. Most of these will be covered in the following sections.

Next, the question of how many factors to extract and retain will be discussed in a separate section. The main reason for including a separate section in addition to a section on methods of extraction is because of the need to introduce a few important "rules-of-thumb" which are found useful by many practitioners.

The section on confirmatory factor analysis is fairly elementary. We will introduce the reader to the notion of empirical confirmation of factor analysis models in general, and then provide illustrations of two simple but important uses of confirmatory factor analysis.

We will then discuss how to build factor scales in order to use them in other studies. We place this after the discussion of confirmatory factor analysis because some of the ways by which inadequacies in factor scale construction can be alleviated require the uses of confirmatory factor analysis.

In the final section, we cover a wide range of questions in a question and answer format. Most of the questions covered here are either not covered in the main text or are deemed important enough to deserve reiteration. Here we also offer some practical advice on issues for which there may not be consensus.

The glossary at the end of the volume is not intended to provide precise technical definitions of each term but, instead, is a convenient way of indicating in what context a term is used in this volume. Finally, the references in the volume are not meant to reflect the historical development or adequately give credit to the original innovations in the field. We have cited sources which we found to be valuable for our own understanding of the subject. The readers are advised to use these references in the same spirit, and we hope we do not offend scholars who have contributed to the development of factor analysis and have not been cited by us.

II. METHODS OF EXTRACTING INITIAL FACTORS

The main objective of the extraction step in exploratory factor analysis is to determine the minimum number of common factors that would satisfactorily produce the correlations among the observed variables. If there are no measurement and sampling errors and the assumption of factorial causation is appropriate for the data, there is an exact correspondence between the minimum number of common factors responsible for a given correlation matrix and the rank of the adjusted correlation matrix. (The adjustment of the correlation matrix requires inserting the communalities in the main diagonal.) That is, given no sampling error and an exact fit between the factorial model and the data, the communalities (actual values, not estimates) can be obtained, as well as the number of common factors, through the examination of the rank of the adjusted correlation matrix. In the presence of sampling errors, however, the rank-theorem cannot be relied on. The objective then becomes one of finding some criterion with which to evaluate the number of common factors in the presence of such sampling errors. As discussed in the preceding volume, the ultimate criterion for determining the minimum number of common factors is how well the assumed common factors can reproduce the observed correlations. Therefore, the objective may be restated as solving a statistical problem which involves finding criteria by which to decide *when to stop extracting common factors.* Following standard statistical logic, this involves determining when the discrepancy between the reproduced correlations and the observed correlations can be attributed to sampling variability.

We will begin by describing the basic strategy that is common to a number of extraction methods. It involves hypothesizing a minimum number of common factors necessary to reproduce the observed correlations. This means, in absence of any knowledge, starting with a one-common factor model. This "hypothesis" is evaluated by applying some criterion to determine whether the discrepancy between the assumed model and the data is trivial. If it is not, a model with one more common factor is estimated and the criterion is applied again. This is continued until the discrepancy is judged to be attributable to sampling error. (The reader should reflect back to Section II of the first volume where we assumed no sampling error, and the criterion was that the discrepancy be exactly zero.) It should be noted that actual computing algorithms may not exactly make such a sequential evaluation, but the principle of extracting the first k factors that account for most of the observed covariation remains valid.

Although in principle this basic strategy is straightforward, its application can take numerous forms because there are many criteria of maximum fit (or minimum discrepancy). Two major types of solutions that follow faithfully the common factor models we have described so far are (1) the maximum likelihood method (Lawley and Maxwell, 1971; Jöreskog, 1967; Jöreskog and Lawley, 1968) whose variants are canonical factoring (Rao, 1955) and procedures based on maximizing the determinants of a residual partial correlation matrix (see Browne, 1968), and (2) the least squares method, whose variants include principal axis factoring with iterated communalities (Thomson, 1934) and Minres (see Harman, 1976). In addition, there are three other major types of extraction methods: (1) Alpha factoring (Kaiser and Gaffrey, 1965), (2) Image analysis (Guttman, 1953; Harris, 1962), and (3) principal component analysis (Hotelling, 1933). The last method will be described first.

Principal Components, Eigenvalues and Vectors

We start with the discussion of principal components analysis for two reasons. First, it will serve as a base model with which the common factor model can be compared and contrasted. Second, it will provide the easiest means of introducing such esoteric concepts as characteristic roots (eigenvalues) and vectors, and their role in factor analytic algorithms. (We are not abandoning our goal of relying on mostly simple algebra, but certain familiarity with these terms is almost essential for a user of many computer programs. We urge you to try to follow our basic presentation.)

Principal components analysis is a method of transforming a given set of observed variables into another set of variables. The easiest way to illustrate its characteristics and underlying logic is to examine it within the bivariate context. Assume that there are two variables, X and Y, and also assume, for ease of presentation, that their distribution is bivariate normal.

A bivariate normal relationship with moderate positive association is depicted in Figure 2 by the use of contour maps. These maps show that because of the positive relationship between X and Y, the data points cluster such that higher values of X tend to be associated with higher values of Y (and vice versa), and therefore, more cases are piled up along the first and third quadrants than along the second and fourth. These contour maps form ellipses, the two axes of which are indicated by dotted lines. The principal axis (P_1) runs along the line on which the most data points are located; the second axis (P_2) runs along the line on which the fewest data points are located.

Now suppose that our task is to represent the relative position of each case in terms of only one dimension or axis. The logical choice for this reference axis is P_1 because in a sense this line is closest to the data points as a whole. The first principal component is then no more than a representation of cases along the principal axis. For one example, a case with a 1 on both X and Y will be represented by a larger value than 1 on P_1 and a smaller value on P_2. If we describe each case with respect to both P_1 and P_2 (in terms of points in a coordinate system), no information is lost and we can describe each case exactly regardless of the relationship between X and Y. However, we may say that the first axis (and the first component) is more informative in describing cases as the association between X and Y becomes stronger. In the extreme case where X and Y are linear functions of each other, the first principal component will contain all the information necessary to describe each case. If X and Y are independent, there will be no principal axis and the use of principal components analysis will not provide any economy.

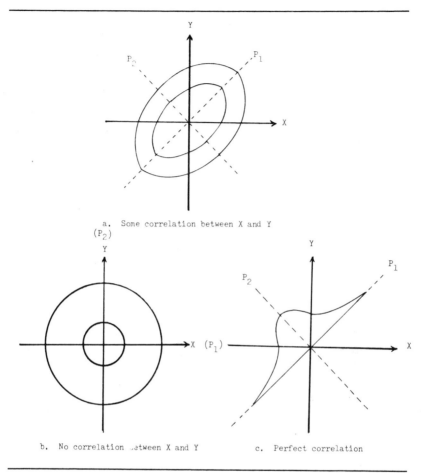

a. Some correlation between X and Y

b. No correlation between X and Y

c. Perfect correlation

Figure 2: Some Examples of Principal Axes for Bivariate Distributions

Although we illustrated the principal axis in terms of an ellipse and a bivariate normal distribution, the concept of principal axes is not confined to relationships which are normal. In general, the principal axis is given by a line from which the sum of the squared distances from each point is a minimum value. A comparison with the least squares principle may help in explaining this. In finding a least squares regression line ($\dot{Y} = a + bX$) we minimize the sum of the squared distances between Y and $\dot{Y}$, i.e., we minimize ($Y - \dot{Y}$), where the distance is measured by a line parallel to the Y axis and perpendicular to the X axis. In finding a principal axis, we minimize the perpendicular distance between the data point and the axis (i.e., the distance is from the point perpendicular to the principal axis,

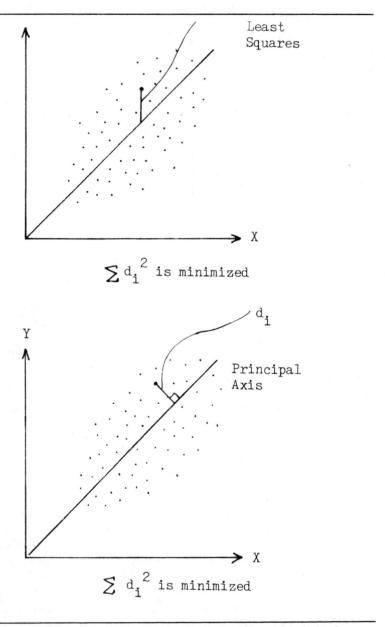

Figure 3: Comparison Between Least Squares Regression Line and Principal Axis

not to X). This difference is illustrated in Figure 3. (See Malinvaud, 1970, for a discussion of least squares vs. orthogonal regressions.)

Once the first component is defined in such a way that the most information is contained in it (it explains the largest amount of variance in the data), the second component is defined in a similar way with the condition that its axis is perpendicular to the first. In the bivariate case, therefore, once the first component is specified, the second component is known automatically. Also keep in mind that unless Y is a linear function of X and vice versa, there will be two principal components (we need two axes to describe the joint distribution completely).

In deriving the principal components, we need not assume the existence of hypothetical factors. The new axes are mathematical functions of the observed variables. Even when principal components analysis is used as a means of achieving economy of representation (this would be the case of examining only the first few components), the objective is not to explain the correlations among variables, but to account for as much *variance* as possible in the data. On the other hand, a factor analytic decomposition would require only one factor (in this bivariate case), and the primary aim would be to account for the *correlation* between the variables. In sum, the former is oriented toward explaining variance, the latter toward explaining covariance.

When there are more than two variables, the basis for defining the principal components is the same. For example, for a trivariate normal distribution, the three dimensional contours will resemble the shape of a partially flattened football (an ellipsoid); the first principal axis is the line running from one tip to the other, thus forming the longest line; the second axis runs across the next longest distance, while being perpendicular to the first axis (this is the part made wider by the flattening); the third axis would be the shortest and would run along the part made less wide by the flattening process.

The primary mathematical tool by which such hierarchical decompositions or transformations are arrived at is referred to as the characteristic equation or eigenequation. Solving this equation produces eigenvalues and eigenvectors associated with a matrix. The characteristic equation (using matrix notation) has the following form:

$$R V = \lambda V \qquad [1]$$

where R is the matrix for which a solution is sought, V is the eigenvector to be found, and λ is an eigenvalue. The solution is eventually based on a simpler determinantal equation of the form:

$$\mathrm{Det}\ (R - I\lambda) = 0, \text{ which translates into a bivariate matrix} \qquad [2]$$

$$\text{Det} \begin{pmatrix} 1-\lambda & r_{12} \\ r_{12} & 1-\lambda \end{pmatrix} = 0 \qquad [3]$$

which can be written out as

$$(1-\lambda)(1-\lambda) - r_{12}(r_{12}) = 0 \qquad [4]$$

(by definition of determinant),

$$= \lambda^2 - 2\lambda + (1 - r_{12}^2) = 0 \qquad [5]$$

(by expanding and grouping in a standard form).

The eigenvalues can now be obtained if you remember how to solve an equation $ax^2 + bx + c = 0$. At any rate the eigenvalues for a bivariate correlation matrix are:

$$\lambda_1 = 1 + r_{12}, \text{ and} \qquad [6]$$

$$\lambda_2 = 1 - r_{12}. \qquad [7]$$

Note that if the correlation between the two variables is perfect, one of the eigenvalues will be 2 and the other zero, and that if the correlation is zero, both eigenvalues will be 1.

Note also that the sum of the eigenvalues, $\lambda_1 + \lambda_2 = (1 + r_{12}) + (1 - r_{12}) = 2$, is equivalent to the number of variables and the product, $(\lambda_1)(\lambda_2) = (1 - r_{12}^2)$, is equivalent to the determinant of the correlation matrix. These properties hold for correlation matrices of any size. Most important, however, is the fact that the largest eigenvalue represents the amount of variance explained by the first principal axis, the second largest eigenvalue represents the amount of the variance explained by the second axis, and so on. Since the sum of all the eigenvalues is equal to the number of variables in the analysis (when the correlation matrix is used), by dividing the first eigenvalue by the m (the number of variables), we can also obtain the *proportion* of the variance explained by a given axis or component:

$$\text{proportion explained by a given component} = \left(\text{corresponding eigenvalue} \right) \Big/ \text{m.} \qquad [8]$$

The associated eigenvectors are found by imposing an arbitrary additional constraint that their lengths be 1. For this reason, the principal component loadings are obtained by multiplying eigenvectors by square roots of the respective eigenvalues, which correctly reflect the relative amount of variances explained by the corresponding data.

The simplest possible example is provided by the components analysis of the two variable (one-common factor) model of Tables 2 and 3 of the previous volume. The eigenvalues (arranged in descending order) are 1.48 and .52, which are equivalent to $(1 + r_{12})$ and $(1 - r_{12})$, respectively. The associated eigenvectors are, respectively, $(\sqrt{1/2}, \sqrt{1/2})$ and $(\sqrt{1/2}, -\sqrt{1/2})$. The "factor loadings" are given then by:

$$\begin{pmatrix} \sqrt{1/2} & \sqrt{1/2} \\ \sqrt{1/2} & -\sqrt{1/2} \end{pmatrix} \begin{pmatrix} 1/\sqrt{1.48} & 0 \\ 0 & 1/\sqrt{.52} \end{pmatrix} = \begin{pmatrix} .86 & .51 \\ .86 & -.51 \end{pmatrix}$$

The last matrix has the factor loadings that would be obtained if principal components analysis is specified in the computer program. Note that $\lambda_1 = (.86)^2 + (.86)^2$ and $\lambda_2 = (.51)^2 + (-.51)^2$.

To facilitate the forthcoming comparison of components analysis with common factor analysis, we will apply the former to the six variable correlation matrix of Table 1. We use error-free data in order to highlight its characteristics without fluctuations introduced by sampling. Table 2 shows the results of the components analysis. Three points should be noted: (1) there will be in general six components (although the last four will be minor and not reported here); (2) the first two components explain more variance than the first two common factors (61.6% vs. 41%); (3) the first two components do not completely account for the observed correlations, whereas the first two factors do (for example, $(b_{11}b_{21}) + (b_{12}b_{22}) = (.747)(.706) + (-.395)(-.409) = .6890$, which is much greater than the underlying correlation of .56).

Principal components analysis is similar to factor analysis in that both methods allow for data reduction. On the basis of the magnitude of eigenvalues, the researcher may have decided to use only the first two components. But to reiterate, it will not necessarily account for the observed correlations even though a two-common factor model can. There is another similarity between the two when they are considered as means of exploring interdependence of variables. Note the fact that if there is no correlation between any variables, there will be no principal component, because every component is as good or as bad as the other; each will account for only a unit variance. As the interrelations among the variables increases, the proportion explained by the first few components will increase.

One way to differentiate between the two is to say factor analysis represents the covariance structure in terms of a hypothetical causal model,

TABLE 2
The First Two Principal Components of the
Correlation Matrix in the Lower Triangle of Table 1

| | Principal Components | | |
Variables	F_1	F_2	$h^{2\,a}$
X_1	.749	−.395	.713
X_2	.706	−.405	.666
X_3	.651	−.417	.597
X_4	.595	.579	.623
X_5	.548	.529	.581
X_6	.488	.526	.514
Eigenvalues	2.372	1.323	Sum = 3.695
Percent of Variance Explained	39.5	22.1	
Cumulative Percent of Variance Explained	39.5	61.6	

a. These are not communality estimates in the strict sense of the term, because principal components analysis does not assume the existence of common factors.

whereas components analysis summarizes the data by means of a linear combination of the observed data. The choice between the two will depend on the researcher's overall objectives. The explanation of the correlation in terms of a smaller number of factors is achieved by an imposition of a hypothetical model. The mathematical representation of the linear combination of observed data does not require imposing what some may consider a questionable causal model, but it does not reveal any underlying causal structure, if such a structure exists.

The orientation of components analysis is, therefore, radically different from that of factor analysis. We wish to reiterate, however, why we have devoted considerable space to it. First, principal components analysis is often considered a variant of factor analysis. Second, principal axis factoring (to be described next) uses similar algorithms (eigen-equations), and the presentation of the factor method is easier with the knowledge of components analysis. Third, and most importantly, one statistic generated with components analysis still serves as the most widely used practical means of solving the number-of-factors question. (This refers to the criterion of "eigenvalue greater than 1," which will be taken up later.)

Variants in the Common Factor Model

Historically speaking, most of the earlier expository treatments of factor analysis identified the common factor model by a *principal axis factoring* procedure, which uses the decomposition strategies of principal components analysis as applied to the adjusted correlation matrix whose diagonal elements (of 1) are replaced by corresponding estimates of communalities.

Commonly used estimates of communalities are the squared multiple correlations of each variable with the remainder of the variables in the set or the highest absolute correlation in a row of a correlation matrix. After inserting these communality estimates in the main diagonal of the correlation matrix, factors are extracted in the manner of principal components analysis. That is, factor solutions are found by applying the same eigenvalue equation to the adjusted correlation matrix as was done in components analysis. (Hence, the name of principal axis factoring.) The equation solved in this case is:

$$\det(R_1 - \lambda I) = 0, \qquad [9]$$

where R_1 is the correlation matrix with communality estimates in the main diagonal. Although this method is still widely used, it is gradually being replaced by the least-squares approaches described below.

LEAST SQUARES APPROACH

The principle behind the least squares approach to common factor analysis is to minimize the residual correlation after extracting a given number of factors, and to assess the degree of fit between the reproduced correlations under the model and the observed correlations (the squared differences are examined). Because one can always reproduce the observed correlations by hypothesizing as many factors as variables, and because the fit will always increase as the hypothesized factors increase, the least squares solution assumes that we start with a hypothesis that k number of factors (k smaller than the number of variables) are responsible for the observed correlations.

The actual procedure for obtaining the solution is roughly as follows. First, assume that k factors can account for the observed correlations. (This step does not present any particular problem in practice because one can start with the hypothesis of one-common factor and increment the number of hypothesized factors until a satisfactory solution is found.) Second, obtain some initial estimates of communalities. (As indicated above, the squared multiple correlation between a variable and the remaining variables is used.) Third, obtain or extract k factors that can best reproduce the observed correlation matrix (according to the least squares principle). At this stage, the mathematical equation to be solved is exactly the same as equation 9 above. Fourth, in order to obtain the factor pattern that can best reproduce the observed correlation or covariance matrix, the communalities are reestimated on the basis of the factor pattern obtained in the previous stage. (The formulae for estimating communalities are given in equation 20 of Section II of the first volume.) Finally, the process is repeated until no improvement can be made. Hence, the name principal axis factoring with iterative estimation of communalities is derived.

The minimum residuals method or Minres (Harman, 1976) also is an iterative solution based on the same principle, but one which uses a somewhat different and more efficient algorithm. For this technique there is an approximate chi-square test which is appropriate for large sample sizes. Harman claims that this approximate test, which is independent of the particular method of factor extraction, can be applied to other methods of extraction, and can be used as a means for checking the completeness of factorization (Harman, 1975:184; for some reservations see McDonald, 1975). Although the test is appropriate when the sample is large, ironically, when the sample size is very large, minor deviations may be statistically significant. Therefore, Harman advises that one should not rely on the formal test alone but consider the number of factors obtained by such a test as only an indication of an upper limit, and try to retain only substantial and theoretically·interpretable factors (preferably after an examination of rotation results).

The application of principal axis factoring with iteration to the correlation matrix in Table 1 is presented in Table 3 below.

SOLUTIONS BASED ON THE
MAXIMUM LIKELIHOOD PROCEDURE

The overall objective of the maximum likelihood solution is the same as the least squares solution: to find the factor solution which would best fit the observed correlations. An informal description of the principle is as follows. We assume that the observed data comprise a sample from a population where a k-common factor model exactly applies, and where the distribution of variables (including the factors) is multivariate normal. What is assumed unknown, however, is the exact configuration of parameters, i.e., the exact loadings on each variable. The objective is then to find the underlying population parameters (under the given hypothesis) that would have the greatest likelihood of producing the observed correlation matrix. A somewhat different criterion based on the same principle involves finding the hypothetical configuration of factors in such a way

TABLE 3
Principal Axis Factoring with Iterated Communalities:
Political Opinion Example

Variables	F_1	F_2	h^2
X_1	.731	-.320	.637
X_2	.642	-.282	.492
X_3	.550	-.241	.360
X_4	.513	.473	.487
X_5	.441	.409	.362
X_6	.367	.340	.251
Eigenvalues	1.842	.746	
Percentage Explained	30.7	12.4	

that the canonical correlation between the k-common factors and the observed variables is the maximum. A third criterion ultimately leading to the same principle involves finding the factor configuration in such a way that the determinant of the residual correlation matrix is the maximum. All of these criteria are rather complex to apply in practice, and various versions based on the same principle vary considerably in the efficiency of the conversion process through the iteration. Jöreskog's (1967) solution is currently considered the best.

We will show in the following that in principle the procedure is not very different from other eigenequation solutions. The basic alogorithm can be expressed in the form of determinantal equations examined previously:

$$\det (R_2 - \lambda I) = 0, \tag{10}$$

where R_2 is given by

$$R_2 = U^{-1}(R - U^2) U^{-1} \tag{11}$$

$$= U^{-1}R_1U^{-1}, \tag{12}$$

where U^2 is the estimate of unique variance at each stage. Equation 10 is different from equation 4 in that it uses the adjusted matrix R_2 in place of R and readjusts it in every iteration, and it is different from the least squares formulation in that R_2 is adjusted at every stage in such a way that greater weight is given to correlations involving less unique variance. Note that the part of equation 11—$(R - U^2)$—is the same as R_1 in equation 9; therefore, the only difference is the weighting factor in equations 11 or 12. In the maximum likelihood solutions, the unique variance is treated as "quasi" error variance, and therefore, the method assigns greater weight to the variables with greater communality (or less unique variance), and this follows the general principle of efficient statistical estimation in which less stable estimates are given less weight.

We mentioned earlier that the optimal procedure should be able to reproduce exact population values if the model is well-defined and data are error-free. Depending on the efficiency of convergence of a given program, some may not produce such a result; in principle, however, a good program should. In Table 4 we present the results of applying the maximum likelihood solution with the two factor hypothesis to the sample correlations presented in the upper triangle of Table 1.

As expected, the significance test indicates that the fit is adequate. The exact formula for calculating the χ^2-value is presented below merely to show that this value is dependent on the sample size, while the degrees

TABLE 4
**Maximum Likelihood Two-Common Factor Solution Applied to
Data in the Upper Triangle of Table 1**

Variables	Unrotated		Communality	Rotated Using Direct Oblimin Criterion	
	F_1	F_2		F_1	F_2
X_1	.747	-.300	.648	.817	-.027
X_2	.701	-.266	.562	.754	-.009
X_3	.599	-.176	.389	.602	.046
X_4	.428	.362	.314	.027	.547
X_5	.505	.605	.621	-.113	.833
X_6	.534	.248	.367	.202	.468
Sum of Squares[a]	2.132	.749		1.652	1.215
χ^2 with 4 degrees of = freedom	.825				

a. Sums of squares are equivalent to eigenvalues in the unrotated solution and this value divided by m gives the proportion of variance explained by that factor. In an obliquely rotated solution, they represent merely what might be called a "direct" contribution of each factor. The joint contribution (including that due to the correlation between the factors) is still equivalent to the sum of eigenvalues in the unrotated solution.

of freedom are independent of the sample size. The χ^2-statistic is given by:

$$U_k = N \left\{ \ln |C| - \ln |R| + \text{tr}(RC^{-1}) - n \right\} \qquad [13]$$

ln = natural logarithm, and tr = trace of a matrix
N = the sample size;
n = number of variables;
R = the covariance matrix;
C = $FF' + U^2$, where
F = Factor loadings and U^2, unique variance.

(In fact, the same formula is used in testing the least squares solution, the only difference being different estimations of F and U.) What is important is that for a fixed correlation matrix, the U_k value goes up directly proportional to N. The associated degrees of freedom are given by

$$df_k = 1/2[(n-k)^2 - (n+k)], \qquad [14]$$

where k is the number of hypothesized factors and n is the number of variables. Note that df_k is not affected by the sample size N.

The most important advantage of this method is that it provides a large sample significance test. If the χ^2 test indicates that the observed data deviate significantly from the k-common factor model, we would determine whether a k + 1 common factor model is appropriate. In an exploratory analysis, we would normally start with the hypothesis of one-common factor and proceed until the significance test indicates that a given factor model does not significantly deviate from the observed data. Although these sequential tests are not independent of each other, they may still be used without too much concern. (See Lawley and Maxwell, 1971.)

In practice, however, the difficulty with relying on the significance test alone is that we will end up with more common factors than are desirable if the sample size is large. Moreover, where the factor model is only an approximation to reality, a minor misfit between the model and the data can produce additional significant factors. Some related issues on how to determine the number of factors will be discussed once again in Section IV.

ALPHA FACTORING

In both least squares and maximum likelihood solutions, it is assumed that the variables one considers constitute the universe, and that the only sampling involved is the sampling of individuals. In Alpha factoring, however, *variables* included in the factor analysis are considered a sample from the universe of *variables*, while assuming that these variables are observed over a given *population* of individuals. Therefore, in Alpha factoring, the key emphasis is on psychometric inference, not on statistical inference in the usual sense.

Kaiser and Caffrey claim that this method is based on the principle that factor loadings are determined in such a way that the common factors so extracted have maximum correlations with corresponding common factors assumed to exist in the universe (1965:5).

Another way to think of this procedure is to consider the unique factors as if they are errors introduced by the psychometric sampling. Consequently, the communality estimates are treated as "reliabilities" in a measurement context. As a first step, the method produces a correlation matrix that is corrected for "attenuation":

$$R_3 = H^{-1}(R-U^2) H^{-1} \qquad [15]$$

where U^2 and H^2 are diagonal matrices of unique components and communalities, respectively. (H^{-1} is a diagonal matrix containing the reciprocals of the square roots of the communalities.) Then the determinantal equation associated with this "corrected" matrix is solved as usual:

$$\det (R_3 - \lambda I) = 0. \qquad [16]$$

Some comments on the similarities and differences between equation 16 and equation 10, and between equation 15 and equation 11, are instructive. The maximum likelihood solution scales the matrix by the unique variance while Alpha factoring scales it by the communality. Or differently stated, the former gives more weight to variables with greater communality, the latter does the reverse. As usual, the actual solution is complicated by the fact that one has to start with initial communalities and iterate these values for the final solution.

In Alpha factoring the number of factors to be retained is determined by the criterion that the associated eigenvalues should be greater than 1. This criterion is equivalent to the criterion that the associated generalizability coefficient, α (hence the name Alpha factoring) in the universe of variables, should be greater than zero. Here, of course, there is no significance test of the usual kind, because it is assumed that the population of individuals is considered.

The results from applying Alpha factoring to the sample correlation matrix reported in the upper triangle of Table 1 are presented in Table 5 along with results of image factoring, to be discussed next.

Image Analysis

Image analysis distinguishes between the common part of a variable and the unique part. The common part of a variable is defined as that part which is predictable by a linear combination of all the other variables in the set, and is called the *image* of the variable. The unique part is that part of the variable not predictable by the linear combination of other variables is called *anti-image*. In defining this decomposition, it is assumed that one is dealing with the universe of variables as well as the population of individuals; sampling of either kind is assumed not to be in operation.

Image analysis also assumes that this universe of variables is potentially infinite. For purposes of comparison we refer back to the two-common factor model specified in Figure 1. For that model the six variables specified constitute a universe in some sense. But in image analysis, the six

TABLE 5
Factor Loadings Based on Alpha and Image Factoring on
Error-Free Correlations Reported in Table 1[a]

	Unrotated Factor Matrices					
	Alpha			Image		
Variables	F_1	F_2	Communality	F_1	F_2	Communality
X_1	.669	.437	.638	.575	.133	.348
X_2	.586	.384	.490	.538	.139	.309
X_3	.502	.329	.361	.477	.131	.245
X_4	.585	-.382	.489	.372	-.270	.211
X_5	.502	-.329	.360	.335	-.263	.182
X_6	.419	-.274	.251	.287	-.239	.140

a. Compare these values with those in Table 10, Kim-Mueller, University Paper 07-013, where the observed correlations were reproduced perfectly. In particular, note that the communality estimates by Alpha are very close to the true communalities whereas the communality estimates by Image factoring are relatively poor.

variables would be considered as a sample from an infinite universe of variables pertaining to the psychometric domain covered by the two-common factors.

If, however, we had all the variables in the potential universe for examination, the squared image of a variable would be equivalent to the *communality* of a variable defined in comon factor analysis, and the squared anti-image of a variable would be equivalent to the unique variance. (It is assumed here that we are dealing with standardized variables.) In other words, the squared multiple correlation between a variable and the remainder of the variables in this universe is the same as the communality of a given variable.

The images and anti-images defined for a sample of variables are called, respectively, partial images and partial anti-images. Although the partial images only approximate the total image, it is completely specified by the observed variables. In that sense, it is a radical departure from common factor analysis in which the common part of a variable is defined to be some linear combination of hypothetical factors, and never to be an exact function of observed variables themselves.

Given a sample of variables and their correlations, the image analysis constructs a partial image covariance matrix, which is given by

$$R_4 = (R - S^2) \, R^{-1} \, (R - S^2) \qquad [17]$$

where R is the correlation matrix and S^2 is the diagonal matrix whose elements are the variance of each variable unexplained by the other variables—or the anti-image variance. The process involved in equation 17 is, (1) to replace the main diagonal of R with the squared multiple correlation of each variable with the rest, and (2) to readjust the off-diagonal elements in order to make the resulting matrix Gramian. Then the eigenequation is applied to this matrix:

$$\det (R_4 - \lambda I) = 0. \qquad [18]$$

The number of factors to retain is, however, not given by the examination of eigenvalues for equation 18 but by the eigenvalues greater than 1 from the equation in which a different matrix $(S^{-1}RS^{-1})$ is put in the place of R_4. Usually, the number of factors so retained is relatively large—approaching one-half of the variables in the analysis. Kaiser suggests that insignificant and uninterpretable factors be dropped after proper rotations. Some statistics generated by image factoring on the sample correlation matrix are presented in Table 5 along with other results.

III. METHODS OF ROTATION

The initial factoring step usually determines the minimum *number* of factors that can adequately account for observed correlations, and in the process determines the communalities of each variable. The next step in factor analysis involves finding simpler and more easily interpretable factors through rotations, while keeping the number of factors and communalities of each variable fixed.

All the solutions examined in the previous section produce initial factors that are orthogonal and that are arranged in a descending order of importance. These two properties of the factor solution are not inherent in the data structure; they are arbitrary impositions placed on data to make the solutions unique and definable in some sense. The consequences of making these arbitrary impositions are that (1) the factorial complexity of variables is likely to be greater than one, regardless of the underlying true model—that is, variables will have substantial loadings on more than one factor; (2) except for the first factor, the remaining factors are bipolar—that is, some variables have positive loadings on a factor while others have negative loadings. (If these descriptions do not seem meaningful, refer to Section II of the preceding volume and examine some of the factor patterns.)

There are basically three different approaches to the rotation problem. The first approach is to examine the pattern of variables graphically as we did in Section II of the previous volume, and then rotate the axis or define new axes in such a way that the new axes best satisfy one's criterion of simple and meaningful structure. When there are clear clusters of variables, well separated from each other (as in Figure 17 of the previous volume), the simple structure would be achieved if each axis is made to run through a cluster. But whenever the pattern is not very clear or there are many factors to examine, such a graphical rotation is not practical for a novice.

The second approach is to rely on some analytic rotation method that is free of subjective judgment, at least after a particular criterion of simplicity is chosen. There are two different subtypes in this approach—one is the method of orthogonal rotation and the other is oblique rotation. Within each subtype there are numerous variations, but only a few well known and widely used versions will be described in this section.

The third approach to rotation is to define a target matrix or configuration before actual rotation. The objective of such rotation is to find the factor patterns that are closest to the given target matrix. Since the specification of target matrix presumes certain knowledge or a hypothesis about the nature of the factor structure, this strategy approaches confirmatory factor analysis.

Graphic Rotation, Simple Structure, and Reference Axes

The graphic rotation procedure is difficult to apply whenever the clustering is not clear or there are more than two factors to examine. We will touch on this subject merely to set the stage for the analytic rotations. (Readers may consult Mulaik (1972) for a good introduction to graphic rotation.)

The manifest goal of all the rotations is to achieve the simplest possible factor structure. Unfortunately, the concept of simplicity itself is not so straightforward as to allow for a formal and undisputed criterion. The most ambitious attempt to define a simple structure is made by Thurstone (1947), but it is generally conceded today that not all of his criteria are definable in analytic terms. Since an understanding of Thurstone's criteria requires knowledge of hyperplanes or subspaces, we merely present Mulaik's (1972:220) excellent account of these criteria for those who have some knowledge of vector spaces. (In Mulaik's description, r refers to the number of common factors, and V is the reference structure matrix consisting of a reference axis.)

(1) Each row of the reference-structure matrix V should have at least one zero. This is the basic assumption of simple structure as implied in the definition of simple structure given at the onset of this section.

(2) For each column k of the reference-structure matrix V there should be a set of at least r linearly independent observed variables whose correlations (as found in the kth column of V) with the kth reference-axis variable are zero. This criterion is needed to overdetermine the corresponding reference axis.

(3) For every pair of columns of V there should be several zero entries in one column corresponding to nonzero entries in the other. This requirement assures the distinctness of the reference axes and their corresponding subspaces of $r - 1$ dimensions of the common-factor space.

(4) When four or more common factors are obtained, each pair of columns of V should have a proportion of corresponding zero entries. This requirement assures that each reference axis is pertinent to only a few of the observed variables and thus guarantees a separation of the observed variables into distinct clusters.

(5) For every pair of columns of V there should be only a small number of corresponding entries in both columns which do not vanish. This criterion further ensures the simplicity of the variables.

These criteria are ultimately based on two somewhat different considerations: (1) the need to define criteria of a simple factor structure, and (2) the need to specify conditions under which a simple structure is unambiguously identified. What makes Thurstone's criteria difficult for novices to understand is the technical and complex literature directed toward the second consideration. For our purposes, however, the first consideration is primary while the second one represents technical requirements which we would rather leave for the specialists to worry about.

Although it is difficult to specify what constitutes a minimum requirement for "simple structure," it is rather easy to specify what constitutes the simplest possible structure, given r number of factors and n variables. The factor structure is the simplest if all the variables have factorial complexity of one—i.e., each variable has nonzero loadings on only one-common factor. Given two or more common factors, this means that in the simplest pattern matrix (1) each row will have only one nonzero element, (2) each column will contain some zeros, and (3) between any pair of columns, the nonzero elements do not overlap.

With real data, one is not likely to see such a simple structure. So the task becomes how to "define" factor structures that are "closest" to the simplest structure. Here, specialists diverge in their definition of "simple" structure among "imperfect" patterns and in their computational approach to arrive at such simple structures. As mentioned earlier, Thurstone's criteria specify empirical conditions under which a simple structure can be identifed unambiguously. One of the empirical specifications is that there should be at least three variables clearly loading on each factor. But the definition of simple structure does not depend on this type of empirical requirement, and it is desirable to separate this definition from actually identifying simple structure in data analysis. This is true because in exploratory factor analysis the researcher will have to be satisfied with whatever variables are at hand, and will be forced to conceptualize what constitutes the simplest structure, before trying to give meaning to the factors.

Historically, a simple structure was first specified in terms of *reference axes*. Although an understanding of these is not absolutely necessary (owing to the development of oblique rotation methods that do not rely on the introduction of reference axes), we will briefly describe them, since many users of factor analysis may have to rely on computer programs that provide oblique rotation methods that depend on the introduction of such axes.

Recall from the previous volume that the initial factor loadings are no more than the projection of variables on the two axes—that is, the loadings are found by dropping lines from each point perpendicular to the two initial orthogonal axes, and reading the values of the intersecting points on the two axes. Also note that a simple structure would exist in this orthogonal solution if all the variables lie on the axes. Also note that in the orthogonal case the notion of simple structure implies that one set of points will have zero loadings (or zero projection) on the other axis or factor. This zero projection is precluded if the angle between the clusters is not orthogonal (i.e., not 90°). Given such an oblique angle, a new procedure is to set up another reference axis that is perpendicular to the hyperplane (in this two factor model it is simply a line) that passes through the cluster of points which one considers to be a primary factor axis. (See Figure 4.)

Thus, it is the same to examine either the condition that a cluster of variables all lie on a primary axis or that a cluster of variables have all zero projections on the reference axes. In our contrived two-common factor model (when examined from the error-free correlation matrix), it is the case that one set of variables, X_1, X_2, X_3, have zero projections or loadings on the reference axis R_2, and variables in another set have zero

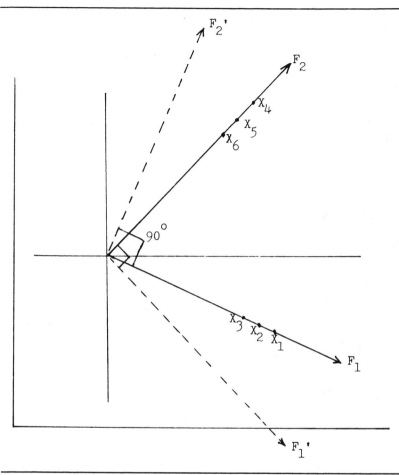

Figure 4: F_1 and F_2 are primary oblique factors and $F_1{}'$ and $F_2{}'$ are corresponding reference axes. The projections of X_1, X_2, and X_3 will be zero on $F_2{}'$, and the projections of X_4, X_5, and X_6 will be zero on $F_1{}'$.

loadings to R_1. In this example, it is not clear why one should rely on the reference axes instead of drawing lines directly through the cluster of variables. We merely note that when there are more than two factors and the clustering is not as clear as in the artificial data, the method of identifying reference .axes, and treating these reference axes as if orthogonal axes in the next step or iteration, allows one to find a better fitting primary axis. What is important to remember from this is that the basic goal of the rotation is still to find a factor *pattern* matrix that is closest to the simplest ideal structure mentioned above.

Methods of Orthogonal Rotation:
Quartimax, Varimax, and Equimax

Since we assume the reader will have to depend on some existing factor
analysis computer program when actually analyzing data, we will only
describe basic principles which underlie each method. In the preceding
section we described the simplest possible structure given k number of
common factors and n number of variables. It is useful here to recapitulate
some of the analytic properties of such a matrix.

Because each variable loads on only one factor, the factorial interpretation of *variables* is the simplest. But such a characterization is insufficient for expressing degrees of simplicity in numerical terms. One
possible numerical measure of simplicity is the variability of the squared
factor loadings for each row (or each variable). (We consider only squared
loadings to avoid the problems of dealing with signs of the loadings.)
Because variance is defined by the average of the squared deviations from
the mean, the variance will be greatest (for a fixed number of factors and
fixed communality) if one element of the squared loadings is equal to the
communality, and all the rest in the row are zeros. In short, the maximum
variance of the squared factor loadings for a variable is equivalent to the
greatest simplicity of factorial complexity for that variable. It is, therefore,
reasonable to quantify the notion of factorial simplicity by:

$$\text{Factorial Complexity of a Variable i} = \frac{1}{r} \sum_{j=1}^{r} (b_{ij}{}^2 - \bar{b}_{ij}{}^2)^2, \qquad [19]$$

where r is the number of columns in a pattern matrix, b_{ij} is the factor
loading of variable i on the factor j, and $\bar{b}_{ij}^2$ is the mean of squared factor
loadings for the row. Equation 19 can be written in the following form:

$$q_i = \frac{\sum\limits_{j=1}^{r} (b_{ij}{}^4) - \left(\sum\limits_{j=1}^{r} b_{ij}{}^2 \right)^2}{r^2} \qquad [20]$$

Once an initial factor solution is given, both r and the communality of
each variable are fixed. Hence, the term after the minus sign remains fixed
because

$$\sum_{j=1}^{r} b_{ij}{}^2 = h_i{}^2$$

in an orthogonal solution. Then the overall measure of simplicity can be obtained by summing q_i for all the variables:

$$q = \sum_{i=1}^{n} q_i = \sum_{i=1}^{n} \frac{\sum_{j=1}^{r} (b_{ij}^4) - \left(\sum_{j=1}^{r} b_{ij}^2 \right)^2}{r^2} . \qquad [21]$$

Application of the *quartimax* criterion results in rotating axes in such a way that the factor loadings maximize q. Maximization of q is, however, equivalent to the maximization of the following terms,

$$Q = \sum_{i=1}^{n} \sum_{j=1}^{r} b_{ij}^4, \qquad [22]$$

because the remaining terms in equation 21 are all constants. Hence, the name quartimax.

In practice, application of this criterion may result in emphasizing the simplicity of interpretation of variables at the expense of simplicity of interpretation of factors. In particular, the interpretation of a variable becomes simpler as fewer common factors are involved in it, whereas the interpretations of a factor will be simpler if a relatively small number of variables have high loadings on the factor and the rest of the variables have zero loadings on it. In general, the quartimax criterion tends to produce final solutions in which there is a general factor with moderate and small loadings on some variables.

The *varimax* rotation uses a slightly different criterion which simplifies each column of the factor matrix. Instead of maximizing variance of squared loadings for each variable, it maximizes the variance of the squared loadings for each factor. The quantity to maximize—the index of simplicity of a factor j—is then:

$$v_j = \frac{n \sum_{i=1}^{n} b_{ij}^4 - \left(\sum_{i=1}^{n} b_{ij}^2 \right)^2}{n^2} \qquad [23]$$

Note that now the sum is over n variables and that the term after the minus sign

$$(\sum_{j=1}^{n} b_{ij}^2)$$

does not remain fixed as does the corresponding term in equation 20. The overall measure of simplicity is given by

$$V = \sum_{j=1}^{r} v_j = \frac{\sum_{j=1}^{r} n \sum_{i=1}^{n} b_{ij}^4 \left(\sum_{i=1}^{n} b_{ij}^2 \right)^2}{n^2} , \qquad [24]$$

which is known as the *row* varimax criterion. It is customary to use normalized factor loadings during the iterations in order to minimize the undesirable predominance of larger initial loadings for the resulting solution. Such a criterion is obtained if one uses b_{ij}^2/h_i^2 in the place of b_{ij}^2 in equation 24 and b_{ij}^4/h_i^4 in the place of b_{ij}^4.

In Table 6 we present the results of applying quartimax and varimax (normalized) rotations to the same data. We note that although the quartimax solution is analytically simpler than the varimax solution, the varimax seemed to give clearer separation of the factors. In general, Kaiser's experiment (1958) showed that the factor pattern obtained by varimax rotation tends to be more invariant than that obtained by the quartimax when different subsets of variables are factor analyzed.

Considering that the quartimax criterion concentrates on simplifying the rows and the varimax criterion concentrates on simplying the columns of the factor matrix, it is logical to consider applying both criteria with some appropriate weights. A general criterion is given by:

$$\alpha Q + \beta V = \text{Maximum}, \qquad [25]$$

where Q is given by equation 22 and V by equation 24 (but multiplied by n for convenience in manipulation and because a constant multiplier does not affect the maximization process), and α and β are weights. This may be written out

$$\sum_{j=1}^{r} \left(\sum_{i=1}^{n} b_{ij}^2 \right)^2 - \gamma \left(\sum_{i=1}^{n} b_{ij}^2 \right)^2/n = \text{maximum}, \qquad [26]$$

where $\gamma = \beta/(\alpha + \beta)$.

If $\gamma = 0$, it reduces to the quartimax criterion; if $\gamma = 1$, it reduces to the varimax criterion. When $\gamma = r/2$, it is called *equimax*, and when $\gamma = .5$, it is called *biquartimax*.

TABLE 6
Varimax and Quartimax Rotations Applied to the Same
Pattern Matrix Shown in Table 4[a]

Variables	Varimax Rotation		Quartimax Rotation	
	F_1	F_2	F_1	F_2
X_1	.787	.167	.793	.133
X_2	.730	.170	.736	.143
X_3	.595	.187	.602	.166
X_4	.154	.539	.173	.533
X_5	.083	.783	.111	.780
X_6	.306	.503	.324	.492

a. In this particular example, the tendency for the first factor in the Quartimax rotation to be a "general" factor is very slight.

Methods of Oblique Rotation

An oblique rotation is more general than an orthogonal rotation in that it does not arbitrarily impose the restriction that factors be uncorrelated. Its advantage over orthogonal rotations is that, after making oblique rotations, if the resulting factors are orthogonal, one can be sure that the orthogonality is not an artifact of the method of rotation. However, because oblique solutions are obtained with the introduction of correlations among factors, a different type of complexity in the interpretation of factor analysis may be introduced. In particular, one may have to assume higher-order factorial causation to explain correlations among the factors. Furthermore, there are two different types of approaches to oblique rotation—one using reference axes and the other using the primary pattern matrix. Since the overall principles for achieving simple structure were discussed in the previous sections, our descriptions of these will be brief.

SOLUTIONS BASED ON REFERENCE AXES

All the solutions included here are based on the fact that if there are definable clusters of variables representing separate dimensions, and if these clusters are correctly identified by primary factors, each cluster of variables will have near-zero projections on all reference axes but one. Therefore, a criterion similar to the quartimax can be defined as a *quartimin criterion:*

$$N = \sum_{i=1}^{n} \sum_{j<k=1}^{r} a_{ij}^2 a_{ik}^2 , \qquad [27]$$

where a_{ij} and a_{ik} are projections on the jth and the kth reference axes. This value will be zero if all the variables are unifactorial. But what we seek in the oblique rotation is factor loadings that will minimize N. (In orthogonal rotations, this criterion is equivalent to the quartimax.)

Parallel to the Varimax modification of the quartimax criterion in orthogonal rotations, there is a *covarimin* or *biquartimin* criterion. The minimized value in this case is the covariance of squared elements of the projections on the reference axes:

$$C = \sum_{j<k=1}^{r} \left(n \sum_{i=1}^{n} a_{ij}^2 a_{ik}^2 - \sum_{i=1}^{n} a_{ij}^2 \sum_{i=1}^{n} a_{ik}^2 \right) \qquad [28]$$

Once again, a version based on normalized values is obtained if we replace a_{ij}^2 with a_{ij}^2 / h_i^2. When applied to the same set of data, the covarimin criterion tends to produce fewer oblique factors while the quartimin criterion produces more oblique factors.

Given the opposite tendencies shown by these two criteria, it is natural to combine them. The most general version is given by:

$B = \alpha N + \beta C/n$ = minimum where α and β are weights to   [29]
be assigned and N and C are given above.

By multiplying equation 29 by n, combining the terms, and setting $\gamma = \beta/(\alpha + \beta)$, we get the general *oblimin* criterion:

$$B = \sum_{j<k=1}^{r} \left(n \sum_{i=1}^{n} a_{ij}^2 a_{ik}^2 - \gamma \sum_{i=1}^{n} a_{ij}^2 \sum_{i=1}^{n} a_{ik}^2 \right). \qquad [30]$$

This general criterion reduces to:

Quartimin when γ = o (most oblique)
Biquartimin when γ = .5 (less oblique)
Covarimin where γ = 1 (least oblique).

We note once again that it is customary to use the normalized oblimin criterion by replacing a_{ij}^2 with a_{ij}^2/h_i^2.

Another criterion closely related to the principles specified in developing oblimin, but based on completely different algorithms, is the binormamin criterion. This is an attempt to objectify the choice of γ in equation 30 as a means of correcting for the "too oblique" bias of quartimin and for the "too orthogonal" bias of covarimin. Compared to biquartimin, which adopts $1/2$ for γ, the binormamin is reported to be more satisfactory if the data are either particularly simple or particularly complex.

SOLUTIONS BASED ON THE
FACTOR PATTERN WITH DIRECT OBLIMIN

In recent years, Jennrich and Sampson (1966) developed a criterion which is based on simplifying loadings on the primary factors (not reference axes) and introduced a successful computer program. The value minimized is defined as exactly parallel to equation 30, with the only difference being the use of primary factor loadings (loadings in the pattern matrix) in the place of loadings on the reference axes. The criterion is:

$$ D = \sum_{j=k=1}^{r} \left[\sum_{i=1}^{n} b_{ij}^2 b_{ik}^2 - d\left(\sum_{i=1}^{n} b_{ij}^2 \sum_{i=1}^{n} b_{ik}^2 \right) / n \right], \qquad [31] $$

where b_{ij} are factor loadings in a pattern matrix, with the slight difference between D and B being the division of the terms by n in D. As in indirect oblimin, the researcher can modify the degree of obliqueness of the final solution by the choice of d in equation 31.

In general, greater values of d produce more oblique solutions and smaller (negative) values produce more orthogonal solutions. If the factor pattern is unifactorial (the simplest possible), the specification of $d = 0$ identifies the correct pattern.

A word of caution is necessary here. Although the formula is similar, choice of d in direct oblimin does not have a known correspondence with the choice of γ in indirect oblimin. To gain a better understanding of the effects of specifying a different d, the reader may consult Harman (1975).

108

OTHER METHODS OF OBLIQUE ROTATION

There are many additional methods of oblique rotation. We will identify a few of the better known solutions.

The *oblimax* criterion (Saunders, 1953) is based on an attempt to simplify the structure by maximizing the number of small and large loadings at the expense of medium loadings. As an objective criterion, it finds a solution which maximizes the kurtosis of doubled factor loadings. (The doubling is done by counting each loading twice, one with the original sign and the other with the reversed one.) This criterion is equivalent to quartimax in orthogonal rotation but leads to a different solution from quartimin (the oblique counterpart of quartimax) when used without restricting to orthogonal axes.

Two more rotation methods need be mentioned at least in passing. Harris and Kaiser's orthoblique method (1964) is gaining wider use, and the Maxplane Method (Cattel and Muerle, 1960; Eber, 1966) is a possible alternative because it is based on a somewhat different criterion of fit than all the others so far examined.

Rotation to a Target Matrix

Instead of applying rotation methods to achieve some analytically defined simple structure, it is possible and sometimes desirable to rotate factors in order to fit a specific simple structure the researcher has in mind or has hypothesized to exist.

The first possibility is that the researcher specifies the exact loadings on each variable, and then makes rotations either with orthogonal restrictions or without such restrictions in such a way that the fit between the specified matrix and the final rotated factor matrix is minimum according to the least squares criterion. This type of rotation is usually performed to examine the congruity of a one factor structure to another factor structure which is already known or presented elsewhere.

The second approach, known as *promax* oblique rotation, is simply a way of obtaining an oblique solution by using some functions of the orthogonal solution as the target matrix (Hendrickson and White, 1964). The rationale behind the promax rotation is that the orthogonal solutions are usually close to the oblique solution, and by reducing the smaller loadings to near-zero loadings, one can obtain a reasonably good simple structure target matrix. Then by finding the best fitting oblique factors for this target matrix, one obtains the desired oblique solution. There are different algorithms for solving for the target structure matrix and for the target pattern matrix, but we will not describe them.

TABLE 7
Target Matrix with 0s and 1s

Variables	Factors 1	2
X_1	1	0
X_2	1	0
X_3	1	0
X_4	0	1
X_5	0	1
X_6	0	1

The third and more general approach is to use a target matrix which is less specific than the preceding ones. Instead of making a least squares fit to a target matrix in which all the values are exactly specified, one may simply specify 0s and 1s. This is the most realistic target matrix in that we usually do not know the exact values to expect, but have some notion about which loadings should be high and which should be low. An example of such a target matrix is given in Table 7.

Such a target matrix can be modified to make it even more general: some are specified to be zero, some are specified to be some other fixed values, and the remainder are left to vary freely. This will be more thoroughly discussed in the section on confirmatory factor analysis.

IV. NUMBER OF FACTORS PROBLEM REVISITED

Although we previously examined various methods of initial factoring, where the objective is to find the minimum number of factors compatible with the data, there are several reasons to reexamine this issue. First, in discussing the initial factoring methods, we essentially assumed that the number of factors question could be resolved without ambiguity, and therefore, did not discuss various technical points pertaining to this question. Second, some of the initial solutions are not satisfactory as a means for answering this question, thus requiring that rotated solutions be examined. Third, we must contend with the problems caused by an imperfect fit between the factor analytic model and the data. Fourth, most existing computer programs will require the user to provide some information regarding the number of factors question, and we want to prepare the reader for this contingency.

There are several rules typically applied in addressing the number of factors question. Some of these are distinct alternatives while some are complementary to each other. The most important rules involve: (1) significance tests associated with the maximum likelihood and least squares solutions, (2) varieties of the eigenvalue criterion, (3) the criterion of substantive importance, (4) the Scree-test, and (5) the criterion of interpretability and invariance.

Significance Tests

The large sample x^2-test associated with the maximum likelihood solution is the most satisfactory solution from a purely statistical point of view, provided that the assumptions of the method are adequately met. Application of the method has shown that for a large sample with many variables, the number of factors retained tends to be much larger than the number of factors the researcher is willing to accept. Although this really is not a defect of the method, it has forced researchers to also apply another criterion—that of substantive significance, which is applied after finding statistical significance.

Monte Carlo experiments usually show that the maximum likelihood criterion is most appropriate when applied to known population models without substantively insignificant minor factors. That is, it is an efficient method to deal with sampling variability, but it is not the best when minor deviations are built into the model. Given sufficient sample size, any of these deviations will be treated as "significant" dimensions that cannot be accounted for by sampling variability. This implies, therefore, that it may be preferable on substantive grounds to ignore some minor factors after proper rotation.

Although we described the use of this method as a fail-safe procedure under which the adequacy of a one-common factor model is tested, and then the adequacy of the two factor model if the data deviate "significantly" from the one factor model, and so on, such a procedure is often too costly to use on large sets of variables. Therefore, one may combine one of the quick methods of determining the number of common factors (to be described below) with the maximum likelihood test. After making the initial "guess" of significant factors, one may increase the number if the data deviate significantly from the assumed model, *or* decrease the number if the initial model is accepted as adequate (to make sure that one has the minimum number of factors that are compatible with the data). From a statistical point of view, the least squares solution is not as efficient as maximum likelihood but the same comments apply to this solution.

Eigenvalue Specification

One of the most popular criteria for addressing the number of factors question is to retain factors with eigenvalues greater than 1 when the correlational (not adjusted) matrix is decomposed. This simple criterion seems to work well, in the sense that it generally gives results consistent with researchers' expectations, and it works well when applied to samples from artifically created population models.

In a population correlation matrix, such a criterion will always establish a lower-bound for the number of common factors. That is, the number of common factors responsible for the correlation matrix will always be equal or greater than the number specified by this criterion. However, this strict inequality need not hold when the sample correlation matrix is considered. Although Kaiser provides several reasons for its success, its acceptance is still based on heuristic and practical grounds. After examining other more "sophisticated" criteria, Kaiser still favors this one (Kaiser, 1974).

Another related eigenvalue criterion is that of retaining vectors with eigenvalues greater than zero when the reduced correlation matrix (with squared multiple Rs in the main diagonal) is decomposed. The rationale behind this criterion is that in a population correlation matrix, it provides an even stricter lower-bound for the number of common factors responsible for the data. But the same may not necessarily apply to the sample correlation matrix, and application to empirical data usually produces more factors than normally accepted on other grounds.

When the communalities are estimated and inserted in the main diagonal, this eigenvalue criterion can be applied. However, when some of the eigenvalues are negative, as will usually be the case, it does not make sense to extract all the factors with the eigenvalues greater than zero. Although the sum of both negative and positive eigenvalues is the same as the sum of all communalities (or variances explained by common factors), the negative values are not meaningfully interpreted within the context of variance, and their presence makes the sum of positive eigenvalues "inflated" in the sense that their sum is greater than the sum of the communalities. Harman (1975:141) suggests that one should stop extracting common factors before the cumulative sum of eigenvalues exceeds the sum of the estimated communalities.

Criterion of Substantive Importance

Considering that the "significance" tests focus on sampling variability and the eigenvalue criterion focuses on some abstract properties of a matrix, a third alternative to use is to focus directly on the criterion of what should be considered a minimum contribution by a factor to be evaluated as substantively significant. This criterion is easy to understand when the initial factoring is based on the decomposition of the unaltered correlation matrix; the proportion to specify is the proportion of the total variance (which is the number of variables) to be explained by the last factor to be retained. (Recall that in every extraction method we discussed, the initial factors were arranged in the order of their magnitude.) One may set the criterion at whatever level is considered substantively important. Some possibilities are one percent, five percent, or ten percent. However, note that the use of "eigenvalue 1" criterion is equivalent to setting the minimum variance explained at $(100/n)$ percent level.

On the other hand, when the altered correlation matrix is factored, as is done in every method we discussed except for principal components, the proportion to specify is the proportion of the last eigenvalue relative to the sum of the eigenvalues (sum of the main diagonal of the matrix to be factored). The major disadvantage of the method is that it uses a subjective criterion. The obvious advantage is that the researcher who is not familiar with the properties of eigenvalue decomposition of a matrix may rely on a measure of relative magnitude which "appears" easier to interpret.

Scree-Test

This is a test advocated by Cattell (1965). The rule directs one to examine the graph of eigenvalues, and stop factoring at the point where the eigenvalues (or characteristic roots) begin to level off forming a straight line with an almost horizontal slope. Beyond this point Cattell describes the smooth slope as "factorial litter or scree" (where scree is the geological term referring to the debris which collects on the lower part of a rocky slope). Its use is illustrated in Figure 5. Based on these results, the re-

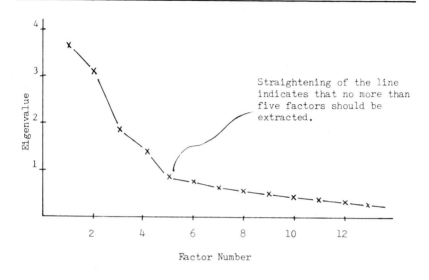

Figure 5: Illustration of Scree-Test

searcher would conclude that not more than five factors should be extracted.

Some Monte Carlo studies indicate that this method is often superior to others where there are minor factors and the interest is in locating only major common factors (Tucker, Koopman and Linn, 1969; Linn, 1968). Some, like Kaiser (1970), argue that this "root-staring" criterion is often very subjective because it is not uncommon to find more than one major break in the root-graph and there is no unambiguous rule to use.

Criteria of Interpretability and Invariance

As a way to protect oneself from accepting results which are dubious, a general rule-of-thumb is to try to combine various rules, accept only those conclusions that are supported by several independent criteria, and consider others as tentative hypotheses (Harris, 1967). Given the complexity as well as uncertainties inherent in the method, the final judgment has to rest on the reasonableness of the solution on the basis of current standards of scholarship in one's own field. This criterion is elusive but, fortunately or unfortunately, all of us must live with it in order to communicate our findings to our fellow scientists.

V. INTRODUCTION TO CONFIRMATORY FACTOR ANALYSIS

Thus far we have concentrated on exploratory factor analysis and have emphasized the fact that in applying the technique, numerous assumptions must be made, the most important of these being the assumptions of factorial causation and parsimony. Since all one does in this type of analysis is to impose a particular model on the data and find a solution that is most compatible with the data, one can legitimately ask whether and to what extent the application of the method generates some empirical support for the factor analytic model itself. As mentioned earlier, whatever the results may be, one can never prove the existence of a particular causal structure from the observation of the covariance structure. One can, however, assess the degree to which the plausibility of factor models is empirically confirmed.

Degree of Empirical Confirmation for the Factor Analytic Model

Compared to exploratory factor analysis, we introduce more specific hypotheses about the factor structure in confirmatory factor analysis and, therefore, the chance that such specific hypotheses will be supported by a given covariance structure is smaller, if in fact some factorial causation is not in operation. In that sense, most confirmatory factor analysis can provide self-validating information. If a given factorial hypothesis is supported by the data, we will in general also have greater confidence in the appropriateness of the factor analytic model for the given data. (Of course, the degree to which such empirical confirmation is provided varies from one analysis to another.) Moreover, even a purely exploratory analysis can provide us with varying degrees of self-validating information. Before introducing confirmatory factor analysis, therefore, it is important to discuss the notion of empirical confirmation in general, and some of the means by which we assess whether or not we have data that are appropriate for factor analysis.

AN ILLUSTRATION

Applying the factor analytical model to a bivariate correlation does not generate information other than what is already known by the researcher. This is so because a one-common factor model is always compatible with a bivariate correlation. Hence, factor analysis is never applied to this situation, not because a factor analytic model is incompatible with the data but because the degree of empirical confirmation of the model (to be called informativeness for short) is zero, and because (though much more trivial) there is no unique solution. Consider the relationship between the first two variables in the model shown in Figure 1. Given any correlation one can arbitrarily choose one factor loading to be between −1 and +1 (except 0) and still find the other factor loading which will be compatible with the observed correlation. In short, there always is a factor solution compatible with data.

The situation changes slightly when factor analysis is applied to a three variable correlation matrix. If one finds that a one-common factor model is compatible with the data, the degree of empirical confirmation obtained is not zero, because some random correlation matrices will not be compatible with a one-common factor model. In particular, for a three variable correlation matrix to be compatible with a one-common factor model the relationships among the three correlation coefficients must meet the conditions that (1) all the correlations are positive or only an even number of them can be negative, and (2) the magnitude of any one coefficient be equal to or greater than the magnitude of the product of the remaining two coefficients:

$$|r_{ij}| \geqslant |r_{ik} r_{jk}|. \tag{32}$$

It is informative to derive the condition specified by equation 32. Consider Figure 18 in the previous volume (or the upper half of Figure 1), and recall that

$$r_{12} = b_1 b_2 \qquad h_1 = b_1^2$$

$$r_{13} = b_1 b_3 \quad \text{and} \quad h_2 = b_2^2$$

$$r_{23} = b_2 b_3 \qquad h_3 = b_3^2.$$

Next, let us multiply two correlation coefficients as follows:

$$r_{12} r_{13} = b_1 b_2 b_1 b_3 = b_1^2 b_2 b_3 = h_1^2 r_{23}. \tag{33}$$

The term after the first equal sign is given by expressing the correlations in terms of factor loadings, the terms after the second sign by rearranging, and the last terms are given by substituting corresponding communalities and correlations for the factor loadings. A slight rearrangement of equation 33 and the fact that communalities cannot be greater than 1 leads to the condition specified by equation 32:

$$h^2 = r_{12} r_{13} / r_{23} \leqslant 1,$$

which implies that $|r_{23}| \geqslant |r_{12}r_{13}|$. In general, all the three variable one-common factor models must meet the condition that $|r_{ij}| \geqslant |r_{ik}r_{jk}|$. To the extent that not all the randomly produced correlation matrices of three variables would satisfy the above condition, finding that one's data meet the requirement of a one-common factor model is informative, but not highly informative because many random matrices can be compatible with the one-common factor model. In other words, the condition specified by equation 32 is met by many random matrices of three correlations.

Recall from Section II of the first volume that a four variable correlation matrix based on a one-common factor model meets three additional conditions, namely:

$$r_{13}r_{24} = r_{14}r_{23} \qquad\qquad [34]$$

$$r_{12}r_{34} = r_{14}r_{23}$$

$$r_{13}r_{24} = r_{12}r_{34}$$

This rule is easy to derive and remember because, using an example, $r_{13}r_{24} = b_1b_3b_2b_4 = (b_1b_4)(b_2b_3) = r_{14}r_{23}$. (The same procedure is employed as in deriving the inequality condition in equation 32.) In general, then, the greater the number of variables, the greater the number of conditions that the correlation matrix has to meet to satisfy the requirements of a particular factor model. Therefore, the fact that a one-common factor model is compatible with a four variable matrix provides the researcher some empirical confirmation that the factor analytic assumption may not be totally arbitrary.

Thus, a factor analytic result can provide some empirical confirmation about the appropriateness of the model itself, in the sense that only when certain constraints are met by the correlation matrix can a given factor model fit the data. Furthermore, the greater the ratio of the number of variables to the number of hypothesized factors, the greater the empirical confirmation of the factor analytic model, because it implies that a greater number of structural constraints do indeed exist in the correlation matrix in order to satisfy the factor analytic model.

Now recall that applying factor analysis implies imposing various assumptions on the data. It is possible then to reject the factor analytic model purely on the grounds that these assumptions are arbitrary or inappropriate. However, one must temper such a judgment when the degree of empirical confirmation is high, because one has to account for the existence of structural constraints in the data (i.e., lack of randomness). Viewed from a slightly different perspective, it can be said that the informativeness of factor analysis varies from application to application;

results of some factor analysis can be much more informative than those of others. Still another way of looking at it is that factor analysis *can* provide self-validating information; the greater the number of empirical constraints a given solution must satisfy, the greater the degree of our confidence in the appropriateness of the factor analytic model for the data. Therefore, depending on the outcome, even an exploratory factor analysis can provide some empirical confirmation about the appropriateness and the economy of the model.

Number of Empirical Constraints Implied by a Model

Given the preceding discussion, it is important to know the number of empirical constraints implied by a given factor model (the number of conditions to be met by a correlation matrix in order to fit a particular model). Fortunately, the number is equivalent to the number of degrees of freedom associated with the significance test for the maximum likelihood solution. (A careful examination of this number is instructive because a clear understanding of the relationship between a factorial hypothesis and the implied degrees of freedom is crucial for the understanding of confirmatory factor analysis to be discussed shortly.)

There are, however, several different ways to specify the number of constraints for a correlation matrix implied by a particular factor model. One way to approach the problem is to use the rank-theorem, which states that if correct communalities are inserted in the correlation matrix (produced by an r-common factor model), the rank (or number of independent dimensions) of the adjusted correlation matrix will be r, which in turn implies that all the submatrices which contain more than r columns and r rows will have zero determinants. From this, one can specify the number of conditions a correlation matrix must satisfy for a given number of factors and variables (e.g., Harman, 1976). The other approach is to examine the degrees of freedom in the context of a significance test. Because the first approach leads to the same number of conditions specified by application of a significance test, we will derive it in the more general context of the second approach.

To illustrate, assume we begin with an empirical correlation matrix. The amount of independent information contained in such a matrix is $(1/2)\, n\, (n-1)$—the number of cells in the upper triangle. Given such data, factor analysis arrives at an initial solution by allowing n x r (where r is the number of common factors) factor loadings to vary in such a way that these loadings best reproduce the observed correlation matrix. But in initial factoring, we require these n x r factor loadings to satisfy the condition that the resulting factors are orthogonal. This implies that

TABLE 8
Degrees of Freedom Associated with n Variables and r Factors[a]

Number of Variables (n)	Number of Factors				Maximum Number of Factors With Positive Degrees of Freedom	Number of Independent Coefficients $\frac{1}{2}n(n-1)$
	1	2	3	4		
3	0	-2	-3	--	none	3
4	2	-1	-3	-4	1	6
5	5	1	-2	-4	2	10
6	9	4	0	-3	2	15
7	14	8	3	-1	3	21
8	20	13	7	2	4	28
9	27	19	12	6	5	36
10	35	26	18	11	5	45
11	44	34	25	17	6	55
12	54	43	33	24	7	66
20	170	151	133	116	14	190
40	740	701	663	626	31	780

a. The general formula is $D = \dfrac{(n-r)^2 - (n+r)}{2}$ = the number of constraints to be satisfied by the data.

$1/2r(r-1)$ arbitrary conditions are imposed. Consequently, we will use the following number of free parameters in arriving at the initial factor solution:

$$nr - (1/2)r(r-1). \qquad [35]$$

Therefore, the number of conditions that an empirical correlation matrix has to satisfy independently of the model is the difference:

Number of Empirical Constraints Required $= 1/2n(n-1) - [nr - 1/2r(r-1)]$ [36]

$$= 1/2[(n-r)^2 - (n+r)],$$

which is the same as the degrees of freedom presented earlier. (When a *covariance* matrix is used in the place of a correlation matrix, the amount of independent information contained in the matrix is $1/2n(n+1)$ instead of $1/2n(n-1)$. However, the final degrees of freedom remains the same because of the additional impositions necessary for the factor analysis model to be applied to the covariance matrix.)

In order to gain some familiarity with what is implied by equation 36, we present in Table 8 actual values for various combinations of number of factors and variables. There are several aspects to note. First, the number of empirical constraints to be satisfied increase, in general, as the ratio of the number of variables to the number of factors increases. Second, when the number is negative, a factor analytic result would not provide any empirical confirmation of the model. Hence, it makes sense in general to consider only those factor models that require some empirical constraints in the data. For example, applying a two-common factor model to a four variable matrix or a three factor model to a matrix with six or less number of variables would not be informative. Third, the number of required constraints increases rapidly as the number of variables increases for a fixed number of factors. Therefore, the addition of a variable to the factor analysis can add a great deal more empirical content to factor analytic results. Fourth, if one uses this number as an index of the empirical confirmation, it would seem to imply that what is really important is not the ratio, but the difference between the number of variables and the number of common factors hypothesized. Notice that the number of constraints to be satisfied is almost the same among the following combinations: 1 factor with 7 variables (14); 2 factors with 8 variables (13); 3 factors with 9 variables (12), and so on. But there is no reason to consider this index to be a direct measure of the degree of empirical confirmation. One alternative is to examine the ratio of (a) the number of constraints to be satisfied to (b) the number of independent coefficients in the observed matrix. Although we do not present these ratios in the table (the base number is given in the last column), we note that such a measure would indicate that the ratio of variables to factors would be more important than the raw index would indicate.

There are two complications that must be taken into consideration in assessing the degree of empirical confirmation provided by factor solutions. The first complication is that the requirements, even if they are met exactly in the population, are not likely to be met exactly in the sample. The second is that even in the population, the factor analytic model may not exactly fit the data; hence, the requirements have to be evaluated taking minor misfits into consideration. The most frustrating part is that in actual analysis there is no way of separating one complication from the other. In practice, therefore, one cannot use equation 36 alone as a measure of empirical confirmation. Given some degree of fit between a factor solution and observed data, a solution which has to meet a greater number of empirical constraints would provide greater confirmation. But to be able to assess that, one must find a way of evaluating the fit.

DEGREE OF EMPIRICAL CONFIRMATION OR RELIABILITY

A significance test associated with some initial factoring methods assesses the degree to which the discrepancy between the hypothesized model and observed data can be attributed to the sampling variability. The significance test is directly dependent upon the sample size; given a sufficiently large sample, any discrepancy between the model and observed data can be made significant. This is the result of the fact that if a factor model fits exactly the population data, the greater the sample size, the smaller the discrepancy between the population values and sample statistic. When sample size is very large, the deviation should be very small.

This statistical principle runs into trouble whenever the researcher suspects the existence of minor factors, and is unwilling or unable to specify their exact nature. In such a case, the significance test may not reveal the adequacy of the model—that is, even if the specified factor model is economical in that it explains a large portion of the observed covariance and brings some order to the data structure, the test may indicate that the model is statistically inadequate. Therefore, we need a descriptive index of adequacy of the factor model, which is conceptually independent of statistical significance.

The statistic we need is a measure of discrepancy between the observed correlation matrix and the reproduced matrix. One possibility, suggested by Harman, is to use the residual-mean-square, in which the squared deviations between the observed correlations and predicted correlations (by the final factor solution) are summed and divided by the number of cells under consideration:

$$\sum_{i \neq j} \sum (r_{ij} - \hat{r}_{ij})^2 / [n(n-1)],$$

where the summation is over all the off-diagonal elements (Harman, 1976:176). This measure, however, does not have a convenient upper limit against which to interpret its relative magnitude.

Another alternative is Tucker and Lewis's reliability coefficient (1973) for the maximum likelihood factor solution. The measure is based on the residual correlations in the matrix after the effects of final factors are taken out; it is therefore ultimately based on the fit between the observed correlations and correlations based on the factor solution. Their reliability coefficient incorporates, however, two additional adjustments: it divides the overall discrepancy by the degrees-of-freedom, thereby adjusting for the potential differences between factor solutions, and it compares the adjusted measure of deviation with the comparable deviation when factors are assumed not operative, thereby making it a measure of proportional reduction in adjusted discrepancy. The coefficient, therefore, ranges between 0 and 1, the former representing the poorest fit and the latter a complete fit. An abbreviated formula is:

$$\text{rho} = \frac{M_o - M_k}{M_o} \qquad [37]$$

where M_0 = Expected χ^2 in the absence of factor effect divided by $(1/2)$ $n(n-k1)$, $M_k = \chi^2$ for the final solution divided by $(1/2)[(n-r)^2 - (n+r)]$. (See also Sörbom and Jöreskog, 1976:4-5). A more useful, but less accurate, description of the formula which converges to equation 37 as sample size gets larger is:

$$\text{Approximate rho} = 1 - \frac{E_1}{E_2}$$

$$\text{where } E_1 = \sum_{i=j} \sum (r_{ij \cdot F})^2 / df_k \text{ and}$$

$$E_2 = \sum_{i=j} \sum (r_{ij})^2 / [1/2 \, n(n-1)],$$

where $r_{ij \cdot F}$ is the partial correlation among variables after the effects of k-factors are taken out, and df, is the degree of freedom, which will be $1/2[(n-r)^2 - (n+r)]$ in an exploratory factor analysis, but will be a larger number in confirmatory factor analysis. (The residual partial correlation is no more than a standardized version of the discrepancy between the predicted correlations and observed ones.)

Another Conception of Empirical Confirmation:
Sampling Adequacy

The conventional statistical tests assume only the sampling of units (objects or entities), but in practice we cannot ignore the fact that a certain degree of psychometric sampling is involved—the variables we analyze are almost always a subset of a potentially larger domain of relevant variables. One must then ask whether the given data (subset of variables) are adequate for factor analysis. (The reader may recall that image factoring and alpha factoring assume such psychometric sampling, but the issue is relevant for any type of factor analysis.)

In general, it is true that other things being equal, the degree of empirical confirmation is greater if (1) the number of variables increases, (2) the number of common factor decreases, (3) the residual correlations decrease, or (4) the greater the degree of factorial determination. The first two conditions are directly related to the increase in the empirical constraints imposed on the data by the factorial model, the third condition measures the degree to which a factor model accounts for the observed covariation, and the last one specifies that the variance of each variable be accounted for mostly by common factors. The last condition is directly related to the notion of sampling adequacy, because the degree of overall factorial determination will increase, other things being equal, with an increase in the number of variables and with an increase in the average magnitude of correlations.

The rule-of-thumb index of sampling adequacy is proposed by Kaiser (1970, 1974), which he calls an overall "measure of sampling adequacy."

$$\text{MSA} = \frac{\underset{j \neq k}{\Sigma \Sigma} \; r_{jk}^2}{\underset{j \neq k}{\Sigma \Sigma} \; r_{jk}^2 + \underset{j \neq k}{\Sigma \Sigma} \; q_{ik}^2} \qquad [38]$$

where r_{ij} is an original correlation and q_{ij} is an element of the anti-image correlation matrix, which is given by $Q = SR^{-1}S$, where R^{-1} is an inverse of the correlation matrix and $S = (\text{diag } R^{-1})^{1/2}$. The index ranges between 0 and 1. In fact, the index becomes 1 if and only if all the off-diagonal elements of the inverse of the correlation matrix are zero, which in turn implies that every variable can be predicted without error from other variables in the set. The guide for interpreting the measure is as follows (Kaiser, 1974):

in the .90's	marvelous
in the .80's	meritorious
in the .70's	middling
in the .60's	mediocre
in the .50's	miserable
below .50	unacceptable.

Kaiser claims that extensive experience with data shows that the magnitude of MSA improves as (1) the number of variables increases,

(2) the number of common factors decreases, (3) the number of cases (entities) increases, and (4) the average magnitude of correlations increases (1970).

To recapitulate, the degree to which data provide empirical evidence that a given factor analytic model is appropriate for the problem at hand varies from one situation to another. The researcher should be aware of the conditions that improve the informativeness of factor analysis. Furthermore, a novice to factor analysis may rely on a rule-of-thumb index such as Kaiser's MSA in order to acquire a rough idea of whether the data are adequate for the technique. Of course, the ultimate decision must be made on the basis of theoretical justification.

Confirmatory Factor Analysis

The minimum requirement of any confirmatory factor analysis is that one hypothesize before hand the number of common factors. However, the hypothesis, if it is to be different from a hunch or guess, must be based on an understanding of the nature of the variables under consideration, as well as on expectations concerning which factor is likely to load on which variables. This cannot be overemphasized because the variety in the actual form of these factorial hypotheses is almost limitless.

We can classify confirmatory factor analysis into two general types: (1) one in which only one group or population is involved, and (2) another in which two or more groups or populations are involved. We begin with the first type.

ONE GROUP OR POPULATION

Given a covariance matrix for a group, in confirmatory factor analysis, one starts with an hypothesis about the factorial structure thought to be responsible for the observed covariance structure. Then one evaluates whether the observed data structure deviates "significantly" from the hypothesized structure. At one extreme, the hypothesis may specify: (a) the number of common factors, (b) the nature of the relationship among factors—either orthogonal or oblique, and (c) the magnitude of factor loadings for each variable. At the other extreme, the hypothesis may be no more than a specification about the number of underlying common factors. There are, of course, numerous possible hypotheses which lie between these extremes.

Because the simplest form of confirmatory factor analysis, where only the number of common factors is specified, is not very different from exploratory factor analysis, only brief comments are necessary. For this type of hypothesis, whether one employs an orthogonal or oblique factor model is immaterial, and a significance test or some other criterion (such as a reliability coefficient) which evaluates the adequacy of initial factor solutions is satisfactory. Therefore, the only difference to note here is that one starts with a number that is based on some prior consideration, whereas, in exploratory analysis one starts with a "safe" number and increments it if the first guess is not adequate. We should also mention that it may not be wise to rely completely on significance tests unless one is willing to accept substantively minor but statistically significant factors. If a judgmental criterion is also to be employed, it is desirable to rotate the solution and then determine whether the emerging structure is meaningful.

The other extreme is also easy to discuss. If the researcher has specific hypotheses about the number of factors, the nature of the relationships among factors, and the specific loadings, it is possible either to check whether the reproduced correlation matrix under the hypothesis is close enough to the observed correlations, or use the hypothesis as a target matrix and find a solution which approximates the target while maximally reproducing the observed correlations. In the former, the check of the adequacy of the hypothesis depends on some test for evaluating similarity between covariance matrices and, in the latter case, some test for evaluating similarity between two factor solutions is required. For more details, the readers may consult a volume in this series (Levine, 1977). In general, it is unrealistic to expect a researcher to possess hypotheses this specific in actual factor analysis. Nevertheless, such an hypothesis can arise if one is comparing the structure of one factor analysis (for one data set) with the structure based on other data. This is the case which can be subsumed under a more general solution to be discussed shortly.

Because Sörbom and Jöreskog's latest confirmatory factor program allows a great deal of flexibility, we will outline some of the important specification options available in that program (Sörbom and Jöreskog, 1976). There are several ways one can specify any parameter. The parameters involved in factor analysis are the factor loadings (nr for common factors) and the correlation coefficients among factors ($1/2\ r(r-1)$). Any of these parameters can be *fixed* at a particular value or left free to vary. Usually, the most useful way of fixing a parameter would be to specify a particular loading to be zero. For example, if all the factor correlations are fixed to be zero, then an orthogonal solution is being specified. Another way of specifying parameters is to *constrain* a parameter to be equal to another parameter.

To make the preceding discussion more concrete we present in Table 9 three examples of specifying *free* and *fixed* parameters. In these examples, x's represent free parameters and zeros represent fixed parameters—fixed

TABLE 9
Three Examples of Specifying Parameters in
Confirmatory Factor Analysis[a]

Variables	Example 1			Example 2			Example 3		
	F_1	F_2	F_3	F_1	F_2	F_3	F_1	F_2	F_3
X_1	X	0	0	X	X	0	X	X	X
X_2	X	0	0	X	X	0	X	X	X
X_3	X	0	0	X	X	0	X	X	X
X_4	0	X	0	X	X	0	X	X	0
X_5	0	X	0	X	0	X	X	X	0
X_6	0	X	0	X	0	X	X	0	0
X_7	0	0	X	X	0	X	X	0	0
X_8	0	0	X	X	0	X	X	0	0

a. X represents free parameters; O represents parameters fixed to be zero.

to be zero. One could fix the parameters at other values, such as 1.0, .5, and so on, but we think it realistic only to expect the researcher to have some notion about where loadings should be high and where they should be low. The first hypothesis specifies a unifactorial structure—the simplest possible type given the number of variables, the second hypothesis anticipates a general factor and two group factors, and the third specifies a special hierarchy. The researcher may, of course, introduce many modifications in these patterns.

Along with the specifications illustrated above, one also has to specify the nature of the relationships among factors. The most usual forms of specifying them are: (1) specifying all the factor correlations to be zero—an orthogonal hypothesis, (2) allowing all the correlations to vary—an oblique hypothesis, or (3) a mixed pattern in which some are assumed to be orthogonal while leaving others to take any value.

An illustration of confirmatory factory analysis is presented in Table 10, using the sample data from Table 1. Suppose that the researcher is willing to hypothesize, (1) that there are two underlying common factors, (2) that the two factors can be correlated, and (3) that one factor has zero loadings on X_4, X_5, X_6 and the other factor has zero loadings on X_1, X_2, X_3.

Note that, compared to exploratory factor analysis, we are making 6 parameters (factorloadings) fixed out of 12 (nr), but making 1 parameter free in the *factor* covariance matrix. Consequently, we are imposing

TABLE 10
Fixed and Free Parameters Specified in Solving the
Oblique Factor Pattern[a]

Variables	Factors	
	F_1	F_2
X_1	X	0
X_2	X	0
X_3	X	0
X_4	0	X
X_5	0	X
X_6	0	X

Correlations Among Factors

	F_1	F_2
F_1	1	
F_2		1

a. Os indicate fixed parameters and Xs represent parameters which are free to vary. The 1s in factor correlation matrices can be considered fixed when the covariance matrix is input. However, in our calculation of degrees of freedom, we counted these values as part of the general specification, so we do not count 1s as fixed.

altogether 5 additional constraints. But not all of these 5 restrictions will be reflected in the increased degrees of freedom. In exploratory analysis, we also use ½ r(r−1) implicit conditions in order to make a particular solution unique. Hence, the degrees of freedom increase is 5−½ r(r−1) = 4. In general, the fit between the models with fixed parameters and the data will be poorer than the fit between the model without fixed parameters. But what is lost in terms of fit usually will be more than compensated for

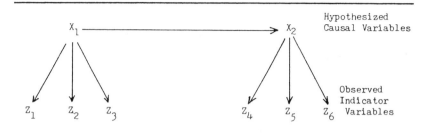

Figure 6: Causal Model Involving Two Hypothetical Variables and Indicator Variables

by the increased degrees of freedom, if the hypothesized model is appropriate.

Also note that it would not make much sense to apply a three-common factor model to a six variable matrix. However, it is quite possible to apply such a model to these data if the hypothesized factor structure has enough constraints to accommodate several degrees of freedom. An example would be: specify that X_1 and X_2 load only on factor 1, that X_3 and X_4 load only on factor 2, and X_5 and X_6 load only on factor 3.

We note that the principle illustrated in this section can be generalized (beyond pure factor analysis) to covariance structures. In particular, it is possible to combine the features of factor analysis with the features of path analysis or regression analysis. For example, if one has a set of variables representing indicators of a theoretical variable (F_1) that affect another theoretical variable (F_2) for which we also have a set of indicator variables, such a system of relationships can easily be analyzed by an extension of confirmatory factor analysis. In this particular example, the model can be specified as a confirmatory factor analysis with two correlated factors as shown in Figure 6. Also note that such a model is not different for the structure specified in Table 9 (sample 1), with no restriction on the correlation between factors. Here we have merely mentioned the most simple extension of confirmatory factor analysis; interested readers should consult Jöreskog (1970), and Sörbom and Jöreskog (1976) for a more complete presentation.

COMPARING FACTOR STRUCTURES

Another use of confirmatory factor analysis is comparing factor structures across several groups. For instance, one may hypothesize that the factor structure of political attitudes for blacks is the same as that of whites, or that the cognitive structure of one society is the same as that of another. It is also possible to specify that certain aspects of the factor structures are the same but others are dissimilar across the groups.

There exists a computer program (COFAMM: Confirmatory Factor Analysis with Model Modifications by Jöreskog and Sörbom) which can handle very general hypotheses. For instance, it allows all the variations that are available in testing factorial hypotheses for a single group—some parameters may be fixed or left to vary freely, or some parameters may be made to be constrained to be equal to the other parameters. In addition, with use of "constrained" parameters, any part of the parameter structure for one group can be made to be equal to that of another group.

As an illustration, consider the example of political attitudes where one is interested in comparing the factor structure of whites to that of blacks. The specific hypothesis may take the form: (1) there are two oblique factors for both whites and blacks, (2) the variables X_1 (money for schools), X_2 (money to reduce unemployment), and X_3 (control of big business) load on the same factor with the same loadings for both whites and blacks; likewise, X_4 (busing programs) and X_5 (job quotas) load on the other factor for both races, (3) but X_6 (headstart program) is expected to load differently for these two groups. In this case, one can specify the parameters for the whites as in a single group analysis and all the parameters for the blacks except one (involving X_6) as constrained to be the same as whites. Fairly extensive examples of confirmatory factor analysis as well as more general "covariance structure" analysis are available in Jöreskog (1976).

VI. CONSTRUCTION OF FACTOR SCALES

After examining factor analysis results, one may construct factor scales for two different reasons. First, having found some underlying dimensions in the data, the researcher may want to examine the cases in terms of these dimensions rather than in terms of each variable separately. Second, the researcher may want to use one or more factors as variables in another study. In fact, with the exception of the psychometric literature, factor analysis seems to have been used more often as a means of creating factor scales for other studies than as a means of studying factor structures per se. In this section, we will examine various procedures for creating factor scales. The methods to be examined are: (1) regression estimates, (2) estimates based on ideal-variables, or the "least squares" criterion, (3) Bartlett's method of minimizing the error variance, and (4) estimates with orthogonality constraints. In addition, we will examine (5) simple summation of variables with high factor loadings, and (6) creation of principal component scales. These methods will be discussed in the context of several important aspects of scaling.

Indeterminancy of Factor Scales

Initially, let us assume we have error-free data, and also that the data have been created by a known one-common factor model. The main objective of factor scale construction is to determine the value for each case on the common factor (F) on the basis of the observed variables, X's. Reflecting on material presented thus far, it should be obvious that it may not be possible to identify exactly the common factor from the variables because each variable also contains a unique component which is inseparably mixed with the common part of the variable. In general, the most one can do is obtain *estimates* of the values of common factors from the variables. For this reason, we say there is always some indeterminancy associated with creating factor scales.

To illustrate this, let us consider a one-common factor model with three variables. In particular, let us assume that all the factor loadings are the same (or that all the correlations have the same magnitude). Such an example is shown in the left half of Figure 7. Recall that given such a model, the observed correlations among variables are given by the multiplication of respective factor loadings, which in this case amounts to the square of one factor loading, because all the factor loadings are the same:

$$r_{ij} = b_i b_j = b_i^2 = b_j^2 = h^2. \qquad [39]$$

This equation also shows that an observed correlation is equivalent to the communality of the variable.

We can then construct an index (or factor scale if you prefer) by combining the observed Xs. Because each variable has the same loading on the common factor, it is reasonable in this case to give equal weight to each and add them. The resulting index is given by

$$\hat{F} = X_1 + X_2 + X_3,$$

with the causal operation depicted in the right half of Figure 7. Note in particular that the index $\hat{F}$ has four ultimate source variables—the common factor F and the three unique factors, U_1, U_2, and U_3. Therefore, because of the presence of unique factors, the correlation between F and $\hat{F}$ will not be perfect. We next will examine the degree of association between the underlying common factor and the factor scale, i.e., the reliability of the scale.

RELIABILITY OF A FACTOR SCALE

The variance of the scale ($\hat{F}$) is easily derivable by applying the algebra of expectations as used in Section II of the first volume. The resulting variance of $\hat{F}$, expressed in terms of variances of the Xs is:

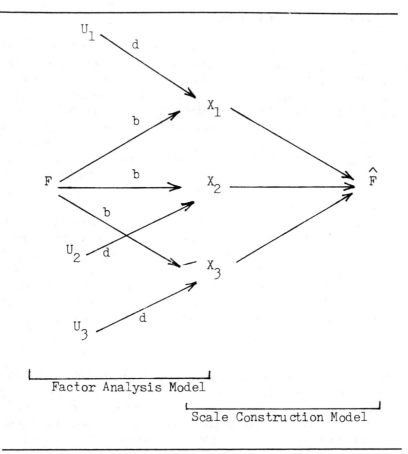

Figure 7: Path model illustrating relationship between factor and factor score

$$\text{var } (\hat{F}) = \text{var } (X_1) + \text{var } (X_2) + \text{var } (X_3) + \qquad [40]$$

$$2[\text{Cov}(X_1,X_2) + \text{Cov}(X_1,X_3) + \text{Cov}(X_2,X_3)].$$

The simplification is due to the weights being 1 in this example. This formula can be simplified further by noting that the variance of each variable is assumed to be 1, and the covariances are not only equal to the correlations but also to each other:

$$\text{Var } (\hat{F}) = n + 2[r_{12} + r_{13} + r_{23}] \qquad [41]$$

$$= n + n(n-1)r$$

(This is in fact no more than summing up all the entries in a correlation matrix of Xs.)

$$= n[1 + (n-1)r]$$

$$= n[1 + (n-1)h^2]$$

because, $r_{12} = r_{13} = r_{23} = r = h_i^2$ (see equation 39).

Some of the variance in $\hat{F}$ is, however, contributed by the unique factors, with their contribution being $\Sigma d_i^2 = \Sigma(1-h_i^2)$, which is further simplified to $n(1-h^2)$ because all the communalities are assumed equal in this example. Therefore, the portion of the variance $\hat{F}$ accounted for by the common factor F is simply

$$
\begin{aligned}
r^2_{(F,\hat{F})} &= \frac{Var(\hat{F}) - n(1-h^2)}{var\ (\hat{F})} \\
&= \frac{n\ [1+(n-1)h^2] - n(1-h^2)}{n\ [1+(n-1)\ h^2]} \\
&= \frac{nh^2}{1+(n-1)h^2} \\
&= \frac{nr}{1+(n-1)r}
\end{aligned}
\qquad [42]
$$

which is equivalent to the Spearman-Brown formula for reliability, a special case of Cronbach's alpha (Cronbach, 1951; Lord and Novick, 1968). (You need to remember that, in this case, h^2 can be replaced by the correlation r.)

To familiarize the reader with the degree of indeterminancy or the degree of expected "reliability" of factor scales, we have presented in Table 11 "reliability" values for some typical combinations of communalities and number of variables. Note that as the number of variables increases for a fixed value of the communality (the factor loadings or the correlation), the reliability increases. Note also that even with fairly high uniform factor loadings (say .8), the reliability is relatively low if one has only a few variables to deal with.

We should also note that in constructing scales, one often standardizes $\hat{F}$ such that its mean = 0 and variance = 1. Such standardization is straightforward and can be incorporated into the weights, but its value is merely cosmetic.

TABLE 11
Expected Reliability (the Correlation Between the
Factor and Its Scale Squared) for Different Values of
Uniform Factor Loadings and Number of Variables[a]

Factor Loadings	.4	.5	.6	.7	.8	.9
Communality (h^2) or Correlation Between Variables	.16	.25	.36	.49	.64	.81
Number of Variables						
2	.276	.400	.529	.658	.780	.895
3	.364	.500	.628	.742	.842	.927
4	.432	.571	.692	.794	.877	.945
6	.533	.667	.771	.852	.914	.962
8	.604	.727	.818	.885	.934	.972
12	.696	.800	.871	.920	.955	.981
20	.792	.870	.918	.951	.973	.988

a. Formula for reliability $(\alpha) = \dfrac{n(r)}{1+(n-1)r} = \dfrac{n(h^2)}{1+(n-1)h^2}$

UNEQUAL FACTOR LOADINGS

Thus far we have assumed not only uniform factor loadings in a one-common factor model but also an error-free model. We will now examine what happens when we complicate the situation. Consider a stituation in which factor loadings in a one-common factor model are not all uniform. This will lead to a matrix of correlation coefficients with varying magnitudes. If one were to build a factor index by simply summing up the observed variables, the resulting scale would have a reliability given by:

$$\text{Cronbach's } a = \frac{\text{Sum of the elements in the reduced correlation matrix}}{\text{Sum of the elements in the correlation matrix}}$$

$$= \frac{\text{Var}(\hat{F}) - \Sigma\, d_i^2}{\text{Var}(\hat{F})} = \frac{\text{Var}(\hat{F}) - \Sigma(1 - h_1^2)}{\text{Var}(\hat{F})} \quad [43]$$

This is equivalent to equation 42 if all the communalties are uniform. In general, given the same amount of average communality (or average correlation), the reliability will be greater when loadings are uniform than when they are not. Therefore, Table 11 gives a fairly good representation of the upper limit of the reliabilities for several sets of loadings which average those given in the table.

But the more crucial question is whether one should use equal weights in constructing the factor scale given different factor loadings. Let us consider an extreme case in which one of the communalities is 1—that is, an observed variable is coterminous with the underlying factor. In that case, one can describe the underlying factor by using that particular variable while ignoring all other variables; adding other variables with communalities less than 1 will simply contaminate the scale.

In general, then, it is not appropriate to simply sum *all* the variables to construct the factor scale when the factor loadings are not uniform. When the one-common factor model fits the data exactly, as is assumed here, the optimal solution is relatively simple; the weights to assign to each variable are obtained by

$$B' (R^{-1}) \tag{44}$$

(where B is the vector of factor loadings and R is the correlation matrix for the Xs)

which is equivalent to regression weights obtained when the factor is regressed on the variables. Here the correlation between F and $\hat{F}$ will be maximized and its squared value is given by:

$$\begin{array}{c}\text{Generalized}\\\text{Reliability}\end{array} = \frac{\text{var}(\hat{F}) - \Sigma(1 - h_i^2)w_i^2}{\text{var}(\hat{F})} \tag{45}$$

where w_i is the regression weight for each variable given by equation 44, and the total variance of the constructed scale is given by

$$\text{var}(\hat{F}) = \sum_i \sum_j w_i w_j r_{ij}, \tag{46}$$

which is equivalent to summing up all the elements in the adjusted correlation matrix—where each element is multiplied by the two respective regression weights w_i and w_j. (The adjusted matrix will contain in its main diagonal squares of each weight for a given variable.) Since this value is equivalent to multiple R^2, it will be not less than the highest communality. Therefore, if one variable is an exact replica of the underlying common factor, that variable will get all the weight and other variables will be ignored.

An additional important point to remember in index construction is that when one uses differential weights, having a variable with a high loading is often more important than just having many variables with moderate loadings. Also keep in mind that the reliability of the scale will be at least as good as the square of the highest factor loading.

Sampling Variability and Different Criteria of Fit

So far we have dealt with an ideal situation in which a one factor model fits the data perfectly and there is no sampling variability. (Of course, this implies that we assume the underlying model is perfectly identified.) When sampling variability is introduced to the data, the relationships observed in the sample will not perfectly correspond to what is true in the population. Even if a one-common factor model fits the data perfectly in the population, such a model will not completely account for the sample correlations observed in the data This complication required that researchers adopt a criterion of fit between the scale and the underlying factor. There are three criteria proposed in the literature:

REGRESSION METHOD

The first criterion is to find a factor scale ($\hat{F}$) in such a way that the correlation between the underlying common factor (F) and the scale ($\hat{F}$) is maximum. Or differently stated, the criterion is to minimize the sum of the squared deviations between the two, that is, minimize $\Sigma(F-\hat{F})^2$. Meeting this criterion involves application of the regression solution. Such a solution is possible because factor analysis provides us with the factor loadings, which are equivalent to the correlations between the factor (to be predicted in scale construction) and the observed variables (to be used as predictors), and the correlations among the predictors which are no more than observed correlations among Xs. These two sets of correlations are all we need to solve the normal equations in regression. The predicted scores are given by

$$\hat{F} = XR^{-1}B, \qquad [47]$$

where B is the matrix of factor loadings, the Xs are the observed variables, and R is the correlation matrix for the Xs. Note that the weighting coefficients are those shown earlier (equation 44). The only difference is that in equation 47 we could have used the predicted correlations (BB') in the place of the actual correlations without altering the principle, because in the error-free population model the two are equivalent. In the present context, the reproduced correlations will in general not be the same as the observed correlations. The expected reliability of the scale will be given by the same formula as equation 45.

LEAST SQUARES CRITERION

In the one-common factor model, each variable is considered as a weighted sum of common and unique factors:

$$X_j = b_j F + d_j u_j.$$

Next, consider inserting in the place of F the predicted $\hat{F}$ for the factor scale. The criterion is to construct $\hat{F}$ in such a way that the following sum of squares is minimum.

$$\text{Minimize} \qquad \sum_i \sum_j (X_{ij} - b_j \hat{F})^2. \qquad [48]$$

Such a criterion leads to the weights given by

$$\hat{F} = X(BB')^{-1}B. \qquad [49]$$

Note that the only important differences between this and equation 47 is that here we use the reproduced correlation (BB') in the place of the observed correlations (R). Therefore, the two criteria would lead to the same index when one is dealing with population variables which fit the one-common factor model perfectly. However, the two diverge as sample correlations diverge from population correlations.

BARTLETT'S CRITERION

The third criterion involves examining the fit while taking the sampling variability into consideration. If we consider, as we did in maximum likelihood factoring, the unique variances as quasi-error variances, it makes sense to give less weight to the variables containing more random errors than the ones with fewer random errors. Hence, the criterion to use here is to minimize the sum of squares given in equation 48 after weighting each element with the reciprocals of the error variance. The criterion involves minimizing:

$$\sum_i \sum_j (X_{ij} - b_j \hat{F})^2 / d_i^2. \qquad [50]$$

The result is that variables with lower communalities are given less weight. Therefore, this criterion will not lead to the same scale as the preceding two whenever the factor loadings are not uniform. The formula (equation 51) for obtaining the factor scale looks formidable, but the underlying principle is not that incomprehensible:

$$\hat{F} = XU^{-2}B(B'U^{-2}B)^{-1}, \qquad [51]$$

where U^2 is the diagonal matrix of unique variances. The presence of U^{-2} may be considered as weighting in the manner described above.

Multiple Common Factors and Additional Complexities

Let us now complicate the situation even further, by assuming we have more than two-common factors. The three criteria discussed in the previous section are generalizable to the multivariate situation, and are generalizable to both orthogonal and oblique factor solutions. In addition, what we have discussed in relation to one-common factor is true in the multivariate case in relation to any specific common factor under consideration. However, the fact that the scales we create will not in general correlate perfectly with the respective underlying factors immediately raises two additional questions in the multifactor context: (1) will the imperfect scales be orthogonal to each other if the underlying factors are orthogonal; (2) will each scale correlate only with the factor it is supposed to measure and not with others (a factor scale is called *univocal* if its partial correlation with other underlying factors is zero after controlling for the factor it is a measure of)? In general these requirements are not simultaneously met by any scaling methods. The factor scales will be correlated among themselves even if the underlying factors are assumed to be orthogonal; also, the correlations among the factor scales will not correctly reflect the underlying correlations among the factors when the oblique factor model is assumed. Finally, a scale for one factor will be correlated with other underlying factors.

There is a special situation in which these requirements are met: (1) the factor analytic model fits the data exactly and there is no sampling or measurement error, and (2) each variable loads only on one factor. If these two conditions are met, one can consider each factor or dimension separately, and the situation reverts to the one-common factor model with error-free data as discussed earlier. We have noted that, under such conditions, there is no ambiguity as to the choice of scale construction—all the criteria we have examined lead to equivalent scales. Unfortunately, such an ideal situation is never found in practice.

There is, however, another situation in which the requirements of orthogonality and univocality of scales are met by some of the scaling methods. If the initial unrotated factors are obtained by means of the maximum likelihood (or canonical method), the factor scales for these unrotated factors would be both orthogonal and univocal if these scales are constructed by either the regression or the Bartlett method. This provides only partial consolation, however, because one is unlikely to expect the underlying factor model to be orthogonal. In addition, after orthogonal rotation, the regression method does not meet either of the requirements, whereas Barlett's method meets only the univocality requirement. None of the methods discussed so far lead to orthogonal scales.

These results provide some motivation for considering the fourth criterion introduced by Anderson and Rubin (1956). The Anderson-Rubin criterion is a modification of Bartlett's; it minimizes the weighted sums of squares used in Bartlett's criterion under the constraint that the created scales be orthogonal to each other. Consequently, regardless of whether the factors are rotated or not, as long as they are based on an orthogonal solution, this criterion produces factor scales that are uncorrelated to each other. However, the scales are not univocal for the rotated solution even if the initial solution is based on the maximum likelihood method.

THE CHOICE

In making a choice among these, the researcher must consider properties that are inherent in the method as well as extra-factor analytic ones. Below we offer some summary remarks about the inherent properties. First, in terms of correlations between the underlying factor and its respective scale, the regression method is superior to Bartlett's, but Bartlett's is superior to the least squares method. In terms of the univocality requirement, Bartlett's method fares best, but in terms of orthogonality requirement, the Anderson-Rubin criterion is preferable. However, assuming that in most research situations the researcher is unlikely to insist on the orthogonality of underlying factors, the real choice seems to be between the regression method and Bartlett's method.

Several additional considerations, some of which complicate the choice and some of which simplify it, should be discussed. First, there is usually a very high correlation among the scales produced by different scaling methods; hence, for many research problems the choice may be academic. One type of scale construction can serve as well as the other (see Horn, 1965; Alwin, 1973). Second, the choice is also dependent upon the specific research problem at hand. Tucker (1971) notes that when factor scales are to be related to outside variables, some methods are better for particular types of analysis. More specifically, he demonstrates that the scales produced by the regression method do not allow one to correctly estimate the underlying correlations between the hypothesized factors and the outside variables, whereas others may allow such estimation. On the other hand, if the major purpose of using factor scales is to use them as predictors of outside variables, the scales based on the regression method are better.

Keep in mind, however, that the discussion so far has been based on the assumption that the factor model fits the data exactly in the population, and thus, any discrepancy between the model and data is assumed to be the result of random sampling error. What happens, however, if such an exact fit is not expected, or if the factor analysis is used only as a heuristic means of sorting out major clusters of variables in the data? Under such circumstances, all of the finer points we have examined may become minor issues in comparison to the extra-factor analytic considerations.

Factor-based Scales

There are two completely different reasons for which one may consider creating *scales utilizing only some of the information* obtained from factor analysis instead of relying on factor scales we have discussed so far. First, one may accept the proposition that the factor analytic model fits the data exactly in the population, but assume that some of the particular values obtained in a factor solution are subject to sampling errors. Here one may ignore specific variations in the factor loadings and consider only one type of information as relevant: either a variable loads on a given factor or it does not. Consequently, a scale is built by summing all the variables with substantial loadings and ignoring the remaining variables with minor loadings. The scale created in this way is no longer a factor scale but merely factor-based. The specific reasons behind such a scale construction are that (1) even if factor loadings are zero for some variables in the population, they will not be zero in a specific sample solution; (2) even if the factor loadings are uniform in the population, they will not be so in a sample. The rule of thumb often used in this context is to consider factor loadings less than .3 as not substantial.

Whether this type of scale construction is justifiable or not depends on the degree to which the specific assumptions underlying it are appropriate. Ideally, one should test these assumptions through the use of confirmatory factor analysis. However, if such a "simple loading pattern" is supported by confirmatory analysis, it is no longer a factor-based scale but a legitimate factor scale. In practice, however, even if such tests were

TABLE 12
Results of Confirmatory Factor Analysis, Using Correlation
Matrix from the Upper Triangle of Table 1 and the
Model Specified in Table 7*

| Variables | Factors | | Communality h^2 |
	F_1	F_2	
X_1	.792	0	.624
X_2	.756	0	.571
X_3	.633	0	.501
X_4	0	.577	.333
X_5	0	.669	.448
X_6	0	.635	.404

$$r_{F_1 F_2} = .501$$

$\chi^2 = 4.6534$
df = 8
probability = .7939

*These results are obtained from LISREL III, not from COFAMM.

made and they show statistically significant deviations, it is a matter of
degree and minor deviations from the simple loadings can still be ignored
for the reasons to be given below.

There is a completely different basis for justifying the practice of simple
index construction. (We are taking for granted that this type of scaling
is the simplest, but this is not the strongest reason for using it.) Often the
factor analytic model is not expected to fit the data completely for several
reasons: (1) non-random measurement errors in the variables, and (2) minor factors unspecified and conceptually unrelated to the domain of
interest, may account for some correlations observed, and these in turn
affect the weights obtained. Therefore, there is a basis for not taking
the specific values obtained in a given factor solution at face value. The
conservative stance is to view the structures found by the factor analysis

as only suggestive, indicating some clustering in the data but no more. Put another way, once we accept that the particular numbers obtained contain substantial "noise," it may be wise to ignore minor distinctions and differences.

It is likely that some will object to the cavalier attitude taken in this type of scale construction. One might be concerned with the fact that the combination of observed variables is not optimal in the sense that some differential weighting can increase the overall correlation between the scale and the observed variables. (That is, the concern is with the efficiency of simple summing as a means of representing information contained in raw variables.) Even on this point, simple weighting can be justified because the multiple correlation between the scale (some combination of variables) and the total set of variables does not change very much for minor variation in the weighting (Wang and Stanley, 1970; Wainer, 1976). One caution, as mentioned in Section III, should be noted. If the factor analytic solution is believed to be faithful to the data, ignoring very high factor loadings—say above .9—and giving them the same weight as the item with a low loading is counter-productive. In summary, we are arguing that both factor scales and factor-based scales have a legitimate place in practical research.

Component Scores

Finally, we would like to comment on scales based on principal components analysis. As noted earlier (rather emphatically), the underlying principle of principal components analysis is different from that of factor analysis. Therefore, one cannot be used as a substitute for the other. But in a larger context of practical research, both have legitimate uses. There are situations in which the component scores may be preferred to the factor scales. In particular, if the objective is some simple summary of information contained in the raw data without recourse to factor analytic assumptions, the use of component scores has a definite advantage over factor scaling. This is why it is important, at least briefly, to comment on component scales.

As noted earlier, the principal components are no more than exact mathematical transformations of the raw variables. Therefore, it is possible to represent the components exactly from the combination of raw variables, and we can speak of component *scores,* instead of *scales* or *estimates.* The scores are obtained by combining the raw variables with weights that are proportional to their component (factor) loadings.

$$\text{Component Score} \quad = \quad \sum_j \left[(b_{ij}/\lambda_i)X_j \right], \qquad [52]$$

where b_{ij} is the component loading for the jth variable on i^{th} component, and λ_1 is the associated eigenvalue. The division by the eigenvalue is cosmetic in that it merely assures that the resulting index has a variance equal to 1.

NOTE

1. When the underlying structure is complex, as in Thurstone's box problem, it is often difficult to recover exactly the underlying pattern from the covariance matrix purely on the basis of some analytical criteria. One may need the aid of fitting hyperplanes and visual rotations.

VII. BRIEF ANSWERS TO QUESTIONS FREQUENTLY ASKED

Questions Pertaining to the Nature of Variables and Their Measurement

(a) *What level of measurement is required for factor analysis?*

Factor analysis requires that the variables be measured at least at the interval level (Stevens, 1946). This requirement is implied by the use of correlation or covariance matrices as the basic input to factor analysis. In addition, the specification of variables as the weighted sum of the underlying factors and the construction of factor scales as a weighted sum of the observed variables is not clearly defined for ordinal or nominal variables.

(b) *Is it appropriate to use measures of association such as Kendall's tau, and Goodman and Kruskal's gamma in place of ordinary correlations?*

The answer is no. As noted above, the operation of addition is not well defined for ordinal variables and, therefore, there is no factor analytic model that incorporates ordinal variables. One may use such a matrix in factor analysis for purely heuristic purposes, but the statistical interpretation to be given to the results is not well defined. (There are some nonmetric scaling methods developed specifically to deal with nonmetric variables.)

(c) *Based on the above answers, must a researcher always avoid using factor analysis when the metric base for the variables is not clearly established?*

Not necessarily. Many variables, such as measures of attitudes and opinions and numerous kinds of items for testing achievement do not have a clearly established metric base. However, it is generally assumed that many "ordinal variables" may be given numeric values without distorting the underlying properties. The final answer to this question really hinges on two considerations: (1) how well the arbitrarily assigned numbers reflect the underlying true distances, and (2) the amount of distortion introduced in the correlations (which become the basic input to factor analysis) by the distortions in the scaling. Fortunately, the correlation coefficients are fairly robust with respect to ordinal distortions in the measurement (Labovitz, 1967, 1970; Kim, 1975). Hence, as long as one can assume that the distortions introduced by assigning numeric values to ordinal categories are believed to be *not* very substantial, treating ordinal variables as if they are metric variables can be justified. Nevertheless, one should be aware of possible distortions, even if minor, in the factor analytic results owing to nonrandom measurement errors.

(d) *What about dichotomous variables? There are people who believe it is okay to use factor analysis on dichotomous variables (1) because assigning numbers to a dichotomy does not really require measurement assumptions, and (2) because, as a result, the phi (ϕ) is equivalent to the Pearson correlation coefficient, which is the appropriate measure of association for factor analysis. Therefore, isn't it appropriate to apply factor analysis to the matrix of phi's?*

The answer is no. For one thing, one cannot express the dichotomous variables within the factor analytic model. To be more specific, recall from Kim/Mueller, University Paper 07-013, Section II, that in factor analysis each variable is assumed to be a weighted sum of at least two underlying factors (one common and one unique). Even if these underlying factors have two values as shown in Table 1 of University Paper 07-013 (which is a very unlikely occurrence in real factor models), the resulting values in the observed variable must contain at least four different values, which clearly is inconsistent with a dichotomous variable. Therefore, nothing can justify the use of factor analysis on dichotomous data except a purely heuristic set of criteria. The following three questions are also relevant.

(e) *But the implications of the preceding answer are quite disturbing. Because we normally conceive of our underlying factors as potentially continuous, we should expect our variables to contain numerous categories. However, most of the variables we deal with usually have a very limited number of categories—yes or no; agree or disagree; at best, strongly agree, agree, neutral, disagree, strongly disagree, etc. Does this really mean we are applying factor analysis to data that are inconsistent with factor analysis models?*

In a sense, yes. The variables with limited categories are in a strict sense not compatible with factor analytic models. If one considers that the observed variables represent the crude measurement or grouping of adjacent values, the question is no longer whether the data are intrinsically incompatible with the factor analysis model but whether and how much the nonrandom measurement errors distort the factor analytic results. Grouping of values certainly affects the correlations, but the extent of this will depend on the degree of coarseness of grouping, the shape of the distribution, and so on. There are, however, some encouraging comments about the use of factor analysis as a heuristic device even under severe measurement distortions (see the next question).

(f) *Under what circumstances can one use factor analysis on data containing dichotomies or variables with a limited number of categories?*

In general the greater the number of categories, the smaller the degree of distortion. Even in dichotomies, the use of phi's can be justified if factor analysis is used as a means of finding general clusterings of variables, and if the underlying correlations among variables are believed to be moderate—say less than .6 or .7. The reason is that dichotomization of continuous variables attenuates the correlations and the attenuation is also affected by the cutting points. However, when the underlying correlations are not very high, the effects of varying cutting points on correlations are negligible. Therefore, the grouping attenuates correlations in general but does not affect the structure of clustering in the data—this is because factor analysis is dependent on the relative magnitude of correlations. If the researcher's goal is to search for clustering patterns, the use of factor analysis may be justified (see Kim, Nie and Verba (1977) for an illustration).

(g) *If the distortion due to the cutting point is more critical than the overall attenuation due to grouping, why not use adjustments such as using ϕ/ϕ_{max} or R/R_{max} in the place of ϕ or r?*

This correction is appropriate only when the underlying distributional shape takes a particular (very unlikely) form (see Carrol, 1961), or when the underlying correlations among the continuous variables are perfect. If the correlations are perfect, there is no point in performing factor analysis. Hence, the use of such a correction is contradictory (see Kim et al., 1977).

(h) *Aren't there some methods that can handle these measurement problems more directly?*

There are two approaches suggested in the literature. Both of these approaches assume that the dichotomous or polychotomous variables are results of some grouping or threshold effects, and these variables are indicators of underlying continuous variables for which the factor analysis models exactly apply. Consequently, in order to solve for the factor structure one has to find out the correlations among the *underlying* variables. One way of doing this is to use tetrachoric correlations instead of phi's. This approach is only heuristic because the calculation of tetrachorics can often break down and the correlation matrix may not be Gramian (see Bock and Lieberman, 1970). Another approach is to directly deal with the underlying multivariate distribution instead of calculating tetrachorics on the basis of bivariate tables. This is a promising line of attack, but currently the computing is expensive even with modern computers (see Christoffersson, 1975).

Questions Pertaining to the Use of Correlation or Covariance Matrices

(a) *Does it make any difference whether one uses the covariance matrix or the correlation matrix?*

It depends on (1) whether the variables have comparable metrics, (2) what type of extraction method is used, and (3) whether or not one is comparing one factor structure to another. If one is considering only one group (or sample) and is using a scale-free extraction method such as the maximum likelihood solution, Alpha factoring, or image analysis, it does not make any difference whether one uses one type of matrix or the other, *when the objective is to identify relevant underlying dimensions*. If the covariance matrix is used and scales vary widely, scale factors will complicate interpretation of the results, however. It is, therefore, advisable to use a correlation matrix if the variances differ from variable to variable and the scales vary substantially (as would be the case if one variable is measured in dollars, another in years or schooling, and a third on a 5-point Likert scale). Furthermore, the use of the correlation matrix is recommended on practical grounds; some computer programs do not accept a covariance matrix, and most examples in the literature are based on correlation matrices.

(b) *When is the use of the covariance matrix preferable then?*

The covariance matrix is preferable when comparison of factors structures between groups are contemplated. The reason is that the correlation matrix is obtained by scaling variables according to sample-specific standards—such as sample means and variances. For this reason, even theoretically invariant parameters involved in factor analysis cannot be expected to be invariant from group to group (or sample to sample) because the measurement scales are restandardized from group to group when the correlations are computed. (See Kim and Mueller (1979) for an expository discussion of the implications of standardizing variables in causal analysis in general; also, Sörbom and Jöreskog, 1976:90.)

(c) *What should be done if the objective is to compare factor structures across the groups when the variables are measured on widely different scales?*

One strategy is to standardize the variables, using a common standard such as the mean and variance of the combined group as a reference group. Then the variance-covariance matrix for each group could be calculated. This is different from using group specific correlation matrices, which implies transforming variables in each group using group (or sample) specific standards.

Questions Pertaining to Significance Tests and Stability of Factor Solution

(a) *When the maximum likelihood solution and associated significance test are used, what is the minimum sample size required?*

The greater the sample size, the better the χ^2 approximation. Lawley and Maxwell (1971) suggest that the test is appropriate if the sample contains at least 51 more cases than the number of variables under consideration. That is, $N - n - 1 \geq 50$, where N is the sample size and n is the number of variables. This is, of course, only a general rule-of-thumb.

(b) *How many variables should one have for each hypothesized factor?*

Thurstone suggests at least three variables for each factor, but this requirement need not be met if confirmatory factory analysis is used. In general, researchers seem to agree that one should have at least twice as many variables as factors. For the minimum number of variables for significance testing, see Table 20 in Section III.

(c) *Is the assumption that variables are multivariate normal always necessary?*

The factor analysis model itself does not require such an assumption. For example, it is possible to build a factor analytic model even using dichotomous factors. However, the maximum likelihood solution and the associated significance test require the assumption. In general, however, the consequences of violating this assumption are not clearly understood.

Other Miscellaneous Statistical Questions

(a) *What is the meaning of the signs of the factor loadings?*

The sign itself has no intrinsic meaning, and in no way should it be used to assess the magnitude of the relationship between the variable and the factor. However, signs for variables for a given factor have a specific meaning relative to the signs for other variables; the different signs simply mean that the variables are related to that factor in opposite directions. For this reason, it is advisable to code the variables in the same direction before factor analyzing them.

(b) *What is the meaning of the eigenvalues associated with rotated factors? What is the relevance of the proportion of variance explained by a given rotated factor?*

The eigenvalues associated with unrotated factors do not have the same meaning given the eigenvalues for rotated factors, with the exception that the eigenvalue sums are the same. In initial factoring, the magnitude of descending values of eigenvalues tells us something about the relative importance of each factor. This is not true for the rotated solution. Once different dimensions are separated out through rotation, it is not crucial to know how much variance in the data as a whole each explains.

(c) *Is it appropriate to factor analyze using the relationships among the factor scales in order to obtain a "higher-order" factor solution?*

No. The correlations among the factor scales are not the same as the correlations among the underlying factors. One should use as the correlation matrix input to the higher-order factoring the correlation matrix produced by the oblique factor solution.

(d) *Can one claim that the underlying factor structure is orthogonal when such a solution is compatible with the data?*

No. Orthogonality is imposed by the researcher. However, if one finds an orthogonal structure when oblique rotations are applied, or if graphical representations show that variable clusterings form right angles, then one can claim that the underlying structure is orthogonal.

(e) *Can one include variables, some of which are causes of others? That is, is it necessary that all the variables be at the same level in the causal ordering?*

In general, the variables should not be causes of each other. The factor model assumes that all the observed variables are caused by the underlying factors. However, an experienced user may apply factor analysis to causal systems of variables for other purposes (see Stinchcombe, 1971).

Questions Pertaining to Books, Journals, and Computer Programs

(a) *Are there any books or articles on factor analysis a novice can read and readily understand?*

Not really. Most require some technical background. However, the following are easier than the others: Rummel (1967); Schuessler (1971); Cattell (1952); Comrey (1973); Fruchter (1954).

(b) *What are the "next-level" books that the serious reader should consider examining?*

Harman (1976); Mulaik (1972); Lawley and Maxwell (1971).

(c) *What are the major journals which regularly publish articles on factor analysis?*

Psychometrika; British Journal of Mathematical and Statistical Psychology; Educational and Psychological Measurement.

(d) *What are some of the general purpose computer packages containing factor analysis programs?*

SPSS; OSIRIS; SAS; BMD.

(e) What are the more specialized programs dealing with factor analysis one should know about?

Kaiser's—Little Jiffy, Mark IV; Sörbom and Jöreskog, COFAMM.

(f) *Where are the major simulation studies reported?*

Tucker, Koopman and Linn (1969); Browne (1968); Linn (1968); Hakstian (1971); Hakstian and Abell (1974).

REFERENCES

ALWIN, D. F. (1973) "The use of factor analysis in the construction of linear composites in social research." Sociological Methods and Research 2:191-214.

ANDERSON, T. W. and H. RUBIN (1956) "Statistical inference in factor analysis." Proceedings of the Third Berkeley Symposium on Mathematical Statistics and Probability 5:111-150.

ASHER, H. (1976) Causal Modeling. Sage University Papers on Quantitative Applications in the Social Sciences, 07-003. Beverly Hills and London: Sage Pub.

BMDP-77: Biomedical Computer Programs (P-Series). W. J. Dixon, Series Editor, M. B. Brown, Editor 1977 edition. Los Angeles: Univ. of California Press, 1977.

BARGMANN, R. E. (1957) A Study of Independence and Dependence in Multivariate Normal Analysis. Mimeo Series No. 186. Chapel Hill, N.C.: Institute of Statistics.

BARTLETT, M. S. (1937) "The statistical conception of method factors." British Journal of Psychology 28:97-104.

BOCK, R. D. and R. E. BARGMANN (1966) "Analysis of covariance structure." Psychometrika 31:507-534.

BOCK, R. D. and M. LIEBERMAN (1970) "Fitting a response model for N dichotomously scored items." Psychometrika 26:347-372.

BOCK, R. D. and A. C. PETERSON (1975) "A multivariate correction for attenuation." Biometrika 62:673-678.

BROWNE, M. W. (1968) "A comparison of factor analytic techniques." Psychometrika 33:267-334.

COFAMM: Confirmatory Factory Analysis with Model Modification User's Guide. Sörbom, D. and Jöreskog, K. G. Chicago: National Educational Resources, Inc., 1976.

CARROLL, J. B. (1953) "Approximating simple structure in factor analysis." Psychometrika 18:23-38.

——— (1961) "The nature of data, or how to choose a correlation coefficient." Psychometrika 26:347-372.

CATTELL, R. B. (1952) Factor Analysis. New York: Harper and Bros.

——— (1965) "Factor analysis: an introduction to essentials. (I) the purpose and underlying models, (II) the role of factor analysis in research." Biometrics 21:190-215, 405-435.

——— (1966) Handbook of Multivariate Experimental Psychology. Chicago: Rand McNally.

——— and J. L. MUERLE (1960) "The 'maxplane' program for factor rotation to oblique simple structure." Educational and Psychological Measurement 20:269-290.

CHRISTOFFERSSON, A. (1975) "Factor analysis of dichotomized variables." Psychometrika 40:5-32.

COMREY, A. L. (1973) A First Course in Factor Analysis. New York: Academic Press.

CRONBACH, L. J. (1951) "Coefficient alpha and the internal structure of tests." Psychometrika 16: 297-334.

DUNCAN, O. D. (1966) "Path analysis: sociological examples." American Journal of Sociology 72:1-16.

EBER, H. W. (1966) "Toward oblique simple structure maxplane." Multivariate Behavioral Research 1:112-125.

FRUCHTER, B. (1954) Introduction to Factor Analysis. New York: Van Nostrand.

GREEN, B. F., Jr. (1976) "On the factor score controversy." Psychometrika 41:263-266.

GUILFORD, J. P. (1977) "The invariance problem in factor analysis." Educational and Psychological Measurement 37:11-19.

GUTTMAN, L. (1953) "Image theory for the structure of quantitative variates." Psychometrika 18:227-296.

——— (1954) "Some necessary conditions for common factor analysis." Psychometrika 19:149-161.

HAKSTIAN, A. R. (1971) "A comparative evaluation of several prominent methods of oblique factor transformation." Psychometrika 36:175-193.

148

–––– and R. A. ABELL (1974) "A further comparison of oblique factor transformation methods." Psychometrika 39:429-444.

HARMAN, H. H. (1976) Modern Factor Analysis. Chicago: University of Chicago Press.

–––– (in press) "Minres method of factor analysis," in K. Enstein, A. Ralston, and H. S. Wilf (eds.) Statistical Methods for Digital Computers. New York: John Wiley.

–––– and W. H. JONES (1966) "Factor analysis by minimizing residuals (Minres)." Psychometrika 31:351-368.

HARMAN, H. H. and Y. FUKUDA (1966) "Resolution of the Heywood case in the Minres solution." Psychometrika 31:563-571.

HARRIS, C. W. (1962) "Some Rao-Guttman relationships." Psychometrika 27: 247-263.

–––– (1967) "On factors and factor scores." Psychometrika 32: 363-379.

–––– and H. F. KAISER (1964) "Oblique factor analytic solutions by orthogonal transformations." Psychometrika 29:347-362.

HENDRICKSON, A. E. and P. O. WHITE (1964) "Promax: A quick method for rotation to oblique simple structure." British Journal of Mathematical and Statistical Psychology 17:65-70.

HORN, J. L. (1965) "An empirical comparison of various methods for estimating common factor scores." Educational and Psychological Measurement 25:313-322.

HORST, P. (1965) Factor Analysis of Data Matrices. New York: Holt Rinehart and Winston.

HOTELLING, H. (1933) "Analysis of a complex of statistical variables into principal components." Journal of Education Psychology 24:417-441, 498-520.

HOWE, W. G. (1955) Some Contributions to Factor Analysis. Report No. ORNL-1919. Oak Ridge, Tenn.: Oak Ridge National Laboratory. Ph.D. dissertation, University of North Carolina.

JENNRICH, R. I. (1970) "Orthogonal Rotation Algorithms." Psychometrika 35:229-235.

–––– (1974) "Simplified formulae in standard errors in maximum likelihood factor analysis." British Journal of Mathematical and Statistical Psychology 27:122-131.

JENNRICH, R. I. and P. F. SAMPSON (1966) "Rotation for simple loadings." Psychometrika 31:313-323.

JÖRESKOG, K. G. (1963) Statistical Estimation in Factor Analysis: A New Technique and Its Foundation. Stockholm: Almquist and Wiksell.

–––– (1966) "Testing a simple structure hypothesis in factor analysis." Psychometrika 31:165-178.

–––– (1967) "Some contributions to maximum likelihood factor analysis." Psychometrika 32:443-482.

–––– (1969) "A general approach to confirmatory maximum likelihood factor analysis." Psychometrika 34:183-202.

–––– (1970) "A general method for analysis of covariance structure." Biometrika 57:239-251.

–––– (1976) Analyzing Psychological Data by Structural Analysis of Covariance Matrices. Research Report 76-9. University of Uppsala, Statistics Department.

JÖRESKOG, K. G. and D. N. LAWLEY (1968) "New methods in maximum likelihood factor analysis." British Journal of Mathematical and Statistical Psychology 21:85-96.

KAISER, H. F. (1958) "The varimax criterion for analytic rotation in factor analysis." Psychometrika 23:187-200.

–––– (1963) "Image analysis," pp. 156-166 in C. W. Harris (ed.) Problems in Measuring Change. Madison: University of Wisconsin Press.

–––– (1970) "A second-generation Little Jiffy." Psychometrika 35:401-415.

–––– (1974) "Little Jiffy, Mark IV." Educational and Psychological Measurement 34: 111-117.

–––– (1974) "An index of factorial simplicity." Psychometrika 39:31-36.

KAISER, H. F. and J. CAFFREY (1965) "Alpha factor analysis." Psychometrika 30:1-14.
KIM, J. O. (1975) "Multivariate analysis of ordinal variables." American Journal of Sociology 81:261-298.
————— and C. W. MUELLER (1976) "Standardized and unstandardized coefficients in causal analysis: An expository note." Sociological Methods and Research 4:423-438.
KIM, J. O., N. NIE and S. VERBA (1977) "A note on factor analyzing dichotomous variables: the case of political participation." Political Methodology 4:39-62.
KIRK, D. B. (1973) "On the numerical approximation of the bivariate normal (tetrachoric) correlation coefficient." Psychometrika 38:259-268.
LISREL III: Estimation of Linear Structural Equation Systems by Maximum Likelihood Methods. (User's Guide). Jóreskog, K. G. and Sörbom, D. Chicago: National Educational Resources, Inc., 1976.
LITTLE JIFFY, MARK IV. (See Kaiser, 1974)
LABOVITZ, S. (1967) "Some observations on measurement and statistics." Social Forces 46:151-160.
————— (1970) "The assignment of numbers to rank order categories." American Sociological Review 35:515-524.
LAND, K. O. (1969) "Principles of path analysis," pp. 3-37 in E. F. Borgatta (ed.) Sociological Methodology. San Francisco: Jossey-Bass.
LAWLEY, D. N. (1940) "The estimation of factor loading by the method of maximum likelihood." Proceedings of the Royal Society of Edinburgh 60:64-82.
————— and MAXWELL, A. E. (1971) Factor Analysis as a Statistical Method. London: Butterworth and Co.
LEVINE, M. S. (1977) Canonical Analysis and Factor Comparison. Sage University Papers on Quantitative Applications in the Social Sciences, 07-006. Beverly Hills and London: Sage Pub.
LI, C. C. (1975) Path Analysis—A Primer. Pacific Grove, Calif.: Boxwood Press.
LINN, R. L. (1968) "A Monte Carlo approach to the number of factors problems." Psychometrika 33:37-71.
LORD, F. M. and W. R. NOVICK (1968) Statistical Theories of Mental Test Scores. Reading, Mass.: Addison-Wesley.
MALINVAND, E. (1970) Statistical Methods of Econometrics. New York: Elsevier.
MAXWELL, A. E. (1972) "Thomson's sampling theory recalled." British Journal of Mathematical and Statistical Psychology 25:1-21.
McDONALD, R. P. (1970) "The theoretical foundations of principal factor analysis, canonical factor analysis, and alpha factor analysis." British Journal of Mathematical and Statistical Psychology 23:1-21.
————— (1974) "The measurement of factor indeterminacy." Psychometrika 39:203-221.
————— (1975) "Descriptive axioms for common factor theory, image theory and component theory." Psychometrika 40:137-152.
————— (1975) "A note on Rippe's test of significance in common factor analysis." Psychometrika 40:117-119.
————— and E. J. BURR (1967) "A comparison of four methods of constructing factor scores." Psychometrika 32:380-401.
MULAIK, S. A. (1972) The Foundations of Factor Analysis. New York: McGraw-Hill.
NEUHAUS, J. O. and C. WRIGLEY (1954) "The method: an analytic approach to orthogonal simple structure." British Journal of Mathematical and Statistical Psychology 7:81-91.
OSIRIS Manual. Ann Arbor, Mich.: Inter-University Consortium for Political Research, 1973.
RAO, C. R. (1955) "Estimation and test of significance in factor analysis." Psychometrika 20:93-111.

150

RUMMEL, R. J. (1967) "Understanding factor analysis." Conflict Resolution 11:444-480.
——— (1970) Applied Factor Analysis. Evanston: Northwestern University Press.
SAS: A User's Guide to SAS 76. Anthony J. Barr, James H. Goodnight, John P. Sall, and Jane T. Helwig. Raleigh, N.C.: SAS Institute, Inc., 1976.
SPSS: Statistical Package for the Social Sciences. Norman H. Nie, C. Hadlai Hull, Jean G. Jenkins, Karin Steinbrenner, and Dale Bent. New York: McGraw-Hill, 1975.
SAUNDERS, D. R. (1953) An Analytic Method for Rotation to Orthogonal Simple Structure. Research Bulletin 53-10. Princeton, N.J.: Educational Testing Service.
——— (1960) "A computer program to find the best-fitting orthogonal factors for a given hypothesis." Psychometrika 25:199-205.
SCHUESSLER, K. (1971) Analyzing Social Data. Boston: Houghton Mifflin.
SÖRBOM, D. and K. G. JÖRESKOG (1976) COFAMM: Confirmatory Factor Analysis with Model Modification User's Guide. Chicago: National Educational Resources, Inc.
STEPHENSON, W. (1953) The Study of Behavior. Chicago: The University of Chicago Press.
STEVENS, S. S. (1946) "On the theory of scales of measurement." Science 103:677-680.
STINCHCOMBE, A. L. (1971) "A heuristic procedure for interpreting factor analysis." American Sociological Review 36:1080-1084.
THOMPSON, G. H. (1934) "Hotelling's method modified to give Spearman's g." Journal of Educational Psychology 25:366-374.
THURSTONE, L. L. (1947) Multiple Factor Analysis. Chicago: University of Chicago Press.
TRYON, C. R. and BAILEY, D. E. (1970) Cluster Analysis. New York: McGraw-Hill.
TUCKER, L. R. (1966) "Some mathematical notes on three mode factor analysis." Psychometrika 31:279-311.
——— (1971) "Relations of factor score estimates to their use." Psychometrika 36:427-436.
———, R. F. KOOPMAN, and R. L. LINN (1969) "Evaluation of factor analytic research procedures by means of simulated correlation matrices." Psychometrika 34:421-459.
TUCKER, L. R. and C. LEWIS (1973) "A reliability coefficient for maximum likelihood factor analysis." Psychometrika 38:1-8.
VELICER, W. F. (1975) "The relation between factor scores, image scores, and principal component scores." Educational and Psychological Measurement 36:149-159.
WAINER, H. (1976) "Estimating coefficients in linear models: it don't make no nevermind." Psychological Bulletin 83:213-217.
WANG, M. W. and J. C. STANLEY (1970) "Differential weighing: a review of methods and empirical studies." Review of Educational Research 40:663-705.

GLOSSARY

ALPHA FACTORING: a method of initial factoring in which the variables included in the analysis are considered samples from a universe of variables; see Kaiser and Caffrey in the references.

ADJUSTED CORRELATION MATRIX: the correlation matrix in which the diagonal elements are replaced by communalities; also used to refer to correlation or covariance matrices which are altered in a variety of ways before extracting factors.

BIQUARTIMIN CRITERION: a criterion applied in obtaining an indirect oblique rotation.

COMMUNALITY (h^2): the variance of an observed variable accounted for by the common factors; in an orthogonal factor model, it is equivalent to the sum of the squared factor loadings.

COMMON PART: that part of an observed variable accounted for by the common factors.

COMMON FACTOR: unmeasured (or hypothetical) underlying variable which is the source of variation in at least two observed variables under consideration.

CONFIRMATORY FACTOR ANALYSIS: factor analysis in which specific expectations concerning the number of factors and their loadings are tested on sample data.

CORRELATION: a measure of association between two variables; generally assumed to be the product-moment r (or Pearson's r); equivalent to the covariance between two standardized variables; also used as a general term for any type of linear association between variables.

COVARIATION: a crude measure of the degree to which two variables co-vary together; measured as the sum of cross-products of two variables which are expressed as deviations from their respective means; also used as a general term for describing the association between variables.

COVARIANCE: a measure of association between two variables; covariation divided by the number of cases involved; expected value of the sum of cross-products between two variables expressed as deviations from their respective means; the covariance between standardized variables is also known as the correlation.

COVARIANCE-STRUCTURE ANALYSIS: an analysis strategy (1) in which the observed covariance is expressed in terms of a very general model which can accommodate hypothetical factors as well as observed variables, and (2) in which the researcher then specifies appropriate parameters to evaluate the adequacy of the specification against the sample covariance structure.

COVARIMIN: a criterion for obtaining an oblique rotation; a variant of indirect oblimin rotation.

DETERMINANT: a mathematical property of a square matrix; discussed as a means of determining the rank (or the number of independent dimensions) of an adjusted correlation matrix.

DIRECT OBLIMIN: a method of oblique rotation in which rotation is performed without resorting to reference axes.

EIGENVALUE (or characteristic root): a mathematical property of a matrix; used in relation to the decomposition of a covariance matrix, both as a criterion of determining the number of factors to extract and a measure of variance accounted for by a given dimension.

EIGENVECTOR: a vector associated with its respective eigenvalue; obtained in the process of initial factoring; when these vectors are appropriately standardized, they become factor loadings.

EQUIMAX: a criterion for obtaining an orthogonal rotation; this criterion is a compromise between varimax and quartimax criteria.

ERROR-FREE DATA: contrived data where the underlying model is presumed known and there is an exact fit between data and model.

EXPECTATION: a mathematical operation through which the mean of a random variable is defined for both discrete and continuous distributions; an expected value is the property of a particular variable.

EXPLORATORY FACTOR ANALYSIS: factor analysis which is mainly used as a means of exploring the underlying factor structure *without* prior specification of number of factors and their loadings.

EXTRACTION OF FACTORS OR FACTOR EXTRACTION: the initial stage of factor analysis in which the covariance matrix is resolved into a smaller number of underlying factors or components.

ERROR COMPONENT: the part of the variance of an observed variable that is due to random measurement errors; constitutes a portion of the unique component.

FACTORS: hypothesized, unmeasured, and underlying variables which are presumed to be the sources of the observed variables; often divided into unique and common factors.

FACTOR LOADING: a general term referring to a coefficient in a factor pattern or structure matrix.

FACTOR PATTERN MATRIX: a matrix of coefficients where the columns usually refer to common factors and the rows to the observed variables; elements of the matrix represent regression weights for the common factors where an observed variable is assumed to be a linear combination of the factors; for an orthogonal solution, the pattern matrix is equivalent to correlations between factors and variables.

FACTOR SCORE: the estimate for a case on an underlying factor formed from a linear combination of observed variables; a by-product of the factor analysis.

FACTOR STRUCTURE MATRIX: a matrix of coefficients where the coefficients refer to the correlations between factors and variables; it is equivalent to a pattern matrix in the orthogonal case.

FACTORICAL COMPLEXITY: a characteristic of an observed variable; the number of common factors with (significant) loadings on that variable.

FACTORIAL DETERMINATION: the overall degree to which variations in observed variables are accounted by the common factors.

GRAMIAN: a square matrix is Gramian if it is symmetrical and all of the eigenvalues associated with the matrix are greater than or equal to zero; unadjusted correlation and covariance matrices are always Gramian.

IMAGE FACTORING: a method of obtaining initial factors; the observed variation is deomposed into (partial) images and anti-images, instead of into common parts and unique parts.

KAISER CRITERION: a criterion of determining the number of factors to extract; suggested by Guttman and popularized by Kaiser; also known as the "eigenvalue greater than one" criterion.

LINEAR COMBINATION: a combination in which variables are combined with only constant weights.

LINEAR SYSTEM: relationship among variables referred to as a whole, in which all the relationships are linear; factor analysis model in which all of the variables are assumed to be linear functions of underlying factors.

LEAST-SQUARES SOLUTION: in general, a solution which minimizes the squared deviations between the observed values and predicted values; a method of extracting initial factors, whose variants include principal axis factoring with iterated communalities and Minres.

MAXIMUM LIKELIHOOD SOLUTION: in general, a method of statistical estimation which seeks to identify the population parameters with a maximum likelihood of generating the observed sample distribution; a method of obtaining the initial factor solution; its variants include canonical factoring (RAO) and a method that maximizes the determinant of the residual partial correlation matrix.

MONTE CARLO EXPERIMENT: a strategy whereby various sample properties based on complex statistical models are simulated.

OBLIMAX: a criterion for obtaining an oblique rotation: it is equivalent to the quartimax criterion in orthogonal rotation.

OBLIMIN: a general criterion for obtaining an oblique rotation which tries to simplify the pattern matrix by way of reference axes; its variants include bi-quartimin, covarimin, and quartimin.

OBLIQUE FACTORS: factors that are correlated with each other; factors obtained through oblique rotation.

OBLIQUE ROTATION: the operation through which a simple structure is sought; factors are rotated without imposing the orthogonality condition and resulting terminal factors are in general correlated with each other.

ORTHOGONAL FACTORS: factors that are not correlated with each other; factors obtained through orthogonal rotation.

ORTHOGONAL ROTATION: the operation through which a simple structure is sought under the restriction that factors be orthogonal (or uncorrelated); factors obtained through this rotation are by definition uncorrelated.

PRINCIPAL AXIS FACTORING: a method of initial factoring in which the adjusted correlation matrix is decomposed hierarchically; a principal axis factor analysis with iterated communalities leads to a least-squares solution of initial factoring.

PRINCIPAL COMPONENTS: linear combinations of observed variables, possessing properties such as being orthogonal to each other, and the first principal component representing the largest amount of variance in the data, the second representing the second largest and so on; often considered variants of common factors, but more accurately they are contrasted with common factors which are hypothetical.

POSTULATE OF FACTORIAL CAUSATION: the assumption that the observed variables are linear combinations of underlying factors, and that the covariation between observed variables is solely due to their common sharing of one or more of the common factors.

POSTULATE OF PARSIMONY: this stipulates that, given two or more equally compatible models for the given data, the simpler model is believed to be true; in factor analysis, only the model involving the minimum number of common factors is considered appropriate.

QUARTIMAX: a criterion for obtaining an orthogonal rotation; the emphasis is on simplifying the rows of the factor pattern matrix.

QUARTIMIN: a criterion for obtaining an oblique rotation; the oblique counterpart of the quartimax rotation; requires the introduction of reference axes.

RANK OF A MATRIX: the number of linearly independent columns or rows of a matrix; the order of the largest square submatrix whose determinant is not zero.

REFERENCE AXES: these refer to axes that are orthogonal to the primary factors; they are introduced to simplify oblique rotation.

SCREE-TEST: a rule-of-thumb criterion for determining the number of significant factors to retain; it is based on the graph of roots (eigenvalues); claimed to be appropriate in handling disturbances due to minor (unarticulated) factors.

SIMPLE STRUCTURE: a special term referring to a factor structure with certain simple properties; some of these properties include that a variable has factor loadings on as few common factors as possible, and that each common factor has significant loadings on some variables and no loadings on others.

SPECIFIC COMPONENT: the part of the variance of an observed variable that is due to a factor which is specific to a given variable; used to designate the part of the unique component that is not due to random errors.

TARGET MATRIX: a matrix of coefficients used as a target in rotation; an initial factor solution may be rotated in such a way that the resulting factor loadings resemble the target matrix maximally.

VARIANCE: a measure of dispersion of a variable; defined as the sum of squared deviations from the mean divided by the number of cases or entities.

VARIATION: a measure of dispersion in a variable; loosely used as a general term for describing any type of dispersion around some central value; sum of squared deviations from the mean.

VARIMAX: a method of orthogonal rotation which simplifies the factor structure by maximizing the variance of a column of the pattern matrix.

UNIQUE COMPONENT: the part of the observed variance unaccounted for by the common factors; the proportion that is unique to each variable; it is often further decomposed into specific and error components.

UNIQUE FACTOR: the factor which is believed to affect only a single observed variable; often stands for all the independent factors (including the error component) that are unique to a variable.

PRINCIPAL COMPONENTS ANALYSIS

PART III

GEORGE H. DUNTEMAN

1. INTRODUCTION

Principal components analysis is a statistical technique that linearly transforms an original set of variables into a substantially smaller set of uncorrelated variables that represents most of the information in the original set of variables. Its goal is to reduce the dimensionality of the original data set. A small set of uncorrelated variables is much easier to understand and use in further analyses than a larger set of correlated variables. The idea was originally conceived by Pearson (1901) and independently developed by Hotelling (1933).

The author has attempted to minimize the use of matrix algebra in this paper. Where matrix algebra is used, the author provides, in some instances, definitions of matrix algebra concepts and examples of their use. For a good elementary introduction to matrix algebra, the reader is referred to an earlier paper in this series, Namboodiri's (1984) *Matrix Algebra: An Introduction.* The reader, with little or no knowledge of matrix algebra is encouraged to read this paper in order to obtain the maximum benefit from the present paper.

This book uses numerous real-life examples to illustrate the myriad applications of principal components analysis. If he or she wishes, the reader can devote less attention to the mathematics and focus his or her attention on the applied examples and still learn a great deal about principal components analysis. The reader will see how principal components can enhance our understanding of the structure of a data set composed of a large number of correlated variables. He or she will also see how principal components can be effectively used in conjunction with other multivariate analysis techniques, such as multiple regression analysis and discriminant analysis.

Many times a social science researcher has numerous correlated measures within a particular domain. In order to both simplify and impose some structure on the domain, the researcher would be interested in reducing the number of variables from p to a much smaller set of k derived variables that retain most of the information in the original p variables. For example, an organizational psychologist may have 20 Likert-type items measuring various aspects of job satisfaction (e.g., pay, working conditions, supervision, co-workers, fringe benefits, etc.). There are clearly too many variables to use as independent, intervening, or dependent variables in a subsequent statistical model. If the variables are correlated, and especially if they are highly correlated, then we can linearly transform the p correlated variables into a relatively small set of k uncorrelated variables such that the k derived variables, if considered as independent variables, will maximize the prediction of the original p variables. The k derived variables which maximize the variance accounted for in the original variables are called principal components. If 3 principal components account for most of the variance in the original 20 job satisfaction measures, then we have reduced the dimensionality of our data set from 20 correlated dimensions to 3 uncorrelated dimensions and thus considerably simplified the structure of the job satisfaction variable domain. The aim of principal components analysis is parsimony.

The technique has been applied to virtually every substantive area including biology, medicine, chemistry, meteorology, and geology, as well as the behavioral and social sciences. For example, Morrison (1976) conducted a principal components analysis of a correlation matrix given by Birren and Morrison (1961) for 11 subscales of the Wechsler Adult Intelligence Scale (WAIS) along with age and years of education completed for a sample of 933 white males and females. The goal was to isolate the dimensions underlying the variation in the WAIS subscales and, in addition, to see how age and education were related to these dimensions. Two principal components, the underlying dimensions, accounted for over 62% of the variation in the original 13 variables. The first principal component, which by itself explained over 51% of the total variance in the 13 variables, had high correlations with all 11 WAIS subtests (i.e., .62 to .83) and was interpreted as a measure of general intellectual ability. Education had a correlation of .75 with this dimension. The second principal component, which accounted for 11% of the total variation in the 13 variables, correlated positively with the verbal subtests and negatively with the performance subtests. It was interpreted as a contrast between verbal and performance subtests. People who scored high on this dimension had high verbal scores and low performance scores. Age correlated .80 with this dimension indicating that older people did better on verbal tests than on performance tests, compared with younger people.

The goal of principal components analysis is similar to factor analysis in that both techniques try to explain part of the variation in a set of observed variables on the basis of a few underlying dimensions. There are, however, as discussed in Chapter 8, important differences between the two techniques. Briefly, principal components analysis has no underlying statistical model of the observed variables and focuses on explaining the total variation in the observed variables on the basis of the maximum variance properties of principal components. Factor analysis, on the other hand, has an underlying statistical model that partitions the total variance into common and unique variance and focuses on explaining the common variance, rather than the total variance, in the observed variables on the basis of a relatively few underlying factors.

Principal components is also similar to other multivariate procedures such as discriminant analysis and canonical correlation analysis in that they all involve linear combinations of correlated variables whose variable weights in the linear combination are derived on the basis of maximizing some statistical property. We have seen that principal components maximize the variance accounted for in the original variables. Linear discriminant function analysis, focusing on differences among groups, determines the weights for a linear composite that maximizes the between group relative to within group variance on that linear composite. Canonical correlation analysis, focusing on the relationships between two variable sets, derives a linear composite from each variable set such that the correlation between the two derived composites is maximized.

Principal components analysis is sometimes used prior to some factor analytic procedures to determine the dimensionality of the common factor space. It can also be used to select a subset of variables from a larger set of variables. That is, rather than substituting the principal components for the original variables we can select a set of variables that have high correlations with the principal components. Principal components analysis is also used in regression analysis to address multicollinearity problems (i.e., imprecise regression parameter estimates due to highly correlated independent variables). The technique is also useful in displaying multivariate data graphically so that, for example, outlying or atypical observations can be detected. This is based on the facts that the principal components represent the variation in the original variables and that there are considerably fewer graphical displays of the principal components to visually examine relative to the original variables. These and other applications of principal components analysis are subsequently discussed in this paper.

Principal components analysis searches for a few uncorrelated linear combinations of the original variables that capture most of the information in the original variables. We construct linear composites routinely, for example, test scores, quality of life indices, and so on. In most of these cases, each variable receives an equal weight in the linear composite. Indices force a p dimensional system into one dimension. For example, a set of p socioeconomic status (SES) indicators such as occupational level, educational level and income, which can be characterized as a p dimensional random vector $(x_1, x_2, \ldots, x_p)$, can be linearly transformed by $y = a_1x_1 + a_2x_2 + \ldots + a_px_p$ into a one dimensional SES index, y. In principal components analysis, the weights (i.e., $a_1, a_2, \ldots, a_p$) are mathematically determined to maximize the variation of the linear composite or, equivalently, to maximize the sum of the squared correlations of the principal component with the original variables. The linear composites (principal components) are ordered with respect to their variation so that the first few account for most of the variation present in the original variables, or equivalently, the first few principal components together have, overall, the highest possible squared multiple correlations with each of the original variables.

Geometrically, the first principal component is the line of closest fit to the n observations in the p dimensional variable space. It minimizes the sum of the squared distances of the n observation from the line in the variable space representing the first principal component. Distance is defined in a direction perpendicular to the line. The first two principal components define a plane of closest fit to the swarm of points in the p dimensional variable space. Equivalently, the second principal component is a line of closest fit to the residuals from the first principal component. The first three components define a three dimensional plane, called a hyperplane, of closest fit, and so on. If there are p variables, then there can be no more than p principal components. There can be fewer if there are linear dependencies among the variables. If all possible principal components are used, then they define a space which has the same dimension as the variable space and, hence, completely account for the variation in the variables. However, there is no advantage in retaining all of the principal components since we would have as many components as variables and, thus, would not have simplified matters.

Algebraically, the first principal component, y_1, is a linear combination of $x_1, x_2, \ldots, x_p$ (i.e., $y_1 = a_{11}x_1 + a_{12}x_2 + \ldots + a_{1p}x_p = \sum_{i=1}^{p} a_{1i}x_i$) such that the variance of y_1 is maximized given the constraint that the sum of the squared weights is equal to one (i.e., $\sum_{i=1}^{p} a_{1i}^2 = 1$). As we shall see, the random variables, x_i, can be either deviation from mean scores or standardized scores. If the variance of y_1 is maximized, then so is the sum of the squared correlations of y_1 with the original variables $x_1, x_2, \ldots, x_p$ (i.e., $\sum_{i=1}^{p} r_{y,x_i}^2$). Principal components analysis finds the optimal weight vector $(a_{11}, a_{12}, \ldots, a_{1p})$ and the associated variance of y_1 which is usually denoted by λ_1. The second principal component, y_2, involves finding a second weight vector $(a_{21}, a_{22}, \ldots, a_{2p})$ such that the variance of

$$y_2 = a_{21}x_1 + a_{22}x_2 + \ldots + a_{2p}x_p = \sum_{i=1}^{p} a_{2i}x_i$$

is maximized subject to the constraints that it is uncorrelated with the first principal component and $\sum_{i=1}^{p} a_{2i}^2 = 1$. This results in y_2 having the next largest sum of squared correlations with the original variables. However, the sum of squared correlations with the original variables, or equivalently, the variances of the principal components get smaller as successive principal components are extracted. The first two principal components together have the highest possible sum of squared multiple correlations (i.e., $\sum_{i=1}^{p} R_{x_i \cdot y_1, y_2}^2$) with the p variables.

This process can be continued until as many components as variables have been calculated. However, the first few principal components usually account for most of the variation in the variables and consequently our interest is focused on these, although, as we shall subsequently see, small components can also provide information about the structure of the data. The main statistics resulting from a principal components analysis are the variable weight vector $a = (a_1, a_2, \ldots, a_p)$ associated with each principal component and its associated variance, λ. As we shall see, the pattern of variable weights for a particular principal component are used to interpret the principal component and the magnitude of the variances of the principal components provide an indication of how well they account for the variability in the data. The relative sizes of the elements in a variable weight vector associated with a particular principal component indicate the relative contribution of the variable to the variance of the principal component, or, equivalently, the relative amounts of variation explained in the variables by the principal components. We will see that the correlations of the variables with a particular principal component are proportional to the elements of the associated weight vector. They can be obtained by multiplying all the elements in the weight vector by the square root of the variance ($\sqrt{\lambda}$) of the associated principal component.

Example

Let us apply the concepts that we have learned so far to a small correlation matrix involving five satisfaction variables generated from data collected from a large recent survey of U.S. armed forces personnel. The satisfaction variables analyzed here were part of a much larger set of satisfaction measures. They are satisfaction with job (SJ), satisfaction with job training (SJT), satisfaction with working conditions (SWC), satisfaction with medical care (SMC), and satisfaction with dental care (SDC). Each respondent was asked to rate their satisfaction on a 1 (very unsatisfactory) to 5 (very satisfactory) scale for each of these five aspects of the military. The correlation matrix among the five variables presented in Table 1.1 was generated for a large subsample of 9,147 married enlisted Army personnel. Note that all of the correlations are positive ranging from a low of .162 to a high of .620.

Since there are five variables, it is possible to extract five principal components from the correlation matrix under the reasonable assumption that for empirical data any one variable does not have a multiple correlation of 1 with the remaining four variables. The basic statistics of the principal components analysis are the five variances (latent roots) $\lambda_1, \ldots, \lambda_5$ ordered by size and the associated variable weight vectors (latent vectors) $a_1, \ldots, a_5$. The total variance in the system is five—the sum of the variances of the five standardized variables (i.e., $\sigma_i^2 = 1$ for $i = 1$ to 5). Each associated weight vector contains five elements, one corresponding to each variable. For example, $a_1 = [a_{11}, a_{12}, a_{13}, a_{14}, a_{15}]$ are the five weights associated with the largest principal component whose variance is λ_1. The latent roots and associated vectors are presented in Table 1.2.

TABLE 1.1

Correlations Among Five Satisfaction Variables for
Married Army Enlisted Personnel (N=9,147)

Variables	SJ	SJT	SWC	SMC	SDC
1) Satisfaction with Job (SJ)	1.000	.451	.511	.197	.162
2) Satisfaction with Job Training (SJT)		1.000	.445	.252	.238
3) Satisfaction with Working Conditions (SWC)			1.000	.301	.227
4) Satisfaction with Medical Care (SMC)				1.000	.620
5) Satisfaction with DentalCare (SDC)					1.000

TABLE 1.2

Latent Roots (Variances) and Latent Vectors of
Correlation Matrix of Satisfaction Variables

Variable	Latent Vector				
	a_1	a_2	a_3	a_4	a_5
SJ	.442	.443	.301	−.716	.074
SJT	.457	.290	−.832	.114	.034
SWC	.479	.308	.454	.658	−.185
SMC	.443	−.531	.095	.060	.714
SDC	.412	−.586	.032	−.191	−.670
λ_i	2.370	1.202	.573	.484	.373

The sum of squares of the five elements in each of these five columns add up to 1. The sum of the cross products of any two columns
add up to 0. The elements in the first column are the weights associated with the linear composite that has maximum variance or, equivalently, has the largest sum of the squared correlations with the five
variables. The linear composite is .442 SJ + .457 SJT + .479 SWC +
.443 SMC + .412 SDC. The weights are about equal so that each satisfaction variable is about equally represented in the linear composite.
Accordingly, the first principal component could be interpreted as a
measure of general satisfaction. The variance of the first principal
component is 2.370. It explains (100 · 2.370/5) or 47.4% of the total
variance of the five variables. The second principal component is the
linear composite .443 SJ + .290 SJT + .308 SWC − .531 SMC −
.586 SDC. Since the first three weights are associated with job related
satisfaction variables and are positive and the last two weights are associated with health care satisfaction variables and are negative, the

TABLE 1.3

Principal Component Loading Matrix for Satisfaction Variables

| Variable | Principal Component | | | | |
	1	2	3	4	5
SJ	.680	.485	.228	−.498	.045
SJT	.704	.318	−.630	.079	.021
SWC	.738	.338	.344	.458	−.113
SMC	.682	−.582	.072	.042	.436
SDC	.634	−.642	−.024	−.133	−.409

second principal component is interpreted as a contrast between job satisfaction and health satisfaction. High scores on this component are associated with higher scores on the three job satisfaction variables and low scores on the two health care satisfaction variables. The second principal component has a variance of 1.202 and accounts for $(100 \cdot 1.202/5)$ or 24.0% of the total variance of the five variables. Together the first two components account for 47.4% + 24.0% or 71.4% of the variance in the five variables. Since the first principal component has all positive weights, the second and subsequent principal components must have a pattern of positive and negative weights since the cross products between any two columns must disappear. The remaining three smaller components will not be interpreted because, as we shall see, they are not important enough by most criteria. Thus, we have reduced the dimensionality of our observations from five to two.

The loadings (correlations) of the variables with the five principal components are presented in Table 1.3. The elements (correlations) in each column are proportional to the corresponding column elements (latent vector) in Table 1.2. The sum of the squared correlations for each column equal the associated latent root, the amount of variance explained. The information presented in each of Tables 1.2 and 1.3 is equivalent, but many researchers prefer to interpret the pattern of correlations rather than the proportional elements in the associated latent vector. The preference for correlations probably stems from the factor analytic tradition of interpreting factor loading matrices which will be discussed subsequently. Also, the size of the correlations for a particular principal component directly reflects the importance of the components in explaining variation in the original variables.

2. BASIC CONCEPTS OF PRINCIPAL COMPONENTS ANALYSIS

The variance of a linear composite

$$\sum_{i=1}^{p} a_i x_i \text{ is } \sum_{i=1}^{p} \sum_{j=1}^{p} a_i a_j \sigma_{ij}$$

where σ_{ij} is the covariance between the ith and jth variables. This is a straightforward generalization of the variance of a linear composite of two variables, $y = a_1 x_1 + a_2 x_2$ which is $a_1^2 \sigma_1^2 + a_2^2 \sigma_2^2 + 2a_1 a_2 \sigma_{12}$. The variance of a linear composite can also be more easily expressed in matrix algebra as $a'C a$ where a is the vector of variable weights and C is the covariance matrix. Principal components analysis finds the weight vector a that maximizes $a'Ca$ given the constraint that

$$\sum_{i=1}^{p} a_i^2 = a'a = 1.$$

The size of the elements of a must be constrained or otherwise we could arbitrarily make the variance of the linear composite large by selecting large weights.

A linear composite can be based on a covariance matrix, as above, or a correlation matrix, R, which is a covariance matrix of standardized variables. Similarly, principal components analysis can be based on either a covariance matrix, C, or correlation matrix, R.

In many cases the units in which the variables are measured are arbitrary. This is particularly true in the behavioral and social sciences where many variables are scales. Even if the variables are measured in the same units, the variances of the variables may differ considerably. For example, anthropomorphic body measurements in centimeters would show a large variation in body height and a relatively small variation in wrist circumference for a sample of adult males. We shall see later that principal components analysis of covariance matrices with large differences in variances among the variables causes problems. The major problem is that variables with large variances automatically get large weights in the principal component and variables with small variances automatically get negligible weights. This is because the way to maximize the variance of a linear composite is to give large weights to the variables with large variances. Most of our discussion and examples will focus on correlation matrices.

If there are no exact linear dependencies among the p variables, then there are as many principal components as variables. A linear dependency means that any one variable in the variable set can be written as an exact linear combination of one or more of the remaining variables. An example of a linear dependency in a set of three variables is $x_1 = \beta_1 x_2 + \beta_2 x_3$. Since there is no error term in the relationship, this is equivalent to a multiple correlation of one between the dependent variable x_1, and the independent variables x_2 and x_3. Exact nonlinear dependencies among the variables such as $x_1 = \beta_1 x_2^2 + \beta_2 x_2 x_3$ have no impact on the dimensionality of a linear space or, consequently, the number of principal components. If there are exact linear dependencies, then the variables are redundant since one or more variables can be dropped from the variable set without any loss of information. We can perfectly predict the values of the excluded variables from the remaining variables. When we have exact linear dependencies, then the dimensionality of the variable space is accordingly reduced. The number of principal components is equal to the dimensionality of the variable space. In most cases, the dimensionality of the variable space is equal to the number of variables since we rarely encounter exact linear dependencies in real empirical data sets. The goal of principal components is to find p linear transformations of the p variables, the principal components.

If we have a set of n observations (e.g., individuals), on p variables, then we can find the largest principal component of R, the correlation matrix, as the weight vector $[a_{11}, a_{12}, a_{13}, \ldots, a_{1p}]$ which maximizes the variance of

$$\sum_{i=1}^{p} a_{1i} x_i \text{ given that } \sum_{i=1}^{p} a_{1i}^2 = 1.$$

In this case, the x_i are standardized variables. We can then define the second largest principal component of R as the weight vector, $[a_{21}, a_{22}, a_{23}, \ldots, a_{2p}]$ which maximizes the variance of

$$\sum_{i=1}^{p} a_{2i} x_i \text{ given that } \sum_{i=1}^{p} a_{2i}^2 = 1$$

and that principal component 2 is linearly independent of principal component 1. The independence condition is specified by the constraint that

$$\sum_{i=1}^{p} a_{1i} a_{2i} = 0.$$

Continuing, we can define a third largest principal component as the weight vector $[a_{31}, a_{32}, a_{33}, \ldots, a_{3p}]$ which maximizes the variance of

$$\sum_{i=1}^{p} a_{3i}x_i \text{ given that } \sum_{i=1}^{p} a_{3i}^2 = 1$$

and that the third principal component, $[a_{31}, a_{32}, \ldots, a_{3p}]$ is orthogonal (i.e., independent) to the first two principal components. These two orthogonality conditions are

$$\sum_{i=1}^{p} a_{3i}a_{1i} = \sum_{i=1}^{p} a_{3i}a_{2i} = 0.$$

We can continue this scenario down to the last or pth principal component.

The sum of the variances of the principal components is equal to the sum of the variances of the original variables. That is

$$\sum_{i=1}^{p} \lambda_i = \sum_{i=1}^{p} \sigma_i^2.$$

where λ_i is the variance of the ith principal component. If the variables are standardized, then

$$\sum_{i=1}^{p} \lambda_i = p.$$

The proportion of variance in the original p variables that k principal components accounts for can be easily calculated as

$$\sum_{i=1}^{k} \lambda_i / p$$

where k is less than p. The proportion of variance that any single principal component accounts for is simply λ_i / p. If the sum of the variances of the first few principal components is close to p, the number of original variables, then we have captured most of the information in the original variables by a few principal components which are linear transformations of the original variables.

It can be shown that the above definition of principal components leads to the matrix equation $Ra = \lambda a$ where λ is the latent root of the correlation matrix R and a is its associated latent vector. Latent roots are sometimes called eigenvalues and latent vectors are sometimes called eigenvectors. They are also called characteristic roots and vectors, respectively. This matrix equation can be solved for λ and a, the basic statistics of principal components analysis. If the matrix R is nonsingular (i.e., no exact linear dependencies among the variables exist), then there are p latent roots, λ_i, and p associated latent vectors a_i, that satisfy the equation. It can be shown that the largest latent root (λ_1) of R is the variance of the first or largest principal component of R and its associated vector

$$a_1 = \begin{bmatrix} a_{11} \\ a_{12} \\ \cdot \\ \cdot \\ a_{1p} \end{bmatrix}$$

is the set of weights for the first principal component that maximize the variance of

$$\sum_{i=1}^{p} a_{1i}x_i.$$

The second largest latent root of R is the variance of the second largest principal component and its associated vector

$$a_2 = \begin{bmatrix} a_{21} \\ a_{22} \\ \cdot \\ \cdot \\ a_{2p} \end{bmatrix}$$

is the set of weights for the second principal component that results in the linear composite or principal component with the next largest variance. The pth or last latent root (λ_p) is the variance of the last or smallest principal component and its associated vector

$$a_p = \begin{bmatrix} a_{p1} \\ a_{p2} \\ \cdot \\ \cdot \\ a_{pp} \end{bmatrix}$$

are the variable weights defining the smallest principal component. If the latent roots are all distinct, then there are p distinct associated latent vectors. This is typically the case for sample correlation and covariance matrices. We will subsequently discuss the case in which some of the latent roots of a correlation or covariance matrix are equal.

Since the principal components are uncorrelated, each one makes an independent contribution to accounting for the variance of the original variables. If, for example, x_i correlates r_{i1} with the largest/first principal component and r_{i2} with the second largest principal component, then, since the two principal components are uncorrelated, the squared multiple correlation of x_i with the first two principal components is $r_{i1}^2 + r_{i2}^2$. The first k largest principal components maximize the sum of these squared multiple correlations across all the variables. This is a generalization of the fact that the first principal component maximizes the sum of the squared simple correlations of the variables with the largest principal component.

Hence, there are p linear transformations (principal components) of the original p variables. They are

$$y_1 = \sum_{j=1}^{p} a_{1j} x_j$$

$$y_2 = \sum_{j=1}^{p} a_{2j} x_j$$

$$\vdots$$

$$y_p = \sum_{j=1}^{p} a_{pj} x_j.$$

They can be expressed more succinctly in matrix algebra as

$$y = A'x$$

where y is a p element vector of principal component scores, A' is a $p \times p$ matrix of latent vectors with the ith row corresponding to the elements of the latent vector associated with the ith latent root, and x is a p element column vector of the original variables. This is a linear transformation of a p element random vector x into a p element random vector y, the principal components.

From the definition of principal components, we have $A'A=I$. Note that A is the matrix with latent vectors as columns, A' is the transpose of A with latent vectors as rows, and I is the $p \times p$ identity matrix with ones in the principal diagonal and zeros elsewhere. $A'A=I$ simply indicates that the cross products of any two latent vectors are 0 and the sum of squares of the elements for a given latent vector are equal to 1.

For example, since $A'A=I$, the element in the 3rd row and 3rd column of I is a 1 (since it is on the principal diagonal of I) and is obtained by multiplying the 3rd row of A' by the 3rd column of A element by element and summing the cross products. That is,

$$\sum_{i=1}^{p} a_{3i}\,a_{3i} = \sum_{i=1}^{p} a_{3i}^2 = 1$$

or in matrix terminology $a_3'a_3 = 1$. The element in the 3rd row and 4th column of I is 0 (since it is an off-diagonal element of I) and is obtained by multiplying the 3rd row of A' by the 4th column of A element by element and summing the products. That is,

$$\sum_{i=1}^{p} a_{4i}\,a_{3i} = 0 \quad \text{or} \quad a_4'a_3 = 0$$

since the latent vectors are orthogonal or perpendicular to one another. Each element of I is the result of the multiplying a row vector from A' by a column vector from A. This is, in fact, the definition of matrix multiplication.

Since the ith latent root and its associated latent root must satisfy the matrix equation $Ra_i = \lambda_i a_i$, we have, premultiplying by a_i', $a_i' Ra_i = \lambda_i a_i'a_i = \lambda_i$ for the variance of the ith principal component since

$$a_i'a_i = \sum_{j=1}^{p} a_{ij}^2 = 1.$$

We can succinctly express the facts that $Ra_1 = \lambda_1 a_1$, $Ra_2 = \lambda_2 a_2$, ..., $Ra_p = \lambda_p a_p$ by combining these relations in one matrix expression as $RA = A\Lambda$ where A is a matrix of eigenvectors as column vectors, and Λ is a diagonal matrix of the corresponding latent roots ordered from largest to smallest.

The elements of Λ, the diagonal matrix of latent roots, have to be in the same order as their associated latent vectors, the columns of A, in order for the matrix equation $RA = A\Lambda$ to hold. That is, the latent root in the ith row and column of Λ must have its corresponding latent vector in the ith column of A. We can use any arbitrary ordering of the latent roots in Λ as long as we use the same ordering of the associated latent roots in A, but it makes more sense to order them with respect to their importance.

We can generalize from $a_i'Ra_i = \lambda_i$ as the equation for the variance of the ith principal component using matrix algebra to obtain the covariance matrix of the principal components as $A'RA = \Lambda$ where A' is the transpose of A (i.e., rows are eigenvectors). That is, since $RA = A\Lambda$, we can premultiply both sides of this expression to obtain $A'RA = A'A\Lambda = \Lambda$ since $A'A = I$. Also, since $RA = A\Lambda$, we can post multiply both sides of this matrix expression by A' to get $RAA' = A\Lambda A'$. Since $AA' = I$, $R = A\Lambda A'$. Thus, we can decompose R into a product of three matrices involving latent vectors and latent roots. The goal of principal components analysis is to decompose the correlation matrix. That is, explain the variation expressed in R in terms of weighting vectors (latent vectors) of the principal components and variances (latent roots) of the principal components. The decomposition of R is a key concept in principal components analysis and we shall discuss it further in a subsequent section.

Many times it is easier to interpret the principal component when the elements of the latent vector are transformed to correlations of the variables with the particular principal components. This can be done by multiplying each of the elements of a particular latent vector, a_i, by the square root of the associated latent root, $\sqrt{\lambda_i}$. Thus the correlations of the variables with the ith principal component is $\sqrt{\lambda_i}a_i$. The correlations of the variables with the principal components are sometimes called loadings, a term borrowed from factor analysis. Variables that correlate highly with a particular principal component give meaning to that component.

Like any other statistical inference problem, we can talk about population parameters associated with the principal components and the sample estimates of them. For example, there are population latent roots and associated latent vectors and sample estimates of them. Procedures have been established for estimating standard errors for these parameters, but the procedures are based primarily on covariance matrices and assume multivariate normality. Inference procedures based on correlation matrices are much more troublesome and consequently not much has been developed in this area. In addition, we use principal components primarily as a tool to describe a sample of observations. We are not interested in testing specific hypotheses, except for possibly the hypothesis that the last latent roots are equal, i.e., $\lambda_k = \lambda_{k+1} = \ldots = \lambda_p$. This test could help us decide how many principal components to retain since, if the last k latent roots are equal, then the latent vectors associated with them are arbitrary, as we shall see, and, hence, should be discarded. For a discussion of statistical inference in principal components analysis the interested reader is referred to Anderson (1963), Lawley (1963), and Morrison (1976).

How many and which principal components to retain depend, in part, on the goals of the analysis. If we simply want to describe a variable set without regard to subsequent uses, then retaining the k largest principal components might be adequate. If we want to use the principal components as predictors of a dependent variable, then we should consider their correlations with the dependent variable as well. Presently, we will be concerned with simply describing a data set by principal components without regard to their subsequent uses as independent variables in a regression analysis or as substitutes for the original variables in multivariate procedures such as discriminant analysis and canonical correlation analysis. The role of principal components analysis in these other analyses will be discussed in the following chapters.

We will now discuss some "rules of thumb" or criteria designed to help us decide on how many principal components to retain. Kaiser (1960) recommends dropping those principal components of a correlation matrix with latent roots less than one. He argues that principal components with variances less than one contain less information than a single standardized variable whose variance is one. In addition, his rule was developed with reference to factor analysis rather than to principal components analysis. Holding rigidly to Kaiser's criteria may result in discarding principal components that, while small, may be important. For example, some variables may not be very well represented by the larger principal components and we may want to retain smaller principal components that better represent those variables.

Jolliffe (1972) has suggested that Kaiser's rule tends to throw away too much information and on the basis of simulation studies has suggested a cutoff of .7 for correlation matrices. Part of his argument is based on the fact that a population latent root ≥1 can result in a corresponding sample latent root considerably less than 1 because of sampling error. This rule can be extended to covariance matrices by using the cutoff $.7\bar{\lambda}$ where $\bar{\lambda}$ is the average size of the latent roots of the covariance matrix.

Cattell (1966) proposes the use of a "scree" graph to help decide on how many principal components to retain. The scree graph involves plotting the latent roots and finding a point where the line joining the points is steep to the left of the point k, and not steep to the right of k. One then retains k principal components. The problem with this method is that steep and non-steep are arbitrary and that for many principal component analyses no such lines are evident.

Another criteria is to retain enough principal components to account for a given percentage of variation, e.g., 80%. All of these rules are arbitrary and should be applied with caution. For example, Jolliffe's criterion of $\lambda = .7$ can, in certain instances, result in retaining twice as many components as Kaiser's criterion of $\lambda = 1$. The more principal components relative to the number of variables that are retained, the less parsimonious our description of the data. In addition, smaller principal components are, in general, harder to interpret than larger ones.

3. GEOMETRICAL
PROPERTIES OF PRINCIPAL COMPONENTS

For a three dimensional random variable characterized by a vector (x_1, x_2, x_3), we can actually plot the observations as points in ordinary three dimensional space. For example, the random vector (5, 4, 8) can be represented as a value of 5 with respect to the x_1 axis, 4 with respect to the x_2 axis, and 8 with respect to the x_3 axis. The x_1, x_2, and x_3 coordinate axes are mutually perpendicular. The coordinates of a point tell us the location of a point in space with respect to the particular set of coordinate axes. If we plot a data set of three dimensional observations, then under certain conditions (e.g., multivariate normality) they will form an egg shaped swarm of points. A line is a one dimensional subspace in this ordinary three dimensional space. A plane is a two dimensional subspace. Sometimes a line or a plane can be found that will lie close to most of the points and then the three dimensional swarm of points can be essentially characterized by a one or two dimensional subspace. This one or two dimensional subspace captures most of the variation (i.e., the distances between observations) in the original three dimensional space.

We can generalize these ideas to higher dimensional spaces where we can no longer plot and visualize the swarm of points. A random vector of 10 variables $(x_1, x_2, \ldots, x_{10})$ can be considered as a point in ten dimensional space where a particular observation, say, (4, 10, \ldots, 3) represents the values on the x_1, x_2, \ldots$x_{10}$ coordinate axes. The coordinates locate the points in the ten dimensional space. In this case, principal component analysis finds a lower dimensional space of say, three dimensions, that provides the best fit to the 10 dimensional swarm of points. We can then represent the points with respect to the coordinate axes, the principal components, defining this subspace. For example, if the best fitting subspace is three dimensional, then three coordinate axes are needed to represent it. An observation can now be represented by its three coordinates on the three new coordinate axes (y_1, y_2, y_3) as contrasted to being represented by the 10 coordinate axes $(x_1, x_2, \ldots, x_{10})$ of the original variables. The idea is to use the first k principal components which are the coordinate axes or basis for a k dimensional subspace of the p dimensional variable space in which most of the variation in the p variables is contained.

The geometrical properties of principal components can be elucidated by some two dimensional figures. Let us assume that we have a sample of observations on two standardized variables, x_1 and x_2. We can use x_1 and x_2 as coordinate axes and plot the standardized scores as in Figure 3.1.

From the shape of the scatterplot we can see that there is a substantial correlation between x_1 and x_2, perhaps a correlation of about .90. There are two variables, and if the variables are not perfectly correlated, two principal components are required to completely account for the variation in the two variables. The first principal component is a new coordinate axis in the variable space which is oriented in a direction that maximizes the variation of the projections of the points on the new coordinate axis, the first principal component. The projection of a point on a coordinate axis is the numerical value on the coordinate axis at which a line from the point drawn perpendicular to the axis intersects the axis. Note that the swarm of points has an elliptical shape and that the first principal component is the principal axis of this ellipse. It turns out that for two standardized variables, the first principal component always forms a 45 degree angle with x_1 and hence x_2 (i.e., it bisects the angle $x_1 0 x_2$) irrespective of the size of the correlation as long as the correlation is not zero. The latent vector associated the largest latent root of the two by two correlation matrix is always

$$a_1 = \begin{bmatrix} .71 \\ .71 \end{bmatrix}.$$

The direction cosine is the cosine of the angle that the principal component coordinate axis makes with a particular variable coordinate axis. It follows that there are as many direction cosines for a particular principal component as there are variables or, equivalently, the number of elements in each latent vector. In fact, the elements of the latent vector are the direction cosines of the first principal component with the x_1 and x_2 axes, respectively. The largest principal component makes an angle of 45 degrees with both x_1 and x_2 and the cosine of 45

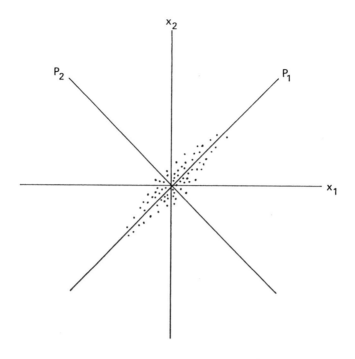

Figure 3.1: Scatterplot of Two Standardized Variables

degrees is .71. As discussed previously, the length of each latent vector is 1 and if we perpendicularly project this unit length vector on both x_1 and x_2, the respective projections are each equal to .71. Thus, the projections of the unit length latent vector variable representing a particular principal component, on each of the variables coordinate axes are equal to the direction cosines. This is illustrated in Figure 3.2. Harman (1976) gives a good discussion of the basic trigonometric and geometric concepts associated with principal components analysis.

For three or more variables, the elements of the latent vector for the largest principal component usually differ from one another. They are only exactly equal if all of the correlations in the correlation matrix are exactly equal. Correlation matrices, especially large ones, rarely have all correlations equal to one another. However, as we shall see later, if the correlations are fairly similar in magnitude, then the elements of the latent vector for the largest principal component will also be similar in magnitude. These elements of the latent vector, the direction cosines, are the directions of the principal component axis

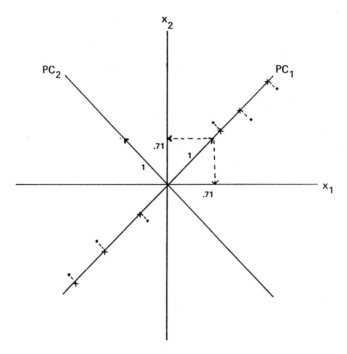

Figure 3.2: One Dimensional Representation by Largest Principal Components of Two Dimensional Data

with respect to each of the variables. For example, in the case of three or more variables, a direction cosine close to one (element of the latent vector) for a particular variable indicates that the direction of the principal component is close to the direction of that variable in the p dimensional space.

If the correlation between the two variables is high, then most of the information contained in the two dimensional swarm of observation can be represented by their projection onto the single largest principal component. This is true for Figure 3.1 and illustrated in more detail with a few observations in Figure 3.2.

There are six observations in Figure 3.2 representing an almost perfect correlation between x_1 and x_2. The perpendicular projections of these six points onto the largest principal component axis are indicated by the dotted lines. These projections are the principal component scores of the linear transformation $y_1 = .71x_1 + .71x_2$. Note that for this pattern of projections, the principal component scores for the largest principal component contains about as much information with regard to the scatter of the observation as the two dimensional scatter in the space of the original two variables, x_1 and x_2. That is because the observations essentially fall on a straight line, the largest principal component. We have captured the information concerning the scatter in a two dimensional space by projecting the points onto a one dimensional subspace, the largest principal component. Another property of the first principal component, evident from Figure 3.2, is that it minimizes the sum of the squared distances of the observations from their perpendicular projections onto the largest principal component. For this reason, the first principal component is sometimes referred to as the line of closest fit.

Since the second principal component is orthogonal, or perpendicular, to the first principal component (i.e., they intersect at a right angle), the vector product $a'_1 a_2$ where

$$a_1 = \begin{bmatrix} .71 \\ .71 \end{bmatrix},$$

the latent vector associated with the largest principal component and

$$a_2 = \begin{bmatrix} a_{21} \\ a_{22} \end{bmatrix}$$

the latent vector associated with the second principal component, must equal 0 by definition. That is, two vectors a and b emanating from the origin at right angles to each other have the property that $a'b = b'a = 0$. Thus,

$$[.71 \ .71] \begin{bmatrix} a_{21} \\ a_{22} \end{bmatrix} = .71 a_{21} + .71 a_{22} = 0.$$

With the constraint that $a_{21}^2 + a_{22}^2 = 1$, it can be shown that $a_{21} = .71$ and $a_{22} = .71$. Thus $a_2 = \begin{bmatrix} -.71 \\ .71 \end{bmatrix}$. The unit vector representing the direction of the second principal component is also shown in Figure 3.2.

The direction cosines of the second principal component are the projections of this unit length vector on the x_1 and x_2 axes, respectively. That is, if we drop a perpendicular line from the tip of the arrow onto the x_1 axis, we find $-.71$ as the value of the projection. The perpendicular projection on x_2 is .71. Note that the variation of points in the direction of the second principal component is considerably smaller than the variation of the points in the direction of the largest principal component. That is, if we project the points perpendicularly onto the second principal component, these are the second principal component scores and their variation on this line is considerably smaller than the variation of the projections onto the first principal component. The perpendicular projections of the six points onto the second principal component would result in principal component scores with virtually no variation when compared to the variation of the projections of these six points on the largest principal component.

Note that the two orthogonal principal components function as just another frame of reference or set of coordinate axes to represent the swarm of observations in the two dimensional variable space. The projections of the observations on the two principal components contain the exact same amount of information as the projections of the observations on the two original variables. For example, distances between points in the two dimensional swarm are the same using either set of coordinate axes. However, if we use as many principal components as variables to represent the swarm of points or observations, then we have not simplified the data because we have not reduced the dimensionality of the data set. The object of principal components analysis is to represent a p dimensional space by a considerably lower dimensional subspace that represents most of the variation in the original p dimensional space. The information is contained in the projections of the p dimensional points onto the k dimensional subspace where k is much smaller than p.

If the two variables are highly correlated as in Figures 3.1 and 3.2, then the two dimensional variable space can be adequately represented by a one dimensional subspace, the first principal component. For example, if x_1 and x_2 had a correlation of .90, then the first principal component $y_1 = .71 x_1 + .71 x_2$ would have a variance equal to $(.71)^2 + (.71)^2 + 2(.71)^2(.90) = 1.90$. Since the variance of each of the two standardized variables is 1, the total variance in the two variable system is 2. The largest principal component has a variance equal to 1.90 so it accounts for a proportion of (1.90/2) or .95 of the variation in the two variables, x_1 and x_2. As we discussed earlier, this turns out to be the largest eigenvalue of the correlation matrix. We can see this by solving the matrix equation $Ra = \lambda a$. For our two variable example,

$$R = \begin{bmatrix} 1 & .90 \\ .90 & 1 \end{bmatrix} \text{ and } a = \begin{bmatrix} .71 \\ .71 \end{bmatrix}$$

so that

$$\begin{bmatrix} 1 & .90 \\ .90 & 1 \end{bmatrix} \begin{bmatrix} .71 \\ .71 \end{bmatrix} = \lambda \begin{bmatrix} .71 \\ .71 \end{bmatrix}$$

Postmultiplying the first row of R, [1 .90], by $\begin{bmatrix} .71 \\ .71 \end{bmatrix}$ we have 1(.71) + .90(.71) = 1.349. Equating the first element on both sides of the matrix equation we have 1.349 = λ .71 or λ = 1.9.

As discussed previously, the latent vectors for the first and second principal components are $\begin{bmatrix} .71 \\ .71 \end{bmatrix}$ and $\begin{bmatrix} -.71 \\ .71 \end{bmatrix}$, respectively, regardless of the magnitude of the correlation. The amount of variation for the original variables, however, explained by each principal component differs depending on the degree of correlation. In the case of a perfect correlation $R = \begin{bmatrix} 1 & 1 \\ 1 & 1 \end{bmatrix}$ and using the relation $Ra = \lambda a$, we have

$$\begin{bmatrix} 1 & 1 \\ 1 & 1 \end{bmatrix} \begin{bmatrix} .71 \\ .71 \end{bmatrix} = \lambda \begin{bmatrix} .71 \\ .71 \end{bmatrix}.$$

Equating the first element on both sides of the equation, we have 1(.71) + 1(.71) = λ(.71) or λ = 2. Thus, the variance of the larger principal component is 2. The total variance in the two standardized variables is 2 so that the first principal component explains 100% (2/2) of the variation in the two standardized variables, x_1 and x_2. Knowing that the latent vector or direction cosines associated with the second principal component is $\begin{bmatrix} -.71 \\ .71 \end{bmatrix}$, we can solve for the associated second largest latent root. Using the matrix equation as before, we find 1(-.71) + 1(.71) = λ (.71) or λ = 0. So the second latent root is zero and the variation in x_1 and x_2 explained by the second principal component is zero. This seems reasonable since we already know that the first principal component explained 100% of the variation in x_1, and x_2. Since the value of the second principal component is a constant of zero for all observations, 0 = -.71 x_1 + .71 x_2 or $x_1 = x_2$. This indicates that x_1 is a perfect linear function of x_2. It tells us that x_1 is perfectly correlated with x_2. So latent vectors associated with zero latent roots indicate dependencies among variables. We shall say more about this later.

Even though the latent root associated with the second principal component is zero, it still has a unique direction given by its associated latent vector, $a_2 = \begin{bmatrix} -.71 \\ .71 \end{bmatrix}$. That is, it has to be perpendicular to the first principal component even if it turns out that all of the observations have a zero projection on it.

Returning to our example with a correlation of .90, we showed that the variance of the first principal component was 1.9. Since the total variability in the system of two standardized variables is 2, we may surmise that the variance of the second principal component is .1. We can verify this by substituting into the principal components equation $Ra = \lambda a$. Substituting we have

$$\begin{bmatrix} 1 & .90 \\ .90 & 1 \end{bmatrix} \begin{bmatrix} -.71 \\ .71 \end{bmatrix} = \lambda \begin{bmatrix} -.71 \\ .71 \end{bmatrix}$$

which gives $\lambda = .1$.

If the two variables have a zero correlation, then the swarm of observations in the variable space typically has a circular appearance as shown in Figure 3.3.

Looking at the circular swarm of points in Figure 3.3, we can see that there is no coordinate axis that maximizes the variance of the projections upon it. That is, there is no unique direction in which we can place a coordinate axis that maximizes variation. One direction is as good as another. So the direction cosines, or elements of the latent vector associated with the largest latent root are not unique. There are an infinite number of directions represented by the latent vector for the largest principal component. Intuitively, we can see that no matter where we place the coordinate axis, the variance of the projections of the points on this axis is always the same since the spread of the points on each possible coordinate axis is equal to the diameter of the circle representing the swarm of points. A few directions are illustrated in Figure 3.3. Each explains the same amount of variance as each of the original variables which is one.

Regression analysis for the two variable cases also results in a line of closest fit. However, the regression line is determined by minimizing the sum of squared distances of the points from the line in the direction of the dependent variable. These distances are not perpendicular to the line as they are in principal components analysis. The differences between the principal component line of best fit and the regression line of best fit is illustrated in Figure 3.4.

When one standardized variable is regressed on another, there can be an infinite number of regression lines, each with a different slope, depending upon the degree of correlation. However, there is only one unique principal component line regardless of the magnitude of correlation for the case of two standardized variables.

Before we leave the two dimensional case, we will briefly return to the problem of conducting a principal components analysis on a covariance matrix from a geometrical perspective. If the variance of one variable is a large multiple of the other variables, then the direction cosine for that variable will be close to 1 and the direction cosines associated with the remaining variables will be close to zero. In other words, the principal component is oriented in the direction of the

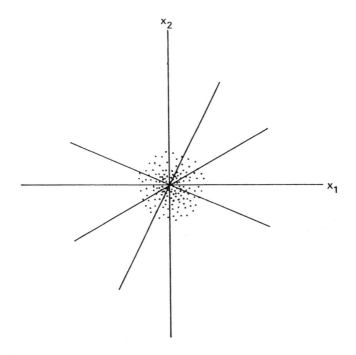

Figure 3.3: Distribution of Two Uncorrelated Variables

variable with the largest variance. This is the direction that maximizes the variation of the largest principal component as illustrated in Figure 3.5.

From Figure 3.5 we can see that the variance of x_1 is high compared to x_2. The largest principal component therefore, has a large direction cosine for x_1 and a small one for x_2 as illustrated in Figure 3.5. It can maximize its variation by orienting itself in the direction of x_1. In a case like this where we have such extreme differences in variances, we could use the variable with the largest variances as a good approximation for the first principal component. Not much is gained by doing a principal component analysis in this situation. We would be better off standardizing the variables so that a single variable would not dominate the analysis. The orientation of the swarm of observations, an approximate ellipse, for a given correlation, and hence the direction of the first principal component, depends on the scales of the variables. It turns out that the solution of a principal component analysis is not invariant with respect to changes in the scales of the variables. Not invariant means that the principal components of

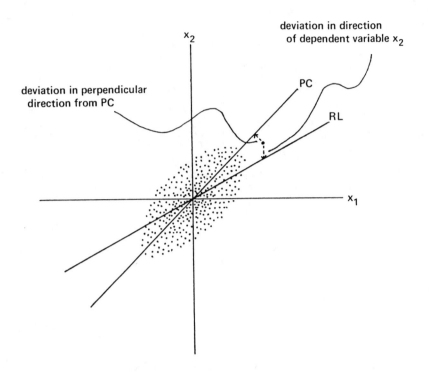

deviation in direction
of dependent variable x_2

deviation in perpendicular
direction from PC

x_2

PC

RL

x_1

Figure 3.4 Principal Component and Regression Line

the covariance matrix have no direct relationship with those of the corresponding correlation matrix. That is, the latent roots and associated latent vectors of a covariance matrix cannot be algebraically transformed into the latent roots and associated latent vectors of the corresponding correlation matrix.

Let us now move from the two dimensional model to a three dimensional model. While no diagrams or figures will be presented, we can still visualize patterns of swarms of observations in three dimensional space. Again, for convenience, we assume that all variables are standardized. If the three variables are uncorrelated, then the swarm of points in the three dimensional space will take the form of a sphere, or ball, with the density of points greatest near the origin and decreasing towards the surface of the sphere. Like the circular density in two dimensional space, there is no unique direction for a coordinate axis that maximizes the variation of the points projected onto it. Every direction has a variance of 1, the same as the original observations. There is no way to simplify the structure of the observations.

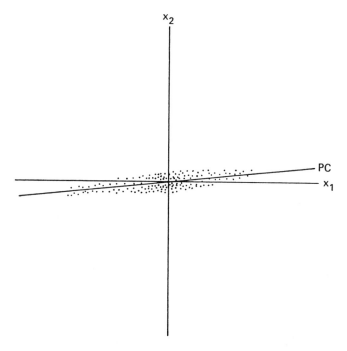

Figure 3.5: Largest Principal Component of Covariance Matrix

We might as well use the original uncorrelated variables. It turns out that all three latent roots are equal to 1, so there is no dominant latent root that would have a unique vector associated with it.

For moderate size correlations among the three variables, the swarm of points would take the shape of an egg or an ellipsoid. The largest principal component would take the direction of the principal axis of the ellipsoid. The second largest principal component would be orthogonal to the first principal component but in a direction that would maximize the variance of the projections of the points on this second coordinate axis. The third largest or smallest principal component would be orthogonal to the first two principal components and, hence, perpendicular to the plane defined by the first two principal components.

If the variables are highly correlated, the swarm of points will have more of a cigar shaped pattern with one large principal component going through the center of the cigar in the direction which the cigar is pointed. The second and third principal components will be orthogonal to the first and be considerably smaller. The second principal component would be orthogonal to the axis of the cigar and be in the

184

direction that maximizes variation. For example, if the cross section of the cigar is elliptically shaped, then the second principal component would be in the direction of the principal axis of that ellipse. The third principal component would be orthogonal to the plane defined by the first two principal components.

If the three variables are perfectly correlated ($r = 1$), then the swarm of points will fall exactly on a straight line. A single principal component captures all of the variation in the original three variables. Since the three variables each have unit variance, and the first principal component accounts for all of this variance, the first principal component has a variance of three. Thus, the largest latent root is three, and the remaining two latent roots are each equal to zero since there is no variation in the points in any direction orthogonal to the largest principal component. The latent vectors associated with the two zero latent roots are not unique since there are no directions in which variance can be maximized. It is zero no matter which direction we go. If the last two principal components are equal, then the variation orthogonal to the first principal component is circular and there is no unique direction for the latent vectors associated with the two equal latent roots.

It very seldom occurs in practice that one or more of the latent roots are exactly equal to zero or two or more of the latent roots are exactly equal to each other. However, there are occasions when one or more of the latent roots are close to zero or two or more of the latent roots are very close to one another in magnitude. In this instance, the resulting latent vectors for a sample correlation matrix could be very unstable.

There are a number of computer algorithms for computing principal components. A detailed discussion of one, the power method, is presented by Dunteman (1984b). Jolliffe (1986) describes the major algorithms and the computer packages in which they are embedded. All of the major computer packages such as SAS and SPSS provide routines for principal components analysis. The outputs for the different programs are quite similar. For example, SAS output includes the following: means and standard deviations of the variables; the variable correlation matrix; the complete set of latent roots and their associated latent vectors; a listing of the principal components scores; and graphical plots of scores for pairs of principal components. SAS also provides for the rotation of the k largest components retained on the basis of various criteria (e.g., $\lambda \geq 1$) or specified a priori by the user. Both the original principal component scores or the rotated component scores can be saved in specified files for use in subsequent analyses.

Example

Let us now illustrate the concepts that we have learned up to now with a data set taken from the 1985 United States Statistical Abstracts. The data involve 1984 crime levels from all 50 states and the District of Columbia for 7 types of crimes. The 7 types of crime levels (the variables), were murder, forcible rape, robbery, aggravated assault, burglary, larceny-theft, and motor vehicle theft—measured for each state (the observations), in offenses per one hundred thousand population. Thus, we have a 51 × 7 data matrix, X. Although all variables are measured in the same metric, number of offenses per one hundred thousand, the variances of the variables ranged from 20.79 for murder, to 481,483 for larceny-theft. Therefore, the first principal component of the covariance matrix would be dominated by larceny-theft since this direction maximizes the variation. Consequently, it seems more reasonable, in this situation, to conduct a principal component analysis on the correlation matrix rather than the covariance matrix.

If the variables are all in the same metric and the variances do not differ widely from one another, then it might be reasonable to conduct a principal components analysis of the covariance matrix rather than the correlation matrix. In the present case, however, the ratio of the largest variance of 481,483 for theft to the smallest variance of 20.79 for murder is 23,159. Even though theft is much more prevalent than murder, its importance should not be such that its influence alone essentially determines the results of the principal components analysis. Two other alternatives come to mind. First, since the mean and variance are positively correlated, the variables could be subjected to a log transformation prior to the computation of the covariance matrix. Second, the crime variables could be weighted according to their relative importance on some key criterion (e.g., seriousness of crime) prior to computing the covariance matrix. The correlations among the seven variables are presented in Table 3.1.

The correlations among the variables are all high and we might suspect that a few principal components would explain most of the variation in the original seven crime variables. For example, if we were going to use this state-level crime data as part of a larger set of state-level social indicators, then tabular presentations would be greatly simplified by interpreting and reporting one or two principal

TABLE 3.1

Correlation Matrix for Seven Crime Indicators

	Murder	Rape	Robbery	Assault	Burglary	Larceny-Theft	MV Theft
Murder	1.000						
Rape	0.651	1.000					
Robbery	0.810	0.501	1.000				
Assault	0.821	0.707	0.722	1.000			
Burglary	0.593	0.740	0.552	0.686	1.000		
Larceny-Theft	0.434	0.641	0.480	0.557	0.751	1.000	
MV Theft	0.490	0.565	0.658	0.563	0.584	0.414	1.000

component scores rather than the seven variable scores. The latent roots and associated latent vectors are presented in Table 3.2.

The correlations of the variables with the principal components, sometimes referred to as component loadings, are obtained by multiplying the elements in a particular column in Table 3.2 by the square root of the corresponding latent root. The principal component loadings as well as the percent of variance explained by each principal component individually and cumulatively are presented in Table 3.3.

As we suspected, the first principal component had a large variance of 4.71 (Table 3.2) which accounted for $\left(\frac{4.71}{7} \times 100\right)$ or 67.3% (Table 3.3) of the variance of the seven crime variables. The second and succeeding components accounted for considerably less variance ranging from 12% for the second principal component to 1.2% for the seventh (smallest) principal component. This pattern of latent roots is typical for highly correlated variables. The first principal component explains a substantial amount of variation in the variables and the remaining components considerably less. In addition, most or all of the variables have high correlations with the dominant principal component. The latent roots are ordered indicating that each succeeding principal component has less variance or, equivalently, explains less variation of the variables. The nature of principal components solutions for correlation matrices exhibiting various patterns of correlations will be discussed in a later section.

The problem now is to decide on how many principal components are needed to adequately represent the data. We previously discussed a number of criteria that are used to decide on how many principal components to retain. They are somewhat arbitrary and the use of different rules sometimes yields conflicting results.

TABLE 3.2

Latent Vectors and Corresponding Latent Roots from the
Correlation Matrix in Table 3.1

	Principal Component						
	1	2	3	4	5	6	7
Murder	.389	.399	.414	.060	.039	.323	−.640
Rape	.387	−.272	.084	.644	.494	.162	.291
Robbery	.380	.462	−.060	−.489	.204	.218	.558
Assault	.410	.168	.288	.148	−.309	−.763	.151
Burglary	.394	−.385	−.054	−.013	−.708	.418	.130
Larceny-Theft	.341	−.590	.066	−.551	.339	−.218	−.257
MV Theft	.340	.169	−.853	.133	.021	−.144	−.298
Latent root (variance)	4.710	.837	.568	.397	.217	.186	.085

TABLE 3.3

Principal Component Loadings for Crime Variables and
Percent Variance Explained

	Principal Component						
	1	2	3	4	5	6	7
Murder	0.845	0.365	0.312	0.038	0.018	0.139	−0.187
Rape	0.839	−0.249	0.063	0.406	0.230	0.070	0.085
Robbery	0.825	0.423	−0.045	−0.308	0.095	0.094	0.163
Assault	0.889	0.154	0.217	0.093	−0.144	−0.329	0.044
Burglary	0.855	−0.352	−0.041	−0.008	−0.330	0.180	0.038
Theft	0.739	−0.540	0.050	−0.347	0.158	−0.094	−0.075
MV Theft	0.738	0.155	−0.643	0.084	0.010	−0.062	−0.087
Percent variance explained individually	67.3%	12.0%	8.1%	5.7%	3.1%	2.7%	1.2%
Percent variance explained cumulatively	67.3%	79.2%	87.4%	93.0%	96.1%	98.8%	100%

The first component explains about two-thirds of the variance in
the seven crime variables. We can use either the latent vectors (Table
3.2) or the principal component loadings (Table 3.3) to interpret the
principal components since the two vectors are proportional to each

other. Relatively large elements in either vector indicate the variables that are important in defining a particular principal component. However, let us use the component loadings (correlations) to interpret the principal components.

The first principal component has large correlations with all seven crime variables. It is, therefore, interpreted as an overall crime dimension. If we were to create a principal component score using the elements of the first latent vector, it would be essentially an equally weighted average of the seven standardized crime scores. If the variables are all positively correlated, then the elements of the latent vector (or principal component loadings) are all positive. If the correlations are of about the same magnitude as they are in this example, then the elements of the first latent vector, or the loadings, are all positive and of about the same magnitude. The largest principal component in these circumstances is sometimes called a size factor. If we wanted only a single index that best summarized the data, then the first principal component is it. This is typically what we do when we construct an index such as a total test score. The test items are usually highly correlated and the correlations are of about the same magnitude. The information in the items is combined in an equally weighted composite of the items to yield a total test score. In situations where the correlations are homogeneous, an equally weighted composite of the variables would have an almost perfect correlation with the first principal component.

If we wanted to retain enough principal components to account for 80% of the variation, then two components would just about suffice since the first two components account for 79.2% of the total variation. The loadings of the second principal component have both positive (4) and negative signs (3). This is the expected pattern of the second and succeeding principal components if the first component has all positive correlations with the variables. The reason for this is that the first principal component must be orthogonal to all the remaining principal components. In order for this condition to be fulfilled, the sum of the cross products of the elements of the first latent vector with the elements of each of the remaining latent vectors must be equal to zero (i.e., $a_1'a_k = 0$ for $k = 1,2, \ldots, p$). Since all of the elements of a_1 are positive, some of the elements in a_k must be negative for $a_1' a_k = 0$. Of course, the signs of any latent vector can be freely reversed since we can multiply both sides of $Ra = \lambda a$ by -1 and still maintain the equality.

When we have an overall size factor the succeeding principal components with alternating positive and negative signs are usually interpreted as contrasts. Our second principal component has high positive correlations (or large weights) with murder and robbery, both violent crimes, and high negative correlations (or large weights) with burglary and theft, both property crimes. Consequently we can interpret this principal component as a contrast between violent crimes and property crimes. That is, we add the violent crimes and subtract the property crimes to compute the second principal component score for a given state. The remaining three variables have smaller correlations or weights so they are given less weight in the interpretation. The negative loading of rape on the second principal component, although low, is somewhat puzzling since it has the same sign as the property crimes. It could be that some rapes are committed during a burglary or theft. The first few principal components are, in many instances, interpretable. They are the ones that explain most of the variation in the set of variables. Frequently, the smaller components are more difficult to interpret. Sometimes researchers prefer to rotate the retained components as in factor analysis. We will discuss this later on.

The sum of squares of all the loadings on a particular principal component is equal to the latent root (variance) associated with that component. This just indicates that the variance of a principal component is equal to the amount of variation that is explained across all of the variables. It is useful to examine the sum of squares of the loadings for each row of the principal component loading matrix as well because the row sum of squares indicates how much variance for that variable is accounted for by the retained principal components. For example, the proportion of variance in murder explained by the first two principal components is $(.845)^2 + (.365)^2$ or .847. Doing likewise for the remaining six rows, we have the proportion of variance that the first two principal components explain for each of the seven variables, as presented in Table 3.4.

Table 3.4 indicates that all the variables except motor vehicle theft have a substantial proportion of their variance explained by the largest two principal components. Motor vehicle theft had only 56.9% of it variance accounted for by the first two principal components whereas all but one of the remaining variables (e.g., rape) had over 80% of their variance explained by the first two principal components. If we wanted to explain at least 75% of the variation in each variable, then we would retain the third principal component as well since motor vehicle theft has a high correlation with the third component. In fact, squaring the motor vehicle loading of .643 on the third component and adding it to .569, the proportion of variance accounted for would increase from .569 to $.569 + (-.643)^2$ or .98. The

TABLE 3.4

Proportion of Variance Accounted for in Crime Variables
by First Two Principal Components

	Proportion of Variance Accounted for
1. murder	.847
2. rape	.766
3. robbery	.860
4. assault	.814
5. burglary	.855
6. theft	.838
7. motor vehicle theft	.569

variance accounted for in the remaining six variables would also increase by retaining the third component, but not to a large extent because their correlations with the third component are considerably smaller. The number of components retained depends on the eventual use of the principal components. If they were going to be used as independent variables in a regression analysis, then we might want to retain three components so that all of the variables would be adequately represented by the principal components. We can always eventually discard the components that do not significantly correlate with the dependent variable.

Let us summarize the application of these criteria for deciding on how many principal components to obtain. We begin by plotting the latent roots in Figure 3.6. Kaiser's criterion calls for retaining only the largest component. Jolliffe's criterion leads to the retention of two components, but we may want to retain the third component because motor vehicle theft is not adequately represented by the first two components but is heavily represented by the third principal component. Using Cattell's scree criterion a steep slope is evident from the first to the second latent roots and the second through the seventh points can be fitted fairly well by a straight line of negligible slope. Consequently, by this criterion, we would retain two components. The various criteria and modifications thereof lead to the retention of one, two, or three principal components. There are no hard and fast rules and the various criteria can give conflicting results. However, three components seem to be a reasonable choice. Three principal components account for 87% of the variation, represent all seven variables well, and are readily interpretable.

We can compute the principal component scores for each of the 51 states by using the appropriate latent vectors. For example, the score

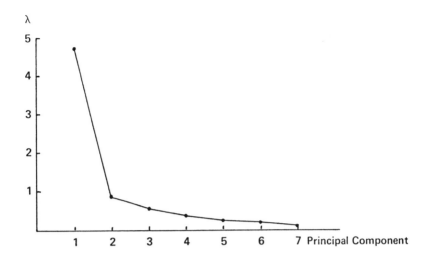

Figure 3.6: Plot of the Eigenvalues of the Crime Variable Correlation Matrix

on the first principal component for the state of Maine is $.389(-1.080) + .387(-1.277) +. 380 (-.761) + .410(-1.030) + .394 (-.675) + .341(-.629) + .340(-.939) = -2.245$, where the values in parentheses are standardized scores for the seven corresponding crime rates. Since the mean score for each principal component is zero, Maine has a low score on the first principal component.

The principal component scores for any pair of principal components can be plotted. The reasons for doing this include checking for outlying observations, searching for clusters and, in general, understanding the structure of the data. The principal component scores on the first two principal components are plotted in Figure 3.7 using SYSTAT® (Wilkinson, 1984). Before plotting, SYSTAT® standardizes the principal component scores so that each principal component has a standard deviation of 1. This means that the distance between points is no longer the Euclidian distance, but the Mahalanobis distance $(x_i - x_j)'R^{-1}(x_i - x_j)$, which takes into account the intercorrelations among the variables. Intuitively, it prevents double counting in that highly correlated variables which are, by definition, redundant are given less weight than lowly correlated variables in defining the distance between two points.

FACTOR (1)

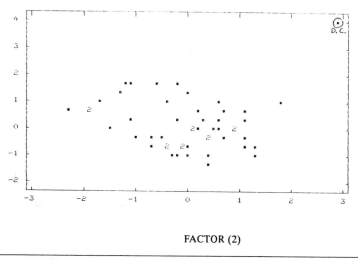

FACTOR (2)

Figure 3.7: Plot of the First Pair of Standardized Principal Components for

This plot will be discussed more fully when we discuss cluster analysis and outliers, but even a cursory examination of the plot indicates a clearly outlying observation, circled and identified as Washington, D.C., in the upper right hand corner of the plot.

4. DECOMPOSITION PROPERTIES OF THE PRINCIPAL COMPONENTS

This chapter describes two important decomposition properties. The principal components can be used both to decompose the variables into additive contributions from the components and to decompose the covariance (correlation) matrix into additive contributions from the components.

Decomposition of the Variables

We have seen that a vector of principal components scores can be expressed as $y = A'x$ where y is a $p \times 1$ vector of principal component scores, A' is the matrix of latent vectors arrayed in rows and x is the $p \times 1$ vector of variable scores. Since A' is an orthogonal matrix,

$AA' = I$ and we can premultiply the left and right side of $y = A'x$ by A to give $Ay = AA'x = x$. Thus, x, the vector of variables, can be expressed as a linear combination of the principal components, y, using A as the linear transformation matrix. Since $x = Ay$, it can also be expressed as $x = A_{(p\times k)}Y_{(k\times 1)} + A_{(p\times(p - k))}Y_{((p - k)\times 1)}$ where $A_{(p\times k)}$ is the matrix of latent vectors for the first k principal components that are retained, $y_{(k\times 1)}$ is the corresponding vector of principal component scores, $A_{(p\times(p - k))}$ is the matrix of latent vectors for the $p - k$ principal components that are discarded and $y_{((p - k)\times 1)}$ is the corresponding vector of principal component scores for the discarded components.

The above equation indicates that we can approximate x by using the first k principal components. The larger the k, the better the approximation of x. For our crime data, we retained the first three principal components so that $A_{(p\times k)}$ equals $A_{(7\times 3)}$, the first three latent vectors, arrayed as columns. That is, we approximate the crime data by using the first three principal components. Thus, the variables x can be decomposed into additive contributions by the principal components. For example, in order to approximate x_1 (murder) for a particular state, we would multiply the score on principal component one by .389, multiply the score on principal component two by .399, multiply the score on principal component three by .414, and sum these products. We get these weights from Table 3.2.

Spectral Decomposition of the Correlation or Covariance Matrix

Another important decomposition is the decomposition of the covariance or correlation matrix with respect to the principal components. Since $x = Ay$, we have $xx' = Ayy'A'$. Taking the expectation of each side we have $E(xx') = R = AE(yy')A' = A \Lambda A'$ where Λ is a diagonal matrix of the latent roots of R or, equivalently, the variances of the principal components, y. In this derivation, we have assumed that x is a vector of standardized scores. The matrix expression $R = A \Lambda A'$ can be written as

$$R = \sum_{i=1}^{p} \lambda_i a_i a_i'.$$

This indicates that R can be decomposed into a sum of the contribution for each of the p principal components. From the form of the last equation, it can be seen that the large principal components (those with large λ's) make more of a contribution to R than the small principal components (those with small λ's).

For our crime data, the contribution of the first principal component to $\mathbf{R}$ is

$$\lambda_1 a_1 a_1' = 4.710 \begin{bmatrix} .389 \\ .387 \\ .380 \\ .410 \\ .394 \\ .341 \\ .340 \end{bmatrix} [.389, .387, .380, .410, .394, .341, .340]$$

$$= \begin{bmatrix} .713 & .709 & .696 & .751 & .722 & .625 & .623 \\ .709 & .705 & .693 & .747 & .718 & .622 & .620 \\ .696 & .693 & .680 & .734 & .705 & .610 & .609 \\ .751 & .747 & .734 & .792 & .761 & .659 & .657 \\ .722 & .718 & .705 & .761 & .731 & .633 & .631 \\ .625 & .622 & .610 & .659 & .633 & .548 & .546 \\ .623 & .620 & .609 & .657 & .631 & .546 & .544 \end{bmatrix}$$

while the contribution of the smallest principal component is

$$\lambda_7 a_7 a_7' = .085 \begin{bmatrix} -.640 \\ .291 \\ .558 \\ .151 \\ .130 \\ -.257 \\ -.248 \end{bmatrix} [-.640, .291, .558, .151, .130, -.257, -.248]$$

$$= \begin{bmatrix} .035 & -.016 & -.030 & -.008 & -.007 & .014 & .016 \\ -.016 & .007 & .014 & .004 & -.003 & -.006 & -.007 \\ -.030 & .014 & .026 & .007 & .006 & -.012 & -.014 \\ -.008 & .004 & .007 & .002 & .002 & -.003 & -.004 \\ -.007 & .003 & .006 & .002 & .001 & -.003 & -.003 \\ .014 & -.006 & -.012 & -.003 & -.003 & .006 & .007 \\ .016 & -.007 & -.014 & -.004 & -.003 & .007 & .008 \end{bmatrix}$$

It can be seen that the elements $\lambda_1 a_1 a_1'$ associated with the first principal component are very large compared to the elements associated with the smallest principal component $\lambda_7 a_7 a_7'$. In fact, $\lambda_1 a_1 a_1'$ is a rough approximation to $\mathbf{R}$. We have already defined the loading (correlations) of the variables on the ith principal component $\mathbf{1}_i$, as $\sqrt{\lambda_i}\,a_i$.

Consequently, R can also be decomposed as $R = \sum_{i=1}^{p} l_i l_i'$.

5. PRINCIPAL COMPONENTS OF PATTERNED CORRELATION MATRICES

The pattern of latent roots and their associated latent vectors depends on the pattern of correlations. For well-defined correlational structures (e.g., variables falling into clearly defined clusters with high correlations within clusters and low correlations between clusters), the pattern of latent roots readily indicates the number of principal components to retain, and those that are retained are easily interpreted from the latent vectors or, equivalently, the loadings. If the pattern of correlations has no well defined structure, then this lack of structure will be reflected in the principal components. They will be difficult to interpret.

In the hypothetical case in which the correlations within a cluster are exactly equal and the correlations between clusters are exactly zero, there is a principal component associated with each cluster whose latent root is $1 + (p_i - 1)\rho_i$ where p_i is the number of variables in the ith cluster of variables and ρ_i is the common correlation among the variables in the ith cluster. There are $p_i - 1$ remaining latent roots associated with the ith cluster, each one equal to $1 - \rho_i$.

The latent vector associated with the ith cluster of variables has an equal element (or loading) for each of the variables comprising the cluster; the remaining elements are zero. Such correlation matrices have a block diagonal form such as the matrix in Table 5.1.

Variables 1 through 3 in Table 5.1 form one cluster, and variables 4 through 7 form another. The latent root associated with the first cluster (variables 1 – 3) is $1 + (3 - 1).80$ or 2.60 and its associated normed latent vector is $[\ 1/\sqrt{3},\ 1/\sqrt{3},\ 1/\sqrt{3},0,0,0,0\ ]$. The latent root associated with the second cluster (variables 4–7) is $1 + (4 - 1).70$ or 3.1 and its associated latent vector is $[0, 0, 0, 1/2, 1/2, 1/2, 1/2]$. The proportion of total variance accounted for by the first two principal components is $(2.6 + 3.1)/7$ or .81. There are five remaining latent roots, two associated with the first cluster and three associated with the second cluster. The two remaining latent roots associated with the first cluster are both equal to $1 - .80$ or .20. The three remaining latent roots associated with the second cluster are equal to $1 - .70$ or .30.

TABLE 5.1
Block Diagonal Correlation Matrix

				Variables			
	1	2	3	4	5	6	7
1	1.00	.80	.80	0	0	0	0
2	.80	1.00	.80	0	0	0	0
3	.80	.80	1.00	0	0	0	0
4	0	0	0	1.00	.70	.70	.70
5	0	0	0	.70	1.00	.70	.70
6	0	0	0	.70	.70	1.00	.70
7	0	0	0	.70	.70	.70	1.00

All of the principal components associated with these five roots would be discarded by any of the criteria discussed above. The elements of the latent vectors of these roots involve contrasts (i.e., a mixture of positive and negative signs) among the variables comprising the cluster. However, because of sphericity, the latent vectors are not unique and, hence, we would not want to interpret them anyway.

In practice, this ideal situation never occurs, but if the correlations within a cluster of variables are fairly homogeneous, and the correlations among variables across clusters are relatively low, then we can use the above principles to approximate a principal components solution. We just replace ρ_i in the above formula with $\bar{\rho}_i$, the average of the correlations within the ith variable cluster.

If all of the variables are equally correlated, then we have one large principal component with latent root equal to $1 + (p - 1)\rho$ where p is the total number of variables and ρ is the common correlation among the variables. The associated latent vector has p elements each equal to $1/\sqrt{p}$. The remaining $p - 1$ latent roots are all equal to $1 - \rho$. For example, the largest latent root of a 10×10 correlation matrix with a common correlation of .50 is $1 + (10 - 1).50$ or 5.5. The remaining nine latent roots are each equal to $1 - .50$ or .50. The nine latent vectors associated with them are arbitrary and would be discarded by any criterion.

Example

Let us take another example. Woodward, Retka, and Ng (1984) present the intercorrelations of seven heroin abuse indicators measured for 24 major metropolitan areas across the nation. The heroin abuse indicators were the number of emergency room episodes due to heroin overdoses (ER); the number of medical examiner episodes indicating death due to heroin overdose (D); the number of heroin users admitted to treatment (T); the number of arrests where opioid was involved (Arr); the number of pharmacy thefts where opioid was stolen (Ph.T); the retail price of heroin (Pr); and the retail purity of heroin (Pur). The correlations among these seven indicators are presented in Table 5.2.

A cursory examination of the correlation matrix in Table 5.2 indicates that the first five variables are all highly intercorrelated, but have relatively low correlations with the last two variables (price and purity of heroin). The latter two variables have a moderate negative correlation of $-.382$. This pattern of correlations indicates two clusters of variables and suggests that two principal components might be adequate for accounting for variation in the seven heroin abuse indicators.

The principal component loadings, latent roots, and percentage of variance accounted for are shown in Table 5.3. Using both Kaiser's and Jolliffe's criteria, two principal components would be retained. If we plotted the eigenvalues, then Cattell's criterion would suggest retaining three principal components since the points for components 3 through 7 fall approximately on a straight line with slope considerably less than the slope of the line joining the second and third components.

Two components account for 77% of the variation. In addition, each indicator has a high loading on at least one component so that each indicator is adequately represented by the first two principal components although some indicators are better represented than others. For example, the first two principal components explain $(.924)^2 + (.253)^2$ or 92.7% of the variation in treatment admissions (Tr), but only $(-.694)^2 + (.448)^2$ or 68.2% of the variation in heroin purity (Pur). In selecting two components we have used Jolliffe's criterion augmented by a check to make sure that each variable is adequately represented. For many cases, all variables are adequately represented using Jolliffe's criterion, but it needs checking.

The first principal component has high loadings on the five indicators which reflect prevalence. Since the loadings are proportional to the elements in the latent vector, this component is essentially an average of the five prevalence indicators. The second principal component has a high positive loading for price and a high negative loading for purity. It is a contrast between price and purity. Those SMSAs which have high scores on the second component are characterized by high heroin prices and low purity. Those with low scores are charac-

TABLE 5.2
Intercorrelations of Seven Heroin Abuse Indicators

	Er	D	T	Ph.T	Arr	Pr	Pur
Er	1.000						
D	0.690	1.000					
T	0.861	0.822	1.000				
Ph.T	0.724	0.671	0.810	1.000			
Arr	0.738	0.543	0.648	0.604	1.000		
Pr	−0.148	0.032	0.032	0.019	−0.190	1.000	
Pur	0.253	0.250	0.205	0.307	0.496	−0.382	1.000

TABLE 5.3
Principal Components Loading Matrix for Heroin Indicator
Correlation Matrix

	Principal Component						
	1	2	3	4	5	6	7
Er	0.907	0.054	−0.233	−0.180	0.017	0.259	0.140
D	0.835	0.221	−0.014	0.373	0.305	−0.124	0.077
Tr	0.924	0.253	−0.110	0.067	−0.005	0.107	−0.231
Ph.T	0.862	0.159	0.068	0.085	−0.446	−0.137	0.054
Arr	0.825	−0.224	0.115	−0.440	0.152	−0.196	−0.024
Pr	−0.129	0.840	0.506	−0.121	0.043	0.065	0.020
Pur	0.448	−0.694	0.529	0.144	−0.002	0.130	−0.005
Latent root	4.017	1.378	.621	.412	.317	0.172	.083
Percent variance	57.38	19.69	8.87	5.89	4.53	2.46	1.19
Cumulative percent	57.38	77.07	85.94	91.83	96.36	98.82	100.00

terized by low prices and high purity. The second principal component can be interpreted as a heroin availability index reflecting illicit drug market forces.

6. ROTATION OF PRINCIPAL COMPONENTS

Even though the retained principal components may be interpretable, some researchers prefer to rotate the principal components as is typically done in factor analysis. An orthogonal rotation is just a shift (rotation) to a new set of coordinate axes in the same subspace spanned by the principal components.

If most of the observations lie near a plane in the variable space, then principal components analysis will find the two coordinate axes, the principal components, that define the plane of closest fit to the essentially two dimensional swarm of points. However, any two other perpendicular coordinate axes lying in the same plane can also be used to describe the observations without any loss of information. Like the principal components, the new coordinate axes are also defined by their correlations (loadings) with the original variables, but hopefully the pattern of loadings on the rotated coordinated axes will be more conceptually appealing, thus allowing for a simpler interpretation of the rotated components.

Varimax rotation (Kaiser, 1958) is probably the most popular orthogonal rotation procedure. By orthogonal rotation we mean that the new coordinate axes, like the principal component axes, are perpendicular to one another. In varimax, the coordinate axes are rotated so as to maximize what is called the varimax criterion. Thus, like the principal components solution, the varimax solution is unique. The varimax criteria maximizes the sum of the variances of the squared loadings within each column of the loading matrix. That is, the varimax criteria results in a new set of orthogonal coordinate axes where each new coordinate axis has either large or small loadings of the variables on it. Since the rotated loading matrix is an orthogonal transformation of the original principal components loading matrix, it can be expressed as $L_r = LT$ where L_r is the $p \times k$ rotated loading matrix, L is the original $p \times k$ principal component loading matrix, and T is the $k \times k$ orthogonal transformation matrix that maximizes the varimax criterion. Kaiser proposed an iterative algorithm to find T. Rotation will be further discussed in a subsequent section comparing principal components and factor analysis.

Example

We will illustrate rotation by taking the loadings on the two principal components of the satisfaction variables from Table 3.1 and subjecting them to a varimax rotation. The result is the rotated loading matrix presented in Table 6.1. Note that each rotated component has either very high or very low loadings by the variables. The first rotated component has very high loadings by the three job-related satisfaction measures and very low loadings by the two health-care satisfaction measures. We would interpret this rotated component as job satisfaction. The second rotated component has very high loadings by the two health care satisfaction measures and very low load-

TABLE 6.1
Rotated Components for Military Satisfaction Variables

Variables	Rotated Components 1	Rotated Components 2
Satisfaction with Job (SJ)	.835	.034
Satisfaction with Job Training (SJT)	.751	.180
Satisfaction with Working Conditions (SWC)	.790	.185
Satisfaction with Medical Care (SMC)	.182	.878
Satisfaction with Dental Care (SDC)	.107	.896
Variance Explained $(\sum_{j=1}^{5} r_{ij}^2, i = 1, 2)$	1.931	1.641

ings by the three job-related satisfaction measures. This rotated component would be interpreted as health care satisfaction. The amount of variance explained by each rotated component is the sum of the squared loadings shown as the last row in Table 6.1. The total amount of variation explained by the two rotated components is 1.931 + 1.641 = 3.52—the same amount of variation explained by the original principal components. This makes sense logically since the rotated coordinate axes lie in the same plane defined by the original principal component axes.

Since both the unrotated and rotated solutions explain exactly the same amount of variation in the variables, the choice between the two hinges upon their interpretability from the researcher's perspective. Each solution is unique with respect to maximizing their respective mathematical criteria. The original principal components solution maximizes the sum of the squared loadings while the varimax rotated solution maximizes, as its name implies, a variance like function of the loading with the components.

7. USING PRINCIPAL COMPONENTS TO SELECT A SUBSET OF VARIABLES

Principal components analysis can be useful in selecting a subset of variables to represent the total set of variables. This discussion does not take into account the use of outside criteria, such as their effectiveness in predicting a particular dependent variable, tō select the subset of variables; only the internal structure of the data is considered. Subsequently, we will consider the joint use of outside criteria as well as the principal components in the selection of variables as independent variables in regression analyses.

The rationale for selecting a subset of variables to represent the variation in a set of variables rather than the principal components themselves is based on two considerations. First, in order to compute the principal component scores, we need measures of all variables in the variable set since each principal component is a linear combination of all of the variables. Some variables may be too difficult or too expensive to measure, and, therefore, collecting data on them in future studies may be impractical. Second, while the variables themselves are usually readily interpretable, the principal components are sometimes uninterpretable. This is not a serious drawback, however, since, as we have seen, the principal components can be rotated to a more interpretable structure by varimax or other rotation algorithms.

If the correlations among the variables are high, or if there are clusters of variables with high intercorrelations, then, in many instances, we can represent the variation in the total set of variables by a much smaller subset of variables. McCabe (1984) calls these principal variables. There are a number of strategies for selecting a subset of variables using principal components analyses. They are summarized in more detail by Jolliffe (1986).

The first step is to decide how many variables to select. One approach is to use Jolliffe's criteria of $\lambda = .70$ to determine which principal components to retain. Then one variable can be selected to represent each of the retained principal components. The variable that has the highest loading or weight on a principal component would be selected to represent that component, provided it has not been chosen to represent a larger variance principal component. In that case, the variable with the next largest loading would be chosen. The procedure would start with the largest principal component and proceed to the smallest retained component.

Another approach is to use the discarded principal components to discard variables. We would start with the smallest discarded component and delete the variable with the largest weight or loading on that component. Then the variable with the largest loading on the second smallest component would be discarded. If the variable had been previously discarded, then the variable with the next highest loading would be discarded. This procedure continues up through the largest discarded component. The rationale for deleting variables with high weights on small components is that small components reflect redundancies among the variables with high weights. Another way to look at it is that components with small variances are unimportant and therefore variables that load highly on them are likewise unimportant.

Example

Let us apply both of these approaches to the crime data example whose principal components are presented in Table 3.3. If we retain two components, then assault would be selected to represent the first component (overall crime level) and theft would be selected to represent the second component (property crimes versus violent crimes). If we use the five discarded principal components to discard five variables, then working from the smallest to the largest principal component we would discard in order murder, assault, burglary, rape, and motor vehicle theft. We are left with robbery and theft as the selected variables. Both of these two variable sets had theft, a property crime, in common. Even though the second variable differed, they both represented violent crimes, robbery and assault. Jolliffe (1986) discusses a number of criteria that can be used to evaluate the efficiency of particular subsets of variables in representing the total set of variables. One criterion that can be used is the total amount of variation the selected variables explain. The total amount of variation that a subset of variables explains is the sum of the variation they explain in each of the discarded variables in addition to the sum of the variances for the variables comprising the subset.

Each discarded variable is regressed on the retained variables and the corresponding squared multiple correlations are summed. If we add to that the variances of the retained variables, which, in this case, are each 1, then we have a measure of the total variation that is accounted for by the variable subset. This formula can be expressed as

$$n_r + \sum_{i=1}^{d} R_{i,r}^2$$

where n_r is the number of retained variables and $R_{i,r}^2$ is the squared multiple correlation of the ith discarded variable with the r retained variables. Assault and theft were selected as a two variable subset from our first approach. The total variance accounted for by these two variables is 2 + .675 + .588 + .530 + .668 + .332 or 4.793, where .675, .588, .530, .668, and .332 are the squared multiple correlations of murder, rape, robbery, burglary, and motor vehicle theft, respectively, with assault and theft.

The total amount of variation explained by the two largest principal components is 5.54 or 79.2% of the variation in the seven crime variables. The total amount of variation explained by our two variable subset (assault and theft) is 4.793 or 68.5% (100 × 4.793/7). The largest two principal components explain more of the total variation than any subset of two variables because the directions of the principal component coordinate axes are defined as those directions which maximize the total variation accounted for in the set of variables. No other set of coordinate axes accounts for as much variability. The coordinate axis of the two variables approximate the direction of the principal component axes but do not define exactly the same two-dimensional subspace. Nevertheless, the two variable subset compares favorably with the first two principal components with respect to the percent of variance accounted for, 68.5% for the variables versus 79.2% for the components.

If we want a subset of variables that will explain at least as much variation as the first two principal components, then we need a subset of variables larger than two. Since the correlations among the variables are high, increasing the subset from two to three should satisfy this requirement. A logical selection for the third variable of the subset is motor vehicle theft which has the highest loading on the third principal component. Regressing murder, rape, robbery, and burglary on assault, theft, and motor vehicle theft we find R^2s of .677, .613, .616, and .699, respectively. Thus, the total amount of variance explained by our three variable subset of assault, theft, and motor vehicle theft is 3 + .677 + .613 + .616 + .699 or 5.605. This is a little larger than the total variance of 5.54 accounted for by the first two components. So three variables explain a little more variation than the two largest principal components (80.1% versus 79.2%). The three variable subset, however, does not explain as much variation as the first three largest principal components. The first three components account for 87.4% of the variation as contrasted to 80.1% for our three variable subset.

Let us now examine the total variability accounted for by our two variable subset (robbery and theft) selected by our second approach, discarding variables associated with small principal components. The squared multiple correlations of murder, rape, assault, burglary, and motor vehicle theft with robbery and theft were .659, .459, .580, .612, and .445, respectively. The total variability explained by robbery and theft is, therefore, 2 + .659 + .459 + .580 + .612 + .445 = 4.755. In this case the second approach performed almost as well as the first approach (67.9% versus 68.5% of the variation explained). The second approach yields robbery, theft, and motor vehicle theft as a three variable subset. Two of these variables (theft and motor vehicle theft) are in common with the three variable subset selected by the first approach. The total variation in the seven variables explained by this three variable subset is 5.426 or 77.5% of the variation. This is a little less than the 80.1% explained by the three variable subset selected by the first approach.

The specific finding here that the first approach is preferable to the second does not mean that this holds in general. In addition, there could be other variable subsets of the same size that account for a larger percentage of the total variability. There are more complex approaches (see Jolliffe, 1986) based on these fundamental principles. The simple approaches discussed here (selected subsets of variables that had conceptual appeal in that they were highly correlated with the principal components), did a good job in representing the total variation in the variable set. Another possibility is to rotate the retained components before using the first approach to select the variable subset. Rotating the first two principal components, we find that robbery and theft had the highest loadings on rotated components one and two, respectively; the same two variable subset that was selected by the second approach of discarding variables.

We may also want to consider a compromise approach lying between selecting a single variable to represent each important principal component and computing the principal component scores which involves using information in all of the variables. The compromise is to represent each important principal component as an equally weighted composite of, say, two, three, or four variables whose loadings exceed some cutoff value such as .40 or .50. This is equivalent to giving a weight of 1 to variables important in defining the principal component and a weight of zero to the less important variables. Simple weighting schemes like this often produce approximate component scores that hold up better under cross-validation than the exact component scores. In addition, we just need a subset of the variables to calculate the "component" scores. This approach is particularly advantageous if the variables in the set are based upon unreliable measures since a composite of unreliable variables can be considerably more reliable than any single variable making up the composite.

8. PRINCIPAL COMPONENTS VERSUS FACTOR ANALYSIS

While both principal components and factor analysis have the common aim of reducing the dimensionality of a variable set, there are some important differences between the two techniques. The most important difference is that principal components analysis decomposes the total variance as we have repeatedly emphasized. In the case of standardized variables, it produces a decomposition of R. We saw earlier that R can be decomposed into the product of three matrices $A \Lambda A'$ where A is the matrix of the latent vectors R arrayed as columns, A' is its transpose (latent vectors arrayed as rows) and Λ is a diagonal matrix of the associated latent roots of R. Because Λ is a diagonal matrix, we saw that this could also be written as

$$\sum_{i=1}^{p} \lambda_i a_i a_i'.$$

We defined the principal component loadings, the correlations of the variables with the components, as $\lambda_i^{1/2} a_i = l_i$ so that in terms of l_i, R can be decomposed as

$$\sum_{i=1}^{p} l_i l_i'$$

or LL' where L is the principal component loading matrix with principal components as columns and L' is its transpose. We can approximate R to any degree desired by retaining k principal components and discarding the remaining p-k. In this way R can be approximated as

$$\underset{(p \times k)}{L} \quad \underset{(k \times p)}{L'}$$

Factor analysis, on the other hand, finds a decomposition of the reduced correlation matrix R-U where U is a diagonal matrix of the unique variances associated with the variables. Unique variances are that part of each variable's variance that has nothing in common with the remaining $p - 1$ variables. If we subtract the unique variances from 1, the elements in the principal diagonal of R, we have what are referred to as communalities in the principal diagonal of the reduced correlation matrix. The communality for each variable is the portion of the total variance that is shared with the remaining $p - 1$ variables, or stated another way, the variance that a particular variable has in common with the remaining $p - 1$ variables. The reduced correlation matrix with communalities in the principal diagonal instead of ones will be referred to as R_c. Factor analysis seeks a decomposition of R_c in terms of a $p \times k$ factor loading matrix L_f with the smallest k such that $R_c = L_f L_f'$. Usually k is much smaller than p. This contrasts with principal components analysis where L must be a $p \times p$ matrix in order for the principal components to fit R perfectly (i.e., for $R = LL'$). In factor analysis it is theoretically possible to find a $p \times k$ factor loading matrix L_f where k is much smaller than p that fits R_c perfectly. Communalities have to be estimated just like the factor loading matrix, L_f. An initial estimate, as we shall see, is the squared multiple correlation of each variable with the $p - 1$ remaining variables.

Since the principal components, y, equal $A'x$ and A' is a non-singular matrix whose inverse is A, $x = Ay$. Thus, the principal components can be expressed as linear functions of the variables or the variables can be expressed as linear functions of the principal components. This is not the case in factor analysis since factor analysis, as we shall see, concentrates on defining the variables as a linear combination of common factors and unique factors. Contrary to principal components analysis, the factor analysis model does not provide a unique transformation from variables to factors.

Principal components analysis is a procedure to decompose the correlation matrix without regard to an underlying model. Most importantly, it does not distinguish between common variance and unique variance as factor analysis does. Factor analysis, on the other hand, has an underlying model that rests on a number of assumptions. The key assumption is that the ith variable in the variable set, x_i, can be expressed as a linear combination of hypothetical unobservable common factors plus a factor unique to that variable. Note that the emphasis here is on explaining x_i as a linear function of unobservable common factors while the emphasis in principal component analysis is expressing the principal component as a linear function of the x_i. The model assumes that the standardized variable x_i can be expressed as

$$\sum_{j=1}^{k} l_{ij} f_j + u_i$$

where l_{ij} is the loading of the ith variable on the jth factor, f_j is the factor score for the jth factor, and u_i is the unique factor score for the ith variable.

The object of factor analysis is to estimate the loadings l_{ij} which together form the factor loading matrix L_f which has p rows corresponding to variables and k columns corresponding to factors where k is considerably smaller than p. In order to estimate L_f, a number of assumptions have to be made. These assumptions are as follows: the mean and variance of f_j equal zero and one, respectively for all j; the correlations among the common factors are zero; the correlations between the common factors and the unique factors are zero, and the correlations between the p unique factors are all zero.

The model and its assumptions can be expressed in matrix algebra as $x = Lf + u$ where x is a vector of p standardized variables, L is the $p \times k$ factor loading matrix, f is a vector of k factor scores, and u is a vector of the p unique factor scores. This equation has the form of a regression equation. If we knew f for each individual then we could estimate L by least squares. However, f is hypothetical so we must use our other assumptions previously discussed to estimate L. Expressed in matrix algebra, they are $E(f) = E(u) = O$; $E(ff') = I$; $E(uu')$ is a diagonal matrix U; and $E(uf') = O$, where E is the expectation operator which is analogous to the operation of computing averages and the averages of cross products for sample data. We can then use these assumptions to show that $R = LL' + U$.

The assumption that $E(ff') = I$, i.e., the factors are uncorrelated, can be relaxed to allow the factors to be correlated. In our subsequent discussion of rotation we will see that L, the factor loading matrix, is not unique. It can be linearly transformed, by a transformation matrix, to another matrix L_r of the same dimensions. Geometrically, this is a rotation of the factor coordinate axes in the same common factor space. We can keep the axes perpendicular to one another using a rigid rotation which will result in uncorrelated factors or we can use a nonrigid rotation where the factor axes are allowed to form oblique angles to one another resulting in correlated factors. Factor analysis with correlated factors is sometimes called oblique factor analysis. In oblique factor analysis we also have to estimate Θ, the matrix of factor intercorrelations, as well as L. For oblique factor analysis, it can be shown that R can be decomposed as $L\Theta L' + U$.

There are a number of ways to estimate U and hence the reduced correlation matrix R_c. Once we have an estimate of R_c, then we can use the principal components algorithm to find L. Principal components analysis is usually used in two ways to estimate the factor loading matrix for the factor analysis model. One method is called iterative principal components analysis. It begins with a principal component analysis of the standard correlation matrix. The eigenvalues are examined and used, along with other considerations, to determine the number of factors accounting for the correlations among the variables. Kaiser's criteria of retaining components with eigenvalues equal or greater than one is often used, but other considerations, as we discussed earlier, can also be used. There are also statistical goodness of fit tests that can be used to determine how well a given number of factors fits the correlation matrix. For more details on determining the number of factors the reader is referred to Kim and Mueller (1978a, 1978b) and Harman (1976).

The number of common factors is determined and an initial communality estimate for each variable is obtained by summing the square of the loadings for the retained components. That is, we compute the sum of squares of the principal component loadings on the retained components for each row (variable) of the loading matrix. Then, these initial communality estimates are substituted for the ones in the principal diagonal of the correlation matrix for an initial estimate of the reduced correlation matrix, R_c. Then a second principal components analysis is done on R_c. Revised communality estimates for each variable are generated from this second component analysis by summing the squared loading on the k largest components where k is the number of common factors determined from the first principal component analysis. These revised communality estimates are now placed in the principal diagonal and a second principal component analysis is conducted on our revised reduced correlation matrix. New communality estimates are generated, and the new reduced correlation matrix is subjected to a third principal component analysis. The procedure continues until the factor loading matrices converge. That is, it continues until all of the corresponding elements of the factor loading matrices for the nth and the $(n + 1)$th principal component analysis are sufficiently close to one another (e.g., a difference of less than .001). Most standard statistical packages have an option for estimating the common factor analysis model by iterated principal components analysis.

Another option available in most standard packages is to replace the 1's in the principal diagonal of the correlation matrix with squared multiple correlations. Each variable is regressed upon the remaining p – 1 variables, and the corresponding squared multiple correlation replaces the 1 in the appropriate position on the principal diagonal. Since the communality is defined as the amount of variance shared with the remaining variables, this seems like a reasonable procedure (Guttman, 1956). A principal component analysis is then conducted on the reduced correlation matrix for estimating the factor loading matrix. The analysis needs only to be done once, an advantage over the iterated principal components analysis procedure. Both procedures give similar results.

There are other factor analysis procedures besides principal components factor analysis. A commonly used alternative approach is maximum likelihood factor analysis (Lawley and Maxwell, 1971). Maximum likelihood factor analysis assumes that the p variables have a multivariate normal distribution whereas principal components factor analysis requires no distributional assumptions. The estimated matrices L, U, and possibly Θ contain the respective estimated parameters which are most likely to have generated the sample data. In maximum likelihood factor analysis we have to specify the number of factors to be extracted. We might also provide certain information about L or the other parameter matrices as discussed below. The initial maximum likelihood estimates can also be rotated. The initial maximum likelihood and principal factor analysis solution tend to be similar. For a brief discussion of maximum likelihood factor analysis as well as other factoring techniques see Kim and Mueller (1978a and 1978b).

If we do not have a particular underlying model of the data in mind, then principal components can be useful in exploring the structure of a data set (e.g., searching for multivariate outliers, and visually clustering observations). It can also be used as an adjunct to other multivariate analysis procedures (e.g., addressing the problem of multicollinearity in regression analysis). Of course, it can be used directly to construct linear composites in order to both simplify the description of a data set and to be used as independent and dependent variables in further analyses.

On the other hand, if the variables contain a substantial amount of measurement error, which is often the case in the behavioral and social sciences, and we can postulate an underlying factor model for the data, then factor analysis has a decided advantage over principal components analysis. The common factors are uncontaminated by measurement error because measurement error is part of the unique variance which is uncorrelated with the common variance. Since, in this case, the principal components will be linear composites of unreliable variables, the principal components will contain measurement error.

While factor analysis can also be exploratory in the sense that nothing need be postulated with respect to either the number of factors or the pattern of variable loadings on these factors, there has been a recent move toward confirmatory factor analysis. Confirmatory factor analysis involves testing specific hypotheses about the underlying factor analysis model with respect to both the number of factors and the pattern of loadings (but not the actual numerical estimates) on each factor. With these constraints, the factor analysis model can be estimated by maximum likelihood and its fit to the observed covariance or correlation matrix can be evaluated in terms of a Chi-square goodness of fit statistic (Long, 1983). Both principal components and factor analysis give similar results if the communalities of the variables are high and/or there are a large number of variables.

Example

Let us illustrate the principal components factor analysis procedure on the crime data using the correlation matrix from Table 3.1. The two largest eigenvalues are 4.710 and .837. This suggests, according to Kaiser, that one common factor would adequately account for the intercorrelations among the crime variables. However, other researchers, using other criteria besides the size of the latent root, might prefer a two factor solution. We will accept two factors, in part, so that we can compare the principal factor analysis solution to the principal components analysis solution previously obtained.

We will estimate communalities by squared multiple correlations. The squared multiple correlations for murder, rape, robbery, assault, burglary, theft, and motor vehicle theft were .831, .710, .800, .756, .727, .640, and .606, respectively. For example, the R^2 of .831 for murder was obtained from regressing murder on the remaining six variables and so on for the remaining six R^2's. These R^2's are fairly high indicating that all seven variables share a high proportion of common variance. Murder has the highest communality, .831, and motor vehicle theft the lowest, .606. Using the R^2's as communality estimates to replace the ones on the principal diagonal of the correlation matrix from Table 3.1, we obtain the reduced correlation matrix presented in Table 8.1.

The principal components analysis of the reduced correlation matrix resulted in the factor loading matrix shown in Table 8.2. The latent roots or, equivalently, the amount of variance explained is also shown. Comparing Tables 3.3 and 8.2, there are a number of differences to be noted between the principal components analysis (Table 3.3) and the factor analysis (Table 8.2) results. First of all, the factors, individually and jointly, explain less of the total variance in the seven crime variables than the principal components.

TABLE 8.1
Reduced Correlation Matrix for Crime Variables

		1	2	3	4	5	6	7
1	MURDER	0.831						
2	RAPE	0.651	0.710					
3	ROBBERY	0.810	0.501	0.800				
4	ASSAULT	0.821	0.707	0.722	0.756			
5	BURGLARY	0.593	0.740	0.552	0.686	0.727		
6	THEFT	0.434	0.641	0.480	0.557	0.751	0.640	
7	MV THEFT	0.490	0.565	0.658	0.563	0.584	0.414	0.606

TABLE 8.2
Factor Loading Matrix for Crime Variables

	Factor	
Variable	1	2
MURDER	0.841	0.340
RAPE	0.810	−0.228
ROBBERY	0.814	0.368
ASSAULT	0.868	0.113
BURGLARY	0.828	−0.313
THEFT	0.702	−0.392
MV THEFT	0.696	0.051
latent root	4.443	.571
percent total variance explained	63.5%	8.2%
percent cumulative variance	63.5%	71.7%

The first principal component (Table 3.3) accounts for 67.3% of the total variance, whereas the first common factor (Table 8.2) accounts for 63.5% of the total variance. Similarly, the second principal component (Table 3.3) accounts for 12% of the total variance while the second common factor (Table 8.2) only accounts for 8.2% of the total variance. Together the first two principal components account for 79.2% of the total variance while the two common factors account for 71.7%.

It should be remembered that factor analysis is concerned with explaining common variance and not total variance. Thus, although the two common factors only account for 72% of the total variance, they, by definition, account for almost all of the common variance. They will not, in general, account for 100% of the common variance in an empirical data set because of sampling fluctuations. If a factor analysis model accounts for 100% of the common variance, then the off diagonal elements in the correlation matrix (i.e., the correlations) can be exactly reconstructed from the factor loading matrix (i.e., $R-U=LL'$). This will rarely be the case. However, the deviations of the correlations from the correlations predicted by the factor model (i.e., residuals) should be small enough to be explained as sampling fluctuations if we are to conclude that the factor analysis model fits the data. As mentioned previously, maximum likelihood factor analysis allows us to statistically test the goodness of fit of a particular factor analysis model to a sample correlation or covariance matrix.

Since the total variance explained by a component or factor is equal to the sum of squares of the loadings for the corresponding column, the principal component loadings will be higher, in general, than the factor loadings. While the principal component loadings are not much larger, in general, there are some noticeable differences. For example, theft has a loading of −.540 on the second principal component but only has a loading of −.392 on the second common factor. While there are differences in the two solutions, overall the differences are not great. This is because the communalities were large, in general, and did not differ substantially from one another. In cases where the communalities approach 1, then principal components analysis can be used as an approximation to factor analysis. However, when the communalities are small or vary considerably, then the two solutions will be quite different. In the case of generally small and varying communalities, the principal component loadings will be considerably larger than the factor loading and, in addition, the ranking of the size of principal component loadings for a particular component may be quite different from the rankings of the factor loadings on the corresponding factor (i.e., the principal component loadings will not be proportional to the corresponding factor loadings).

As the number of variables increases, the ratio of off-diagonal to diagonal elements becomes large and, consequently the size of the communalities, the diagonal elements, will have little effect on the solution. Factor analysis and principal components analysis will yield similar results. That is, the pattern of the two loading matrices will be the same. Each column of one loading matrix will be proportional to the corresponding column of the other. However, the principal component loadings will be larger than the factor loadings because the former is attempting to account for the total variation and the latter for the smaller amount of common variation.

Factor Rotation

We previously discussed the fact that the investigator can rotate the retained principal components if he prefers. This is sometimes done if the unrotated components are difficult to interpret. It also illustrates the fact that there is not a unique orthogonal decomposition of the correlation or covariance matrix. However, the principal components analysis decomposition is unique in that each succeeding component has maximal variance. Equivalently, the sum of the squared loading for each component is maximized. This desirable mathematical property, especially if the components are readily interpretable, precludes the need for rotation.

In factor analysis, the initial factor solution, which also has optimal properties with respect to successive maximization of explained common variance, is considered arbitrary and there is the need to transform the original solution to a rotated solution that has desirable properties with respect to the simplicity and interpretability of the rotated factor loading matrix. Rotations, like principal components analysis, optimize a particular mathematical criterion that results in a rotated factor loading matrix with certain desirable properties sometimes called simple structure (Thurstone, 1947).

Rotation brings about simple structure by either simplifying the rows (variables) or columns (factors) of the rotated factor loading matrix. Varimax rotation, as discussed earlier, simplifies the columns of the factor loading matrix by maximizing the variance of the squared loadings. It results in a unique rotated factor loading matrix. That is, there is only a single unique factor loading matrix that maximizes the varimax criterion. Other definitions of simple structure have been defined analytically for computer implementation (Harman, 1976). Each definition leads to a different unique factor loading matrix, although there may be similarities among them. Varimax, by far, is the most commonly used rotation algorithm. The point is that while L is not unique, it is unique with respect to a particular analytical criterion. Rotations result in variables loading primarily on one factor and having either high or low loadings on a factor and, hence, in many instances, bring about a simplification of the initial solution where variables might have moderate loadings across a number of factors. The simplicity of the rotated factor loading matrix makes for ease of interpretation.

The idea is to find an initial arbitrary solution for the factor loading matrix L such that $LL' = R_c$. Then the unique orthogonal transformation matrix T is found that maximizes the varimax criterion. The

TABLE 8.3
Rotated Factor Loading Matrix for Crime Variables

Variables	Factors 1	2
MURDER	0.846	0.328
RAPE	0.434	0.722
ROBBERY	0.845	0.290
ASSAULT	0.710	0.512
BURGLARY	0.389	0.795
THEFT	0.242	0.767
MV THEFT	0.542	0.439
Total Variance explained	2.625	2.389

unique rotated factor loading matrix L_R is then $\underset{(p \times k)}{L} \ \underset{(k \times k)}{T}$ where k is the number of factors. LT is a solution since $R_c = LT(LT)' = LL'$ since $LT(LT)' = LTT'L'$ and $TT' = I$. The varimax solution is presented in Table 8.3.

Factor 1 has high loadings for violent crimes and relatively low loadings for property crimes. Conversely, the property crimes, burglary and theft, have the highest loadings on Factor 2. However, rape and assault, violent crimes, also have appreciable loadings on this factor so that while we might label this factor, property crimes, it is not as structurally simple as our first factor. Note that whereas Factor 1 explained most of the variance in the unrotated solution, the rotated solution distributes the total variance almost equally between the two rotated factors (Table 8.3). Under circumstances such as this when an orthogonal rotation such as varimax does not result in a clear cut simple structure, some researchers prefer to relax the restriction that the common factors be orthogonal or uncorrelated in order to improve the simple structure of the factor loadings and, hence, the interpretability of the factors. They argue that there is no conceptual reason why factors have to be inherently uncorrelated. Rotations that simplify the structure of the unrotated factor loading matrix but allow for correlated factors are called oblique rotations. There is a tradeoff when using oblique rotations. We are improving the simple structure of the factor loadings at the cost of having to consider, in the interpretation, the correlations among factors. For more details on oblique rotation the reader is referred to Kim and Mueller (1978a, 1978b) or Harman (1976).

9. USES OF PRINCIPAL COMPONENTS IN REGRESSION ANALYSIS

Principal components analysis can be used in regression analysis in a number of ways. If the independent variables are highly correlated, then they can be transformed to principal components and the principal components can be used as the independent variables. If we do not want to transform the independent variables, then principal components can be used indirectly to improve the precision of the regression parameter estimates associated with the independent variables. Principal components analysis can also be used as a diagnostic tool to detect multicollinearities among the independent variables. Multicollinearity means that one or more independent variables are essentially linear combinations of other independent variables. Principal components analysis can also be used to select a subset of independent variables from a larger set.

Regression on Principal Components

If we have a large set of correlated independent variables, then the possibility of transforming the independent variables to principal components should be considered. If the principal components are interpretable, and there are near dependencies (i.e., multicollinearities) among the original independent variables, then there are considerable advantages to be gained. (If the principal components are uninterpretable, then we could rotate the retained components prior to the regression analysis.) If multicollinearity is a problem, then a number of the estimated regression parameters will have large standard errors. The estimated regression parameters associated with the principal components have variances that are proportional to the inverse of the variances of the principal components themselves. Let P be the $n \times p$ matrix of principal component scores, then $P'P$ is the $p \times p$ matrix of the sum of squares and cross products of the principal component scores. Since the principal components are uncorrelated, this will be a diagonal matrix with the sum of squares for the various components as the diagonal elements. The sum of cross products is zero by definition. The sum of squares for the ith principal component is $n\lambda_i$ since the variance of the ith principal component is the ith latent root, λ_i, of R and since we can convert a variance into a sum of squares by multiplying it by its sample size, n. The matrix expression for the variance-covariance of the estimated regression parameters is $\sigma^2(X'X)^{-1}$. For principal components, the matrix corresponding to $(X'X)^{-1}$ is $(P'P)^{-1}$.

The latter matrix is a diagonal matrix with $1/n\lambda_i$ as the p diagonal elements. Thus, the variance of the estimated regression parameter associated with the ith principal component is proportional to $1/n\lambda_i$.

We can easily see from this formula that the estimated regression parameters associated with the large principal components have small standard errors and, conversely, the estimated regression parameters associated with small principal components have large standard errors. If the larger principal components are the most important in predicting a particular dependent variable, then their associated regression parameters will be precisely estimated. However, as Jolliffe (1986) warns, this is not always the case. He presents examples where very small components ($\lambda \le .10$) are better predictors than much larger components ($\lambda \ge 1$). Another advantage of using principal components as independent variables is that since they are uncorrelated, each regression coefficient can be estimated independently of the other components. That is, the regression coefficient for a particular component remains constant regardless of which other components are either added to or discarded from the model. For correlated independent variables, the regression parameter for a particular variable depends upon which other independent variables are included in the model. The statistical independence of principal components makes it easy to choose the optimal set of predictors of any size. We select those principal components in the order of their correlation with the dependent variable. For example, the best set of size three would contain those principal components with the three highest correlations with the dependent variable.

Principal Components Regression

There may be instances where the variables themselves are of theoretical interest. In this situation, a principal components transformation would be of no direct use. However, if a multicollinearity problem exists, then principal components analysis can be used indirectly to improve the precision of the regression parameter estimates for the original variables. A multicollinearity problem exists if one or more of the latent roots of the correlation (covariance) matrix are very small (e.g., .001). As explained earlier, this means that a linear combination of the independent variables using the elements of the associated latent vector is essentially zero. Consequently, one variable can be nearly expressed as a linear combination of the other variables. This results in large standard errors for the variables involved in these near dependencies. For a further discussion of multicollinearity see Lewis-Beck (1980). We can use the spectral decomposition theorem to substantially reduce the standard errors of the variables associated with multicollinearities. We saw earlier that the correlation matrix R could be decomposed with respect to its latent roots and latent vectors. That is,

$$R = \sum_{i=1}^{p} \lambda_i a_i a_i'.$$

It can be shown that the inverse of the correlation matrix R^{-1} can also be decomposed as

$$\sum_{i=1}^{p} \frac{1}{\lambda_i} a_i a_i'.$$

The latent vector associated with the largest latent root of R is associated with the smallest latent root of R^{-1}, the latent vector associated with the second largest latent root of R is associated with the second smallest latent root of R^{-1} and so on. Since the inverse of $Z'Z$, where Z is an $n \times p$ matrix of standardized variables, is used to compute the variances and covariances of the regression parameter estimates, we need to decompose $(Z'Z)^{-1}$ rather than R^{-1}. Since $Z'Z = nR$, $(Z'Z)^{-1} = (nR)^{-1} = 1/n\ R^{-1}$. The latent vectors of $1/n\ R^{-1}$ are identical to those of R^{-1} and the associated latent roots of $1/n\ R^{-1}$ are proportional to those of R^{-1} where the constant of proportionality is $1/n$ (i.e., the ith latent root of $(Z'Z)^{-1}$ is $1/n\lambda_i$). Thus, $(Z'Z)^{-1}$ can be spectrally decomposed as

$$\sum_{i=1}^{p} \frac{1}{n\lambda_i} a_i a_i'.$$

Since the variance-covariance matrix of the parameter estimates is $\sigma^2(Z'Z)^{-1}$ where σ^2 is the error variance for the regression model, the decomposition of $\sigma^2(Z'Z)^{-1}$ is

$$\sigma^2 \sum_{i=1}^{p} \frac{1}{n\lambda_i} a_i a_i'.$$

From this decomposition we can see that the small principal components make large contributions to the variance-covariance matrix of the regression parameter estimates. They reduce the precision of our regression parameter estimates. In particular, very small principal components reduce the precision of those regression parameter estimates that correspond to large elements in the associated latent vector.

We are usually most interested in the diagonal elements of $\sigma^2(\mathbf{Z}'\mathbf{Z})^{-1}$ since they correspond to the variances (or squared standard errors) of the estimated regression parameters. Using this decomposition, we can express the variance of the kth regression parameter as

$$\sigma^2 \sum_{i=1}^{p} \frac{1}{n\lambda_i} a_{ik}^2$$

where a_{ik} is the kth element of the latent vector associated with the ith principal component. We can clearly see that if λ_i is very small and the associated a_{ik} is very large, then the corresponding principal component makes a large contribution to the standard error of the kth regression parameter. If the associated component does not predict the dependent variable, then it seems reasonable to subtract out its substantial contribution to the variance of kth regression parameter. For example, if the latent root associated with the smallest principal component was very small, then we would drop the last term in the decomposition and use

$$\sigma^2 \sum_{i=1}^{p-1} \frac{1}{n\lambda_i} a_i a_i'$$

as our estimator of the variance-covariance matrix of the regression parameter estimates. If there were two small principal components, then our estimator of the parameter variance-covariance matrix would be

$$\sigma^2 \sum_{i=1}^{p-2} \frac{1}{n\lambda_i} a_i a_i'.$$

If we drop one or more components, then the variance of certain parameter estimates may be substantially reduced. However, some bias may now be introduced into our estimate of the regression parameters, since, in order to be consistent, we must use

$$\sum_{i=1}^{p-k} \frac{1}{n\lambda_i} a_i a_i' \mathbf{Z}' y'$$

where k is the number of "small" components that have been dropped as our estimator of β, the vector of regression parameters, rather than $(Z'Z)^{-1} Z'y$. If the discarded components are uncorrelated with the dependent variable, then no bias in the regression parameter estimates will result. However, even if they are correlated with the dependent variable, the reduction in the variance of the estimate may more than offset the bias that is introduced.

Example

In order to illustrate the concepts introduced above and to introduce some new concepts, we shall examine a correlation matrix presented in Levine (1977) which in turn was based on data drawn from Taylor and Hudson (1970). The data were originally collected to see if the distribution of expenditures for defense, education, and health could be explained on the basis of six sociodemographic and political characteristics of 58 countries which had data on all characteristics. The six independent variables were population size (POP), population density (DENS), literary rate (LIT), energy consumption per capita (ENERGY), gross national product per capita (GNP/POP), and electoral irregularity score (ELECT). Although there are three dependent variables, we will, for the moment, only consider educational expenditures as a percent of the gross national product (EDUC). The intercorrelations among the seven variables are presented in Table 9.1.

Table 9.1 indicates that all six independent variables have a positive correlation with the dependent variable, educational expenditures (EDUC). LIT, ENERGY, and GNP/POP have high correlations of .610, .640, and .640, respectively, with EDUC. Consequently, regressing EDUC on the six independent variables, should yield a high multiple correlation. Looking at the correlations among the six independent variables we see some high correlations. In particular, ENERGY and GNP/POP have a correlation of .93. We suspect that we might have a multicollinearity problem. Let us look at the results of the regression analysis presented in Table 9.2. The multiple correlation of .689 based on six independent variables is not appreciably higher than the largest single correlation of .64 between either ENERGY or GNP/POP and EDUC. This indicates that the remaining five independent variables do not add much unique variance that is systematically related to EDUC. Even so, the F ratio indicates that the multiple correlation is highly significant (p < .0005). While the estimated regression parameters associated with LIT, ENERGY, and GNP/POP are large as we would have expected from their high corre-

TABLE 9.1

Correlations Among National Socioeconomic and Political Variables

		1	2	3	4	5	6	7
1	POP	1.000						
2	DENS	0.050	1.000					
3	LIT	0.200	0.450	1.000				
4	ENERGY	0.350	0.230	0.710	1.000			
5	GNP/POP	0.330	0.190	0.740	0.930	1.000		
6	ELECT	0.040	0.320	0.360	0.190	0.360	1.000	
7	EDUC	0.300	0.230	0.610	0.640	0.640	0.170	1.000

TABLE 9.2

Multiple Regression of EDUC on Six Independent Variables

Variable	Regression Parameter Estimate	Standard Error	t ratio	Probability
POP	.101	.109	.925	.360
DENS	.028	.125	.224	.824
LIT	.300	.172	1.747	.087
ENERGY	.161	.322	.501	.619
GNP/POP	.257	.348	.737	.465
ELECT	−.074	.130	−.569	.572

multiple correlation = .689, F-ratio = 7.663 with 6 and 51 degrees of freedom (p < .0005).

lations with EDUC, none of them are significant at the .05 level. In fact, only LIT even approaches significance. The problem is that while some of the estimated regression parameters are large, so are their standard errors. These regression results are typical of data sets with multicollinearity problems. The overall multiple correlation is highly significant, but all of the estimated regression parameters are insignificant. While various indices of multicollinearity have been proposed in the literature (Dillon and Goldstein, 1984), a rule of thumb is to suspect multicollinearity if the R^2 is highly significant, many of the independent variables have highly significant correlations with the dependent variables, and all, or most, of the multiple regression parameters do not approach statistical significance. If this rule of thumb points towards multicollinearity, then one or more extremely small latent roots of $X'X$ will provide further support.

Let us see how we can apply principal components analysis to address this multicollinearity problem. A principal components analysis of the correlation matrix of the six independent variables is presented in Table 9.3.

The principal components show the typical pattern of the first component reflecting overall size and the remaining components reflecting various contrasts. Table 9.4 presents the correlation of each principal component with the dependent variable, EDUC, and the regression parameter associated with each principal component along with its associated standard error and t ratio.

Except for the standard error of the last coefficient, the standard errors for the principal component regression coefficients are all smaller than the standard errors of the coefficients associated with the original variables. The size of the standard errors are inversely related to the size of the principal components. The largest component has the smallest standard error and the smallest component has the largest standard error. Whereas none of the original estimated regression parameters were statistically significant, the estimated regression parameter associated with the largest principal component was highly significant. While Jolliffe's criteria ($\lambda \geq .70$) would tell us to retain the first four components, for the purpose of predicting .EDUC we need only retain the first component.

The six principal components together explain exactly the same amount of variance in EDUC as the six original variables. For our transformed parameters, the independence property of principal components allows us to easily select the best subsets with respect to predicting the dependent variable. The best single component subset is the component with the highest correlation with the dependent variable; the best two component subset is comprised of the two components with the highest correlations with the dependent variable, and so on.

If the principal components are difficult to interpret, then the k components with significant correlations with the dependent variable could be rotated to simple structure using varimax or some other rotational procedure. The dependent variable could then be regressed on the rotated components.

Let us suppose that we are not interested in using the principal components as independent variables, but, for conceptual reasons, are interested in the regression parameters associated with the original six independent variables. We saw that we can increase the precision of

222

TABLE 9.3
Latent Vectors and Roots of the Correlation Matrix of Socioeconomic
and Political Variables (N=58)

Variable	Latent Vector					
	1	2	3	4	5	6
POP	.235	−.510	.810	.128	−.108	.005
DENS	.268	.584	.418	−.565	.291	.097
LIT	.503	.113	−.154	−.192	−.817	−.065
ENERGY	.514	−.266	−.242	−.113	.403	−.660
GNP/POP	.529	−.193	−.262	.115	.263	.729
ELECT	.277	.527	.136	.775	.047	−.152
Latent Root	3.036	1.165	.783	.710	.259	.047
Cumulative percent variance explained	50.61	70.02	83.07	94.91	99.21	100

TABLE 9.4
Results from Regressing EDUC on the Six Principal Components

Principal Component	Correlation with EDUC	Regression Coefficient	Standard Error	t ratio
1	.662	.380	.054	7.04 (p < .0001)
2	−.143	−.132	.088	1.50
3	−.061	−.069	.107	.64
4	−.090	−.107	.112	.96
5	−.059	−.116	.118	.98
6	.012	.055	.440	.13

those regression parameter estimates that are involved in near dependencies by deleting the very small principal components that reflect these dependencies. In the present example, there is only one very small latent root, the last root whose value is .047. The latent vector contains two large elements, −.660 for ENERGY and .729 for GNP/POP. The remaining elements are small so that the near dependency can be written as −.660 ENERGY + .729 GNP/POP = 0, or ENERGY = 1.105 GNP/POP. We already noticed the correlation of .93 between ENERGY and GNP/POP so this should not surprise us. Since the elements −.660 and .729 are large and λ = .047 is small our spectral decomposition of $(Z'Z)^{-1}$ tells us that if we drop this component from the regression equation, the standard errors associated with the ENERGY and GNP/POP regression parameters should be reduced considerably. Besides, we have seen that the smallest component has no value in predicting EDUC. Let us use the decomposition theorem to see how much the standard errors are reduced by discarding the last component and then see how much our parameter estimates have changed because of this deletion.

The contribution of the last component to the variance of the estimated regression coefficient ENERGY is

$$\frac{\hat{\sigma}^2}{n\lambda_6} a_{4,6}^2$$

where $\hat{\sigma}^2$ is the error variance estimate from the regression model. Since we are using standardized variables, $\hat{\sigma}^2$ is estimated as $1 - R^2$ or $1-(.689)^2 = .525$. Substituting the appropriate values in our equation for the contribution of the last component, we have

$$\frac{.525(-.660)^2}{58(.047)} = .084.$$

The regression estimate of the variance associated with this parameter (Table 9.2) was $(.322)^2 = .104$. Subtracting out the contribution of the last component to the variance we have $.104 - .084 = .02$. This is the revised principal components estimate of the variance of the estimated ENERGY regression parameter. We have reduced the variance of our estimate by approximately 80%. Taking the square root of $.02$, our new standard error becomes $.14$. This is considerably smaller than the conventional least squares estimate of $.32$ presented in Table 9.2. Proceeding similarly we find that the contribution of the last principal component to the variance of the estimated regression coefficient for GNP/POP is

$$\frac{\hat{\sigma}^2}{n\lambda_6} a_{5,6}^2 = \frac{.525(.729)^2}{58(.047)} = .102.$$

Subtracting this from the variance of the estimated regression coefficient for GNP/POP, we find $(.348)^2 - .102 = .019$. So our revised standard error becomes $\sqrt{.019} = .138$. We have reduced our standard error from $.348$ to $.138$, the same magnitude of reduction as in the case of ENERGY.

We must also revise our estimates of the regression parameters associated with ENERGY and GNP/POP by subtracting out the contribution of the last principal component to the estimator of β, the estimated vector of regression coefficients. From the previous section, we find that this contribution is

$$\frac{1}{n\lambda_p} a_p a_p' \, Z \, y'.$$

Since

$$Z y' = n r_{x,y}$$

where $r_{x,y}$ is the vector of correlations of the independent variables with y, the dependent variable, we can express the contribution of the last component to the regression parameter estimates as

$$\frac{1}{n\lambda_p} a_p a_p' \, Z \, y' = \frac{1}{n\lambda_p} a_p a_p' \, n r_{x,y} = \frac{1}{\lambda_p} a_p a_p' \, r_{x,y}$$

for standardized variables. Substituting into this formula, we have

$$\frac{1}{.047} \begin{bmatrix} .005 \\ .097 \\ -.065 \\ -.660 \\ .729 \\ -.152 \end{bmatrix} [.005 \ .097 \ -.065 \ -.660 \ .729 \ -.152] \begin{bmatrix} .30 \\ .23 \\ .61 \\ .64 \\ .30 \\ .17 \end{bmatrix} = \begin{bmatrix} .01 \\ .01 \\ .02 \\ -.03 \\ .04 \\ -.01 \end{bmatrix}$$

We can see that the contribution of the last principal component to the values of the estimated regression coefficients is small. Subtracting this vector from the original vector of estimated regression parameters leads to a revised estimator that does not differ appreciably from the original estimator.

Sometimes a very small principal component can have a substantial correlation with the dependent variable (Jolliffe, 1986). Therefore, before we discard one or more very small components we should make sure that their correlation(s) with the dependent variable are small and insignificant. Otherwise, we shall be discarding information that is useful in predicting the dependent variable. Discarding predictive components with very small variances will still reduce the standard errors of the regression coefficients associated with those variables with large weights in the latent vector (i.e., those variables involved in the multicollinearities), but, at the same time, considerable bias will be introduced in our principal components estimators of the regression coefficients associated with the original variables. The bias introduced may more than offset the gains in reducing their standard errors.

10. USING PRINCIPAL COMPONENTS TO DETECT OUTLYING AND INFLUENTIAL OBSERVATIONS

A major advantage of principal components analysis is that if the first two principal components account for a substantial portion of the total variation, then we can approximate the distribution of the observations in the variable space by plotting the principal component scores. This two-dimensional representation of the p-dimensional observations can be used in a number of ways. The plot can be examined for outlying observations, for influential observations, or it can be used to see if the observations can be visually clustered. Outlying observations are observations that lie at a considerable distance from the bulk of the observations or do not conform to the general pattern the observations exhibit. Outlying observations are called influential observations if their deletion from a particular analysis leads to different results (e.g., different parameter estimates in a regression equation or different latent roots and associated latent vectors in a principal components analysis). Outliers, depending on the analysis, do not have to be influential. The use of principal components plots in cluster analysis will be discussed in the next chapter. We presented a plot of the scores for the first two principal components for our state level crime data in Figure 3.7.

Recall that the first two principal components accounted for over 79% of the variation in the seven state level crime variables. So this plot is a good approximation of the distribution of the observations in the original seven-dimensional space. There is nothing unusual about the swarm of points except that Washington, DC, is off by itself in the upper right corner of the plot. It has extreme standardized scores on both principal components. Since all seven crime variables had high loadings or weights on the first component, it might be expected that Washington, DC, had extreme values on one or more of the crime variables. The seven crime scores for the District of Columbia are presented in Table 10.1 along with the means, standard deviations, and other statistics for the total sample of 51 states.

Table 10.1 indicates that Washington, DC, had extremely high values for all seven crime variables. For murder, robbery, assault, and theft it had the maximum sample value. The District of Columbia would have been judged an outlier by looking at its values on the original variables. However, some outliers are picked up by principal component plots that would not be identified by examining their scores one variable at a time. We usually try to find a reason for an observation being an outlier before we decide to delete it from an

TABLE 10.1
Crime Variable Scores for DC and Overall Sample Statistics

Crime	D.C.	Mean	Standard Deviation	Minimum Sample Value	Maximum Sample Value
murder	28.6	6.63	4.56	1.0	28.6
rape	63.7	33.60	15.63	12.9	91.6
robbery	1014.0	147.06	159.17	8.0	1014.0
assault	693.0	253.24	132.25	32.0	693.0
burglary	1767.0	1140.69	374.63	399.0	1978.0
theft	4521.0	2755.39	693.89	1347.0	4521.0
motor vehicle theft	711.0	343.43	194.37	109.0	866.0

analysis. In some cases, the outlying observation could be due to data coding errors and measurement errors. In other cases, it could be due to the special circumstances in which the observation was measured. When we look at the table in the U.S. Statistical Abstracts from which this data was taken, we find a footnote attached to Washington, DC. The footnote indicates the crime rates for the city include offenses reported by the U.S. Park police and Zoological police. Washington, DC, may be somewhat different from other states with respect to the way in which crime statistics are aggregated. Nevertheless, it is quite different from the remaining states and consideration should be given to deleting it from the data set and redoing the principal components analysis to see if the Washington, DC, observation had an influential effect on the results of the analysis.

The latent roots for the first three principal components in the original principal components analysis were 4.71, .837, and .568. With Washington, DC, deleted, the corresponding latent roots were 4.451, .935, and .717. Right away we see that we would have retained a third component in the reduced data set by Jolliffe's criterion. In this sense, it is certainly an influential observation since it changes our representation of the observations from two- to three-dimensions. It reduced the variance of the first component by 5% (i.e., (4.71 − 4.51)/4.71) and increased the variance of the second and third components by 12% (i.e., (.935 − .837)/.837) and 22% (i.e., (.717 − .568)/.568), respectively.

There are also differences between the two analyses in the corresponding elements of the latent vectors, but the interpretation of the first three components in either case is essentially the same. Outliers on the first few PCs are those that typically inflate correlations. For example, Washington, DC, was extremely high on all variables that inflated the correlations among the seven crime variables. When it was removed, the variance of the first component, which reflects the overall size of the correlations, was reduced by 5%. This is a substantial reduction when we realize that only a single observation was removed.

Examining plots of the smallest components is also a worthwhile undertaking. Very small components reflect the correlational structure of the observations since the latent vector associated with a small component indicate, as discussed earlier, how one variable is linearly related to the remaining $p - 1$ variables. An outlier on a small component is an observation that does not fit the correlational structure represented by that component. The direction of the last principal component is orthogonal to the $p - 1$ dimensional subspace defined by the first $p - 1$ principal components. Thus, the first $p - 1$ components are defined by minimizing the sum of squares of the observations in the direction perpendicular to the space defined by the first $p - 1$ principal components. This is the direction of the smallest principal component. Consequently, outliers on the last component are those observations that could influence the directions of the first $p - 1$ components in the space of the p variables.

The scores on the last two principal components were plotted, but not shown here. Texas was identified as a clear outlier in the upper left hand corner of the plot. It appeared to deviate from the correlational structure in the observations represented by the last two components. Like Washington, DC, we can determine how much influence Texas has on our principal components analysis by deleting Texas and redoing the components analysis. A comparison between the principal components results, with and without Texas, showed virtually no differences with respect to both the sizes of the latent roots and the sizes of the corresponding elements in all of the latent vectors. Texas is clearly an outlier, but it is not an influential observation, whereas Washington, DC, was both an outlier and an influential observation since it changed the correlational structure of the crime variables as reflected in the results of the principal components analysis.

Thus, Washington, DC, might also have an influence on the results of a subsequent regression analysis in which the seven crime variables would play the role of independent variables. Therefore, principal components analysis can be used to identify observations that might also be influential observations in other analyses besides principal components analysis.

11. USE OF PRINCIPAL COMPONENTS IN CLUSTER ANALYSIS

If the first two or three principal components account for a substantial proportion of the total variation, as in the state level crime data, then we can also use the plots to visually identify clusters. A cluster is a group of observations that are "closer" to each other than they are to observations in another cluster or group. The plot of the scores on the first two principal components for the crime data does not reveal a clear pattern of clusters. If asked to define three clusters, however, we might come up with the cluster definitions presented in Figure 11.1. They seem to be natural clusters and not arbitrarily defined by a linear partition of the space of the first two principal components. Note that two observations were not included in any of the three clusters. From our definition of the structure of the data in terms of three clusters, we have defined another outlier, New York, in addition to Washington, DC. If asked to define four clusters, we might divide the large cluster into two subclusters. The possibilities are endless unless there are homogeneous clumps of observations with large distances between them.

There are a large number of clustering algorithms that are used to cluster data. For a good discussion of clustering see Aldenderfer and Blashfield (1984). There is no advantage in transforming the original observations to principal component scores prior to the clustering since the same information is contained in the original and the transformed data. That is, for any distance function, the distances among observations computed from principal component scores are equal to the corresponding distances computed from the original variable scores using an equivalent but different distance function.

The only advantage of employing principal components in cluster analysis is to be able to plot the component scores and visually search for clusters of observations as we have done above. Principal components can also be used to verify the clusters determined on the basis of another clustering algorithm. We can see if the previously defined clusters are homogeneous, distinct, and aesthetically appealing to the eye. Clustering algorithms will define clusters even if none exist, i.e., if the observations are evenly spread throughout the variable space. In

FACTOR (1)

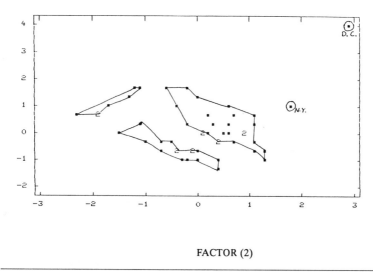

FACTOR (2)

Figure 11.1: Three Clusters of States Defined by Principal Components of Crime Data

this case, the clustering algorithm merely defines an arbitrary partition of the observations into clusters.

Different algorithms lead to both different numbers of clusters and cluster membership with respect to the observations. In fact, the same algorithm when repeated on the same data can sometimes result in a different solution if the rows of the matrix representing the similarity among observations are reordered. For these reasons, a plot of the data on the first two principal components can be informative if they account for a large portion of the total variance. If the data are to be arbitrarily clustered, then visual clustering in the space of the first two principal components is just as good as any other clustering procedure. If the first two principal components do not account for a substantial amount of variation, then it is useful to supplement the plot with information from the third principal component. This can be done in numerous ways. For example, for each plotted point we could represent the score on the third principal component by a minus (–) or plus (+) with the minus sign indicating a high negative score on the third component, the plus sign indicating a high positive score, and a blank (no symbol on the diagram) indicating a score in the middle of the distribution of the third component.

12. USE OF PRINCIPAL COMPONENTS ANALYSIS IN CONJUNCTION WITH OTHER MULTIVARIATE ANALYSIS PROCEDURES

In both linear discriminant function analysis and canonical correlational analysis there is an advantage in transforming the original variables to principal components before undertaking either of these analyses. This is particularly true if the variables are highly correlated and the resulting principal components (or rotated components) have a conceptually appealing interpretation.

Use of Principal Components in Discriminant Analysis

Linear discriminant function analysis is a maximization problem like principal components. It even involves solving for the latent roots and associated latent vectors of a particular matrix. The object of discriminant analysis is to determine one or more linear functions of a set of variables, measured on a number of groups, that maximize the between group variation relative to within group variation on the derived linear composite. In matrix terminology discriminant analysis involves finding a vector of variable weights, a, such that $a'Ba$ is maximized relative to $a'Wa$ where B is the between group sum of squares and cross products matrix and W is the common within group sum of squares and cross products matrix. The solution to this problem involves finding the latent roots and associated latent vectors of the matrix $W^{-1}B$. The number of latent roots (discriminant functions) is equal to the number of groups minus one or the number of variables, whichever is less.

The elements of the latent vector, a_1, associated with the largest latent root, λ_1, are the variable weights associated with the linear discriminant function that maximizes the between to within group variation. The largest latent root, λ_1, is the ratio of the between to within group variation for that linear function. If there are at least three groups or two variables, then there is a second largest latent root, λ_2, and associated vector, a_2 which maximizes the between to within group variation on $a_2'x$ and is uncorrelated with the first discriminant function. The latent root, λ_2, measures the between to within group variation on this second linear discriminant function. Since it is smaller than λ_1, the second orthogonal linear discriminant function has less power to discriminate among groups than the discriminant function associated with the largest root. We continue this process of extracting successively smaller latent roots and associated latent vectors, as in principal components analysis, until all of the between group relative to within group variation is totally accounted for. This occurs, as mentioned above, when we have extracted k linear discriminant functions where k is the lesser of the number of groups minus 1 or the number of variables used to discriminate among the groups. For a further discussion of linear discriminant function analysis see Dunteman (1984b) and Klecka (1980).

If we have a large number of groups and a large number of highly correlated variables, then conducting a discriminant analysis on a subset of the principal components is especially appealing. Since the principal components are uncorrelated, we can test the statistical significance of each one independently of the others by an F ratio associated with a one-way analysis of variance. We can then elect to use only those principal components that individually discriminate between groups. With the original correlated variables, this simple variable selection scheme is not feasible. A variable that alone discriminates among groups, may not add independent discriminatory power when used together with other variables. In most cases, the largest principal components will be the most discriminatory components, but there are always exceptions, as Jolliffe (1986) so forcibly points out. This mainly occurs because a small component is defined primarily by a single variable that adds discriminatory power. For example, Figure 12.1 illustrates a case where the largest principal component does not discriminate among three groups, as well as the second one does. In fact, the second principal component discriminates perfectly among the three groups while the projections of observations on the first principal component would show considerable overlap.

Example

Let us return to our crime data where the 51 states can be subdivided into 9 geographical regions. We can use the principal component scores, rather than the original variables, to conduct a discriminant analysis. Since the seven principal components are statistically independent, each one makes an independent contribution with respect to discriminating among the nine regions. We can thus conduct a one-way analysis of variance for each principal component with regions as the categorical independent variable and the particular principal component score as the dependent variable. The seven analysis of variances indicate that only principal components two and three are statistically significant. The F ratios were 6.623 and 6.253,

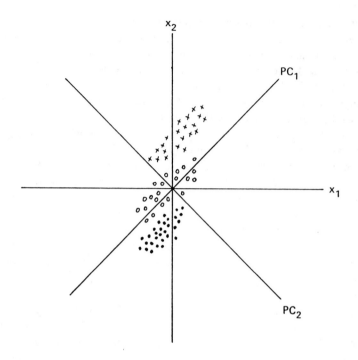

Figure 12.1: Distribution of Groups on the First Two Principal Components

respectively, and with 8 and 42 degrees of freedom each one was highly significant ($p < .0001$).

The F ratio associated with the largest principal component was not significant at the .05 level although it approached significance. By itself, the largest principal component, although accounting for over 67% of the total variation in the seven crime variables, did not significantly discriminant among the nine regions. We noted that this largest principal component reflected overall crime level. Thus, regions don't differ very much with respect to overall crime level, but differ with respect to patterns of crime which are represented by the second and third components. We previously interpreted the second principal component as a contrast between violent personal crimes and property crimes. Since the third component had a latent root less than .70 (.57) we did not interpret it. It seems to be primarily defined by motor vehicle theft. We see the danger of arbitrarily discarding principal components if they are to be used in subsequent analyses. If we only retained the first two principal components, then we would have included one component, the first, that was relatively useless in discriminating among the nine regions and rejected one, the third, which exhibited extremely high discriminatory power.

The discriminant analysis indicated that only the first two discriminant functions were statistically significant. Both were highly significant at the .0001 level. The canonical correlations associated with these two discriminant functions were .819 and .801, respectively. These correlations indicate a high association between the regions and each of the two discriminant functions. The canonical correlations are identical to those that would have been obtained if we had used the seven original crime variables since the seven principal components completely account for the variation in the seven crime variables.

Let us now examine the vector of weights shown in Table 12.1 for these two discriminant functions. The weights are for the principal component scores after these each have been standardized to have a within region standard deviation of 1. Principal component 3 has by far the largest weight on the first discriminant function, and likewise, the second principal component has the largest weight, by far, on the second discriminant function. The results are consistent with the univariate F ratios discussed above. Let us see how well we can do by using these two principal components alone with respect to discriminating among the nine regions. We can do this by conducting a linear discriminant function analysis with only components 2 and 3 and comparing the canonical correlations derived from this analysis with those from the discriminant analysis discussed above which used the information in all seven crime variables. Since there are only two variables and nine regions, all of the between region differences are captured by two linear discriminant functions. Both of the discriminant functions were highly significant (p < .0001). The standardized weights and canonical correlations are presented in Table 12.2. The second principal component essentially defines discriminant function 1 and the third principal component essentially defines discriminant function 2. The two canonical correlations are high, .752 and .732, respectively, indicating strong associations between the geographical regions and the second and third principal components.

If we take the ratio of the corresponding squared canonical correlations for each of the two discriminant functions, putting the smaller one on top, this gives us the proportion of discriminatory power that the two-component linear discriminant function has in comparison with the full seven component discriminant analysis. The ratios are

TABLE 12.1
Standardized Linear Discriminant Function Weights for
Crime by Region Data

	Discriminant Function	
Principal Component	1	2
1	.252	−.457
2	.269	.978
3	.911	−.234
4	.539	.165
5	−.345	−.222
6	.309	.118
7	−.514	.283
canonical correlation	.819	.801

TABLE 12.2
Standardized Linear Discriminant Function Weights for Components
Two and Three Analysis

	Discriminant Function	
Principal Component	1	2
2	.873	−.489
3	.513	.859
canonical correlation	.752	.732

$$\frac{(.752)^2}{(.819)^2} = .84 \text{ and } \frac{(.732)^2}{(.801)^2} = .84,$$

respectively. These high ratios indicate that most of the discriminatory information resides in just components two and three. The dimensions that discriminate among regions are violent personal crimes versus property crimes and motor vehicle thefts.

Some researchers prefer to use the pooled within group covariance or correlation matrix to determine the principal components for a discriminant analysis rather than using the total correlation matrix as we did. The preference depends on whether we want to emphasize the within group characteristics of the discriminant function or emphasize the discriminatory structure of the data as a whole. Depending on the pattern of differences among the groups, the pooled within group correlation matrix can differ considerably from the total correlation matrix.

If between group differences on the variates are large relative to within group variation, then the largest principal components will be oriented in the direction of between group differences. On the other hand, the largest principal components of the pooled within groups covariance matrix, in this case, are not necessarily those that account for a significant proportion of between group variation. Using the principal components from the pooled within group covariance matrix does, however, allow us to determine if the same principal components that account for most of the within group variation account for most of the between group differences. If the separate within group covariance matrices differ from one another, then pooling is not justified in the first place. In this instance, it makes more sense to either use the principal components of the total covariance matrix or use a nonlinear discriminant analysis where information concerning the differences in the covariance matrices is used to discriminate among groups. The choice is somewhat arbitrary in that the total set of principal components generated by either approach will completely account for between group differences.

The discriminant analysis can be done using both approaches and the choice of one approach over the other can be based upon factors such as the interpretability of the resulting principal components, the number of principal components required for adequately discriminating among groups, and whether or not it is the largest or smallest components that are discriminating among the groups. If the between group variation on the variables is not large relative to within group variation, then either approach will yield essentially the same results.

A principal component analysis of the pooled within groups correlation matrix, for our crime data, not presented here because of space limitations, showed a strong similarity to the principal components for the total correlation matrix which we used in our discriminant analysis. So, in this instance, either choice yields the same results.

Use of Principal Components in Canonical Correlation Analysis

Canonical correlation analysis, originated by Hotelling (1935), involves partitioning a set of variables into two subsets and finding pairs of linear composites, one composite representing each variable set, that are maximally correlated. The variables are often partitioned into a set of independent and dependent variables, although canonical correlation analysis makes no assumptions about the direction of causality; each of the two variable sets is given equal status. Canonical correlation analysis has conceptual similarities to both principal components and discriminant analysis. If the set of p variables is divided into two subsets of p_1 and p_2 variables with $p_1 \leq p_2$, then we can solve for p_1 pairs of linear composites where each pair of composites has the maximum correlation and is uncorrelated with the linear composites making up the other pairs. For example, the largest canonical correlation is obtained by finding the pair of weight vectors $[a_{11}, a_{12}, \ldots, a_{1p}]$ and $[b_{11}, b_{12}, \ldots, b_{1p}]$ such that the correlation between

$$\sum_{i=1}^{p_1} a_{1i} x_i \text{ and } \sum_{i=1}^{p_2} b_{1i} y_i$$

is maximized. This involves finding the largest latent root and associated latent vectors of matrix products involving the within subset and between subset correlation matrices and their inverses. Like principal components analysis and discriminant analysis, we can continue solving for canonical correlations and their associated weighting vectors until all of the independent linear relationships between the two variable sets are accounted for. For more details the reader is referred to Mardia, Kent, and Bibby (1979), Levine (1977), and Thompson (1984).

Rather than using the original variables for the canonical correlation analysis, we can, as we did in our discriminant analysis example, transform the original variables into principal components before conducting the canonical correlation analysis. In this case, we would conduct a principal components analysis within each of the two variable sets and use the principal components rather than the original variables in the canonical correlation analysis. Once again, the advantage is simplicity and interpretability. This is especially true if the number of large principal components within each variable set are relatively small and turn out to have high loadings (correlations) on their respective canonical variates. In this situation, the analysis would indicate that the dimensions that account for most of the variation within variable sets are also important in determining relationships across variable sets. An obvious advantage is that we would have less canonical loadings to interpret.

Another approach would be to conduct a single principal components analysis on the total set of variables. We can then see which components reflect mainly the structure of the data within each of the variable sets and which components explain significant variation across both variable sets. The reason for conducting a principal components analysis on the total set of variables, keeping in mind the distinction between the two variable sets when interpreting the principal components, is that canonical correlation analysis has some serious shortcomings due to its singular focus on maximizing the correlation between linear composites across the variable sets. Specifically, while a linear composite (canonical variate) from one variable set may correlate highly with the corresponding canonical variate from the other data set, the correlation of each variable with its corresponding canonical variate may be low, indicating that each canonical variate explains little of the variation in the individual variables within its respective variable set. Furthermore, each canonical variate from one variable set may not explain much of the variation in the individual variables from the other variable set. Principal components analysis helps balance the objectives of finding both dimensions that explain variation across both data sets and dimensions that explain variation primarily within one data set or the other. For example, if two variable sets are highly related, then one or more large principal components will have substantial loadings from both variable sets. Other principal components, hopefully, the smaller ones, will be defined primarily by one variable set or the other.

13. OTHER TECHNIQUES RELATED TO PRINCIPAL COMPONENTS

Principal Coordinate Analysis

We have seen that we can decompose a covariance or correlation matrix in terms of its latent roots and latent vectors. That is,

$$R = \lambda_1 a_1 a_1' + \lambda_2 a_2 a_2' + \ldots + \lambda_p a_p a_p' = \sum_{i=1}^{p} \lambda_i a_i a_i'.$$

Principal coordinate analysis (Gower, 1966) involves decomposing an $n \times n$ similarity matrix in the same manner. Instead of decomposing a $p \times p$ correlation or covariance matrix of variables, we decompose an $n \times n$ matrix whose elements are measures of similarity between all pairs of observations. The correlation or covariance matrix summarizes the similarity among the p variables rather than the n observations. The similarity measures can be of any type as long as the $n \times n$

similarity matrix, S, is positive-semidefinite and symmetrical like a correlation matrix. Positive-semidefinite means that there are no negative latent roots.

If the matrix S fulfills the two conditions, then we can use the spectral decomposition theorem to decompose S in terms of its latent roots and latent vectors. That is,

$$S = \lambda_1 a_1 a_1' + \lambda_2 a_2 a_2' + \ldots + \lambda_n a_n a_n' = \sum_{i=1}^{n} \lambda_i a_i a_i' .$$

If we let $b_i = \sqrt{\lambda_i}\, a_i$, then the decomposition of S can be written as

$$S = \sum_{i=1}^{n} b_i b_i' .$$

If we consider the n observations as points in n-dimensional space, then the vector b_1 contains the coordinates of the n observations on the first dimension, b_2 contains the coordinates on the second dimension, and so on through b_n which contains the coordinates of the n observations on the nth dimension.

The first stage of principal coordinate analysis is to solve for the b_i. The second and final stage of principal coordinate analysis is to treat the n b_i vectors as the data set (i.e., $[b_1 b_2 \ldots b_n]$) and conduct a principal component analysis on this data set. We can then plot the principal component scores with respect to the first k principal components where k is determined by the same criteria as discussed earlier and used throughout this book.

Gower (1966) points out that principal coordinate analysis and principal components analysis are equivalent if the similarity measure is proportional to Euclidean distance. It turns out that two widely used similarity measures are proportional to Euclidean distance. The first of these two similarity measures is the covariance or correlation between the observations. In this case, S is an $n \times n$ matrix of covariances or correlations among observations rather than variables. We then use this particular S as our starting point for the two steps in our principal coordinate analysis. The second widely used similarity measure is applicable to binary data. It is sometimes called a matching coefficient. This similarity measure is the proportion of the p variables that take the same value for any pair of individuals or observations. Binary variables take only two values, by most conventions, 0 or 1. The similarity between the jth and kth individual or observation is simply the number of times that the patterns 0,0 or 1,1 occur divided by the total number of variables. The patterns 0,0 and 1,1 are matches while the patterns 1,0 or 0,1 are mismatches. The matching similarity coefficient is equivalent to a Euclidean distance measure.

It should be emphasized that if the similarity measure is not proportional to Euclidean distance then principal coordinate analysis and principal component analysis do not produce equivalent results. Principal coordinate analysis is most useful when we do not have measures for p variables on n observations that are required for principal components analysis, but instead have only the similarity measures among the n observations. The latter situation occurs, for example, if we have people rate the similarity between pairs of objects or people with respect to a set of attributes. The aims of principal coordinate analysis in this case are to determine the number of dimensions people use to judge similarity among a particular set of objects or people and to plot the scores for the objects or people in a, hopefully, low dimensional space. If we have the $n \times p$ data matrix, then we might as well do a principal components analysis to begin with unless we want to use this $n \times p$ data matrix to create an $n \times n$ similarity matrix containing non-Euclidean similarity measures. In any event, principal components and principal coordinate analysis have similar goals, to reduce dimensionality, and rely on the spectral decomposition theorem to decompose their respective matrices in terms of their latent roots and latent vectors.

Correspondence Analysis

Correspondence analysis is another multivariate technique related to principal components analysis. Its goal is to summarize the information in a two-way contingency table with r rows and c columns. Our previous applications of principal components analysis were focused on n by p data matrices where p variables were measured on n individuals or observations. The goal was to transform the $n \times p$ matrix to an $n \times k$ matrix of principal component scores where k was considerably less than p. In correspondence analysis we deal with two categorical variables (e.g., geographical region, sex, ethnicity, type of community, etc.) that are crossed to define cells for which frequencies are available from a sample of observations.

We can consider the rows of the contingency table as observations and the columns of the table as variables and conduct a principal components analysis of a transformation of the contingency table in order to generate principal component score vectors for the rows. We also want to generate principal component scores summarizing information in the columns of the contingency table. We do this by transposing the transformed contingency table so that the columns are now rows and conducting a principal components analysis of this matrix in order to generate the scores associated with columns. We usually only generate the scores associated with the two largest principal components associated with the transformed contingency table and its transpose. This is because we usually want to plot the scores associated with the rows and columns of the transformed contingency table in a two dimensional figure so that we see the correspondence between row and column scores.

Jolliffe (1986) used correspondence analysis on a contingency table where a large number of bird species were cross classified with a large number of geographical sites. The rows (bird species) and columns (sites) of the contingency table were each summarized by two dimensions. Jolliffe then plotted in the two dimensional space the scores for bird species and the scores for the geographical areas, which were wetland sites in Ireland. The plot of the pair of r scores for species and the pair of c scores for sites in the two dimensional space was informative in two respects. Species that are close to each other in the two dimensional space are similar to each other with respect to their original data. The same holds for sites. Second, it indicated which species tended to inhabit which sites. A species that is near a particular site in the two dimensional plot indicates that the species is likely to inhabit that site.

An application of correspondence analysis for social scientists might be to summarize the data in a contingency table cross classifying different types of drug abuse treatment programs with client types. Drug treatment programs (e.g., outpatient drug free as one category) could be considered the row variable with r categories and client type (e.g., young, black, females as one category) could be considered the column variable with c columns. This $r \times c$ contingency table would contain, for a sample of n observations, the distribution of the observations across the r times c cells. The outcome of the correspondence analysis would be a set of scores for the rows of the table which represent treatments and a set of scores for the columns which represent client types.

We would retain only two scores representing the r treatment programs and only two scores representing the c client types so that the scores for both treatment programs and client types could be plotted in the same two dimensional space. Since there are r treatments, there would be r values for each of the two score distributions characterizing treatments. Similarly, since there are c client types, there would be c values for each of the two score distributions characterizing client types. If we plot the treatment scores and the client type scores in the same two dimensional space, then we can see if treatments or client types form clusters and, more importantly, if certain treatments and client types occupy the common regions of the two dimensional space which would indicate a correspondence between treatment and client types. That is, we can determine which treatments certain types of clients are more likely to enter.

Correspondence analysis involves, as mentioned above, first transforming the contingency table which, for a data set of n observations, contains the number of observations falling into each of the cells defined by the intersection of a particular row and column. The number of observations falling into the cell defined by the ith row and jth column is denoted as n_{ij}. The first step in the transformation is to divide each cell frequency, n_{ij}, by n to convert the cell counts into probabilities, p_{ij}. In analyzing a contingency table, we are interested in the association between the row and column variable. If the two variables are independent, then each cell probability, p_{ij}, is equal to the product of the corresponding row and column marginal probabilities which are denoted by p_i and p_j, respectively. That is, if the two variables are independent, then $p_{ij} - p_i p_j = 0$ for all i and j. If the two variables are not independent, the $p_{ij} - p_i p_j$ take a nonzero value for some values of i and j. The $p_{ij} - p_i p_j$ can be considered as residuals under the model of independence. If the two categorical variables are highly related, then some of these residuals will be large. This indicates that the model of independence does not fit the data in the contingency table very well. Correspondence analysis focuses on these residuals rather than the original cell probabilities. Its goal is to summarize the pattern of residuals by generating scores associated with rows and scores associated with columns. Note that for a regular $n \times p$ data set, we do not usually do a principal components analysis on the raw data matrix, but first subtract out the mean for each variable. We are interested in summarizing patterns of deviations from the mean.

Correspondence analysis involves yet another transformation on the residuals $p_{ij} - p_i p_j$. Each residual is divided by the product of the square root of the associated marginal probabilities. That is, the new cell entries become

$$\frac{p_{ij} - p_i p_j}{\sqrt{p_i}\sqrt{p_j}}$$

This last step in the transformation adjusts the residuals with respect to the size of the marginal probabilities. This is similar to standardizing a deviation score cross product by dividing it by the product of the standard deviations. Our transformation is now complete.

The next step is to conduct two principal components analyses on the $r \times c$ matrix with the transformed cell entries. The first principal components analysis considers the rows as observations and the columns as variables and, hence, generates score vectors associated with rows. The second principal components analysis is conducted on the transpose of the transformed data matrix so that now the columns are treated as observations in the analysis and score vectors can be generated for columns. The scores associated with the largest two principal components for each analysis are then plotted so that clusters can be identified and, more importantly, correspondences between the row and column variables can be visually identified.

In a sense, correspondence analysis is a graphical procedure for clustering both the row categories (with respect to the column categories) and the column categories (with respect to the row categories). Both row categories and column categories are represented by scores from their respective two largest principal components so that the information can be plotted in two dimensions. Obviously, correspondence analysis is most useful when both the number of row and column categories are large. Otherwise, we could "see" the similarity between rows or between columns by directly examining the contingency table. The reader desiring more details or further applications is referred to Greenacre (1984).

14. SUMMARY AND CONCLUSIONS

Principal components analysis is useful in significantly reducing the dimensionality of a data set characterized by a large number of correlated variables. Many times the principal components have a natural interpretation; if not, they can be rotated. The principal component scores can be plotted to identify clusters of observations as well as outlying and influential observations. In general, principal components analysis helps us understand the structure of a multivariate data set. If we do not want to transform our original variables to principal components, principal components analysis can still be useful in selecting a small subset of variables that contains most of the statistical information in the much larger original set of variables.

In addition, principal components analysis is useful when used in conjunction with other multivariate procedures. It addresses the multicollinearity problem in multiple regression analysis. Multicollinearity is evidenced by the presence of principal components with extremely small variances. This shows that both large and small variance principal components are useful in understanding the structure of a data set. In some cases, the substitution of a few principal components for the original variables can enhance our understanding of a linear discriminant function analysis or a canonical correlation analysis. In fact, all three procedures involve finding linear composites that maximize a particular criterion. The procedure is so fundamental that it is closely related to other techniques that appear, on the surface, to be quite different. We have seen, for example, its relationship to principal coordinate analysis and its use in analyzing contingency table data by correspondence analysis. The reader who is interested in further details on principal components analysis presented in a more rigorous fashion is referred to the excellent book by Jolliffe (1986).

We will conclude with a word of caution. It makes no sense to conduct a principal components analysis on a hodge podge of variables that have low intercorrelations. It will take nearly as many principal components as there are original variables to account for a major portion of variance in the original variables. If we rotated these components we would find ourselves back to where we started in the sense that most of the rotated components will be defined essentially by a single variable.

244

REFERENCES

ALDENDERFER, M. S., & BLASHFIELD, R. K. (1984). Cluster Analysis. Beverly Hills, CA: Sage.

ANDERSON, T. W. (1963). "Asymptotic theory for principal components analysis." Annuals of Mathematical Statistics, 34: 122-148.

BIRREN, J. E., & MORRISON, D. F. (1961). "Analysis of WAIS subtests in relation to age and education." Journal of Gerontology, 16: 363-369.

CATTELL, R. B. (1966). "The scree test for the number of factors." Multivariate Behavioral Research, 1: 245-276.

DILLON, R., & GOLDSTEIN, M. (1984). Multivariate analysis: Methods and applications. New York: John Wiley.

DUNTEMAN, G. H. (1984a). Introduction to linear models. Beverly Hills, CA: Sage.

DUNTEMAN, G. H. (1984b). Introduction to multivariate analysis. Beverly Hills, CA: Sage.

GOWER, J. C. (1966). Some distance properties of latent root and vector methods used in multivariate analysis. Biometrika, 53: 325-328.

GREENACRE, M. J. (1984). Theory and applications of correspondence analysis. London: Academic Press.

GUTTMAN, L. (1956). "Best possible systematic estimates of communalities." Psychometrika, 21: 273-285.

HARMAN, H. H. (1976). Modern factor analysis. Chicago: University of Chicago Press.

HOTELLING, H. (1933). "Analysis of a complex of statistical variables into principal components." Journal of Educational Psychology, 24: 417-441, 498-520.

HOTELLING, H. (1935). "The most predictable criterion." Journal of Educational Psychology, 26: 139-142.

JOLLIFFE, I. T. (1972). "Discarding variables in a principal component analysis, I: Artificial data." Applied Statistics, 21: 160-173.

JOLLIFFE, I. T. (1986). Principal component analysis. New York: Springer-Verlag.

KAISER, H. F. (1958). "The varimax criterion for analytic rotation in factor analysis." Psychometrika, 23: 187-200.

KAISER, H. F. (1960). "The application of electronic computers to factor analysis." Educational and Psychological Measurement, 20: 141-151.

KIM, J., & MUELLER, C. W. (1978a). Introduction to factor analysis. Beverly Hills, CA: Sage.

KIM, J., & MUELLER, C. W. (1978b). Factor analysis. Beverly Hills, CA: Sage.

KLECKA, W. R. (1980). Discriminant analysis. Beverly Hills, CA: Sage.

LAWLEY, D. N. (1963). "On testing a set of correlation coefficients for equality." Annuals of Mathematical Statistics, 34: 149-151.

LAWLEY, D. N., & Maxwell, A. E. (1971). Factor analysis as a statistical method. New York: American Elsevier.

LEVINE, M. S. (1977). Canonical analysis and factor comparison. Beverly Hills, CA: Sage.

LEWIS-BECK, M. (1980). Applied regression: An introduction. Beverly Hills, CA: Sage.

LONG, J. S. (1983). Confirmatory factor analysis. Beverly Hills, CA: Sage.

MARDIA, K. V., KENT, J. T., & BIBBY, J. M. (1979). Multivariate analysis. London: Academic Press.

McCABE, G. P. (1984). "Principal variables." Technometrics, 26: 137-144.

MORRISON, D. F. (1976). Multivariate statistical methods (2nd ed.). New York: McGraw-Hill.

NAMBOODIRI, K. (1984). Matrix algebra: An introduction. Beverly Hills, CA: Sage.

PEARSON, K. (1901). On lines and planes of closest fit to systems of points in space. Phil., May 2:559-572.

Statistical Abstracts of the United States (1985). Washington, DC: U.S. Department of Commerce, Bureau of Census.

TAYLOR, C. L., & HUDSON, M. C. (1972). World handbook of social and political indicators (2nd ed.). New Haven, CT: Yale University Press.

THOMPSON, R. (1984). Canonical correlation analysis: Uses and interpretation. Beverly Hills, CA: Sage.

THURSTONE, L. L. (1947). Multiple factor analysis. Chicago: University of Chicago Press.

WILKINSON, L. (1986). SYSTAT: The system for statistics. Evanston, IL: SYSTAT.

WOODWARD, J. A., RETKA, R. L., & NG, L. (1984). "Construct validity of heroin abuse estimators." International Journal of the Addictions, 19: 93-117.

CONFIRMATORY FACTOR ANALYSIS
A Preface to LISREL

PART IV

J. SCOTT LONG

Notation

Boldface letters are used to indicate matrices and vectors. For example, $\mathbf{B}$ indicates that B is a matrix. Dimensions of matrices and vectors are indicated by "$(r \times c)$" for a matrix with r rows and c columns. Subscripts to lower-case letters indicate elements of a matrix. For example, the $(i,j)^{th}$ element of $\mathbf{B}$ is indicated as b_{ij}; the ith element of the vector $\mathbf{x}$ is indicated as x_i. The symbol "'" indicates the transpose of a matrix; thus $\mathbf{B}'$ is the transpose of $\mathbf{B}$. The symbol "-1" as a superscript of a matrix indicates the inverse of the matrix $\mathbf{B}$; $\mathbf{B}^{-1}$ is the inverse of $\mathbf{B}$. "COV" is the covariance operator. If the arguments of the operator are two variables, say x_i and x_j, then $COV(x_i,x_j)$ indicates the covariance between x_i and x_j. If the argument of the covariance operator is a vector, say $\mathbf{x}$ of dimension $(n \times 1)$, then $COV(\mathbf{x})$ is the $(n \times n)$ covariance matrix whose $(i,j)^{th}$ element (for $i \neq j$) is the covariance between x_i and x_j, and whose $(i,i)^{th}$ element is the variance of x_i. Similarly, "COR" is used as the correlation operator. $COR(x_i,x_j)$ indicates the correlation between x_i and x_j. $COR(\mathbf{x})$ is the $(n \times n)$ correlation matrix whose $(i,j)^{th}$ element (for $i \neq j$) is the correlation between x_i and x_j, and whose $(i,i)^{th}$ element is one. "E" is the expectation operator. If x_i is a random variable, $E(x_i)$ is the expected value of x_i. If $\mathbf{x}$ is a vector, then $E(\mathbf{x})$ is a vector whose i^{th} element is the expected value of the random variable x_i.

Figures, equations, and tables are numbered sequentially within chapters. Thus Table 2.3 is the third table in Chapter 2. The same examples are developed throughout the text and are referred to by the same example number. Thus, if Example 2 is discussed in Chapter 4, the reader should realize that it is a continuation of Example 2 from earlier chapters.

The literature on the confirmatory factor model uses Greek letters. People who have not encountered these "squiggles" before may experience unnecessary anxiety and confusion. For those who have not mastered the Greek alphabet, it is worthwhile to spend some time learning the following Greek letters.

NAMES OF GREEK LETTERS

Upper Case	Lower Case	Name
A	α	alpha
B	β	beta
Υ	γ	gamma
Δ	δ	delta
E	ϵ	epsilon
Z	ζ	zeta
H	η	eta
Θ	θ	theta
I	ι	iota
K	κ	kappa
Λ	λ	lambda
M	μ	mu
N	ν	nu
Ξ	ξ	xi
O	o	omicron
Π	π	pi
P	ρ	rho
Σ	σ	sigma
T	τ	tau
Υ	υ	upsilon
Φ	ϕ	phi
X	χ	chi
Ψ	ψ	psi
Ω	ω	omega

Preface

This monograph presents a statistical method known as confirmatory factor analysis. Two groups of people should find this method to be of interest: first, those who are currently using the more traditional technique of exploratory factor analysis may find that their research problems are more appropriately analyzed with confirmatory factor analysis. Second, those who are interested in the analysis of covariance structures, more commonly known as the LISREL model, will find study of the confirmatory factor model to be a useful first step in understanding the more complex LISREL model. It is for this reason that the monograph has been subtitled *A Preface to LISREL*. Members of the first group are likely to find themselves evolving into members of the second group, since the advantages of the confirmatory factor model over the exploratory factor model are more than equaled by the advantages of the covariance structure model over the confirmatory factor model.

Upon mastery of the materials in this monograph, the reader will be ready to study the more complex covariance structure model. To this end, a second monograph in the Sage series on Quantitative Applications in the Social Sciences is available. This monograph, entitled *Covariance Structure Models: An Introduction to LISREL*, was written in conjunction with the current monograph. The reader of *Confirmatory Factor Analysis* can read *Covariance Structure Models* with no loss of continuity.

Matrix algebra is a necessary prerequisite for studying the confirmatory factor model. While the proofs presented are simple, the reader must feel comfortable with matrix multiplication, inversion, and transposition, and with the distributive property of matrices. Notes at the end of the monograph provide brief reviews for each matrix operation or property when it is used for the first time in the text. Readers who need a more thorough review are encouraged to consult an introductory text in matrix algebra such as Namboodiri (forthcoming) or Chapter 1 of Hohn (1973). The basic statistical concepts presented in texts such as Hays (1981) or Blalock (1979) are also assumed.

A full understanding of the confirmatory factor model requires the application of the model to actual data. Readers are encouraged to replicate the analyses presented in the text. The correlations and standard deviations necessary for such replications are contained in Appendix I. If the results you obtain match those presented in the text, you have a good indication that you understand the confirmatory factor model. To estimate the confirmatory factor model it is generally necessary to use software designed to estimate the covariance structure model (e.g., LISREL, MILS). Appendix II describes how such software can be used to estimate the confirmatory factor model.

A number of people generously gave of their time to comment on various portions of this monograph. I would especially like to thank Paul Allison, Carol Hickman, Karen Pugliesi, Jay Stewart, Blair Wheaton, Ronald Schoenberg, and two anonymous reviewers. The final product is far better for their efforts. Remaining errors and lack of clarity are the result of not heeding the advice of those listed above.

1. INTRODUCTION

Some variables of theoretical interest cannot be directly observed. This is the fundamental idea underlying the factor analytic model. These unobserved variables are referred to as either *latent* variables or *factors*. While latent variables cannot be directly observed, information about them can be obtained indirectly by noting their effects on *observed* variables. Factor analysis is a statistical procedure for uncovering a (usually) smaller number of latent variables by studying the covariation among a set of observed variables.

Exploratory Versus Confirmatory Factor Analysis

Figure 1.1 illustrates an *exploratory* factor model. In this figure, as in later figures, observed variables are represented by squares and latent variables are represented by circles. A straight arrow pointing from a latent variable to an observed variable indicates the causal effect of the latent variable on the observed variable. Curved arrows between two latent variables indicate that those variables are correlated.

The circles at the top of Figure 1.1 correspond to the latent variables ξ_1, ξ_2, and ξ_3. The curved arrows between these factors indicate that they are correlated with one another. Each of these factors causally affects each of the observed variables, contained in the boxes labeled x_1 to x_7, as indicated by the arrows from the ξ's to the x's. The factors labeled with ξ's are called *common* factors, since their effects are shared in common with more than one of the observed variables. The circles at the bottom of the figure, labeled δ_1 to to δ_7, are called *unique* factors, or errors in variables. Unlike the common factors, their effects are unique to one and only one observed variable. In the exploratory factor model, unique factors are assumed to be uncorrelated with one another and with the common factors, as indicated by the lack of curved arrows between them in Figure 1.1.

The model represented by Figure 1.1 is referred to as an exploratory factor model to reflect the fact that beyond the specifications of the numbers of common factors and observed variables to be analyzed, the researcher does not specify the structure of the relationships among the variables in the model. The researcher must assume that

(1) *all* common factors are correlated (or, in some types of exploratory factor analysis, that *all* common factors are uncorrelated);
(2) *all* observed variables are directly affected by *all* common factors;
(3) unique factors are uncorrelated with one another;
(4) *all* observed variables are affected by a unique factor; and
(5) all ξ's are uncorrelated with all δ's.

These assumptions are made regardless of the substantive appropriateness. Additional and generally arbitrary assumptions must then be imposed in order to estimate the model's parameters. The exploratory factor model's inability to incorporate substantively meaningful constraints, and its necessary imposition of substantively meaningless constraints, has earned it the scornful label of garbage in/garbage out (GIGO) model.

The limitations of the exploratory factor model have been largely overcome by the development of the *confirmatory* factor model (Jöreskog, 1967, 1969; Jöreskog and Lawley, 1968). In the confirmatory factor model, the researcher imposes *substantively motivated* constraints. These constraints determine (1) which pairs of common factors are correlated, (2) which observed variables are affected by which common factors, (3) which observed variables are affected by a unique factor, and (4) which pairs of unique factors are correlated. Statistical tests can be performed to determine if the sample data are consistent with the imposed constraints or, in other words, whether the data *confirm* the substantively generated model. It is in this sense that the model is thought of as confirmatory.

The distinction between exploratory and confirmatory factor models can be seen by comparing the exploratory model in Figure 1.1 to the confirmatory model in Figure 1.2. In the confirmatory model, the

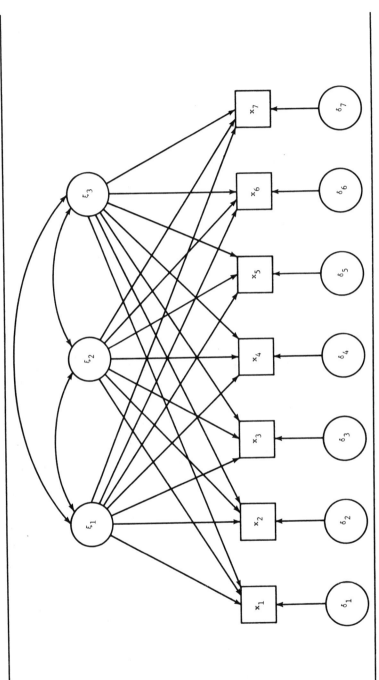

Figure 1.1 An Exploratory Factor Model

253

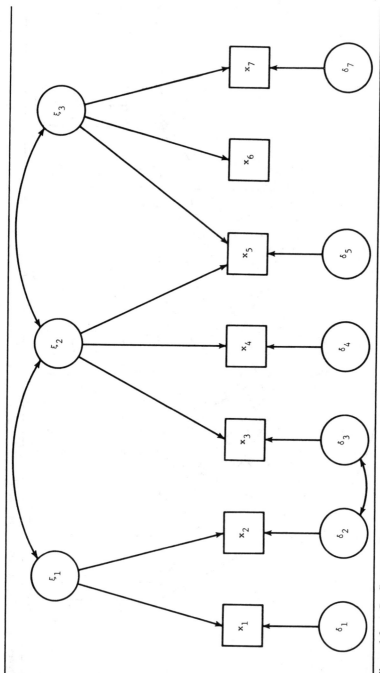

Figure 1.2 A Confirmatory Factor Model

common factors ξ_1 and ξ_3 are assumed to be uncorrelated, whereas in the exploratory model all common factors are necessarily assumed to be correlated (or alternatively, they may all be assumed to be uncorrelated). In the confirmatory factor model, the observed variables are affected by only some of the common factors (e.g., x_1 is assumed not to be affected by ξ_2 and ξ_3), whereas all observed variables are affected by all common factors in the exploratory model. In the example of the confirmatory factor model, two of the unique factors are assumed to be correlated (δ_2 and δ_3 are correlated as indicated by the curved arrow connecting them), and one of the observed variables is assumed to have no error factor associated with it (x_6 has no unique factor associated with it), whereas in the exploratory model all unique factors are uncorrelated, and a unique factor is associated with each observed variable.

In practice, the researcher may not have a single, compelling model in mind. Instead, a handful of equally reasonable models may be suggested by substantive theory. Or, the researcher may find that the single model suggested by theory does not fit. In either case, the confirmatory factor model can be used in an exploratory fashion. A specification search (Leamer, 1978) can be conducted in which the selection of a model is based on prior examination of the data. Procedures for the exploratory use of confirmatory factor analysis are presented in Chapter 5.

Structural Relations Among Common Factors

Factor models explain the covariation in a set of observed variables in terms of a (usually) smaller number of common factors. The common factors are often of significant theoretical interest, and accordingly most researchers are interested in the structural relations among these factors. While the confirmatory factor model can provide correlations among common factors, these are generally insufficient for determining the structural parameters of interest. Estimating structural parameters requires the application of a structural equation model to the common factors, in the same way that structural equation models are commonly applied to observed variables. For example, Figures 1.2 and 1.3 contain the same observed and latent variables. Figure 1.3 differs in that it assumes that the common factor ξ_1 causally affects ξ_2 and that ξ_1 and ξ_2 causally affect ξ_3. The incorporation of structural relations among latent variables can be accomplished by what is known as the *covariance structure model* or, more popularly, the LISREL model. This more general model is beyond the scope of the current monograph, but is the subject of the companion volume in this series, *Covariance Structure Models*.

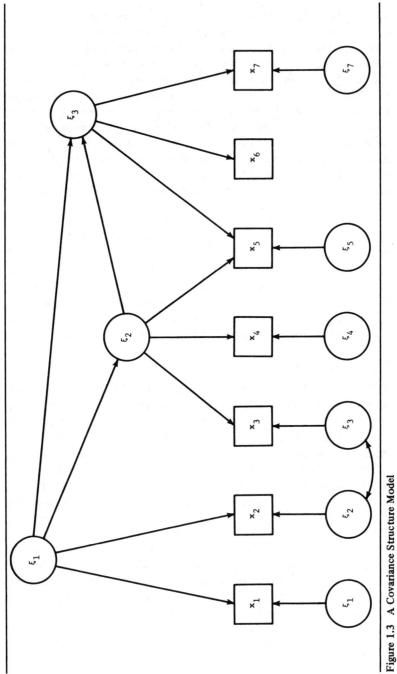

Figure 1.3 A Covariance Structure Model

While the confirmatory factor model is limited by not allowing structural relations among the common factors, it is still an extremely flexible model that can deal with a variety of important applications. These include: (1) measurement models in which latent variables are estimated to eliminate errors in measurement; (2) multiple indicator models in which several indicators of each latent variable are available and a factor model is used to determine the correlations among the common factors (an extension of methods for correcting for attenuation); and (3) multimethod-multitrait models in which each substantive factor is measured with several methods in the hope of eliminating the distorting effects of the methods of measurement. References to specific applications of the confirmatory factor model are given in the concluding chapter.

Organization of the Monograph

The confirmatory factor model is presented in four steps, corresponding to Chapters 2 through 5. Chapter 2 presents the specification of the mathematical model. This involves formal definitions of the various components of the model and a statement of the assumptions. Since the confirmatory factor model allows the researcher to impose constraints specific to the application at hand, this chapter demonstrates how substantive considerations can be translated into constraints on the model. After a model has been specified, it must be determined if the model is identified, the subject of Chapter 3. Identification involves determining if there is a unique solution for the parameters of the model. If a model is not identified, parameters of the model cannot be estimated, and the specification of the model must be reconsidered. Once identification has been established, estimation can proceed. Chapter 4 considers how information from a sample can be used to obtain estimates of population parameters. After a model has been estimated, an assessment of its fit can be made. This involves conducting hypothesis tests as well as making specification searches. These issues are considered in Chapter 5.

2. SPECIFICATION OF THE CONFIRMATORY
FACTOR MODEL

Specification of the confirmatory factor model requires making formal and explicit statements about (1) the number of common factors; (2) the number of observed variables; (3) the variances and covariances among the common factors; (4) the relationships among observed variables and latent factors; (5) the relationships among unique factors and observed variables; and (6) the variances and covariances among the unique factors. The great flexibility of the confirmatory factor model comes from its ability to specify each of these components according to the demands of a given application.

An Informal Introduction

Before providing a formal description, the basic components of the confirmatory factor model are illustrated using a portion of a model analyzed by Wheaton (1978) describing the sociogenesis of psychological disorders. This example is used throughout and is referred to as Example 1.

Example 1: an informal specification. This model measures psychological disorders for a sample of 603 adult heads of household from the Hennepin area of rural Illinois at two points in time (1967 and 1971). Since a single, adequate measure of psychological disorders is not available, a measurement model is proposed in which two latent variables are assumed: psychological disorder at time 1, referred to as ξ_1, and psychological disorder at time 2, referred to as ξ_2. These common factors are represented by the circles at the top of Figure 2.1.

Psychological disorder at each point in time is imperfectly measured by two observed variables. ξ_1 is linked to the number of psychological **symptoms at time 1, x_1, and the number of psychophysiological symp**toms at time 1, x_2. Similarly, ξ_2 is linked to the corresponding observed variables x_3 and x_4 measured at time 2. In the terminology of factor analysis, we state that x_1 and x_2 load on ξ_1, and x_3 and x_4 load on ξ_2. The observed variables are indicated by the squares in Figure 2.1, and the loadings are indicated by the *solid*, straight arrows connecting the latent variables to the observed variables. Note that the observed variables do

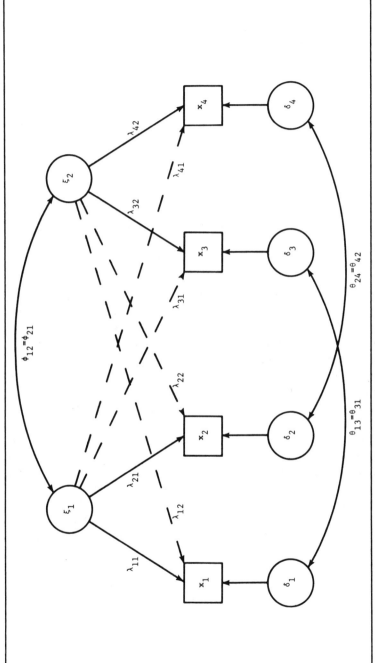

Figure 2.1 A Model for the Measurement of Psychological Disorders

not have direct links to all common factors. For example, while x_1 loads on ξ_1 (i.e., a solid arrow connects ξ_1 to x_1), x_1 does not load on ξ_2 (i.e., a solid arrow does not connect ξ_2 to x_1).

The relationships among the observed variables and factors are specified in a set of equations, referred to as *factor equations*. For our example these equations are

$$x_1 = \lambda_{11}\xi_1 + \delta_1 \qquad\qquad x_2 = \lambda_{21}\xi_1 + \delta_2$$

$$x_3 = \lambda_{32}\xi_2 + \delta_3 \qquad\qquad x_4 = \lambda_{42}\xi_2 + \delta_4 \qquad\qquad [2.1]$$

δ_i is the unique factor affecting x_i. λ_{ij} is the loading of the observed variables x_i on the common factor ξ_j.

The factor equations are similar to a simple linear regression:

$$Y = \alpha + \beta X + e \qquad\qquad [2.2]$$

where Y is an observed dependent variable, X is an observed independent variable, and e is an error term indicating that X does not perfectly predict Y. Factor equations can be thought of as the regression of observed variables (our x's) on unobserved variables (our ξ's). The factor loadings (the λ's in equation 2.1) correspond to slope coefficients (the β in equation 2.2). In equation 2.2, β indicates that a unit change in the independent variable X results in an expected change of β units in the dependent variable Y. Similarly, the factor loadings indicate how a unit change in a common factor affects an observed variable. The factor equations differ from the regression equation in that they have no intercept. Or equivalently, they have an intercept fixed to zero. This is because in factor analysis it is usually assumed that variables are measured from their means, an issue discussed in more detail below. As in regression analysis, the relationship between independent and dependent variables is not exact. This is reflected by the error term e in equation 2.2 and the unique factors δ_i in the factor equations. These unique factors are represented by the circles labeled with δ's at the bottom of Figure 2.1.

If our model were an exploratory factor model, each observed variable would load on each common factor. These additional loadings are represented by *broken arrows* in Figure 2.1. If these loadings were included in our confirmatory model, the resulting factor equations would be

$$x_1 = \lambda_{11}\xi_1 + \lambda_{12}\xi_2 + \delta_1 \qquad x_2 = \lambda_{21}\xi_1 + \lambda_{22}\xi_2 + \delta_2$$

$$x_3 = \lambda_{31}\xi_1 + \lambda_{32}\xi_2 + \delta_3 \qquad x_4 = \lambda_{41}\xi_1 + \lambda_{42}\xi_2 + \delta_4 \qquad [2.3]$$

If these equations were used rather than those in equation 2.1, the loadings would be interpreted as regression coefficients in multiple regression. For example, the loadings in the equation for x_1 would be interpreted as follows: A unit increase in ξ_1 results in an expected increase of λ_{11} units in x_1, holding ξ_2 constant; and, a unit increase in ξ_2 results in an expected increase of λ_{12} units in x_1, holding ξ_1 constant. In our example the decision to use equation 2.1 as opposed to equation 2.3 is based on substantive considerations. If the specification in equation 2.3 were considered preferable, it could have been used. The point distinguishing confirmatory factor analysis from exploratory factor analysis is that equation 2.3 *must* be used in an exploratory analysis, even if the specification in equation 2.1 is substantively preferable.

It is reasonable to expect that the factor representing psychological disorder at time 1 (ξ_1) is correlated with the factor representing psychological disorder at time 2 (ξ_2). A person with a high level of psychological disorder at time 1 would generally be expected to have a high level of psychological disorder at time 2; conversely, a person with a low level of psychological disorder at time 1 would be expected to have a low level of psychological disorder at time 2. The possibility of such a relationship is represented in Figure 2.1 by the curved arrow labeled ϕ_{12} connecting ξ_1 and ξ_2. If ξ_1 and ξ_2 are assumed to have unit variances, ϕ_{12} would correspond to a correlation between ξ_1 and ξ_2; if ξ_1 and ξ_2 are not assumed to have unit variances, ϕ_{12} would correspond to the covariance between ξ_1 and ξ_2.

The unique factors may also be correlated. If δ_1 corresponds to random error in the measurement of psychological symptoms at time 1 (variable x_1), and δ_3 corresponds to random error in the measurement of psychological symptoms at time 2 (variable x_3), these errors in measurement might be correlated over time. That is, large errors in measurement at time 1 might correspond to large errors at time 2, and small errors at time 1 might correspond to small errors at time 2. This possibility is represented by the curved arrow labeled θ_{13} between δ_1 and δ_3. Similarly, covariation between δ_2 and δ_4 is represented by the curved arrow labeled θ_{24}. At this point the confirmatory factor model again distinguishes itself from the exploratory factor model. In the exploratory model all errors in measurement are assumed to be uncorrelated. For this example, this would mean that θ_{13} and θ_{24} would be assumed to equal zero. //[1]

This informal specification of a simple measurement model serves to introduce the basic issues involved in specifying a confirmatory factor model. At this point it is necessary to provide a more formal specification using matrix algebra.

A Formal Specification

Factor analysis attempts to explain the variation and covariation in a set of observed variables in terms of a set of unobserved factors. Each observed variable is conceptualized as a linear function of one or more factors. These factors are of two types: common factors that may directly affect more than one of the observed variables, and unique or residual factors that may directly affect one and only one observed variable. Mathematically the relationship between the observed variables and the factors is expressed as [2]

$$\mathbf{x} = \Lambda \xi + \delta \qquad [2.4]$$

where $\mathbf{x}$ is a $(q \times 1)$ vector of observed variables; ξ is a $(s \times 1)$ vector of common factors; Λ is a $(q \times s)$ matrix of factor loadings relating the observed x's to the latent ξ's; and δ is a $(q \times 1)$ vector of the residual or unique factors. It is assumed that the number of observed variables in $\mathbf{x}$ is greater than the number of common factors in ξ; that is, $q > s$.

Both the observed and latent variables in equation 2.4 are assumed to be measured as deviations from their means. Thus, the expected value of each vector is a vector containing zeros: $E(\mathbf{x}) = \mathbf{0}$; $E(\xi) = \mathbf{0}$; and $E(\delta) = \mathbf{0}$.[3] Since this assumption involves only a change in origin, it does not affect the covariances among the variables and, hence, does not limit the flexibility of the model.[4] For example, let U and V be two variables with means μ and v, and let $u = U - \mu$ and $v = V - v$, then COV(U,V) = COV(u,v).[5] Thus, if we are interested in only the covariance between U and V, it does not matter if we use the original variables or the variables measured as deviations from their means. A practical advantage of assuming zero means is that covariances are equivalent to expectations of the products of variables with zero means. Thus, while $E(UV) \neq COV(U,V)$, it holds that (see Note 5)

$$E(uv) = E[(U - \mu)(V - v)] = COV(U,V) = COV(u,v)$$

Assuming zero means for the observed and latent variables in the confirmatory factor model allows us to define the covariance matrix of a vector of variables in terms of expectations of vector products. Let q be a $(n \times 1)$ vector of random variables such that $E(q) = 0$. Let Q be defined as $E(qq')$, where the $(i,j)^{th}$ element of Q is labeled q_{ij}. For example, assume that q contains three variables ($n = 3$). Then[6]

$$qq' = \begin{bmatrix} q_1 \\ q_2 \\ q_3 \end{bmatrix} [q_1 \ q_2 \ q_3] = \begin{bmatrix} q_1q_1 & q_1q_2 & q_1q_3 \\ q_2q_1 & q_2q_2 & q_2q_3 \\ q_3q_1 & q_3q_2 & q_3q_3 \end{bmatrix}$$

and

$$Q = E(qq') = \begin{bmatrix} E(q_1q_1) & E(q_1q_2) & E(q_1q_3) \\ E(q_2q_1) & E(q_2q_2) & E(q_2q_3) \\ E(q_3q_1) & E(q_3q_2) & E(q_3q_3) \end{bmatrix}$$

$$= \begin{bmatrix} q_{11} & q_{12} & q_{13} \\ q_{21} & q_{22} & q_{23} \\ q_{31} & q_{32} & q_{33} \end{bmatrix} \quad [2.5]$$

Thus, the $(i,j)^{th}$ element of Q, q_{ij}, is the expected value of the product of q_i and q_j.

Since it was assumed that the q_i's are measured as deviations from their means, $q_{ij} = COV(q_i,q_j)$ and $q_{ii} = COV(q_i,q_i) = VAR(q_i)$. Accordingly,

$$ Q = \begin{bmatrix} VAR(q_1) & COV(q_1,q_2) & COV(q_1,q_3) \\ COV(q_2,q_1) & VAR(q_2) & COV(q_2,q_3) \\ COV(q_3,q_1) & COV(q_3,q_2) & VAR(q_3) \end{bmatrix} $$

Since the covariance of x_i and x_j is equivalent to the covariance if x_j and x_i, $q_{ij} = q_{ji}$ and Q is a symmetric matrix (i.e., $Q = Q'$). Matrices such as Q are called variance/covariance matrices, or simply covariance matrices.

A number of definitions and assumptions can now be stated. These and other results are summarized in Table 2.1. The population covariance matrix for the observed variables contained in x is defined as $\Sigma = E(xx')$, a $(q \times q)$ symmetric matrix. The $(i,j)^{th}$ element of Σ, σ_{ij}, is the population value of the covariance between x_i and x_j, and can be defined as $\sigma_{ij} = E(x_i x_j)$. If the x's were standardized to have a variance of one, $E(x_i x_j)$ would be the correlation between x_i and x_j, and Σ would be the population correlation matrix.

The covariances among the common factors are contained in Φ, an $(s \times s)$ symmetric matrix. An individual element of Φ, say ϕ_{ij}, is the covariance between the latent variables ξ_i and ξ_j. Since the factors have zero expectations, $\phi_{ij} = E(\xi_i \xi_j)$ or $\Phi = E(\xi\xi')$. If one assumed that the common factors were uncorrelated, the off-diagonal elements of Φ would be restricted to zeros. If each of the common factors was standardized with a unit variance, Φ would be a correlation matrix with ones on the diagonal and correlations between common factors on the off-diagonals.

The covariances among the residual factors are contained in the population matrix Θ, a $(q \times q)$ symmetric matrix. The $(i,j)^{th}$ element of Θ, θ_{ij}, is the covariance between unique factors δ_i and δ_j. The unique factors are assumed to have means of zero, in the same way that the errors in equations in regression analysis are assumed to have means of zero. It follows that $\theta_{ij} = E(\delta_i \delta_j)$, or in matrix notation, that $\Theta = E(\delta\delta')$. In most treatments of both the exploratory factor model and the confirmatory factor model, all off-diagonal elements of Θ are assumed to be zero, indicating that the unique factor δ_i affecting the observed variable

TABLE 2.1
Summary of the Confirmatory Factor Model

Matrix	Dimension	Mean	Covariance	Dimension	Description
$\boldsymbol{\xi}$	$(s \times 1)$	**0**	$\boldsymbol{\Phi} = E(\boldsymbol{\xi}\boldsymbol{\xi}')$	$(s \times s)$	common factors
x	$(q \times 1)$	**0**	$\boldsymbol{\Sigma} = E(\mathbf{xx}')$	$(q \times q)$	observed variables
$\boldsymbol{\Lambda}$	$(q \times s)$	—	—	—	loadings of **x** on $\boldsymbol{\xi}$
$\boldsymbol{\delta}$	$(q \times 1)$	**0**	$\boldsymbol{\Theta} = E(\boldsymbol{\delta}\boldsymbol{\delta}')$	$(q \times q)$	unique factors

Factor Equation: $\mathbf{x} = \boldsymbol{\Lambda}\boldsymbol{\xi} + \boldsymbol{\delta}$ [2.4]

Covariance Equation: $\boldsymbol{\Sigma} = \boldsymbol{\Lambda}\boldsymbol{\Phi}\boldsymbol{\Lambda}' + \boldsymbol{\Theta}$ [2.11]

Assumptions:

  a. Variables are measured from their means: $E(\boldsymbol{\xi}) = \mathbf{0}$; $E(\mathbf{x}) = E(\boldsymbol{\delta}) = \mathbf{0}$.

  b. The number of observed variables is greater than the number of common factors; i.e., $q > s$.

  c. Common factors and unique factors are uncorrelated: $E(\boldsymbol{\xi}\boldsymbol{\delta}') = \mathbf{0}$ or $E(\boldsymbol{\delta}\boldsymbol{\xi}') = \mathbf{0}$.

x_i is uncorrelated with the unique factor δ_j affecting x_j (for all $i \neq j$). In our treatment of the confirmatory factor model, off-diagonal elements of $\boldsymbol{\Theta}$ need not be constrained to equal zero. This allows the unique factor affecting one observed variable to be correlated with the unique factor affecting some other observed variable.[7] Allowing correlated errors is particularly useful in test/retest models and panel models.

While the common factors are allowed to be correlated among themselves and the unique factors are allowed to be correlated among themselves, it is assumed that all common factors are uncorrelated with all unique factors. Mathematically this can be expressed as $E(\xi_i\delta_j) = 0$ for all ξ_i and δ_j. In matrix algebra this assumption can be expressed as $E(\boldsymbol{\xi}\boldsymbol{\delta}') = \mathbf{0}$, or equivalently, $E(\boldsymbol{\delta}\boldsymbol{\xi}') = \mathbf{0}$.

To illustrate the structure and assumptions of the confirmatory factor model, Example 1 is presented again—this time in matrix notation—and a second example is introduced. These examples are extended in later chapters to illustrate the ideas of identification, estimation, and hypothesis testing.

Example 1: a formal specification. The model for the measurement of psychological disorders is reproduced in Figure 2.2. The relationships

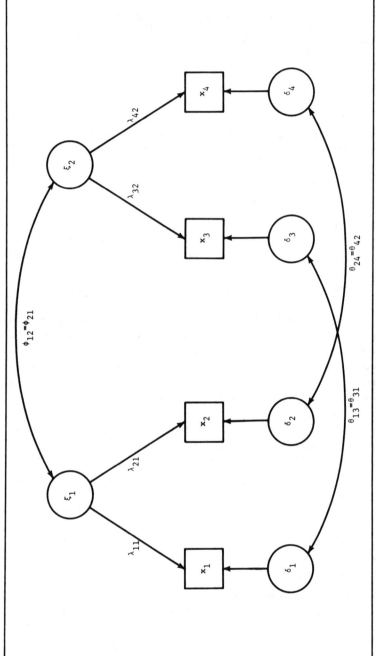

Figure 2.2   A Model for the Measurement of Psychological Disorders

among the observed variables and the common and unique factors were presented in equation 2.3. To translate this equation into a form compatible with the matrix formulation in equation 2.4, it is useful to write the factor equations thus:

$$x_1 = \lambda_{11}\xi_1 + \underline{0}\xi_2 + \delta_1 \qquad \text{[2.6a]}$$

$$x_2 = \lambda_{21}\xi_1 + \underline{0}\xi_2 + \delta_2 \qquad \text{[2.6b]}$$

$$x_3 = \underline{0}\xi_1 + \lambda_{32}\xi_2 + \delta_3 \qquad \text{[2.6c]}$$

$$x_4 = \underline{0}\xi_1 + \lambda_{42}\xi_2 + \delta_4 \qquad \text{[2.6d]}$$

which can be written in matrix form as:

$$
\begin{bmatrix} x_1 \\ x_2 \\ x_3 \\ x_4 \end{bmatrix} =
\begin{bmatrix} \lambda_{11} & \underline{0} \\ \lambda_{21} & \underline{0} \\ \underline{0} & \lambda_{32} \\ \underline{0} & \lambda_{42} \end{bmatrix}
\begin{bmatrix} \xi_1 \\ \xi_2 \end{bmatrix} +
\begin{bmatrix} \delta_1 \\ \delta_2 \\ \delta_3 \\ \delta_4 \end{bmatrix}
\qquad \text{[2.7]}
$$

(Here, and in later chapters, parameters are underlined if they have been constrained to equal the given value.) The reader is encouraged to carry out the necessary matrix operations to reconstruct equation 2.6 from equation 2.7.

Consider equation 2.6a, predicting the observed variable x_1: $x_1 = \lambda_{11}\xi_1 + \underline{0}\xi_2 + \delta_1$. x_1 is defined as a linear combination of the latent variables ξ_1, ξ_2, and δ_1. The coefficient for ξ_1 is λ_{11}, indicating that a unit change in the latent variable ξ_1 results in an average change in x_1 of λ_{11} units. The coefficient for ξ_2 is fixed as zero, indicating that changes in ξ_2 do not directly cause changes in x_1.

In examining the equations 2.6a to 2.6d, one sees that each observed variable loads on only one common factor, with loadings on the other common factors being constrained to zero. In the confirmatory factor model it is up to the researcher to determine which loadings are to be estimated and which are to be constrained to some fixed value. For example, if it made substantive sense to do so, the loading of x_1 on ξ_2 could be freed and the parameter λ_{12} would be estimated.

Each observed variable x_i is also affected by a single residual or unique factor δ_i. The factor δ_i is residual in the sense that it corresponds to that portion of the observed variable x_i that is *not* explained by one or more common factors. Such residual factors are often thought of as random measurement error, unique to each observed variable. Accordingly, they are generally given little substantive consideration.

The curved arrows in the Figure 2.2 correspond to covariances among factors. The arrow connecting ξ_1 and ξ_2 represents the covariance between ξ_1 and ξ_2, which is labeled $\phi_{12} = \phi_{21}$ in $\mathbf{\Phi}$:

$$\mathbf{\Phi} = \begin{bmatrix} \phi_{11} & \phi_{12} \\ \phi_{21} & \phi_{22} \end{bmatrix} \qquad \text{[2.8]}$$

The diagonal elements of $\mathbf{\Phi}$ are the variances of the common factors, and as such define the scale of these unmeasured variables. The importance of the scale of a latent variable is discussed in Chapter 3.

The variances and covariances among the residual factors are contained in $\mathbf{\Theta}$:

$$\mathbf{\Theta} = \begin{bmatrix} \theta_{11} & 0 & \theta_{13} & 0 \\ 0 & \theta_{22} & 0 & \theta_{24} \\ \theta_{31} & 0 & \theta_{33} & 0 \\ 0 & \theta_{42} & 0 & \theta_{44} \end{bmatrix} \qquad \text{[2.9]}$$

The diagonal elements correspond to the variances of the unique factors. The off-diagonal elements indicate a covariance between the unique factor in the equation explaining one observed variable and the unique factor in the equation explaining another observed variable. Thus, the curved arrow between δ_2 and δ_4 in Figure 2.2, designated by **the coefficient θ_{24}, indicates that the unique factor δ_2 in the equation** 2.6b explaining x_2 and the unique factor δ_4 in equation 2.6d explaining

x_4 are correlated. In this particular example, x_2 and x_4 are variables measured with the same instrument at two points in time. Accordingly, it is likely that their errors in measurement (i.e., unique factors) would be correlated. Covariances between unique factors associated with observed variables that have been measured by different methods have been restricted to zero, as indicated by $\underline{0}$'s in equation 2.9.

The assumption that the unique and common factors are uncorrelated (i.e., $E(\boldsymbol{\xi\delta'}) = \boldsymbol{0}$) is represented by the *lack* of curved arrows between the ξ's and δ's in Figure 2.2 //

In Example 1 each observed variable was affected (i.e., loaded on) by only one common factor. In many applications it is reasonable to assume that an observed variable loads on more than one factor. This is the case in the multimethod-multitrait (MMMT) model. In the MMMT model each of a set of traits is measured by each of a set of methods. If the measurement of a trait is not affected by the method used in measurement, the observed variable would load on only the common factor for that trait, and not on the common factor for that method. However, if there is an effect of the method of measurement, then each observed variable would load on both the factor for that particular trait and the factor for the particular method used. The MMMT model attempts to disentangle the effects of different substantive concepts from the methods of measurement used to measure those concepts. This model can be easily formulated as a confirmatory factor model, as our next example illustrates. For more details on the MMMT model, see Alwin (1974); Kenny (1979); and Sullivan and Feldman (1979).

Example 2: the multimethod-multitrait model. Consider a study in which three traits are being measured with each of three methods. Let the three traits correspond to the trait factors ξ_1, ξ_2, and ξ_3, and let the three methods correspond to the method factors ξ_4, ξ_5, and ξ_6. There are nine observed variables: x_1 to x_3 are measures of traits ξ_1 to ξ_3 by method ξ_4; x_4 to x_6 are measures of traits ξ_1 to ξ_3 by method ξ_5; and x_7 to x_9 are measures of traits ξ_1 to ξ_3 by method ξ_6.

Figure 2.3 shows the loadings of the observed variables on the factors. A given method factor is assumed to affect only those observed variables measured by that method. For example, since x_1 to x_3 are all measured by method ξ_4, they load on ξ_4 but not ξ_5 and ξ_6. Similarly, a given trait factor is assumed to affect only those observed variables that are measures of that trait. For example, x_1, x_4, and x_7 are measures of trait ξ_1 by each of the methods and load on the trait factor ξ_1, but not on

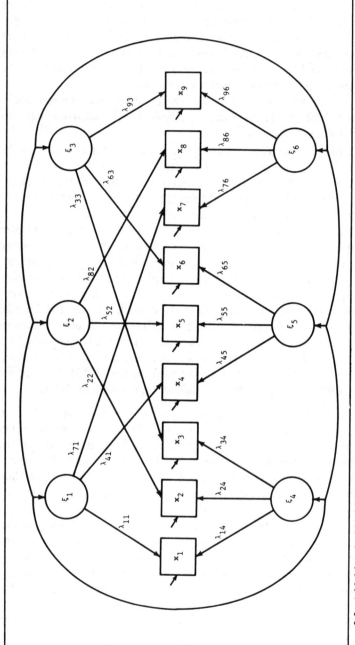

Figure 2.3   A Multimethod-Multitrait Model

the trait factors ξ_2 and ξ_3. This information is contained in the loading matrix Λ:

	Trait Loadings			Method Loadings			
$\Lambda =$	λ_{11}	$\underline{0}$	$\underline{0}$	λ_{14}	$\underline{0}$	$\underline{0}$	x_1
	$\underline{0}$	λ_{22}	$\underline{0}$	λ_{24}	$\underline{0}$	$\underline{0}$	x_2
	$\underline{0}$	$\underline{0}$	λ_{33}	λ_{34}	$\underline{0}$	$\underline{0}$	x_3
	λ_{41}	$\underline{0}$	$\underline{0}$	$\underline{0}$	λ_{45}	$\underline{0}$	x_4
	$\underline{0}$	λ_{52}	$\underline{0}$	$\underline{0}$	λ_{55}	$\underline{0}$	x_5
	$\underline{0}$	$\underline{0}$	λ_{63}	$\underline{0}$	λ_{65}	$\underline{0}$	x_6
	λ_{71}	$\underline{0}$	$\underline{0}$	$\underline{0}$	$\underline{0}$	λ_{76}	x_7
	$\underline{0}$	λ_{82}	$\underline{0}$	$\underline{0}$	$\underline{0}$	λ_{86}	x_8
	$\underline{0}$	$\underline{0}$	λ_{93}	$\underline{0}$	$\underline{0}$	λ_{96}	x_9
	ξ_1	ξ_2	ξ_3	ξ_{44}	ξ_5	ξ_6	

The x's and ξ's are added as borders to indicate which observed variables and common factors are being linked by a particular loading.

Covariances among latent variables are contained in Φ, a (6×6) symmetric matrix. These covariances are indicated by the continuous curve connecting all common factors in Figure 2.3. This matrix contains covariances among trait factors, covariances among method factors, and covariances between trait factors and method factors. If all factors are assumed to be correlated, we have

$$
\Phi = \begin{bmatrix}
\phi_{11} & \phi_{12} & \phi_{13} & \phi_{14} & \phi_{15} & \phi_{16} \\
\phi_{21} & \phi_{22} & \phi_{23} & \phi_{24} & \phi_{25} & \phi_{26} \\
\phi_{31} & \phi_{32} & \phi_{33} & \phi_{34} & \phi_{35} & \phi_{36} \\
\phi_{41} & \phi_{42} & \phi_{43} & \phi_{44} & \phi_{45} & \phi_{46} \\
\phi_{51} & \phi_{52} & \phi_{53} & \phi_{54} & \phi_{55} & \phi_{56} \\
\phi_{61} & \phi_{62} & \phi_{63} & \phi_{64} & \phi_{65} & \phi_{66}
\end{bmatrix} = \begin{bmatrix}
\text{trait/} & \text{trait/} \\
\text{trait} & \text{method} \\
\text{method/} & \text{method/} \\
\text{trait} & \text{method}
\end{bmatrix}
$$

The trait/trait block contains covariances among the trait factors. To understand these covariances it is useful to contrast them with the covariances among the observed variables. For example, σ_{12} is the covariance between the observed variable x_1, which measures trait ξ_1 with method ξ_4, and x_2, which measures trait ξ_2 with the same method. Ideally we would like to know the covariance between the traits ξ_1 and ξ_2, uncontaminated by the effects of the method of measurement used. Even though σ_{12} reflects this covariance, it also reflects the variance in the method factor ξ_4 (ϕ_{44}), the covariances between the trait factors ξ_1 and ξ_2 and the method factor ξ_4 (ϕ_{14} and ϕ_{24}), and the loadings of the x_1 and x_2 on the factors ξ_1, ξ_2, and ξ_4 (λ_{11}, λ_{14}, λ_{22}, and λ_{24}). This can be seen by multiplying the factor equation $x_1 = \lambda_{11}\xi_1 + \lambda_{14}\xi_4 + \delta_1$ by the factor equation $x_2 = \lambda_{22}\xi_2 + \lambda_{24}\xi_4 + \delta_2$ and taking expectations

$$
\begin{aligned}
E(x_1 x_2) = \; & \lambda_{11}\lambda_{22}E(\xi_1\xi_2) + \lambda_{14}\lambda_{22}E(\xi_2\xi_4) + \lambda_{22}E(\xi_2\delta_1) \\
& + \lambda_{11}\lambda_{24}E(\xi_1\xi_4) + \lambda_{14}\lambda_{24}E(\xi_4\xi_4) + \lambda_{24}E(\xi_4\delta_2) \\
& + \lambda_{11}E(\xi_1\delta_2) + \lambda_{14}E(\xi_4\delta_2) + E(\delta_1\delta_2)
\end{aligned}
$$

Since ξ_1, ξ_2, and ξ_4 are assumed to be uncorrelated with δ_1 and δ_2, and δ_1 and δ_2 are assumed to be uncorrelated, it follows that

$$\sigma_{12} = \lambda_{11}\lambda_{22}\phi_{12} + \lambda_{14}\lambda_{22}\phi_{24} + \lambda_{11}\lambda_{24}\phi_{14} + \lambda_{14}\lambda_{24}\phi_{44}$$

The factors contaminating the covariances between observed variables are eliminated by the trait/trait covariance in Φ. Indeed, a primary motivation in applying the MMMT model is to estimate covariances (or correlations) among traits that are unaffected by method.

Variances and covariance among the unique factors are contained in Θ. In the MMMT model the unique factors are usually assumed to be uncorrelated. The unique factors are represented by the unlabeled arrows in Figure 2.3 //

The Covariance Structure

In these examples the relationships among the observed variables and the latent variables have been specified in a manner similar to multiple regression analysis. One important difference exists, however. While the dependent variables are observed in both regression analysis and factor analysis, the independent variables are unobserved in factor models. Consequently, the parameters of the model cannot be directly estimated by regressing the dependent x's on the independent ξ's.

Since the factor equation 2.4 cannot be directly estimated, it is necessary to examine the structure of the covariances among the observed variables (contained in the matrix Σ) in terms of the structure implied by the right-hand side of equation 2.4. This is accomplished by multiplying equation 2.4 by its transpose and taking expectations

$$\Sigma = E(\mathbf{xx'}) = E[(\Lambda\xi + \delta)(\Lambda\xi + \delta)']$$

Since the transpose of a sum of matrices is equal to the sum of the transpose of the matrices, and the transpose of a product of matrices is the product of the transposes in reverse order, it follows that

$$\Sigma = E[(\Lambda\xi + \delta)(\xi'\Lambda' + \delta')]$$

Using the distributive property for matrices and taking expectations

$$\Sigma = E[\Lambda\xi\xi'\Lambda' + \Lambda\xi\delta' + \delta\xi'\Lambda' + \delta\delta']$$

$$= E[\Lambda\xi\xi'\Lambda'] + E[\Lambda\xi\delta'] + E[\delta\xi'\Lambda'] + E[\delta\delta']$$

The parameter matrix Λ does not contain random variables, since the population values of the parameters are constant (even if unknown). This allows us to write

$$\Sigma = \Lambda E[\xi\xi']\Lambda' + \Lambda E[\xi\delta'] + E[\delta\xi']\Lambda' + E[\delta\delta'] \qquad [2.10]$$

Finally, since $E[\xi\xi']$ is defined as Φ, $E[\delta\delta']$ is defined as Θ, and δ and ξ are assumed to be uncorrelated, equation 2.10 can be simplified to:

$$\Sigma = \Lambda\Phi\Lambda' + \Theta \qquad [2.11]$$

This important equation is referred to as the *covariance equation*.

While some readers may not follow the matrix manipulations in the last derivation, it is important to understand what has been accomplished. The left side of the equation contains $q(q + 1)/2$ distinct variances and covariances among the observed variables.[8] The right side of the equation contains qs possible loadings from Λ, $s(s + 1)/2$ independent variances and covariances among the ξ's; and $q(q + 1)/2$ independent variances and covariances among the δ's. Thus, equation 2.11 decomposes the $q(q + 1)/2$ distinct elements of Σ into $[qs + s(s + 1)/2 + q(q + 1)/2]$ unknown, independent parameters from the matrices Λ, Φ, and Θ. The unknown parameters that are to be estimated have been tied to the population variances and covariances among the observed variables. Unlike the parameters in Λ, Φ, and Θ, these variances and covariances can be directly estimated with sample data. It is this link that makes estimation possible. Before estimation can proceed, however, it is necessary to determine whether it is possible to obtain unique estimates of the parameters. This is the problem of *identification*.

3. IDENTIFICATION OF THE CONFIRMATORY FACTOR MODEL

Estimation and Identification

While justification for estimating the parameters is contingent upon the identification of the model, identification and estimation are distinct issues (see, for example, Wonnacott and Wonnacott, 1979: 276). Estimation involves using *sample* data to make estimates of *population* parameters. In the confirmatory factor model this involves using the sample matrix of covariances, called **S**, to estimate the parameters in Λ, Φ, and Θ. Concern is with such issues as bias (are the estimates on average equal to the true parameters?) and efficiency (are the sample data being used in the most effective way?). Identification is concerned with whether the parameters of the model are *uniquely* determined. If a model is not identified, it is impossible to uniquely determine the parameters even if the values for each observed variable are known for the entire population. In the confirmatory factor model this means that even if the population covariance matrix Σ were known (i.e., did not have to be estimated with a sample matrix **S**), it would be impossible to uniquely solve the covariance equation $\Sigma = \Lambda\Phi\Lambda' + \Theta$ for the parameters in Λ, Φ, and Θ. If the model were not identified, it would be possible to find an infinite number of values for the parameters, each set of which would be consistent with the covariance equation.

Estimation assumes that the model is identified. Sample data contained in **S** and information about the structure of the model (i.e., knowledge about the constraints on the parameters that are to be estimated) is used to find estimates $\hat{\Lambda}$, $\hat{\Phi}$, and $\hat{\Theta}$ of the population parameters. These estimates result in predictions of the population variances and covariances of the observed variables according to the equation $\hat{\Sigma} = \hat{\Lambda}\hat{\Phi}\hat{\Lambda}' + \hat{\Theta}$. The problem of estimation is finding $\hat{\Lambda}$, $\hat{\Phi}$, and $\hat{\Theta}$ such that the predicted covariance matrix $\hat{\Sigma}$ is as close as possible to the observed variances and covariances contained in **S**. How this is accomplished and what is meant by "as close as possible" is the subject of Chapter 4. For now, this is the critical issue relating identification and estimation: *Attempts to estimate models that are not identified result in arbitrary estimates of the parameters and meaningless interpretations.* Note well that computer programs will estimate identified as well as unidentified models, providing useful information in the case of identified models and useless information in the case of unidentified models. Identification *must* be established before estimation proceeds.

Identification is not an issue unique to the confirmatory factor model. For example, identification is an important issue in simultaneous equation models and exploratory factor models. One important practical difference exists between identification in the confirmatory factor model and these other models. For simultaneous equation models and exploratory factor models there are rules that can be routinely applied to a large class of commonly encountered models. For simultaneous equation models these are the well-known rank and order conditions (see, for example, Wonnacott and Wonnacott, 1979); for the exploratory factor model these are rules on the number of parameters relative to the number of variances and covariances among observed variables (see, for example, Lawley and Maxwell, 1971). For the confirmatory factor model the rules that are avaiable apply to only a limited number of special cases. Consequently, proving that a model is identified presents one of the greatest practical difficulties in using the confirmatory factor model.

Identification

To understand why identification is a problem, it is useful to recast the problem as follows. Consider the factor model presented in equation 3.1:

$$\mathbf{x} = \Lambda \xi + \delta \qquad [3.1]$$

As shown in Chapter 2, this model implies that the variances and covariances of the observed variables and the parameters Λ, Φ, and θ are related according to the covariance equation

$$\Sigma = \Lambda \Phi \Lambda' + \Theta \qquad [3.2]$$

Unless restrictions are imposed on the parameters in Λ, Φ, and Θ, if there is one set of parameters that satisfies equation 3.2, there will be an infinite number of such sets. To see why this is so, let $\mathbf{M}$ be any (s × s) invertible matrix.[9] If we define $\ddot{\Lambda} = \Lambda \mathbf{M}^{-1}$; $\ddot{\xi} = \mathbf{M}\xi$; and $\ddot{\Phi} = \mathbf{M}\Phi\mathbf{M}'$, both the Λ, Φ, and Θ matrices, and the $\ddot{\Lambda}$, $\ddot{\Phi}$, and $\ddot{\Theta}$ matrices satisfy equations 3.1 and 3.4. This can be easily demonstrated.

$$\ddot{\Lambda}\, \ddot{\xi} + \delta = (\Lambda \mathbf{M}^{-1})(\mathbf{M}\xi) + \delta$$

$$= \Lambda(\mathbf{M}^{-1}\mathbf{M})\xi + \delta$$

$$= \Lambda\xi + \delta \qquad [3.3]$$

Thus, if $\mathbf{x} = \Lambda \xi + \delta$, it is also true that $\mathbf{x} = \ddot{\Lambda}\, \ddot{\xi} + \delta$. Applying the same procedures to the covariance equation 3.2,

$$\ddot{\Lambda} \, \ddot{\Phi} \, \ddot{\Lambda}' \; + \; \Theta \; = \; (\Lambda M^{-1}) \, (M \Phi M') \, (M^{-1} \Lambda') \; + \; \Theta$$

$$= \; \Lambda (M M^{-1}) \, \Phi (M' M'^{-1}) \, \Lambda' \; + \; \Theta$$

$$= \; \Lambda \, \Phi \, \Lambda' \; + \; \Theta \; = \; \Sigma \qquad [3.4]$$

Thus, if $\Sigma = \Lambda \, \Phi \, \Lambda' + \Theta$, it is also true that $\Sigma = \ddot{\Lambda} \, \ddot{\Phi} \, \ddot{\Lambda}' + \Theta$. Since the "··" matrices do not equal the original matrices unless $M = I$, each of the infinite number of invertible M matrices provides an *equally satisfactory* solution to the model. That is, the model is unidentified.

Example 1: the covariance structure. To illustrate this idea, consider the model from Wheaton (1978). Assume, for purposes of demonstration, that the population covariance matrix for the four observed variables is

$$\Sigma = \begin{bmatrix} 0.50 & 0.16 & 0.12 & 0.08 \\ 0.16 & 1.00 & 0.12 & 0.20 \\ 0.12 & 0.12 & 1.60 & 1.44 \\ 0.08 & 0.20 & 1.44 & 2.00 \end{bmatrix}$$

Assume that the population parameter matrices Λ, Φ, and Θ are unknown except that they must reproduce the population covariance matrix Σ given above when substituted into this equation $\Sigma = \Lambda \, \Phi \, \Lambda' + \Theta$.

Consider the matrices $\Lambda^{(1)}$, $\Phi^{(1)}$, and $\Theta^{(1)}$ as possibilities for the population parameters. If they are defined as

$$\Lambda^{(1)} = \begin{bmatrix} 0.20 & 0.00 \\ 0.40 & 0.00 \\ 0.00 & 0.60 \\ 0.00 & 0.80 \end{bmatrix} \qquad \Phi^{(1)} = \begin{bmatrix} 2.00 & 0.50 \\ 0.50 & 3.00 \end{bmatrix}$$

and

$$\mathbf{\Theta}^{(1)} = \begin{bmatrix} 0.42 & 0.00 & 0.06 & 0.00 \\ 0.00 & 0.68 & 0.00 & 0.04 \\ 0.06 & 0.00 & 0.52 & 0.00 \\ 0.00 & 0.04 & 0.00 & 0.08 \end{bmatrix}$$

then the equality $\mathbf{\Sigma} = \mathbf{\Lambda}^{(1)}\mathbf{\Phi}^{(1)}\mathbf{\Lambda}^{(1)\prime} + \mathbf{\Theta}^{(1)}$ holds. (The reader is encouraged to carry out the necessary matrix operations to verify this statement.) Thus, the $10 = [q(q + 1)/2]$ independent elements of $\mathbf{\Sigma}$ are decomposed into—hence are reproduced by—the $21 = qs + [s(s + 1)/2] + [q(q + 1)/2]$ independent elements of the matrices $\mathbf{\Lambda}^{(1)}$, $\mathbf{\Phi}^{(1)}$, and $\mathbf{\Theta}^{(1)}$. The "(1)" matrices satisfy the conditions required of the true parameter matrices: They are of correct dimension and they reproduce the population covariance matrix. The only remaining question is, are they unique, or are there other matrices of correct dimension that also reproduce the population covariance matrix? That is, is the model identified?

To illustrate why the model as currently stated is not identified, let $\mathbf{M}^{(1)}$ and $\mathbf{M}^{(1)^{-1}}$ be defined as

$$\mathbf{M}^{(1)} = \begin{bmatrix} -1.0 & 1.0 \\ 2.0 & -3.0 \end{bmatrix}$$

and

$$\mathbf{M}^{(1)^{-1}} = \begin{bmatrix} -3.0 & -1.0 \\ -2.0 & -1.0 \end{bmatrix}$$

New Λ and Φ matrices can be formed by carrying out the following matrix multiplications on the first set of parameter matrices:

$$\Lambda^{(2)} = \Lambda^{(1)}M^{(1)^{-1}} = \begin{bmatrix} -0.60 & -0.20 \\ -1.20 & -0.40 \\ -1.20 & -0.60 \\ -1.60 & -0.80 \end{bmatrix}$$

and

$$\Phi^{(2)} = M^{(1)}\Phi^{(1)}M^{(1)\prime} = \begin{bmatrix} 4.0 & -10.5 \\ -10.5 & 29.0 \end{bmatrix}$$

with $\Theta^{(1)}$ remaining unchanged. These new parameter matrices have the same dimensions as the first set of matrices, which satisfies the first requirement. Substituting the "(2)" parameters into the covariance equation reproduces the population covariance matrix Σ. That is, $\Sigma = \Lambda^{(2)}\Phi^{(2)}\Lambda^{(2)\prime} + \Theta^{(1)}$. Hence, the second requirement is satisfied. (Once again, the reader should verify this fact.) Since both sets of parameter matrices reproduce Σ, they can both be thought of as solutions to the covariance equation.

While both solutions are acceptable in terms of reproducing the covariance matrix, each suggests a different structure. In $\Lambda^{(1)}$ each observed variable loads on only one common factor, while in $\Lambda^{(2)}$ each observed variable loads on both common factors. In $\Phi^{(1)}$ the common factors are positively correlated, while in $\Phi^{(2)}$ they are negatively correlated. Since both sets of parameters are equally acceptable in terms of reproducing the covariances among observed variables, any interpretation of the parameters is misleading.

To distinguish between the two sets of potential parameters, additional criteria must be used. Recall that in originally describing the model (see Figure 2.2) it was argued that each observed variable should load on only one common factor (i.e., $\lambda_{12} = \lambda_{22} = \lambda_{31} = \lambda_{41} = 0$). With respect to these substantively motivated constraints on the λ's, the (1) solution would be acceptable, while the (2) solution would not. Thus, by imposing constraints on some of the loadings, at least one possible set of parameters is eliminated. The model is identified if the first solution set is the only set of parameters that can reproduce the variances and covariances among the observed variables and maintain the imposed constraints. Whether or not this is the case is considered below.//

Our example illustrates that the factor model is not identified if there are no constraints imposed on the parameters. Without constraints an indeterminacy exists, which allows more than one set of acceptable parameter values. In the exploratory factor model this indeterminacy is often eliminated by imposing the constraint that $\Lambda'\Theta^{-1}\Lambda$ is a diagonal matrix whose elements are distinct, positive, and arranged in descending order (Lawley and Maxwell, 1971: 8).[10] The model is identified since the diagonality constraint eliminates all but one set of possible parameters. The problem is that the constraint is substantively arbitrary. In the confirmatory factor model identification is achieved by imposing constraints based on substantive considerations. Examples of the types of constraints that can be imposed illustrate the advantage of this approach.

Fixing an element of Λ, say λ_{ij}, to zero means that the observed variable x_i is not causally affected by the common factor ξ_j; that is, x_i does not load on ξ_j. Fixing an element of Φ, say ϕ_{ij} where $i \neq j$, to zero means that the common factors ξ_i and ξ_j are uncorrelated. If all off-diagonal elements of Φ are zero ($\phi_{ij} = 0$ for all $i \neq j$), the factor structure is said to be orthogonal. Since Φ is symmetric, fixing $\phi_{ij} = 0$ implies that $\phi_{ji} = 0$; hence only one independent constraint is being imposed. If diagonal elements of Φ are set to zero, say $\phi_{ii} = 0$, the common factor is in effect eliminated, since it has no variation. Similar constraints can be imposed on Θ. If $\theta_{ij} = 0$ for $i \neq j$, then the unique factor affecting x_i is independent of the unique factor affecting x_j. Setting $\theta_{ii} = 0$ indicates that x_i is perfectly determined by the common factors of the model, with no unique component.

Equality constraints can also be imposed. For example, if there are multiple measurements of an underlying factor one might assume that $\lambda_{1j} = \lambda_{2j} = \ldots = \lambda_{qj}$, meaning that all indicators depend on the underlying factor ξ_j in the same way. With equality constraints the value of the parameters constrained to be equal is unknown. Thus, if four parameters are constrained to be equal, only three independent constraints are being imposed, since the value to which they are all equal is unknown.

The confirmatory factor model is identified if the constraints have been imposed in such a way that there is a unique set of parameters that generate Σ according to the covariance equation 3.2. The constraints on parameters in the confirmatory factor model have the same effect as the diagonalization assumption in the exploratory factor model. The major difference is that in the exploratory factor model the diagonalization assumption *always* eliminates all but one set of values for the parameters; hence the model is known to be identified (even if the imposed constraints are substantively meaningless). In the confirmatory factor model the user cannot readily determine if the imposed constraints eliminate all but one set of values for the parameters; hence identification must be proven individually for each model. Example 1 illustrates this point.

Example 1: identification. When this example was initially described, a set of constraints was imposed on Λ. It was assumed that $\lambda_{12} = \lambda_{22} = \lambda_{31} = \lambda_{41} = 0$; that is, x_1 and x_2 load only on ξ_1, while x_3 and x_4 load only on ξ_2. The loading matrix $\Lambda^{(1)}$, defined above, retains these constraints, but $\Lambda^{(2)}$ does not. Thus, the constraints imposed on Λ eliminated at least one possible loading matrix. Nonetheless, the constraints imposed on the loadings are not sufficient to identify the model. This can be seen by considering the matrix $\mathbf{M}^{(3)}$, a diagonal matrix with 1.0 as the $(1,1)^{\text{th}}$ element and 2.0 as the $(2,2)^{\text{th}}$ element. With this matrix another set of Λ and Φ matrices can be constructed that both reproduces the covariance matrix Σ (as did the matrices constructed with $\mathbf{M}^{(1)}$) and maintains the imposed constraints (as $\Lambda^{(2)}$ did not). These new matrices are

$$\Lambda^{(3)} = \Lambda^{(1)}\mathbf{M}^{(3)^{-1}} = \begin{bmatrix} 0.2 & 0.0 \\ 0.4 & 0.0 \\ 0.0 & 0.3 \\ 0.0 & 0.4 \end{bmatrix}$$

and

$$\Phi^{(3)} = \mathbf{M}^{(3)}\Phi^{(1)}\mathbf{M}^{(3)\prime} = \begin{bmatrix} 2.0 & 1.0 \\ 1.0 & 12.0 \end{bmatrix}$$

The reader should verify that $\Sigma = \Lambda^{(3)}\Phi^{(3)}\Lambda^{(3)\prime} + \Theta^{(1)}$, where Σ and $\Theta^{(1)}$ are defined in our earlier example. Thus, while some parameter matrices can be eliminated by the constraints on Λ, not all can. Once again it must be concluded that the model is not identified. //

Conditions for Identification

While it is known that imposing constraints will eliminate at least some possible solutions to the factor model, what is required is a set of easily verifiable conditions that determine unambiguously whether a model is identified. Such conditions are of three types: (1) necessary conditions, which if *not* satisfied indicate that a model is not identified, but if satisfied do not necessarily mean that the model is identified; (2) sufficient conditions, which if met imply that the model is identified, but if not met do not imply that the model is unidentified (although it may be that it is unidentified); and (3) necessary and sufficient conditions, which if satisfied imply that the model is identified, and if not satisfied imply that the model is not identified.

The simplest necessary condition relates the number of independent covariance equations to the number of independent, unconstrained parameters. Covariance equation 3.2 contains $q(q + 1)/2$ independent equations, one for each of the independent elements of the $(q \times q)$ symmetric matrix Σ. If there are more independent parameters than covariance equations, there will be many solutions to equation 3.2 and the model will not be identified. Since there are $qs + [s(s + 1)/2] + [q(q + 1)/2]$ possible independent parameters in Λ, Φ, and Θ, a confirmatory factor model is unidentified unless *at least* $qs + [s(s + 1)/2]$ constraints are imposed. Hence, a necessary but not sufficient condition for identification is that the number of independent, unconstrained parameters in the model must be less than or equal to $q(q + 1)/2$. This condition is easy to apply, as is now illustrated.

Example 1: testing a necessary condition for identification. In this example there are four observed variables and thus, $10 = 4(4 + 1)/2$ distinct variances and covariances in Σ. There are thirteen independent parameters. These are numbered in the following matrices; elements marked with * are fixed.

$$
\Lambda = \begin{bmatrix} 1 & * \\ 2 & * \\ * & 3 \\ * & 4 \end{bmatrix}
\qquad
\Phi = \begin{bmatrix} 5 & 6 \\ 6 & 7 \end{bmatrix}
$$

and

$$
\Theta = \begin{bmatrix} 8 & * & 9 & * \\ * & 10 & * & 11 \\ 9 & * & 12 & * \\ * & 11 & * & 13 \end{bmatrix}
$$

Since the number of independent parameters is greater than the number of independent covariance equations (13 > 10), the necessary condition for identification is not satisfied and the model is not identified. If the number of independent parameters had been less than or equal to the number of independent covariance equations, it would not necessarily mean that the model was identified, since the condition is necessary, but not sufficient. //

Jöreskog (1969:186) described what were thought to be two sufficient conditions, originally presented by Howe (1955). First, if $\Phi = I$ and the columns of Λ are arranged such that column k contains at least $(k - 1)$ fixed elements, the model is identified. Second, if Φ is not diagonal but its diagonal elements are ones (i.e., all factors are standardized to have unit variance), the model is identified if there are at least $(s-1)$ fixed elements in each of the columns of Λ. These conditions have been presented and applied frequently (Werts et al., 1973; Bielby and Hauser, 1977; Burt et al., 1978; Long, 1976), but recent research has shown that these conditions are *not* sufficient (Dunn, 1973; Jennrich, 1978; Burt et al., 1979). Jöreskog (1979) has found one sufficient condition that does hold, however. A confirmatory factor model is identified if (1) Φ is a symmetric, positive definite matrix with diagonal elements equal to one;[11] (2) Θ is diagonal; (3) Λ has at least (s – 1) fixed zeros (nonzero fixed elements do not count) in each column, where s is the number of common factors; and (4) Λ^k has rank (s – 1), where Λ^k (for k = 1, 2, . . . s) is the submatrix of Λ consisting of the rows of Λ that have fixed zero elements in the kth column.[12] An application of this condition is given below.

This condition is limited in two respects. First, it does not apply to many useful models (e.g., models with fixed values not equal to zero; models with equality constraints). Second, it is only a sufficient condition. If a model does not satisfy the condition, it does not necessarily mean that the model is unidentified. Rather, all that is known is that identification cannot be proven with this sufficient condition, and other methods of proving identification must be considered. Accordingly, a more broadly applicable condition for identification is needed.

In general, the most effective way to demonstrate that a model is identified is to show that through algebraic manipulations of the model's covariance equations each of the parameters can be solved in terms of the population variances and covariances of the observed variables. This is a necessary and sufficient condition for identification. If the condition is satisfied, the model is identified; if the condition is not satisfied, the model is not identified. In the case in which the variables are standardized, as noted by Werts et al. (1973: 1473), solving the equations for the parameters is equivalent to solving the path equations. Duncan (1975) and Kenny (1979) are two useful sources dealing with techniques for solving path equations.

With this approach, parameters are identified on an individual basis. If a parameter can be solved for in terms of the variances and covariances of the observed variables, it is identified. If a parameter can be solved in more than one way, the parameter is overidentified—a special case of being identified. The model as a whole is identified if all of the individual parameters are identified. If a model is identified, but some or all of the parameters are overidentified, the model is said to be overidentified—a special case of being identified. Finally, if the covariance equations cannot be solved for a particular parameter, the parameter is unidentified and the model as a whole is unidentified. Note that individual parameters can be identified when the model as a whole is not identified. These identified parameters can be estimated, even though the unidentified parameters cannot. This point is illustrated below.

In practice, solving the covariance equations can be time-consuming. It is tempting to forgo the task and to assume that the model is identified, as all too many retractions for published findings illustrate. It cannot be emphasized strongly enough that if a model is not identified, estimates of the parameters that are not identified are arbitrary and interpretations are meaningless. *Identification must be established before attempts are made to estimate a model.*

Jöreskog and Sörbom (Jöreskog, 1979; Jöreskog and Sörbom, 1981) have recently argued that the computer can be used to determine identification. In computing maximum likelihood estimates of the parameters (a topic discussed in Chapter 4), the information matrix for the parameters can be computed. (See Kmenta [1971: 174-186] for a technical discussion of the information matrix.) Roughly speaking, the information matrix corresponds to a matrix of variances and covariances for the parameter estimates. Jöreskog and Sörbom (1978:11) stated, "if [the information matrix] is positive definite it is *almost certain* that the model is identified. On the other hand, if the information matrix is singular, the model is not identified" (italics added). The software can check these conditions and indicate whether or not the model appears to be identified. Even though this is a tempting solution to the identification problem, the reader is warned that it is not a necessary and sufficient condition for identification. If the information matrix is positive definite, it is possible, even if unlikely, that the model is not identified. If a user happens to estimate a model for which the "almost certain" condition is satisfied, but the model is not identified, the resulting analyses are meaningless. The emphatic recommendation: Always prove that your model is identified by solving the model's parameters in terms of the variances and covariances of the observed variables.[13] On the other hand, if identification has been "proven" by solving the parameters in terms of the covariances among the observed variables, and the program indicates that the information matrix is *not* positive definite, an error in the proof of identification or in running the program may have been made.

Example 1: identification. To illustrate how identification is proven and what components characterize an unidentified model, a variety of models are considered for the measurement of psychological disorder. To make the presentation easier to follow, Table 3.1 provides a summary of each model that is considered here or later in the text. Figure 3.1

TABLE 3.1
Models Considered in Example 1

Model	λ_{11}	λ_{21}	λ_{32}	λ_{42}	ϕ_{11}	ϕ_{22}	ϕ_{12}	θ_{11}	θ_{22}	θ_{33}	θ_{44}	θ_{13}	θ_{24}
M_a	*	*	*	*	*	*	*	*	*	*	*	0	0
M_b	A	B	A	B	*	*	*	*	*	*	*	0	0
M_c	*	*	*	*	1	1	*	*	*	*	*	0	0
M_d	1	*	1	*	*	*	*	*	*	*	*	0	0
M_e	A	B	A	B	1	1	*	*	*	*	*	0	*
M_f	A	B	A	B	1	1	*	*	*	*	*	*	*
M_g	1	A	1	A	B	B	*	*	*	*	*	0	0
M_h	1	A	1	A	B	B	*	*	*	*	*	0	*

NOTE: * indicates that a parameter is estimated; pairs of capital letters indicate that those parameters have been constrained to be equal; numbers indicate fixed value for a parameter.

illustrates the model with all of the parameters that are to be considered.

Consider model M_a described in Table 3.1. There are eleven parameters (λ_{11}, λ_{21}, λ_{32}, λ_{42}, ϕ_{11}, ϕ_{22}, ϕ_{12}, θ_{11}, θ_{22}, θ_{33}, θ_{44}), but only 10 [= $q(q + 1)/2$] variances and covariances. Therefore, the necessary condition for identification is not satisfied, and M_a is not identified.

In longitudinal models with multiple indicators, such as the current example, it is often reasonable to assume that the factor loadings for a given measure at different points in time are identical. For the current example this involves imposing the equality constraints $\lambda_{11} = \lambda_{32}$ and $\lambda_{21} = \lambda_{42}$. M_b adds these constraints to M_a. By imposing two constraints, two of the original eleven independent parameters have been eliminated, leaving nine. Accordingly, the necessary condition for identification is satisfied, and an attempt can be made to solve the covariance equations for the parameters. To facilitate such a solution it is useful to rewrite the factor equations (equation 2.6 above) incorporating the constraints:

$$x_1 = \lambda_{11}\xi_1 + \delta_1 \qquad x_2 = \lambda_{21}\xi_1 + \delta_2$$

$$x_3 = \lambda_{11}\xi_2 + \delta_3 \qquad x_4 = \lambda_{21}\xi_2 + \delta_4 \qquad [3.5]$$

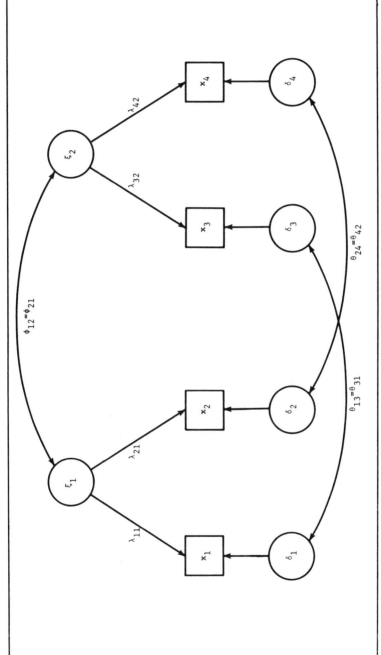

Figure 3.1 A Model for the Measurement of Psychological Disorders

287

The elements of the covariance equations are obtained by multiplying the factor equations 3.5 by one another and taking expectations. For example, multiplying the equation for x_1 by itself results in

$$x_1 x_1 = \lambda_{11}^2 \xi_1 \xi_1 + \delta_1 \delta_1 + 2\lambda_{11}\xi_1\delta_1$$

Taking expectations,

$$E(x_1 x_1) = E(\lambda_{11}^2 \xi_1\xi_1 + \delta_1\delta_1 + 2\lambda_{11}\xi_1\delta_1)$$

$$= E(\lambda_{11}^2 \xi_1\xi_1) + E(\delta_1\delta_1) + E(2\lambda_{11}\xi_1\delta_1)$$

$$= \lambda_{11}^2 E(\xi_1\xi_1) + E(\delta_1\delta_1) + 2\lambda_{11}E(\xi_1\delta_1)$$

Since the x's, ξ's, and δ's are assumed measured from their means, the expectations of the products are equal to variances or covariances.

$$VAR(x_1) = \lambda_{11}^2 VAR(\xi_1) + VAR(\delta_1) + 2\lambda_{11}COV(\xi_1, \delta_1)$$

$$= \lambda_{11}^2 \phi_{11} + \theta_{11} + 0$$

which follows by substituting the symbols used for $VAR(\xi_1)$ and $VAR(\delta_1)$, and using the assumption that $COV(\xi_1, \delta_1)$ is zero. Thus, we conclude that

$$\sigma_{11} = \lambda_{11}^2 \phi_{11} + \theta_{11}$$

Applying the same procedures to all possible pairs of equations, the following results are obtained:

$$\sigma_{11} = \lambda_{11}^2\phi_{11} + \theta_{11} \qquad\qquad \sigma_{22} = \lambda_{21}^2\phi_{11} + \theta_{22}$$

$$\sigma_{33} = \lambda_{11}^2\phi_{22} + \theta_{33} \qquad\qquad \sigma_{44} = \lambda_{21}^2\phi_{22} + \theta_{44}$$

$$\sigma_{12} = \lambda_{11}\lambda_{21}\phi_{11} \qquad \sigma_{13} = \lambda_{11}^2\phi_{12} \qquad \sigma_{14} = \lambda_{11}\lambda_{21}\phi_{12}$$

$$\sigma_{23} = \lambda_{11}\lambda_{21}\phi_{12} \qquad \sigma_{24} = \lambda_{21}^2\phi_{12} \qquad \sigma_{34} = \lambda_{11}\lambda_{21}\phi_{22}$$

$$[3.6]$$

To demonstrate identification, the parameters of the model must be solved for in terms of these equations.

Consider the parameters ϕ_{11} and ϕ_{22}. In solving for these parameters the variance equations $\sigma_{11}, \sigma_{22}, \sigma_{33}$, and σ_{44} are not helpful, since each contains an unknown parameter corresponding to the variance of a unique factor (parameters $\theta_{11}, \theta_{22}, \theta_{33}$, and θ_{44}, respectively). Accordingly, the variance equations cannot be used to solve for ϕ_{11} and ϕ_{22} until the values of $\theta_{11}, \theta_{22}, \theta_{33}$, and θ_{44} are known. But solutions for $\theta_{11}, \theta_{22}, \theta_{33}$, and θ_{44} cannot be obtained until the parameters $\lambda_{11}, \lambda_{21}, \phi_{11}$, and ϕ_{22} have been solved for. Consequently, if equation 3.6 can be solved for ϕ_{11} and ϕ_{22}, the equations for $\sigma_{11}, \sigma_{22}, \sigma_{33}$, and σ_{44} will not be helpful.

The equations for σ_{ij} ($i \neq j$) can be solved for ratios of ϕ_{11}, ϕ_{22}, and ϕ_{12}. The ratios $\phi_{11}/\phi_{12}, \phi_{11}/\phi_{22}$, and ϕ_{12}/ϕ_{22}, can be solved for in several ways; hence these *ratios* of parameters are overidentified. One set of solutions is

$$\frac{\sigma_{12}}{\sigma_{14}} = \frac{\phi_{11}}{\phi_{12}} \qquad \frac{\sigma_{12}}{\sigma_{34}} = \frac{\phi_{11}}{\phi_{22}} \qquad \frac{\sigma_{14}}{\sigma_{34}} = \frac{\phi_{12}}{\phi_{22}}$$

While there are three equations in three unknowns, they cannot be solved for the parameters ϕ_{11}, ϕ_{22}, and ϕ_{12}. (The reader is encouraged to try to solve these equations; such systems of equations are frequently encountered in attempts to identify a model.) Since the covariance equations cannot be solved for the parameters in Φ, these parameters are not identified.

A similar result occurs in attempting to solve for loadings λ_{11} and λ_{21}. While the ratio $\lambda_{11}/\lambda_{21}$ can be solved for in terms of covariances (e.g., $\lambda_{11}/\lambda_{21} = \sqrt{\sigma_{13}/\sigma_{24}}$), there are no solutions for λ_{11} and λ_{12} individually.

None of the parameters of model M_b are identified; hence the model is unidentified. The reason for this is that there is a *scale indeterminacy*, a basic problem in factor analytic models. //

Scale Indeterminacy and Setting a Metric

A factor analytic model cannot be identified until the metric, or scale, of the common factors has been established. If the scale of a factor is not established, there exists an indeterminacy between the variance of a common factor and the loadings of observed variables on that factor. This makes it impossible to distinguish between the case in which a factor has a large variance and the loadings on it are small, and the case in which the variance is small and the loadings on it are large. In terms of the parameters of the model, the problem is that if the loadings in Λ are not fixed, they must be estimated. If the diagonal elements of Φ (i.e., the variances of the common factors) are not fixed, they must be estimated. But it is not possible to estimate both the loadings on and the variances of common factors.

For example, let ξ be a common factor, let x be an observed variable that loads on ξ with loading λ, and let δ be the unique factor affecting x. For this example, subscripts have been dropped to simplify the presentation. The factor equation for x is

$$x = \lambda\xi + \delta \qquad [3.7]$$

Using the techniques and assumptions described above, it follows that

$$VAR(x) = \lambda^2 VAR(\xi) + VAR(\delta) \qquad [3.8]$$

To see why the loading of x on ξ and the variance of ξ are not identified, suppose that there is a second common factor, ξ^*, that differs from ξ only by a change in scale. That is, $\xi^* = \alpha\xi$, where α is any constant not equal to one or zero. For example, if ξ is measured in dollars and ξ^* is measured in cents, then α would equal 100 and ξ^* would equal $100 \times \xi$.

Now assume that the loading of x on ξ^* equals $\lambda^* = \lambda/\alpha$, resulting in the factor equation $x = \lambda^*\xi^* + \delta$. This equation is identical to equation 3.7, as can be easily shown:

$$x = \lambda^*\xi^* + \delta$$

$$= (\lambda/\alpha)(\alpha\xi) + \delta$$

$$= \lambda\xi + \delta \qquad [3.9]$$

Since $\xi^* = \alpha\xi$, it follows that $VAR(\xi^*) = VAR(\alpha\xi) = \alpha^2 VAR(\xi)$. This allows us to demonstrate that the variance of $x = \lambda^*\xi^* + \delta$ is equivalent to the variance of $x = \lambda\xi + \delta$ as defined in equation 3.8:

$$VAR(x) = \lambda^{*2} VAR(\xi^*) + VAR(\delta)$$

$$= (\lambda/\alpha)^2 VAR(\alpha\xi) + VAR(\delta)$$

$$= (\lambda^2/\alpha^2) \alpha^2 VAR(\xi) + VAR(\delta)$$

$$= \lambda^2 VAR(\xi) + VAR(\delta) \qquad [3.10]$$

Since the common and unique factors are unobserved, there is no way to tell if the observed variable x was generated by ξ and δ with a loading λ, or by ξ^* and δ with a loading λ^*. The change in scale occurring in the change from ξ to ξ^* is absorbed by an offsetting change in the loading from λ to $\lambda^* = \lambda/\alpha$. The loading of x on ξ and the variance of ξ cannot be identified since they are indistinguishable from the loading of x on ξ^* and the variance of ξ^*.

Example 1: scale indeterminacy. This important point can be further illustrated by considering the sets of specific values for Λ, Φ, and Θ presented above. Consider the observed variable x_3. The variance of x_3 was assumed to equal 1.60, or $\sigma_{33} = 1.60$. Set (1) of parameters included these values: $\lambda_{32}^{(1)} = 0.60$, $\phi_{22}^{(1)} = 3.0$, and $\theta_{33}^{(1)} = 0.52$. These values satisfy the covariance equation for x_3:

$$\sigma_{33} = \lambda_{32}^{(1)^2}\phi_{22}^{(1)} + \theta_{33}^{(1)}$$

or, substituting specific values,

$$1.60 = (0.60)^2\, 3.0 + 0.52$$

Now consider set (3) of parameters: $\lambda_{32}^{(3)} = 0.30$, $\phi_{22}^{(3)} = 12.00$, and $\theta_{33}^{(3)} = \theta_{33}^{(1)} = 0.52$. The loading λ_{32} decreases by a factor of 0.5 and the common factor variance ϕ_{22} increases by a factor of 4.0. Above it was demonstrated that if a common factor's scale is changed by a factor of α, the variance of the common factor changes by a factor of α^2, and the loadings on that factor change by a factor of $1/\alpha$. Thus, $\lambda_{32}^{(3)} = \lambda_{32}^{(1)}/\alpha$ and $\phi_{22}^{(3)} = \alpha^2\phi_{22}^{(1)}$, and α must equal 2.0. In moving from the parameters in set (1) to those in set (3), the decrease in the loading from 0.60 to 0.30 ($= 0.60 \times 1/2.0$) is offset by an increase in the variance of ξ_2 from 3.0 to 12.0 ($= 0.30 \times 2.0^2$). These results imply that

$$\sigma_{33} = \lambda_{32}^{(3)^2}\phi_{22}^{(3)} + \theta_{33}^{(3)} = (\lambda_{32}^{(1)}/\alpha)^2\alpha^2\phi_{22}^{(1)} + \theta_{33}^{(1)}$$

or, substituting specific values,

$$1.60 = (0.30)^2 12.0 + 0.52 = (0.60/2.0)^2[(2.0)^2 3.0] + 0.52$$

Thus, in terms of reproducing the variance of the observed variable x_3, the two sets of parameters are indistinguishable. The two solutions, as well as any other obtained by choosing a diagonal **M** matrix, differ only by the arbitrary scales of the common factors. The reader is encouraged to choose another diagonal **M** matrix and verify this statement. //

The indeterminacy caused by a lack of scale or metric for the common factors can be eliminated in either of two ways: (1) by fixing the variances of the common factors or (2) by fixing one loading on each factor to a nonzero value. To illustrate these two approaches, consider again the factor equation $x = \lambda\xi + \delta$. Above it was noted that if the scale of the common factor is not known, it is impossible to distinguish the common factor ξ from the common factor $\xi^* = \alpha\xi$. If the variance of ξ is fixed to some constant value, say 1, then $VAR(\xi)$ and $VAR(\xi^*)$ must both equal one. Given the equality $VAR(\xi^*) = \alpha^2 VAR(\xi)$, it follows that α equals one and ξ is identical to ξ^*. Thus, the indeterminacy has been eliminated.

Alternatively, if the loading of the observed variable on the common factor is fixed to some constant value, say 1, the equality $\lambda\xi + \delta = \lambda^*\xi^* + \delta$ reduces to $\xi + \delta = \xi^* + \delta$ or $\xi = \xi^*$, and the indeterminacy has been eliminated. By fixing a loading to one, the common factor is given the scale of the observed variable. This can be seen by considering the factor equation $x = \lambda\xi + \delta$, which is now simplified by the assumption that $\lambda = 1.0$ to this: $x = \xi + \delta$. If ξ increases by some constant, an equivalent change is produced in the observed variable x. Since a common factor's scale is determined by a single fixed loading, it is unnecessary and overly restrictive to fix the loadings of more than one observed variable on any common factor.

In general, if the variances of the common factors are fixed or if one loading on each common factor is fixed, the scale indeterminacy is eliminated from the confirmatory factor model. This does not necessarily mean that the model is identified, for other sources of indeterminacy may still exist. These points are illustrated with Example 1.

Example 1: identification. The first method of fixing the scale in the model is to constrain the diagonal elements of Φ to equal 1.0: $\phi_{11} = \phi_{22} = 1.0$. Let M_c be the model formed from M_a (see Table 3.1 for a summary of the models used in this example) by imposing the constraints $\phi_{11} = \phi_{22} = 1.0$. The resulting covariance equations are

$$\sigma_{11} = \lambda_{11}^2 + \theta_{11} \qquad\qquad \sigma_{22} = \lambda_{21}^2 + \theta_{22}$$

$$\sigma_{33} = \lambda_{32}^2 + \theta_{33} \qquad\qquad \sigma_{44} = \lambda_{42}^2 + \theta_{44}$$

$$\sigma_{12} = \lambda_{11}\lambda_{21} \qquad \sigma_{13} = \lambda_{11}\phi_{12}\lambda_{32} \qquad \sigma_{14} = \lambda_{11}\phi_{12}\lambda_{42}$$

$$\sigma_{23} = \lambda_{21}\phi_{12}\lambda_{32} \qquad \sigma_{24} = \lambda_{21}\phi_{12}\lambda_{42} \qquad \sigma_{34} = \lambda_{32}\lambda_{42}$$

From these equations we find that $\sigma_{12} = \lambda_{11}\lambda_{21}$ and $\sigma_{13}/\sigma_{23} = \lambda_{11}/\lambda_{21}$. Solving these two equations in two unknowns results in $\lambda_{21} = \sqrt{\sigma_{12}\sigma_{23}/\sigma_{13}}$ and $\lambda_{11} = \sigma_{12}/\lambda_{21}$. Similarly, $\lambda_{42} = \sqrt{\sigma_{34}\sigma_{14}/\sigma_{13}}$ and $\lambda_{32} = \sigma_{34}/\lambda_{42}$. Then, $\phi_{12} = \sigma_{13}/\lambda_{11}\lambda_{32}$. The remaining parameters are solved for as

$$\theta_{11} = \sigma_{11} - \lambda_{11}^2$$

$$\theta_{22} = \sigma_{22} - \lambda_{21}^2$$

$$\theta_{33} = \sigma_{33} - \lambda_{32}^2$$

$$\theta_{44} = \sigma_{44} - \lambda_{42}^2$$

Note that in proving that parameters are identified, once a parameter is shown to be identified, its value can be assumed known in proving that other parameters are identified. For example, once it was shown that λ_{21} was identified, λ_{21} was used to solve for λ_{11}.

Since each of the parameters is identified, the model is identified. Further, the model is overidentified. For example, parameter λ_{21} can also be solved for as $\lambda_{21} = \sqrt{\sigma_{12}\sigma_{24}/\sigma_{14}}$. Other parameters are also overidentified, as the reader should verify.

A second method of fixing the scales of the common factors is by fixing one of the loadings for each common factor to equal one. For example, constrain $\lambda_{11} = \lambda_{32} = 1.0$. Call this model M_d. The covariance equations are now

$$
\begin{array}{lll}
\sigma_{11} = \phi_{11} + \theta_{11} & & \sigma_{22} = \lambda_{21}^2\phi_{11} + \theta_{22} \\[2mm]
\sigma_{33} = \phi_{22} + \theta_{33} & & \sigma_{44} = \lambda_{42}^2\phi_{22} + \theta_{44} \\[2mm]
\sigma_{12} = \lambda_{21}\phi_{11} & \sigma_{13} = \phi_{12} & \sigma_{14} = \lambda_{42}\phi_{12} \\[2mm]
\sigma_{23} = \lambda_{21}\phi_{12} & \sigma_{24} = \lambda_{21}\phi_{12}\lambda_{42} & \sigma_{34} = \lambda_{42}\phi_{22}
\end{array}
$$

$$[3.11]$$

The parameters can be easily solved for as $\phi_{12} = \sigma_{13}$; $\lambda_{42} = \sigma_{14}/\phi_{12}$; $\lambda_{21} = \sigma_{23}/\phi_{12}$; $\phi_{11} = \sigma_{12}/\lambda_{21}$; $\phi_{22} = \sigma_{34}/\lambda_{42}$; $\theta_{11} = \sigma_{11} - \phi_{11}$; $\theta_{22} = \sigma_{22} - \lambda_{21}^2\phi_{11}$; $\theta_{33} = \sigma_{33} - \phi_{22}$; and $\theta_{44} = \sigma_{44} - \lambda_{42}^2\phi_{22}$. Hence, the model is identified.

Now consider a modification to Model M_b. The model, M_e, assumes that

$$\Lambda = \begin{bmatrix} \lambda_{11} & \underline{0} \\ \lambda_{21} & \underline{0} \\ \underline{0} & \lambda_{11} \\ \underline{0} & \lambda_{21} \end{bmatrix} \qquad \Phi = \begin{bmatrix} \underline{1} & \phi_{12} \\ \phi_{21} & \underline{1} \end{bmatrix}$$

and

$$\Theta = \begin{bmatrix} \theta_{11} & \underline{0} & \underline{0} & \underline{0} \\ \underline{0} & \theta_{22} & \underline{0} & \theta_{24} \\ \underline{0} & \underline{0} & \theta_{33} & \underline{0} \\ \underline{0} & \theta_{42} & \underline{0} & \theta_{44} \end{bmatrix}$$

The resulting covariance equations are

$$\sigma_{11} = \lambda_{11}^2 + \theta_{11} \qquad\qquad \sigma_{22} = \lambda_{21}^2 + \theta_{22}$$

$$\sigma_{33} = \lambda_{11}^2 + \theta_{33} \qquad\qquad \sigma_{44} = \lambda_{21}^2 + \theta_{44}$$

$$\sigma_{12} = \lambda_{11}\lambda_{21} \qquad \sigma_{13} = \lambda_{11}^2\phi_{12} \qquad \sigma_{14} = \lambda_{11}\phi_{12}\lambda_{21}$$

$$\sigma_{23} = \lambda_{21}\phi_{12}\lambda_{11} \qquad \sigma_{24} = \lambda_{21}^2\phi_{12} + \theta_{24} \qquad \sigma_{34} = \lambda_{11}\lambda_{21}$$

$$[3.12]$$

The parameters can be solved for as $\phi_{12} = \sigma_{23}/\sigma_{12}$; $\lambda_{11} = \sqrt{\sigma_{13}/\phi_{12}}$; $\lambda_{21} = \sigma_{34}/\lambda_{11}$; $\theta_{24} = \sigma_{24} - \lambda_{21}^2\phi_{12}$; and the θ_{ii} parameters are solved for similarly to the earlier models. Consequently, M_e is identified. Indeed, the model is overidentified, as the reader should attempt to verify.

As a final model, M_f in Table 3.1, modify M_e by relaxing the constraint $\theta_{13} = 0$. The only equation that changes in equation set 3.12 is $\sigma_{13} = \lambda_{11}^2\phi_{12} + \theta_{13}$. The covariance between ξ_1 and ξ_2 (which is now a correlation since ξ_1 and ξ_2 have variances of one), can still be solved, and is in fact overidentified: $\phi_{12} = \sigma_{23}/\sigma_{34} = \sigma_{14}/\sigma_{34} = \sigma_{14}/\sigma_{12} = \sigma_{23}/\sigma_{12}$. The covariance equations cannot be solved for any other parameters; therefore the model is unidentified. It is important to realize that even though the model is not identified, it would be possible to estimate ϕ_{12}, since it is identified. If a researcher were primarily concerned with the correlation between the two common factors, it could be estimated, even though the other parameters could not. //

This concludes our discussion of identification. While the algebraic manipulations may seem far removed from the substantive interest motivating a particular analysis, identification is a crucial component of the confirmatory factor model.

4. ESTIMATION OF THE CONFIRMATORY FACTOR MODEL

After identification has been established, estimation can proceed. The general objective in estimating the factor model is to find estimates of the parameters that reproduce the sample matrix of variances and covariances of the observed variables as closely as possible in some well-defined sense. In this chapter several methods of estimation are presented. While a formal statistical justification of these methods is beyond the scope of this monograph, it is possible to present the general characteristics of each method. For technical details, see Browne, (1974), Jöreskog and Goldberger (1972), Bentler and Bonett (1980), and the literature cited therein.

The researcher begins with a sample of observed data. From the sample data it is possible to construct the sample covariance matrix S with elements s_{ij}. Diagonal elements are variances of the observed variables, and off-diagonal elements are covariances. If the data are standardized, S contains the correlations among the observed variables.

The population covariance matrix Σ is related to the population parameters by the covariance equation $\Sigma = \Lambda \Phi \Lambda' + \Theta$. In the same way an estimate of Σ is defined in terms of estimates of the population parameters through the covariance equation $\hat{\Sigma} = \hat{\Lambda} \hat{\Phi} \hat{\Lambda}' + \hat{\Theta}$, where the $\wedge$ indicates that the matrices contain estimates of population parameters. These estimates must satisfy the constraints that have been imposed on the model. Estimation involves finding values of $\hat{\Lambda}$, $\hat{\Phi}$, and $\hat{\Theta}$ that generate an estimated covariance matrix $\hat{\Sigma}$ that is as close as possible to the sample covariance matrix S.

It is useful to think of the process of estimation as follows. Consider all possible sets of matrices having the dimensions of the matrices Λ, Φ, and Θ. Many of these possible matrices must be excluded from consideration because they do not incorporate the constraints imposed on Λ, Φ, and Θ. Let Λ^*, Φ^*, and Θ^* be any matrices that incorporate the imposed constraints. This set of matrices define a matrix Σ^* according to the formula $\Sigma^* = \Lambda^* \Phi^* \Lambda^{*'} + \Theta^*$. If Σ^* is "close" to S, one might conclude that Λ^*, Φ^*, and Θ^* are reasonable estimates of the population parameters. This would be justified since the value of Σ^* implied by Λ^*, Φ^*, and Θ^* is consistent with the observed data. The problems of estimation are to measure how close Σ^* is to S, and to find the values of Λ^*, Φ^*, and Θ^* that produce the Σ^* that is as close as possible to S.

A function that measures how close a given Σ^* is to the sample covariance matrix S is called a *fitting function*. A fitting function is designated as $F(S; \Sigma^*)$; or, to indicate that Σ^* is defined by Λ^*, Φ^*, and

Θ^*, it may be written as $F(S;\Lambda^*, \Phi^*, \Theta^*)$. This function is defined over all possible matrices Λ^*, Φ^*, and Θ^* that satisfy the constraints on Λ, Φ, and Θ. If one set of "*"ed matrices produces the matrix Σ_1^*, and a second set produces the matrix Σ_2^*, if $F(S;\Sigma_1^*) < F(S; \Sigma_2^*)$, Σ_1^* is considered to be closer to S than is Σ_2^*. Those values of Λ^*, Φ^*, and Θ^* that minimize the fitting function for a given S are the sample estimates of the population parameters and are designated as $\hat{\Lambda}$, $\hat{\Phi}$, and $\hat{\Theta}$.

Three fitting functions are commonly used in confirmatory factor analysis. These functions correspond to the methods of unweighted least squares (ULS), generalized least squares (GLS), and maximum likelihood (ML).

Unweighted Least Squares

ULS for the confirmatory factor model corresponds to the method of iterated principal factors or MINRES in exploratory factor analysis (see Harmon, 1976: chaps.8, 9). The ULS estimators of Λ, Φ, and Θ are those values that minimize the fitting function:

$$F_{ULS}(S;\Sigma^*) = tr[(S - \Sigma^*)^2] \qquad [4.1]$$

where "tr" is the trace operator indicating the sum of the diagonal elements of a matrix. [14] The fitting function for ULS is an intuitively reasonable way of assessing the difference between two matrices. Though not immediately obvious from equation 4.1, the fitting function computes the sum of the squares of corresponding elements of S and Σ^*. Estimation involves minimizing this sum of squares, in much the same way that ordinary or unweighted least squares for regression analysis minimizes the sum of the squared residuals.

Beyond this intuitive justification, the ULS estimator can be shown to be consistent without making any assumptions about the distribution of the x-variables (Bentler and Weeks, 1980). This means that for large samples, ULS is approximately unbiased. Not having to make distributional assumptions about the observed variables is an advantage, but it is offset by two limitations. First, there are no statistical tests associated with ULS estimation of the confirmatory factor model. Second, ULS estimators have a property known as *scale dependency*.

Scale Dependency

The scale of a variable changes if the unit of measurement changes. Accompanying a change in scale of a variable is a corresponding change in the standard deviation of that variable. For example, if income is measured in cents rather than dollars, the change in scale is accompanied by an increase by a factor of 100 (the number of cents in a dollar) in the standard deviation. A particularly useful change in scale involves standardization. If a variable is divided by its standard deviation, the resulting variable has a standard deviation of one and the covariance between two such standardized variables is the correlation between those variables.

A method of estimation is scale free if the minimum of the fitting function is independent of the scale of the variables. Accordingly, the minimum of the fitting function for a scale free estimator is identical, whether the sample covariance matrix or the sample correlation matrix is analyzed. The parameter estimates would change, but only to reflect the change in scale of the observed variables being analyzed. An example clarifies this point.

Let x be an observed variable that measures income in dollars, and let ξ be a common factor measuring income. Let $\lambda = 5$ be the loading of x on ξ, indicating that a unit change in ξ results in a five-dollar change in x. If the scale of x is changed from dollars to cents, a change by a factor of 100, the value of λ changes to 500 to reflect the change in scale. Thus, a change in ξ of one unit would result in a change in the rescaled x of 500 cents, the new unit of measurement. (Recall that we are assuming the estimates are obtained by a scale-free method of estimation.) Clearly this is a transparent change, since 500 units in the rescaled x is equal to five units in the original x. That is, 500 cents is equal to five dollars.

If a method is scale dependent, changes in scale result in different minimums for the fitting function, and changes in the estimates do not simply reflect the change in scale. ULS is a method of estimation that is scale dependent. Accordingly, the results obtained may differ when different units of measurement are used. For example, analyzing data in which income is measured in dollars can lead to substantively different results than those obtained from analyzing the same data measured in cents, pounds, or yen. Since the scales of variables are often arbitrary, it is generally suggested that when a scale-dependent method is used, the scales of the observed variables should be standardized by analyzing a correlation matrix.

Generalized Least Squares and Maximum Likelihood

GLS and ML are two methods that have the advantage of being scale free. These methods are now considered.

The fitting function for GLS is more complex than that for ULS, with differences between S and Σ being weighted by elements of S^{-1} (see Jöreskog and Goldberger, 1972). The GLS fitting function is [15]

$$F_{GLS}(S;\Sigma^*) = tr[(S - \Sigma^*)S^{-1}]^2 \qquad [4.2]$$

As Σ^* approaches S, the value of F_{GLS} becomes smaller. If S equals Σ^*, the function necessarily equals zero.

The ML estimator minimizes the fitting function defined as

$$F_{ML}(S;\Sigma^*) = tr(S\Sigma^{*-1}) + [\log | \Sigma^*| - \log | S |] - q \qquad [4.3]$$

where $\log | \Sigma^* |$ is the log of the determinant of the matrix Σ^*.[16,17] The statistical justification of this function is beyond the scope of this discussion, but it is possible to indicate how the function reflects the distance between S and Σ^*. (See Jöreskog [1969] for a derivation of the ML fitting function.) If S and Σ^* are similar, their inverses will be similar. Accordingly, $S\Sigma^{*-1}$ becomes closer to a (q × q) identity matrix as Σ^* and S become closer. Since the trace of a (q × q) identity matrix equals q (the sum of the q ones on the diagonal), the first term in the fitting function approaches the value of q as S and Σ^* become closer. The second term in F_{ML} is the difference in the logs of the determinants of S and Σ^*. As S and Σ^* become closer, their determinants (and logs of determinants) become closer and the second term approaches zero. The last term in the fitting function is the constant q, which serves to cancel the value approached by the first term. Accordingly, if S and Σ^* are equal, the fitting function will equal zero.

If x has a multivariate normal distribution, both GLS and ML have desirable asymptotic properties, that is, properties that hold as the sample size gets large. The ML estimator is approximately unbiased, has as small a sampling variance as any other estimator, and is approximately normally distributed. This means that if the assumptions about the distribution of x hold, as the sample size gets larger, (1) the expected value of the sample estimates get closer and closer to the true population parameters; (2) the variance of the sampling distribution of the ML estimators becomes as small as possible with any estimator; and (3) the sampling distribution of the estimators becomes normal. In the confirmatory factor model, GLS is asymptotically equivalent to ML (Lee, 1977; Browne, 1974). Both methods of estimation are scale invariant and have desirable properties for statistical testing, a topic discussed in the next chapter.

Note that these are asymptotic properties. Strictly speaking, they are justified only as the sample approaches an infinite size. An important practical question is, How large must a sample be in order to take advantage of the desirable asymptotic properties? Unfortunately, there is no definitive answer to this question. Boomsma (1982) has obtained some results for two factor models with either six or eight observed variables. For such models he concluded that it is dangerous to use sample sizes smaller than 100. One would expect that more complex models with more factors and more observed variables would require larger samples. Further, he found that the robustness of the ML estimator depends on the magnitudes of the parameters being estimated. Further research is needed in this area.

The mathematical justification for both GLS and ML require assumptions of normality, with GLS being justified under slightly less restrictive assumptions than ML (Browne, 1974). Unfortunately, very little is known about the effects of violations of the assumption of normality on the properties of either GLS or ML estimators for the confirmatory factor model.

Practical Considerations

In general, none of these estimators (ULS, GLS, and ML) have closed-form solutions.[18] That is to say, the values that minimize the fitting functions must be found by numerically searching over possible values of Λ, Φ, and Θ. The estimates are those values that make the fitting function as small as possible. Technical details on how the search is conducted need not concern us, even though without computer programs implementing efficient search procedures the application of the confirmatory factor model would not be possible. Three practical problems are, however, worth noting.

First, it is possible for search procedures to locate what is called a "local minimum." This is a value of the fitting function that appears to be the smallest possible when actually there are other smaller values. Such occurrences are thought to be rare, but are nonetheless possible (see Jöreskog and Sörbom, 1981: I.31).

Second, the values of the parameters that minimize the fitting function may be outside the range of feasible values. For example, a variance may be estimated to be negative or a correlation to be greater than 1.0. Such occurrences are thought to result from misspecified models or insufficiently large sample sizes. This issue is discussed in more detail in the next chapter.

Third, numerical searches can be costly in computer time. The computer time required for estimating a given model is based on several things: (1) The larger the number of independent elements in the covariance matrix for the observed variables, the more costly it is to estimate a given model. Note that the number of elements in S goes up according to the formula $q(q + 1)/2$, which increases much more quickly than the number of observed variables, q. (2) The more parameters to be estimated, the more computer time required. (3) The better the guess of the values of the parameters to estimated, the less computer time required. Software estimating the confirmatory factor model requires start values for each parameter that is to be estimated. Start values are guesses that the user supplies, which are used to compute the first Σ^*. The software proceeds by refining these initial guesses. The closer the start values, the easier it will be to find the final estimates. Unfortunately, choosing start values can be difficult. If there are similar models using similar data that have been analyzed by others, these can provide suggestions of start values. Alternatively, the user must guess start values on the basis of knowledge of the process being modeled. On the brighter side, the most recent version of LISREL (Jöreskog and Sörbom, 1981) has incorporated an algorithm for generating start values for most models. This can save the user a great deal of time and substantially reduce the cost of estimating models.

In this discussion of the cost of estimating a model, there has been a conspicuous lack of concern for sample size. This is because once the covariance matrix for the observed variables has been computed (an operation whose cost does depend on sample size), the cost of estimating a confirmatory factor model is independent of sample size. This can be seen by noting that none of the fitting functions includes a term reflecting the number of observations in the sample.

5. ASSESSMENT OF FIT IN
THE CONFIRMATORY FACTOR MODEL

Estimating the parameters of a confirmatory factor model is only the first step. In a confirmatory analysis there are specific hypotheses to test; in an exploratory analysis some indication of how to improve the fit of the model is desired. A variety of techniques are available for these purposes. The values of individual parameter estimates and their standard errors can be used to test the statistical significance of individual parameters. A chi-square goodness-of-fit test can be used to assess the overall fit of a model and to compare competing, nested models (defined below). Indices based on derivatives of the fitting function can be used to suggest better-fitting models. The following discussion of these techniques draws heavily upon Jöreskog and Sörbom (1981) and Bentler and Bonnet (1980).

Examining Values of the Parameters

In most programs that estimate the confirmatory factor model no constraints are imposed to ensure that the estimates have meaningful values. Consequently, it is possible to obtain negative estimates of variances and/or correlations that exceed 1.0 in absolute value. Even if all other measures of goodness of fit suggest that the model is adequate, unreasonable estimates indicate that one of the following problems has occurred (Jöreskog and Sörbom, 1981: I.36).

First, the model may be misspecified. This can be the case even when the overall fit of the model is adequate.

Second, there may be violations of the assumed normality of the observed variables. Very little is known about the robustness of ML and GLS estimation of the confirmatory factor model when the assumption of normality has been violated. Since estimation by ULS does not require assumptions of normality, violations of normality cannot be the cause of unreasonable ULS estimates.

Third, the sample may be too small to justify the use of the asymptotic properties of the method of estimation. Boomsma (1982) found that small samples often result in negative estimates of variances.

Fourth, the model may be nearly unidentified, making the estimation of some parameters difficult and unstable. This problem is sometimes referred to as empirical underidentification (Kenny, 1979: 40, 143, 155). It occurs when the model can be proven identified, but the sample data are such that the method of estimation has a difficult time distinguishing between two or more of the parameters. This issue is discussed further in the next section in relation to the correlations among estimates.

Fifth, the covariance matrix may have been computed by pairwise deletion of missing data. When missing data is a problem, researchers often construct covariance or correlation matrices by using all of the data available for a given pair of variables to compute the covariance or correlation between those two variables (see Hertel, 1976). As a result, each covariance or correlation is based on a different sample. This can lead to a covariance matrix that is inappropriate to use for estimation. In extreme cases programs for ML or GLS estimation may detect the inappropriate matrix and refuse to analyze it; in less extreme cases the matrix may be analyzed, but may result in erroneous estimates. ULS estimation generally proceeds, regardless of the inputted covariance matrix. A pairwise covariance matrix should be used only if there are a small number of missing observations scattered evenly across the variables and cases.

Variances and Covariances of the Estimates

Using the assumptions justifying either ML or GLS estimation, it is possible to estimate the variances of individual parameter estimates, which can be used to test hypotheses about individual parameters. Let ω be any parameter to be estimated from the model; let $\hat{\omega}$ be an estimate of ω; and let $\hat{\sigma}$ be the estimate of the standard deviation of the sampling distribution of $\hat{\omega}$. Under the assumptions justifying ML or GLS estimation, for large samples $\hat{\omega}$ is distributed approximately normally with a standard deviation estimated as $\hat{\sigma}$. This result allows us to test hypotheses of the sort, H_0: $\omega = \omega^*$, where ω^* is a fixed value (generally zero). To test this hypothesis the test statistic $z = (\hat{\omega} - \omega^*)/\hat{\sigma}$ can be used. For large samples z is approximately normally distributed with a mean of zero and a variance of one.[19] For example, if $\hat{\phi}_{12} = 0.78$ and $\hat{\sigma}_{\phi_{12}} = 0.56$, then $z = (0.78 - 0.00)/0.56 = 1.39$, and the null hypothesis (H_0: $\phi_{12} = 0$) would not be rejected at the .05 level. The researcher would conclude that ϕ_{12} is not significantly different from zero.

Under the assumptions of ML and GLS, covariances among estimates can also be estimated. Let ω_1 and ω_2 be any two parameters, estimated as $\hat{\omega}_1$ and $\hat{\omega}_2$. Let their standard deviations be estimated as $\hat{\sigma}_1$ and $\hat{\sigma}_2$, and their covariance estimated as $\hat{\sigma}_{12}$. The correlation between the estimates of ω_1 and ω_2 can be computed as $\hat{\rho}_{12} = \hat{\sigma}_{12}/\hat{\sigma}_1\hat{\sigma}_2$. If $\hat{\rho}_{12}$ is large, this indicates that changes in the estimate of ω_1 are associated with corresponding changes in the estimate of ω_2. Accordingly, it is statistically difficult to disentangle these two parameters, even though both are identified. This is the problem of empirical underidentification that was discussed earlier. Readers familiar with multiple regression should recognize this as being comparable to the effects of extreme multicollinearity (Jöreskog and Sörbom, 1981: I.36: Judge et al., 1980: chap. 12).

Chi-Square Goodness-of-Fit Tests

Under the assumptions justifying ML and GLS, a chi-square goodness-of-fit measure can be computed. (See Bentler and Weeks [1980] for a statistical justification of this test.) This statistic allows a test of the null hypothesis H_0 that a given model provides an acceptable fit of the observed data. The fit of the model is assessed by comparing the observed covariance matrix S with the covariance matrix estimated by the equation $\hat{\Sigma} = \hat{\Lambda}\hat{\Phi}\hat{\Lambda}' + \hat{\Theta}$. $\hat{\Sigma}$ will not perfectly reproduce S, since the values that $\hat{\Sigma}$ can assume are limited by the constraints imposed on the model's parameters. The chi-square goodness-of-fit test compares the imperfect fit under H_0 to the perfect fit under the alternative hypothesis H_1 that Σ is any covariance matrix. The larger the differences between S and $\hat{\Sigma}$, the larger the chi-square.

As with any chi-square statistic, there are degrees of freedom associated with the test. In the confirmatory factor model the degrees of freedom are computed as

$$df = \text{number of independent parameters under } H_1 \text{ minus}$$
$$\text{number of independent parameters under } H_0 \qquad [5.1]$$

The number of independent parameters under H_1 is easily computed. Since H_1 provides a perfect fit of the data, there must be one independent parameter for each independent element of Σ—specifically, $q(q + 1)/2$ independent parameters, where q is the number of observed variables. The number of independent parameters associated with H_0 varies with each model. The only difficulty in counting the parameters involves determining which are independent. Since covariance matrices are symmetric, if parameters above the diagonal are counted, those below the diagonal must not be counted. For example, since $\phi_{12} = \phi_{21}$, if ϕ_{12} is counted as an independent parameter, then ϕ_{21} cannot be counted. Further, equality constraints must be taken into account. If several parameters are constrained to be equal, only one of those parameters is independent. For example, if the model assumes that $\lambda_{11} = \lambda_{12} = \lambda_{13}$, then only one of the three λ parameters can be counted as independent. Examples of counting degrees of freedom are given below.

Testing proceeds by finding the critical value at the α level of significance of the chi-square distribution with df degrees of freedom. Call this value $\chi_{1-\alpha}(df)$. Values of the chi-square larger than the critical value result in the rejection of the null hypothesis and the conclusion that the proposed model did not generate the observed data; values smaller than the critical value result in the acceptance of the null hypothesis and the conclusion that the proposed model did generate the observed data.

While the chi-square test can be derived theoretically under the assumptions necessary for ML or GLS estimation, Bentler and Bonett (1980) and Jöreskog and Sörbom (1981: I.38) noted that applications of the chi-square test are often unjustified in practice. To apply the test it must be assumed that (1) the observed variables are normally distributed, (2) the analysis is based on a sample covariance matrix rather than a sample correlation matrix, and (3) the sample size is large enough to justify the asymptotic properties of the chi-square test. At least one of these assumptions is generally violated in applications of the confirmatory factor model. Consequently, Jöreskog and Sörbom suggested that the chi-square test be used as an indicator of how well the model reproduces the observed covariance matrix S, rather than as a formal test of a hypothesis. A large value of the chi-square indicates a poor reproduction of S, and a small value indicates a good reproduction.

Nested Models and Difference of Chi-Square Tests

In many cases it is useful to compare the hypothesis implied by a given model to the hypothesis implied by some competing model. Such tests are possible when the two models are *nested*.

For any two models (call them M_1 and M_2) M_1 is nested in M_2 if M_1 can be obtained from M_2 by constraining one or more of the free parameters in M_2 to be fixed or equal to other parameters. Thus, M_1 can be thought of as a special case of M_2. Two examples illustrate this concept.

Example 1: nested models. Consider the models M_d, M_g, and M_h for the measurement of psychological disorders:

Model	λ_{11}	λ_{21}	λ_{32}	λ_{42}	ϕ_{11}	ϕ_{22}	ϕ_{12}	θ_{11}	θ_{22}	θ_{33}	θ_{44}	θ_{24}
M_d	1	*	1	*	*	*	*	*	*	*	*	0
M_g	1	A	1	A	B	B	*	*	*	*	*	0
M_h	1	A	1	A	B	B	*	*	*	*	*	*

An * indicates that the parameter is free; numbers indicate the value that a parameter has been constrained to equal; and letters indicate pairs of parameters that are constrained to be equal.

M_g can be formed from M_d by imposing the constraints $\lambda_{21} = \lambda_{42}$ and $\phi_{11} = \phi_{22}$. Accordingly, M_g is nested in M_d. Similarly, M_g is nested in M_h, since M_g can be formed from M_h by constraining θ_{24} to equal zero. M_d is not nested in M_h, nor is M_h nested in M_d, since neither model can be formed by imposing constraints on the other model. //

Example 2: nested models. As originally specified, our multimethod-multitrait model assumed that all trait and method factors were correlated. Except for ones on the diagonal, Φ was unconstrained. Call this version of the MMMT model M_A. In some applications it is reasonable to assume that trait factors are independent of method factors. For our example this implies that

$$
\Phi = \begin{bmatrix}
1.0 & \phi_{12} & \phi_{13} & 0.0 & 0.0 & 0.0 \\
\phi_{21} & 1.0 & \phi_{23} & 0.0 & 0.0 & 0.0 \\
\phi_{31} & \phi_{32} & 1.0 & 0.0 & 0.0 & 0.0 \\
0.0 & 0.0 & 0.0 & 1.0 & \phi_{45} & \phi_{46} \\
0.0 & 0.0 & 0.0 & \phi_{54} & 1.0 & \phi_{56} \\
0.0 & 0.0 & 0.0 & \phi_{64} & \phi_{65} & 1.0
\end{bmatrix} = \begin{bmatrix}
\text{trait/} & \text{trait/} \\
\text{trait} & \text{method} \\
\text{method/} & \text{method/} \\
\text{trait} & \text{method}
\end{bmatrix}
$$

Call this version of the MMMT model M_B. A third version of the model—call it M_C—assumes that all factors are uncorrelated. That is, that $\Phi = I$, an identity matrix.

M_B can be formed from M_A by constraining correlations in the method/trait and trait/method blocks of Φ to equal zero. Hence, M_B is nested in M_A. M_C can be formed from M_A by constraining all off-diagonal elements of Φ to zero; accordingly, it is also nested in M_A. Finally, M_C is nested in M_B, since it can be formed from M_B by constraining the remaining off-diagonal elements of Φ to zero.

The reader should realize that for models M_B and M_C to be estimated, they must be identified, which in fact they are. For details on these models, see Alwin (1974). //

Nested models can be statistically compared. If M_1 is nested in M_2, a difference of chi-square test can be used to compare M_1 with the more general model M_2. The more general model M_2 necessarily fits as well as or better than M_1, since it has at least one additional unconstrained parameter to aid in reproducing the observed covariance matrix. The estimated covariance matrix Σ_2 obtained from estimating M_2 will be closer to S than Σ_1 obtained from estimating M_1. As a consequence, the X_1^2 with df_1 degrees of freedom from testing M_1 will necessarily be larger than the X_2^2 with df_2 degrees of freedom obtained from testing M_2. Whether this improvement in fit obtained by adding additional parameters to M_1 is statistically significant is determined by a difference of chi-square test. For large samples, $X^2 = X_1^2 - X_2^2$ is distributed as chi-square with df $=$ df$_1$ $-$ df$_2$ degrees of freedom if M_1 is the true model. If X^2 exceeds the chosen critical value for the chi-square distribution with df degrees of freedom, the hypothesis that the constraints imposed on M_2 to form M_1 are valid can be rejected. That is, relaxing the constraints results in a statistically significant improvement in fit of M_2 over M_1.

Example 1: difference of chi-square test. Consider models M_g with a chi-square of X_g^2 and df$_g = 3$ degrees of freedom, and M_h with X_h^2 and df$_h = 2$. Model M_g differs from M_h in that the parameter θ_{24} is constrained to equal zero in M_g. To test the hypothesis H_0: $\theta_{24} = 0$ in M_h, the difference of chi-square test $X^2 = X_g^2 - X_h^2$ with df $=$ df$_g$ $-$ df$_h$ $= 1$ can be used. If X^2 exceeds the critical value of the chi-square distribution with one degree of freedom at a given level of significance, the null hypothesis that $\theta_{24} = 0$ would be rejected. Note that H_0 could also be tested with the z-test described above.

The difference of chi-square test is particularly useful in testing more complex hypotheses. Consider models M_g with X_g^2 and df$_g = 3$, and M_d with X_d^2 and df$_d = 1$. Model M_g differs from M_d in that the loading of x_2 on ξ_1 is constrained to equal the loading of x_4 on ξ_2 (i.e., $\lambda_{21} = \lambda_{42}$) in M_g, and the variance of ξ_1 is constrained to equal the variance of ξ_2 (i.e., $\phi_{11} = \phi_{22}$) in M_g. To test the hypothesis H_0: $\lambda_{21} = \lambda_{42}$ and $\phi_{11} = \phi_{22}$ in M_g, the difference of chi-square test $X^2 = X_g^2 - X_d^2$ with df $=$ df$_g$ $-$ df$_d = 2$ can be used. If X^2 exceeds the critical value of the chi-square distribution with df degrees of freedom at a given level of significance, the null hypothesis would be rejected. Note that this complex hypothesis could not be tested with a simple z-test. //

Example 2: difference of chi-square test. For the MMMT model, let X_A^2, X_B^2, and X_C^2 be the chi-square test associated with models M_A, M_B, and M_C with df$_A$, df$_B$, and df$_C$ degrees of freedom. Recall that in M_A, Φ is unconstrained except for ones on the diagonal; in M_B the method/trait blocks of Φ are constrained to zeros; and in M_C, Φ is constrained to equal I. The hypothesis that all factors are uncorrelated can be tested by comparing M_A with M_C. The resulting test statistic is: $X^2 = X_C^2 - X_A^2$ with df $=$ df$_C$ $-$ df$_A$. If X^2 exceeded the appropriate critical value, the hypothesis that the factors were uncorrelated would be rejected. The hypothesis that the method/trait correlations are zero, but the method/method and trait/trait correlations are not zero can be tested by comparing models M_A and M_B. The appropriate test statistic is $X^2 = X_B^2 - X_A^2$ with df$_B$ $-$ df$_A$ degrees of freedom. //

Specification Searches

If the hypothesized model does not fit, it is often of interest to find a model that does fit. Given that the model suggested by theory has already been rejected, there may be little theoretical guidance as to how to improve the fit of the model. Consequently, the results obtained from estimating the rejected model will have to be used to suggest additional, perhaps better-fitting, models. This process is called a specification search.

While a specification search can provide useful information, it is important to realize that since the sample data are used to select a model, the same data cannot be used to formally assess the fit of that model (Leamer, 1978). The model selected must be viewed as tentative, in need of verification with a second, independent sample. With this important warning in mind, procedures for searching for a model are considered.

The first and most obvious way to improve the fit of a model is to eliminate parameters that are not significant, as indicated by a z-test. Restricting such parameters cannot reduce the magnitude of a chi-square obtained, but can improve the overall fit by recovering degrees of freedom with little accompanying increase in the chi-square. For example, assume that a model—call it M_1—with five degrees of freedom was fit with a resulting chi-square of 10.4. Since the critical value at the .10 level of significance is 9.24, M_1 would be rejected. Now suppose that M_1 had five parameters with very small z-values, indicating that they were not significantly different from zero. By constraining these parameters to zero a second model, M_2, is formed with 10 degrees of freedom. The .10 critical value for the chi-square test is increased to 15.99 as a result of the added degrees of freedom. The chi-square obtained in testing M_2 also increases, since M_2 has fewer parameters with which to reproduce the observed covariance matrix. Nevertheless, if the resulting chi-square is still less than 15.99, M_2 would be considered an acceptably fitting model. The increase in the chi-square would have been offset by the accompanying increase in degrees of freedom.

The ability of a model to reproduce the observed covariance matrix can also be improved by the addition of parameters. To determine which parameters might improve the fit of a model, it is sometimes proposed that the matrix of differences between the observed covariance matrix S and the predicted matrix $\hat{\Sigma}$ be studied. The argument is that large differences reflect the portion of the model that is misspecified. This notion is misleading, however, since the methods of estimation used for the confirmatory factor model are full-information techniques. A full-information technique *simultaneously* fits all of the parameters in all of the equations of the model. Specification errors in one equation affect the estimation of other, correctly specified equations. Accordingly, modifying a model on the basis of the differences in $S - \hat{\Sigma}$ does not necessarily result in an improvement in fit (Sörbom, 1975).

A more promising approach is based on the partial derivatives of the fitting function with respect to each of the fixed parameters of the model (Sörbom, 1975). The partial derivatives indicate the rate of change in the fitting function for a very small change in a fixed parameter. Thus, if a derivative with respect to a particular fixed parameter is large, relaxing that parameter might lead to a large decrease in the minimum of the fitting function, hence, a substantial improvement in the fit of the model. Unfortunately, this is not always the case. A fixed parameter that has a large derivative may have a fixed value very close to the value that would be estimated if that parameter were freed. If this were the case, the improvement in fit would be small.

To remedy this problem, Jöreskog and Sörbom (1981: I.42) have proposed a *modification index* that is equal to the expected decrease in the chi-square if a single constraint is relaxed. The actual decrease in the chi-square may be larger than the expected value, but it should not be smaller. The greatest improvement in fit for a given model is obtained by freeing the parameter with the largest modification index. Since freeing a single parameter results in a loss of one degree of freedom, the modification index approximates a chi-square test of the hypothesis that the parameter to be freed is equal to its fixed value. If the value of the modification index for a parameter does not exceed 3.84—the 0.05 critical value for a chi-square test with one degree of freedom—no appreciable gain in fit is likely to result from freeing that parameter.

In using the modification index (or the derivative), it is suggested that only one parameter be relaxed at a time, since freeing one parameter may reduce or eliminate the improvement in fit possible by freeing a second parameter. The parameter to be relaxed should have the largest modification index *and* it must make substantive sense to relax that parameter.[20] This procedure continues, relaxing one parameter at a time, until an adequate fit is found or no further improvement in fit is possible. This is a blatantly exploratory approach. The resulting model should be verified with a second, independent sample. Further, there is no guarantee that the models suggested by the modification indices are identified. The user must prove identification for each model estimated in a specification search.

This concludes our survey of the basic techniques for assessing goodness of fit and carrying out specification searches in the confirmatory factor model. Additional techniques and greater detail can be found in Jöreskog and Sörbom (1981) and Bentler and Bonett (1980). This chapter concludes with an extended example and a discussion of standardized solutions.

Example 1: estimation and hypothesis testing. The model for the measurement of psychological disorders, though quite simple, can be used to illustrate a number of basic ideas. First, results of the three methods of estimation are compared.[21] Second, various ways of establishing the metric of the latent variables are demonstrated. Third, a specification search is performed. And finally, the idea of scale invariance is extended to deal with models containing equality constraints.

The first model considered, M_d, corresponds to the solid lines in Figure 5.1. The metric is set by constraining the loadings for x_1 and x_3 to equal 1.0 ($\lambda_{11} = \lambda_{32} = 1$). Table 5.1 presents the ULS, GLS, and ML estimates for this model. The GLS and ML estimates are extremely close, while the ULS estimates are slightly different. This pattern of similarities is found in a variety of models using various data sets. The best way to assess the similarity of the results is to determine if the substantive interpretations that each set of estimates generate are similar. In a factor model of this sort there are two functions of parameters that are of primary interest: correlations between common factors and reliabilities of observed variables.

Estimates of correlations among the latent variables differ from the correlations among the observed variables, since the latter correlations are affected by errors in measurement. To estimate the correlation between ξ_1 and ξ_2, the general formula for the correlation coefficient can be used:

$$COR(\xi_1, \xi_2) = COV(\xi_1, \xi_2) \,/\, \sqrt{VAR(\xi_1)\,VAR(\xi_2)}$$

$$= \phi_{12} \,/\, \sqrt{\phi_{11}\phi_{22}}$$

The correlations between the latent variables in M_d range from 0.63 to 0.66 (see Table 5.1), indicating that the latent variables for psychological disorders at time 1 and time 2 share between 40% ($= 0.63^2$) and 44% ($= 0.66^2$) of their variation in common. The correlations between the observed variables are uniformly smaller. The correlation between the number of psychological symptoms at the two times is 0.53, and the

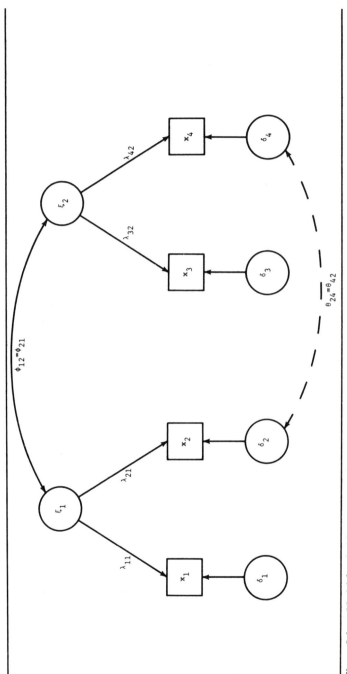

Figure 5.1   A Model for the Measurement of Psychological Disorders

311

TABLE 5.1
Estimation Model M_d, by ULS, GLS, and ML

Parameter	Method of Estimation		
	ULS	GLS	ML
λ_{11}	<u>1.000</u>	<u>1.000</u>	<u>1.000</u>
λ_{21}	0.188	0.205	0.205
λ_{32}	<u>1.000</u>	<u>1.000</u>	<u>1.000</u>
λ_{42}	0.268	0.270	0.271
ϕ_{11}	1.938	1.800	1.781
ϕ_{22}	1.424	1.431	1.408
ϕ_{12}	1.051	1.046	1.045
θ_{11}	0.164	0.300	0.322
θ_{22}	0.239	0.220	0.233
θ_{33}	0.480	0.467	0.497
θ_{44}	0.150	0.141	0.150
$COR(\xi_1, \xi_2)$	0.633	0.652	0.660
$REL(\xi_1, x_1)$	0.922	0.857	0.847
$REL(\xi_1, x_2)$	0.222	0.286	0.244
$REL(\xi_2, x_3)$	0.748	0.755	0.739
$REL(\xi_2, x_4)$	0.407	0.443	0.407
df	1	1	1
Chi-square	–	17.32	18.31
prob	–	0.000	0.000

NOTE: Underlines indicate those parameters that have been constrained to equal the given value.

correlation between the number of psychophysiological symptoms is 0.31 (see Appendix I). The attenuation in the correlation between the observed variables has been eliminated in the estimation of the correlation between the latent variables.

The second parameter of interest is the reliability of the observed variables. The reliability is defined as the squared correlation between a latent variable and its observed indicator. As such it indicates the percentage of variation in an observed variable that is explained by the common factor that it is intended to measure. To illustrate the computation of reliabilities, consider the observed variable x_2, which is a measure of ξ_1. The factor equation for x_2 is $x_2 = \lambda_{21}\xi_1 + \delta_2$. Since the variables are measured as deviations from their means, $COV(\xi_1, x_2) = E[\xi_1 x_2] = E[\xi_1(\lambda_{21}\xi_1 + \delta_2)]$. Using the fact that ξ_1 and δ_2 are assumed uncorrelated, $COV(\xi_1, x_2) = \lambda_{21}\phi_{11}$. Since the correlation between x_2 and ξ_1 is the covariance divided by the standard deviations of x_2 and ξ_1, the squared correlation or reliability is defined as

$$REL(\xi_1, x_2) = (\lambda_{21}\phi_{11})^2 / (\sigma_{22}\phi_{11})$$

$$= \lambda_{21}{}^2\phi_{11}/\sigma_{22}$$

See Sullivan and Feldman (1979), Bagozzi (1981), and Kenny (1979) for details on the computation of reliabilities in other types of models.

The reliabilities computed for M_d are given in Table 5.1 for each method of estimation. The measures of psychological symptoms (x_1 and x_3) are much more reliable than the measures of psychophysiological symptoms (x_2 and x_4) for all methods of estimation. One might conclude that this is due to the fixed loadings linking x_1 to ξ_1 and x_3 to ξ_2. This is not the case, however, as is demonstrated by considering alternative methods for setting the metric.

Table 5.2 presents ML estimates of M_d for five different ways of setting the scale. For the model just considered, the scale is set by fixing λ_{11} and λ_{32} to equal 1.0. The scale of ξ_1 is determined by x_1 and the scale of ξ_2 by x_3. Differences in the variables x_1 and x_3 are reflected in the different variances of ξ_1 ($\phi_{11} = 1.78$) and ξ_2 ($\phi_{22} = 1.41$). The factor correlations and reliabilities for this model were discussed above. This version of M_d will be referred to as M_{d1}.

In a second version of M_d, M_{d2}, the scale is set by fixing to 1.0 the loadings of ξ_1 on x_2 and ξ_2 on x_4. While the estimates of Λ and Φ differ from those for M_{d1}, the chi-square, the correlation between ξ_1 and ξ_2, and the reliabilities are the same. The change in the loadings simply reflects a change in the scale of the common factors. To see this, consider the effect on x_1 of a one-standard deviation change in ξ_1. For M_{d1} this involves a change in ξ_1 of 1.335 ($= \sqrt{\phi_{11}}$). The increase in x_1 equals 1.335 times the loading of x_1 on ξ_1 ($= 1.00$), or an increase of 1.335. For M_{d2} a standard deviation increase in ξ_1 equals 0.274 ($= \sqrt{\phi_{11}}$). The increase in x_1 equals 0.274 times the loading of x_1 on ξ_3 ($= 4.874$), or an increase of 1.335. Thus, the larger variances of the latent variables in M_{d1} as opposed to M_{d2} are exactly compensated for by the smaller loadings in M_{d1}.

TABLE 5.2
ML Estimates of M_d with Different Constraints to Set the Metric

Parameter	Model Estimated M_{d1}	M_{d2}	M_{d3}	M_{d4}	M_{d5}
λ_{11}	1.000	4.874	2.000	1.335	0.944
λ_{21}	0.205	1.000	0.410	0.274	0.194
λ_{32}	1.000	3.694	2.000	1.187	0.839
λ_{42}	0.271	1.000	0.541	0.321	0.227
ϕ_{11}	1.781	0.075	0.445	1.000	2.000
ϕ_{22}	1.408	0.103	0.352	1.000	2.000
ϕ_{12}	1.045	0.058	0.261	0.660	1.320
θ_{11}	0.322	0.322	0.322	0.322	0.322
θ_{22}	0.233	0.233	0.233	0.233	0.233
θ_{33}	0.497	0.497	0.497	0.497	0.497
θ_{44}	0.150	0.150	0.150	0.150	0.150
$COR(\xi_1, \xi_2)$	0.660	0.660	0.660	0.660	0.660
$REL(\xi_1, x_1)$	0.847	0.847	0.847	0.847	0.847
$REL(\xi_1, x_2)$	0.244	0.244	0.244	0.244	0.244
$REL(\xi_2, x_3)$	0.739	0.739	0.739	0.739	0.739
$REL(\xi_2, x_4)$	0.407	0.407	0.407	0.407	0.407
df	1	1	1	1	1
Chi-square	18.31	18.31	18.31	18.31	18.31
prob	0.000	0.000	0.000	0.000	0.000

NOTE: Underlines indicate those parameters that have been constrained to equal the given value.

Model M_{d3} illustrates that the scale can also be set by fixing one loading on each factor to any constant. In this case the loadings are arbitrarily fixed to 2.0. The chi-square, the factor correlation, and the reliabilities are unchanged. Differences in other parameters simply reflect changes in scale.

Often it is convenient to directly set the scale of the common factors by fixing the diagonal of Φ. In model M_{d4} this is done by standardizing the factors to unit variance, and in model M_{d5} by standardizing to a variance of 2.0. The only differences in these models are the scale of the latent variables and the compensating changes in the magnitudes of the loadings.

In general, changes in the scale of the common factors do not affect the substantive results of the analyses. An exception to this rule occurs when equality constraints are used. This topic is discussed below.

While M_d is useful for demonstrating the interpretation of various parameters in the model and the basic ideas of establishing metrics, its fit is not adequate, as indicated by the chi-square of 18.3 with one degree of freedom. To improve the fit, coefficients that are not statistically different from zero can be considered for dropping from the model. In column 2 of Table 5.3 the z-values for each parameter in M_d are given. All are statistically significant beyond the .0001 level, except for the parameter θ_{11}. To fix this parameter to zero, while statistically convenient, does not make substantive sense. Accordingly, other types of constraints should be considered.

Since the model includes the same variables measured at two points in time, it might be reasonable to assume that both the loadings of the observed variables on the common factors and the variances of the common factors are identical at both points. This corresponds to assuming that $\lambda_{11} = \lambda_{32}$, $\lambda_{21} = \lambda_{42}$, and $\phi_{11} = \phi_{22}$. Since λ_{11} and λ_{32} are already constrained to equal 1.0, they are implicitly constrained to be equal. Thus, only two constraints are being added, with a gain of two degrees of freedom. The resulting model, designated as M_g in our earlier discussion (see Table 3.1), has a chi-square of 22.57 with three degrees of freedom. To test the hypothesis H_0: $\lambda_{21} = \lambda_{42}$ and $\phi_{11} = \phi_{22}$, a difference of chi-square test comparing M_d and M_g can be computed. The resulting chi-square is 4.21 with two degrees of freedom, and the hypothesis cannot be rejected at the .10 level of significance. The constraints are supported by the data.

It may also be possible to improve the fit by freeing parameters. In M_g the maximum modification index is 15.09 for θ_{42}. This means that if θ_{42} is freed, the minimum decrease in the chi-square will be 15.09 with a loss of one degree of freedom. The model formed by freeing θ_{42} is labeled M_h (see the broken and solid arrows in Figure 5.1) and was proven identified in Chapter 3; hence, it may be estimated. The actual improvement in fit is 16.71, which is highly significant, although the overall fit of the model is marginal with a chi-square of 5.86 with two degrees of freedom and a probability level of .053.

The maximum modification index for M_h is 3.19 for λ_{22}. Relaxing this parameter would allow the number of psychophysiological symp-

TABLE 5.3
ML Estimates of M_d, M_g, and M_h

Parameter	M_d Estimate	M_d z-value	M_g Estimate	M_g z-value	M_h Estimate	M_h z-value
λ_{11}	1.000	–	1.000	–	1.000	–
λ_{21}	0.205	7.88	0.244[A]	13.69	0.227[A]	12.14
λ_{32}	1.000	–	1.000	–	1.000	–
λ_{42}	0.271	11.14	0.244[A]	13.69	0.227[A]	12.14
ϕ_{11}	1.781	7.88	1.538[B]	11.68	1.658[B]	11.90
ϕ_{22}	1.408	9.30	1.538[B]	11.68	1.658[B]	11.90
ϕ_{12}	1.045	11.36	1.038	11.32	1.046	11.39
θ_{11}	0.322	1.67	0.519	4.44	0.412	3.33
θ_{22}	0.233	14.88	0.225	15.12	0.230	15.34
θ_{33}	0.497	4.43	0.405	3.77	0.271	2.23
θ_{44}	0.150	12.78	0.156	14.06	0.163	14.42
θ_{42}	0.000	–	0.000	–	0.035	4.04
df	1		3		2	
Chi-square	18.31		22.57		5.86	
prob	0.000		0.000		0.053	

NOTE: Underlines indicate those parameters that have been constrained to equal the given value. As are values constrained to be equal; Bs are values constrained to be equal.

toms at time 1 (x_2) to load on the psychological disorder factor at time 2 (ξ_2). Since this makes no substantive sense, relaxing λ_{22} should not be considered. The second-largest modification index is for θ_{41}, which is also substantively inappropriate to relax. The third-largest modification index is for θ_{31}, which does make substantive sense, indicating correlated errors in measurement of the same variable measured at two points in time. If this parameter were relaxed, the resulting model (which adds the parameter θ_{31} to M_h) is not identified. Accordingly, the specification search ends.

The final model, M_h, was constructed through an exploratory search. Even though the search was guided by substantive considerations, the resulting parameter estimates and statistical tests must be viewed with caution. Ideally, the model should be verified with an independent sample. //

Standardization

A final issue to consider is standardization, which has two distinct meanings in the factor model. First, the *observed* variables can be standardized so that S is a correlation matrix rather than a covariance matrix. Second, the *latent* variables can be standardized by constraining the diagonal elements of Φ to equal one. These two meanings of standardization are linked through the concept of scale invariance which can be illustrated by reconsidering models M_d and M_g.

Table 5.4 contains four sets of parameters for M_d. In column 1 the metric is established by the fixed loadings on $\lambda_{11} = \lambda_{32} = 1.0$, and the observed variables are unstandardized. That is, a covariance matrix rather than a correlation matrix is analyzed. In column 2 the metric is established by the fixed variances of ξ_1 and ξ_2, and the observed variables are unstandardized. In both cases the chi-square is 18.31 with one degree of freedom. Further, the parameters are the same except for the change in scale. For example, the loading of x_1 on ξ_1 in column 1 is fixed at 1.0; in column 2 the loading is estimated to be 1.335. These differences are offset by the differences in the variances of ξ_1. For column 1, the standard deviation of ξ_1 is 1.335 ($= \sqrt{\phi_{11}}$), compared to the fixed standard deviation of 1.0 in column 2. Accordingly, a change in the latent variable of some fixed amount Δ in column 1 corresponds to a change of $\Delta / 1.335$ in column 2. For both versions of M_d the resulting change in the observed variable is the same.

In columns 3 and 4 comparable results are presented for the analysis of the correlation matrix rather than the covariance matrix; that is, the observed variables have been standardized. Column 3 has λ_{11} and λ_{32} fixed to 1.0; column 4 has fixed variances for ξ_1 and ξ_2. The correlations between ξ_1 and ξ_2, the reliabilities, and the chi-squares are the same for all versions of M_d. Differences in Λ and Φ simply reflect the differences in the scales of the observed variables and common factors.

For M_d the decision to analyze the covariance matrix as opposed to the correlation matrix, or to set the metric by fixing loadings as opposed to fixing variances, makes no substantive difference when a scale-free estimator (such as ML or GLS) is used. These results would not hold, however, if a method such as ULS, which is scale dependent, were used.

TABLE 5.4
ML Estimates of M_d and M_g with Standardized Observed
Variables and/or Standardized Common Factors

	Model M_d				Model M_g			
O.V. Standardized?[a]	no	no	yes	yes	no	no	yes	yes
L.V. Standardized?[b]	no	yes	no	yes	no	yes	no	yes
Parameter								
λ_{11}	1.000	1.335	1.000	0.920	1.000	1.240[B]	1.000	0.885[B]
λ_{21}	0.205	0.274	0.536	0.493	0.244[A]	0.303[A]	0.645[A]	0.571[A]
λ_{32}	1.000	1.187	1.000	0.860	1.000	1.240[B]	1.000	0.885[B]
λ_{42}	0.271	0.321	0.743	0.639	0.244[A]	0.303[A]	0.645[A]	0.571[A]
ϕ_{11}	1.782	1.000	0.847	1.000	1.538[B]	1.000	0.782[B]	1.000
ϕ_{22}	1.408	1.000	0.739	1.000	1.538[B]	1.000	0.782[B]	1.000
ϕ_{12}	1.045	0.660	0.522	0.660	1.038	0.675	0.522	0.667
θ_{11}	0.322	0.322	0.153	0.153	0.519	0.519	0.222	0.222
θ_{22}	0.233	0.233	0.757	0.757	0.225	0.225	0.733	0.733
θ_{33}	0.497	0.497	0.261	0.261	0.405	0.405	0.213	0.213
θ_{44}	0.150	0.150	0.592	0.592	0.156	0.156	0.623	0.623
VAR(x_1)	2.102	2.102	1.000	1.000	2.102	2.102	1.000	1.000
VAR(x_2)	0.308	0.308	1.000	1.000	0.308	0.308	1.000	1.000
VAR(x_3)	1.904	1.904	1.000	1.000	1.904	1.904	1.000	1.000
VAR(x_4)	0.253	0.253	1.000	1.000	0.253	0.253	1.000	1.000
COR(ξ_1, ξ_2)	0.660	0.660	0.660	0.660	0.675	0.675	0.667	0.667
REL(ξ_1, x_1)	0.847	0.847	0.847	0.847	0.753	0.753	0.778	0.778
REL(ξ_1, x_2)	0.244	0.244	0.244	0.244	0.269	0.269	0.267	0.267
REL(ξ_2, x_3)	0.739	0.739	0.739	0.739	0.787	0.787	0.787	0.787
REL(ξ_2, x_4)	0.407	0.407	0.407	0.407	0.383	0.383	0.377	0.377
df	1	1	1	1	3	3	3	3
Chi-square	18.31	18.31	18.31	18.31	22.57	22.57	24.59	24.59

NOTE: Underlines indicate those parameters that have been constrained to equal
the given value. As are values constrained to be equal; Bs are values constrained to
be equal.
a. O.V. = observed variables.
b. L.V. = latent variables.

Quite different results are found in analyzing M_g. Recall that M_g
differs from M_d in that the equality constraints $\phi_{11} = \phi_{22}$, $\lambda_{11} = \lambda_{32}$, and
$\lambda_{21} = \lambda_{42}$ have been imposed. The choice of how to establish the metric
of the common factors in M_g has no substantive effect, as was the case in

M_d. The reader is encouraged to verify this using the estimates in columns 5 and 6. The choice of whether or not to standardize the observed variables, however, affects the substantive results obtained, even though a scale-free method of estimation is used. The models in columns 5 and 7 of Table 5.4 differ from one another only in the standardization of the observed variables in column 7. While such standardization did not affect the results for M_d, in M_g the chi-squares, reliabilities, and correlations between common factors differ. This is a consequence of the imposed equality constraints.

To standardize the observed variables and hence, Σ, requires the pre- and post-multiplication of the covariance equation $\Sigma = \Lambda \Phi \Lambda' + \Theta$ by a diagonal matrix D, where $d_{ii} = 1/\sqrt{s_{ii}}$ and s_{ii} is the variance of x_i. The resulting covariance equation is $D\Sigma D = (D\Lambda) \Phi (D\Lambda)' + D\Theta D$. Thus Λ changes from

$$\Lambda = \begin{bmatrix} \underline{1} & \underline{0} \\ \lambda_{21} & \underline{0} \\ \underline{0} & \underline{1} \\ \underline{0} & \lambda_{21} \end{bmatrix} \text{ to } D\Lambda = \begin{bmatrix} d_{11} & \underline{0} \\ d_{22}\lambda_{21} & \underline{0} \\ \underline{0} & d_{33} \\ \underline{0} & d_{44}\lambda_{21} \end{bmatrix}$$

where the underlined values are constants that have been fixed in the specification of the model. The only way that the equality constraints in Λ can be maintained in $D\Lambda$ is if $d_{11} = d_{33}$ and $d_{22} = d_{44}$, which will not be true unless $s_{11} = s_{33}$ and $s_{22} = s_{44}$. Unless these variances are equal in the sample (which is almost certainly not the case), scale invariance must be given up in order to maintain the imposed equality constraints. In the current example the loss of scale invariance does not have a major effect on the results obtained since the variances of x_1 and x_3, and x_2 and x_4 are similar in the sample data. As a general rule, however, in the presence of equality constraints the decision to analyze the correlation matrix as opposed to the covariance matrix can have significant substantive effects on the results obtained. In general it is preferable to analyze the covariance matrix.

6. CONCLUSIONS

The confirmatory factor model is a powerful statistical model. Its ability to test specific structures suggested by substantive theory gives it a major advantage over the exploratory factor model. The examples presented in Chapters 1 through 5 are quite simple, having the advantage of allowing a relatively simple presentation of the basic concepts and techniques. The reader should not be left with the impression, however, that more complex models cannot be analyzed. Complexities can be readily added by increasing the number of observed variables, common factors, correlations among error factors, and factor loadings. While the resulting models are more complex, the issues of specification, identification, estimation, and hypothesis testing are unchanged.

For the interested reader the following applications are recommended as examples of the flexibility of the model.

(1) Bagozzi (1981) gave a detailed presentation of the use of the confirmatory factor model for studying validity and reliability.
(2) Jöreskog (1969) presented the statistical justification of the confirmatory factor model and details on numerical issues related to estimation, along with a number of examples. The paper is mathematically demanding.
(3) Jöreskog and Sörbom (1981) is the manual accompanying LISREL V. The example on pages III.1-III.21 provides an extensive discussion of the interpretation of a confirmatory factor model.
(4) Kenny (1979) is useful in a number of respects. Early chapters develop the algebraic techniques necessary for proving that a model is identified. While many of the models considered in the book cannot be incorporated into the confirmatory factor model, most of those presented in Chapters 7 and 8 can. Recasting these models into the framework presented in this monograph and then estimating them is a useful exercise.
(5) Sullivan and Feldman (1979) considered a variety of models for multiple indicators, including the MMMT model. Most of these models can be estimated with the confirmatory factor model, which would also be a useful exercise.
(6) Zeller and Carmines (1980) considered the general issue of measurement in the social sciences. Their Appendix demonstrates how many of these issues can be addressed with the confirmatory factor model. Note in particular pages 176-184.

The reader is strongly encouraged to consult these sources and the references they contain. The best way to obtain a clear understanding of the confirmatory factor model is to study applications and to apply the model to actual data. The above references are extremely useful in both respects.

Even with the flexibility of the confirmatory factor model and its advantage over the exploratory factor model, it is limited by its inability to incorporate structural relationships among common factors and by a lack of provisions for qualitative data. Both of these limitations can, however, be overcome by extensions of the basic model.

Qualitative data can be handled in two ways. First, confirmatory factor models can be compared across populations. This essentially involves the simultaneous estimation of confirmatory factor models for different groups, and the testing of the hypothesis that the factor structures are the same in all groups. Jöreskog (1971), Sörbom (1974), and Werts et al. (1979) discussed this extension of the model. Second, the observed, x-variables can be categorical. This extension of the model, recently proposed by Jöreskog and Sörbom (1981: chap. 4), involves computations of polychoric, tetrachoric, and polyserial correlations.

To analyze structural relations among common factors requires the unification of the confirmatory factor model (CFM) and the structural equation model. This important extension is accomplished in the covariance structure model, sometimes referred to as the LISREL model. This is the subject of the companion volume in this series, *Covariance Structure Models*.

APPENDIX I

Correlations and Standard Deviations from Wheaton/Hennepin Sample (N = 603)

Variables	PSY67	PHY67	PSY71	PHY71
PSY67	1.000			
PHY67	0.454	1.000		
PSY71	0.526	0.247	1.000	
PHY71	0.377	0.309	0.549	1.000
S.D.	1.45	0.555	1.38	0.503

SOURCE: Wheaton (1978: 395).

Variable Identifications:
PSY67 = psychological disorders 1967 (x_1)
PHY67 = psychophysiological disorders 1967 (x_2)
PSY71 = psychological disorders 1971 (x_3)
PHY71 = psychophysiological disorders 1971 (x_4)

APPENDIX II: SOFTWARE TO ESTIMATE THE CONFIRMATORY FACTOR MODEL (CFM)

In general, the easiest way to estimate the CFM is with software designed for the covariance structure model. LISREL (versions I through V) and MILS (Schoenberg, 1982b) are the most commonly available programs. Information on obtaining LISREL can be obtained from International Educational Services, 1525 East 53rd Street, Suite 829, Chicago, IL 60615. Information on obtaining MILS can be obtained from Dr. Ronald Schoenberg, National Institutes of Health, Bldg. 31, Room 4C11, Bethesda, MD 20205. To understand how to estimate the CFM using the more general covariance structure model, it is necessary to briefly describe the covariance structure model. More details can be found in the companion volume in this series, *Covariance Structure Models.*

The covariance structure model consists of three matrix equations:

$$\mathbf{x} = \Lambda_x \boldsymbol{\xi} + \boldsymbol{\delta} \qquad \text{[II.1]}$$

$$\mathbf{y} = \Lambda_y \boldsymbol{\eta} + \boldsymbol{\epsilon} \qquad \text{[II.2]}$$

$$\eta = \mathbf{B}\eta + \mathbf{\Gamma}\xi + \zeta \qquad [\text{II}.3]$$

This last equation is sometimes written as

$$\ddot{\mathbf{B}}\eta = \mathbf{\Gamma}\xi + \zeta \qquad [\text{II}.3']$$

$\ddot{\mathbf{B}} = (\mathbf{I} - \mathbf{B})$. $\mathbf{x}$ and $\mathbf{y}$ are vectors of observed variables. η and ξ contain common factors. $\mathbf{\Phi}$ is the covariance matrix for ξ. δ, ϵ, and ζ contain error factors, with covariance matrices $\mathbf{\Theta}_\delta$, $\mathbf{\Theta}_\epsilon$, and $\mathbf{\Psi}$, respectively.

The CFM can be formed by imposing the following constraints:

$$\mathbf{B} = 0 \text{ (or } \ddot{\mathbf{B}} = \mathbf{I}) \qquad \mathbf{\Lambda}_y = 0$$
$$\mathbf{\Gamma} = 0 \qquad\qquad\quad \mathbf{\Theta}_\epsilon = 0 \qquad [\text{II}.4]$$
$$\mathbf{\Psi} = 0$$

This, in effect, eliminates equations II.2 and II.3. Equation II.1, along with the covariance matrices $\mathbf{\Phi}$ and $\mathbf{\Theta}_\delta$, can be used to estimate the CFM. The $\mathbf{x}$ in our presentation corresponds to the $\mathbf{x}$ in equation II.1. $\mathbf{\Lambda}_x$ corresponds to our $\mathbf{\Lambda}$. ξ corresponds to our ξ. $\mathbf{\Phi}$ corresponds to our $\mathbf{\Phi}$. Finally, $\mathbf{\Theta}_\delta$ corresponds to our $\mathbf{\Theta}$.

NOTES

1. The symbol "//" will be used to designate the end of an example.
2. Equation 2.4 requires two matrix operations: addition and multiplication. Matrix addition requires that the two matrices to be added are of the same dimension. This means that they must have the same number of rows and columns. For example, adding the (3×2) matrices $\mathbf{A}$ and $\mathbf{B}$ results in

$$\mathbf{A} + \mathbf{B} = \begin{bmatrix} 1 & 2 \\ 3 & 4 \\ 5 & 6 \end{bmatrix} + \begin{bmatrix} 7 & 8 \\ 9 & 10 \\ 11 & 12 \end{bmatrix} = \begin{bmatrix} 1+7 & 2+8 \\ 3+9 & 4+10 \\ 5+11 & 6+12 \end{bmatrix}$$

Assume that we want to multiply $\mathbf{C}$ of dimension $(q \times r)$ by $\mathbf{D}$ of dimension $(s \times t)$: $\mathbf{CD}$. Matrix multiplication requires that the number of columns in the first matrix equal the number of rows in the second matrix, or for multiplying **CD**, that r = s. The other dimensions need not be equal. The resulting matrix will be of dimension (q × t). For example, if **C** is (2 × 3) and **D** is (3 × 2):

$$CD = \begin{bmatrix} 1 & 2 & 3 \\ 4 & 5 & 6 \end{bmatrix} \begin{bmatrix} 7 & 8 \\ 9 & 10 \\ 11 & 12 \end{bmatrix} = \begin{bmatrix} (1*7 + 2*9 + 3*11) & (1*8 + 2*10 + 3*12) \\ (4*7 + 5*9 + 6*11) & (4*8 + 5*10 + 6*12) \end{bmatrix}$$

3. "E" is the expectation operator. If X is a random variable, E(X) is the expected value of X, or for our purposes, the mean of X. If **x** is a (q × 1) vector of random variables, E(**x**) is a (q × 1) vector containing the expected values or means of the random variables in **x**. When the expectation operator is applied to a matrix, the expected value of each element of the matrix is taken.

4. This assumption affects some types of analyses that compare factor models across populations, and particularly models with structured means. These models are beyond the scope of our presentation. For details, see Jöreskog (1971), Sörbom (1974, 1982), and Jöreskog and Sörbom (1981).

5. "COV" is the covariance operator. If X and Y are two random variables, COV(X,Y) indicates the covariance between X and Y. Recalling that the covariance between X and Y is the average of the product of the deviations of X and Y from their means, COV (X, Y) can be written as $E[(X - \mu_x)(Y - \mu_y)]$, where μ_x and μ_y are the means of X and Y.

6. " ' " indicates the transpose of a matrix. Transposing involves taking rows of a matrix and standing them on end to make them columns. For example, consider **A**, a (2 × 3) matrix. If

$$A = \begin{bmatrix} 1 & 2 & 3 \\ 4 & 5 & 6 \end{bmatrix}$$

then

$$A' = \begin{bmatrix} 1 & 4 \\ 2 & 5 \\ 3 & 6 \end{bmatrix}$$

7. Some programs for estimating the confirmatory factor model do not allow the unique factors to be correlated. This is not a real limitation since unique factors can be

allowed to correlate in these programs by treating them as though they are common factors that load on only one observed variable and that are uncorrelated with the "real" common factors. For details on making this change, see Long (1981).

8. To count the unique elements of a covariance matrix it is necessary to keep in mind that the matrix is symmetric. For Σ, a (q × q) covariance matrix, this means that if σ_{ij} is counted, σ_{ji} should not be counted (for i ≠ j). The unique elements can be counted as follows: Of the q^2 elements in Σ, the q diagonal elements are variances. The remaining $q^2 - q$ elements are covariances, half of which are redundant. Thus, there are $q + (q^2 - q)/2 = q(q + 1)/2$ unique elements in Σ.

9. A square matrix $\mathbf{A}$ of dimension (r × r) is said to be invertible or nonsingular if there exists a square matrix $\mathbf{A}^{-1}$ of dimension (r × r), such that $\mathbf{A}\mathbf{A}^{-1} = \mathbf{I}$, where $\mathbf{I}$ is a (r × r) identity matrix.

10. In exploratory factor analysis equation 3.2 is generally replaced by $\Sigma = \mathbf{\Lambda}\mathbf{\Lambda}' + \mathbf{\Theta}$. This involves assuming that $\mathbf{\Phi} = \mathbf{I}$, or that the factors are orthogonal. This does not really constrain the exploratory model since the assumption is relaxed after estimation, when factor rotations are made (see, Lawley and Maxwell, 1971: 66-86).

11. If $\mathbf{X}$ is a real, symmetric matrix of dimension (r × r) and $\mathbf{a}$ is any (r ×1) vector, $\mathbf{X}$ is positive definite if $\mathbf{a'Xa} > 0$ for all possible $\mathbf{a}$. All nonsingular variance/covariance matrices are positive definite (Kmenta, 1971:606).

12. A submatrix of $\mathbf{A}$ is defined as a matrix formed from $\mathbf{A}$ by deleting one or more rows and/or columns of $\mathbf{A}$. The rank of a matrix is defined as the size of the largest nonsingular submatrix contained in $\mathbf{A}$.

13. The technical problem with computational methods for determining whether a model is identified is that identification is a property of the specification of a model, not of the estimation of a model. If a model appears to be identified for a particular set of estimates based on the positive definiteness of the information matrix, this may result from having drawn an unusual sample rather than from the fact that the model is identified. For a more technical discussion of this issue, see Schoenberg (1982a) and McDonald and Krane (1979).

14. The fitting function for unweighted least squares is sometimes written as $F_{ULS} = \frac{1}{2}\text{tr}[(\mathbf{S} - \hat{\mathbf{\Sigma}})^2]$, dividing the function given in the text by ½. This change in scale does not affect the values obtained as estimates of $\mathbf{\Lambda}$, $\mathbf{\Phi}$, and $\mathbf{\Theta}$.

15. The fitting function for generalized least squares is often written as $F_{GLS} = \frac{1}{2}\text{tr}[(\mathbf{S} - \mathbf{\Sigma}^*)\mathbf{S}^{-1}]^2$. The difference in scale caused by the multiplication by ½ will not affect the values of the estimates obtained.

16. The determinant of a square matrix can be defined as follows. Consider a square matrix, say $\mathbf{X}$, of order (r × r), with individual elements designated as x_{ij}. The determinant of $\mathbf{X}$ is defined as

$$|\mathbf{X}| = \Sigma \pm x_{1j_1} x_{2j_2}. \ . \ . \ x_{rj_r}$$

where the sum is over permutations of the second subscript, and the sign is positive for even permutations and negative for odd permutations. For example, if $\mathbf{X}$ is a (2 × 2) matrix, $|\mathbf{X}| = x_{11}x_{22} - x_{12}x_{21}$. If $\mathbf{X}$ is a (3 × 3) matrix, $|\mathbf{X}| = x_{11}x_{22}x_{33} - x_{12}x_{21}x_{33} + x_{12}x_{23}x_{31} - x_{13}x_{22}x_{31} + x_{13}x_{21}x_{32} - x_{11}x_{23}x_{32}$. For more details, see Hohn (1973).

17. The fitting function for maximum likelihood estimation is often written in the alternative form: $F_{ML} = \text{tr}(\mathbf{S}\mathbf{\Sigma}^{*-1}) + [\log|\mathbf{\Sigma}^*| - \log|\mathbf{S}|]$. This function differs from the text by the subtraction of q, where q is the number of independent variables. This is only a change in origin of the function which will not affect the values of the parameters that minimize the function. The function in the text is used since it has a close relationship to

the computation of the chi-square statistic discussed in Chapter 5. The fitting function is sometimes simplified by making use of the equality $\log |\Sigma^{-1}S| = \log|S| - \log|\Sigma|$, resulting in $F_{ML} = tr(S\Sigma^{*-1}) - \log|\Sigma^{*-1}S| - q$.

18. If a model is just identified, closed-form solutions can be obtained by solving the covariance equations for each parameter.

19. This z-statistic is labeled as a t-statistic in the program LISREL and in many applications of the confirmatory factor model. It does not, however, have a t-distribution.

20. In an exploratory search there is generally a class of parameters that could reasonably be included in the model, although there is no strong substantive reason for either including them or excluding them. On the other hand, there is usually another class of parameters that make no substantive sense. Parameters from this second class should not be freed, even if the modification index suggests that freeing one of them will result in the maximum improvement of fit in the model. Little is gained if a model is constructed that reproduces the observed data but can be given no substantive interpretation.

21. Estimates were obtained using MILS (Schoenberg, 1982b) and LISREL V (Jöreskog and Sörbom, 1981).

REFERENCES

ALWIN, D. F. (1974) "Approaches to the interpretation of relationships in the multitrait-multimethod matrix," pp.79-105 in H. L. Costner (ed.) Sociological Methodology 1973-1974. San Francisco: Jossey-Bass.

BAGOZZI, R. P. (1981) "An examination of the validity of two models of attitude." Multivariate Behavioral Research 16: 323-359.

BENTLER, P. M. and D. G. BONETT (1980) "Significance tests and goodness-of-fit in the analysis of covariance structures." Psychological Bulletin 88: 588-606.

BENTLER, P. M. and D. G. WEEKS (1980) "Linear structural equations with latent variables." Psychometrika 45: 289-308.

BIELBY, W. T. and R. M. HAUSER (1977) "Response error in earning functions for nonblack males." Sociological Methods and Research 6: 241-280.

BLALOCK, H. M. (1979) Social Statistics. New York: McGraw-Hill.

BOOMSMA, A. (1982) "The robustness of LISREL against small sample sizes in factor analysis models," pp. 149-173 in H. Wold and K. Jöreskog (eds.) Systems Under Indirect Observation. New York: Elsevier North-Holland.

BROWNE, M. W. (1974) "Generalized least-squares estimators in the analysis of covariance structures." South African Statistical Journal 8: 1-24.

BURT, R. S., M. G. .FISCHER, and K. P. CHRISTMAN (1979) "Structures of well-being: sufficient conditions for identification in restricted covariance models." Sociological Methods and Research 8: 111-120.

BURT, R. S., J. A. WILEY M. J. MINOR, and J. R. MURRAY (1978) " Structures of well-being." Sociological Methods and Research 6: 365-407.

DUNCAN, O. D. (1975) Introduction to Structural Equation Models. New York: Academic.

DUNN, J. E. (1973) "A note on a sufficiency condition for uniqueness of a restricted factor matrix." Psychometrika 38: 141-143.

HARMON, H. H. (1976) Modern Factor Analysis. Chicago: University of Chicago Press.

HAYS, W. L. (1981) Statistics. New York: Holt, Rinehart & Winston.

HERTEL, B. R. (1976) "Minimizing error variance introduced by missing data routines in survey analysis." Sociological Methods and Research 4: 459-474.

HOHN, F. E. (1973) Elements of Matrix Analysis. New York: Macmillan.

HOWE, H. G. (1955) Some Contributions to Factor Analysis. Report ORNL-1919. Oak Ridge, TN: Oak Ridge National Laboratory.

JENNRICH, R. I. (1978) "Rotational equivalence of factor loading matrices with specified values." Psychometrika 43: 421-426.

JÖRESKOG, K. G. (1979) "Author's addendum to: A general approach to confirmatory maximum likelihood factor analysis," pp. 40-43 in K. G. Jöreskog and D. Sörbom (eds.) Advances in Factor Analysis and Structural Equation Models. Cambridge, MA: Abt Books.

——— (1971) "Simultaneous factor analysis in several populations." Psychometrika 36: 409-426.

——— (1969) "A general approach to confirmatory factor analysis." Psychometrika 34: 183-202.

——— (1967) "Some contributions to maximum likelihood factor analysis." Psychometrika 34: 183-202.

——— and A. S. GOLDBERGER (1972) "Factor analysis by generalized least squares." Psychometrika 37: 243-260.

JÖRESKOG, K. G. and D. SÖRBOM (1981) LISREL V. User's Guide. Chicago: National Educational Resources.

——— (1978) LISREL IV. User's Guide. Chicago: National Educational Resources.

JUDGE, G. G., W. E. GRIFFITHS, R. C. HILL, and T. C. LEE (1980) The Theory and Practice of Econometrics. New York: John Wiley.

KENNY, D. A. (1979) Correlation and Causality. New York: John Wiley.

KMENTA, J. (1971) Elements of Econometrics. New York: Macmillan.

LAWLEY, D. N. and A. E. MAXWELL (1971) Factor Analysis as a Statistical Method. New York: American Elsevier.

LEAMER, E. E. (1978) Specification Searches. New York: John Wiley.

LEE, S. Y. (1977) "Some algorithms for covariance structure analysis." Ph.D. dissertation. University of California, Los Angeles.

LONG, J. S. (1981) "Estimation and hypothesis testing in linear models containing measurement error," pp. 209-256 in P. V. Marsden (ed.) Linear Models in Social Research. Beverly Hills, CA: Sage.

——— (1976) "Estimation and hypothesis testing in linear models containing measurement error." Sociological Methods and Research 5: 157-206.

McDONALD, R. P. and W. R. KRANE (1979) "A Monte Carlo study of local identifiability and degrees of freedom in the asymptotic likelihood ratio test." British Journal of Mathematical and Statistical Psychology 32: 121-132.

SCHOENBERG, R. (1982a) Identification and the Condition of the Information Matrix in Maximum Likelihood Estimation of Structural Equation Models. Working Paper. Washington, DC: National Institute of Mental Health.

——— (1982b) MILS: A Computer Program to Estimate the Parameters of Multiple Indicator Linear Structure Models. Bethesda, MD: National Institutes of Health.

SÖRBOM, D. (1982) "Structural equation models with structured means," pp. 183-195 in H. Wold and K. Jöreskog (eds.) Systems under Indirect Observation. New York: Elsevier North-Holland.

———— (1975) "Detection of correlated errors in longitudinal data." British Journal of Mathematical and Statistical Psychology 28: 138-151.

———— (1974)"A general method for studying differences in factor means and factor structure between groups." British Journal of Mathematical and Statistical Psychology 27: 229-239.

SULLIVAN, J. L. and S. FELDMAN (1979) Multiple Indicators. Beverly Hills, CA: Sage.

WERTS, C. E., K. G. JORESKOG, AND R. L. LINN (1973) "Identification and estimation in path analysis with unmeasured variables." American Journal of Sociology 73: 1469-1484.

WERTS, C. E., D. A. ROCK, and J. GRANDY (1979) "Confirmatory factor analysis applications." Multivariate Behavioral Research 14: 199-213.

WHEATON, B. (1978) "The sociogenesis of psychological disorder." American Sociological Review 43: 383-403.

WONNACOT, R. J. and T. H. WONNACOTT (1979) Econometrics. New York: John Wiley.

ZELLER, R. A. and E. G. CARMINES (1980) Measurement in the Social Sciences. New York: Cambridge University Press.

Additional References

BENTLER, Peter M. (1989) EQS:Structural Equations Program Manual. Los Angeles: BMDP Software.

BOLLEN, Kenneth A. (1989) Structural Equations with Latent Variables. New York: John Wiley.

JÖRESKOG, Karl G., and D. SÖRBOM (1988) LISREL 7: A Guide to the Program and Applications. Chicago: SPSS, Inc.

COVARIANCE STRUCTURE MODELS

PART V

An Introduction to LISREL

J. SCOTT LONG

Notation

Boldface letters are used to indicate matrices and vectors. For example, **B** indicates that B is a matrix. Dimensions of matrices and vectors are indicated by "$(r \times c)$" for a matrix with r rows and c columns. Subscripts to lower case letters indicate elements of a matrix. For example, the $(i,j)^{th}$ element of **B** is indicated as b_{ij}; the ith element of the vector **x** is indicated as x_i. The symbol "$'$" indicates the transpose of a matrix; **B$'$** is the transpose of **B**. The symbol "-1" as a superscript of a matrix indicates the inverse of the matrix; **B**$^{-1}$ is the inverse of **B**. "COV" is the covariance operator. If the arguments of the operator are two variables, say x_i and x_j, then $COV(x_i, x_j)$ indicates the covariance between x_i and x_j. If the argument of the covariance operator is a vector, say **x** of dimension $(n \times 1)$, then $COV(\mathbf{x})$ is the $(n \times n)$ covariance matrix whose $(i,j)^{th}$ element (for $i \neq j$) is the covariance between x_i and x_j, and whose $(i,i)^{th}$ element is the variance of x_i. Similarly, "COR" is used as the correlation operator. $COR(x_i, x_j)$ indicates the correlation between x_i and x_j. $COR(\mathbf{x})$ is the $(n \times n)$ correlation matrix whose $(i,j)^{th}$ element (for $i \neq j$) is the correlation between x_i and x_j, and whose $(i,i)^{th}$ element is one. "E" is the expectation operator. If x_i is a random variable, $E(x_i)$ is the expected value of x_i. If **x** is a vector, then $E(\mathbf{x})$ is a vector whose i^{th} element is the expected value of the random variable x_i.

Figures, equations, examples, and tables are numbered sequentially within chapters. Thus, Table 2.3 is the third table in Chapter 2. Examples are also numbered sequentially within chapters. Thus Example 3.2 refers to the second example in Chapter 3. Some examples are developed in several steps throughout a chapter. Thus, if Example 3.2 appears several times in Chapter 3, the reader should realize that it is the development of the same example.

Preface

This monograph presents a statistical model referred to variously as the covariance structure model, the analysis of covariance structures, the linear structural relations model, the moments structure model, latent variable equation systems in structured linear models, and (perhaps most commonly) the LISREL model. "Covariance structure model" is probably the most general term—hence the name of this monograph. Estimating the covariance structure model requires the use of sophisticated software. LISREL, written by Jöreskog and Sörbom, is by far the most commonly used program for estimating the covariance structure model. The importance of LISREL is evidenced by the fact that the term LISREL has come to stand for not only software but also a statistical model and an approach to data analysis. This importance is reflected by the subtitle of the monograph, "An Introduction to LISREL." The monograph is not, however, an introduction to the control cards necessary to use a particular software package.

While many readers may be unfamiliar with the covariance structure model in its full complexity, it is likely that most have already, even if unwittingly, mastered parts of the model, since the covariance structure model consists of two components, each of which is a powerful and well-known statistical technique in its own right. The first component is the confirmatory factor model considered in psychometrics; the second component is the structural equation model considered in econometrics. This monograph is designed to take advantage of a reader's familiarity with one or both of these components.

The reader is assumed to be familiar with the confirmatory factor model and the mathematical tools presented in a companion volume in the Sage Series on Quantitative Applications in the Social Sciences: *Confirmatory Factor Analysis: A Preface to LISREL.* Since results from that volume are referred to frequently, it is designated simply as *CFA.* The reader whose primary interest is in the structural equation model will find our discussion to be particularly useful for the estimation of models with equality constraints and correlated errors across some but not all equations (e.g., panel models).

A full understanding of the covariance structure model requires the application of the model to actual data. Readers are encouraged to replicate the analyses presented in the text, using the data contained in the Appendix. If the results you obtain match those presented in the text, you have a good indication of your understanding. To estimate the covariance structure model it is generally necessary to use software not contained in such packages as the Statistical Package for the Social Sciences (SPSS), the Statistical Analysis System (SAS), and BMDP statistical software. The concluding chapter briefly describes the software that can be used.

A number of people generously gave of their time to comment on various portions of this monograph. I would like to thank Paul Allison, Greg Duncan, Karen Pugliesi, Jay Stewart, Blair Wheaton, Ronald Schoenberg, and two anonymous reviewers. Carol Hickman read several drafts of both *Confirmatory Factor Analysis* and this manuscript. Her comments greatly improved the accuracy and clarity of the final product. Remaining errors and lack of clarity are the result of not heeding the advice of those listed above.

1. INTRODUCTION

Models for the analysis of covariance structures attempt to explain the relationships among a set of observed variables in terms of a generally smaller number of unobserved variables. As the name of this technique implies, the relationships among the observed variables are characterized by the covariances among those variables, contained in the matrix Σ. This matrix is decomposed by a model that assumes that *unobserved* variables are generating the pattern or structure among the *observed* variables. Using a measurement model linking the observed variables to the unobserved variables, and a structural model relating the unobserved variables, an analysis of the covariance matrix Σ is made to describe its structure.

The term "analysis of covariance structures" was introduced by Bock and Bargmann (1966) to describe what would now be called a confirmatory factor model. Since then, numerous authors (including Browne, Bentler, Goldberger, Jöreskog, Lee, Sörbom, McDonald, and Múthen) have added to the complexity and generality of the model. The model has grown from the factor analytic model of Bock and Bargmann to an extremely general model in which the covariance matrix Σ is considered to be any function of any set of parameters, with many intermediate forms of the model appearing along the way. See Bentler and Weeks (1979) for a review of these models, or Bentler (1980) for a less mathematically demanding review.

Though progress has been made in the estimation and application of these extremely general forms of the model, our emphasis is on the more limited, albeit still quite general, form introduced by Jöreskog (1973;

Jöreskog and van Thillo, 1972), Keesling (1972), and Wiley (1973). In this more restrictive model the covariances among the observed variables are decomposed in two conceptually distinct steps. First, the observed variables are linked to unobserved or latent variables through a factor analytic model, similar to that commonly found in psychometrics. Second, the causal relationships among these latent variables are specified through a structural equation model, similar to that found in econometrics. The covariance structure model, in the form considered here, consists of the simultaneous specification of a factor model and a structural equation model, and as such represents a fruitful unification of psychometrics and econometrics. This synthesis was greatly facilitated by Goldberger's (1971) programmatic article and the Conference on Structural Equation Models, organized by Goldberger in 1970 (Goldberger and Duncan, 1973).

The application of the covariance structure model in any form requires the use of efficient numerical methods for the maximization of functions of many variables. A major breakthrough in this area was made by K. Jöreskog in 1966 while working at Educational Testing Service. A series of increasingly general programs were developed leading to the well-known and widely available program LISREL (Jöreskog and van Thillo, 1972; Jöreskog and Sörbom, 1976, 1978, 1981), now in its fifth enhancement. This program has played such a vital role in the acceptance and application of the covariance structure model that such models are often referred to as "LISREL models."

The form of the covariance structure model that is presented here is esentially that incorporated in LISREL and will be referred to simply as the covariance stucture model. The decision to restrict attention to this form of the model is motivated by three considerations. First, a number of programs are available for estimation. This is an important consideration, since without such software the model cannot be applied. Second, the mathematical development of the more general models requires techniques beyond those assumed for this monograph. Third, this form of the model includes a wide variety of useful applications, including confirmatory factor analysis, second-order factor models, multiple indicator models, simultaneous equation systems, panel models, and structural equation models with errors in equations and errors in variables. Thus, it should be sufficient for the needs of most researchers.

Our approach to developing the covariance structure model is to present the factor analytic and structural equation models separately before merging them to create the covariance structure model. In the companion volume—*Confirmatory Factor Analysis* (CFA)—in this series, the confirmatory factor model was developed. In Chapter 2 of this volume the measurement component of the covariance structure model is presented as a pair of confirmatory factor models, each similar to the model in *CFA*. In Chapter 3 the structural equation model is presented as a special case of the covariance structure model, consisting only of the structural component of the model. Chapter 4 presents the covariance structure model as a synthesis of the factor model of Chapter 2 and the structural equation model of Chapter 3.

Before beginning, a general overview of the mathematical structures of each model is useful.

The Mathematical Models

The factor analytic model assumes that the observed variables are generated by a generally smaller number of unobserved or latent variables called factors. Observed variables are considered to be measured with error. Thus, the factor model is basically a measurement model. For example, consider the model in Figure 1.1. The squares correspond to observed variables that are measured with error; the circles correspond to unobserved variables. Each of the circles at the top is linked to two observed variables, indicating that the observed variables are generated by the unobserved variables, called common factors. The circles at the bottom of the figure are each linked to one observed variable. They correspond to that portion of the observed variable that cannot be accounted for by one of the common factors. As such, they are called unique factors or errors in measurement. While the covariances among the observed variables are known, they are assumed to be contaminated by errors in their measurement. To eliminate the effects of measurement error, the model estimates the covariance between the two common factors at the top of the figure.

For the example in Figure 1.1, the relationships between the latent variables and observed variables can be written as

$$x_1 = \lambda_{11}\xi_1 + \delta_1 \qquad x_2 = \lambda_{21}\xi_1 + \delta_2$$
$$x_3 = \lambda_{32}\xi_2 + \delta_3 \qquad x_4 = \lambda_{42}\xi_2 + \delta_4 \qquad [1.1]$$

The x's are the observed variables, the ξ's are the common factors, and the δ's are the unique factors. The λ's are loadings, which indicate how a change in a common factor affects an observed variable.

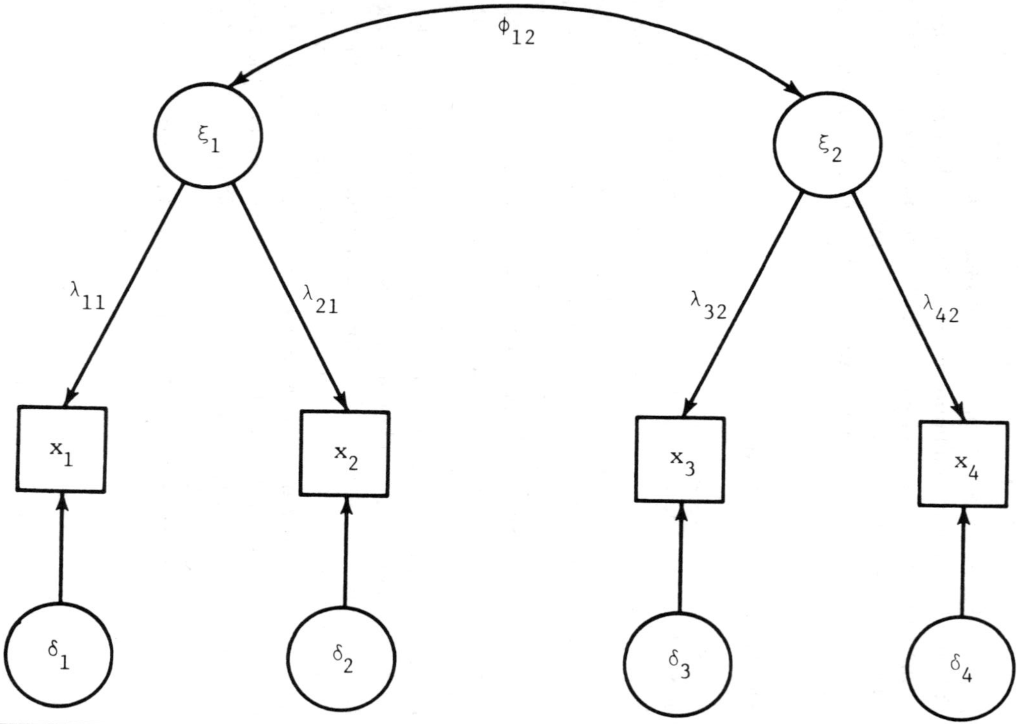

Figure 1.1 The Measurement Component of the Covariance Structure Model

In its general form, the relationships between the observed and latent variables are represented by the matrix equation (equation 2.4 of *CFA*):

$$\mathbf{x} = \Lambda \boldsymbol{\xi} + \boldsymbol{\delta} \qquad [1.2]$$

where $\mathbf{x}$ is a vector of observed variables, $\boldsymbol{\xi}$ is a vector of common factors, and $\boldsymbol{\delta}$ is a vector of unique factors. Statistically, the task is to explain the interrelationships among the observed variables, as indicated by the covariances among these variables, in terms of relationships among the observed and latent variables defined by equation 1.2. This model was the subject of *CFA*.

The structural equation model has received widespread use in the social and behavioral sciences. In its simplest form it consists of the regression of a single dependent variable on one or more independent variables. An example of such a model, where all variables are assumed to be measured from their means, is

$$y = \beta_1 x_1 + \beta_2 x_2 + e \qquad [1.3]$$

where y is a dependent variable; the x's are independent variables related to the dependent variables by the slope coefficients β_1 and β_2; and e is an *error in equation,* indicating that the x's do not perfectly predict y. In the notation to be used in Chapters 3 and 4, equation 1.3 would be written as

$$\eta_1 = \gamma_{11} \xi_1 + \gamma_{12} \xi_2 + \zeta_1$$

More realistic models are constructed using multiple equation systems, both with and without reciprocal causation. An example of such a model is contained in Figure 1.2. This model states that the observed variable η_1 is causally determined by the observed variables η_2, ξ_1, and ξ_2. That these three variables do not perfectly explain η_1 is reflected by the error in equation ζ_1. Similarly, η_2 is causally determined by η_1, ξ_2, and ξ_3, with an error in equation ζ_2. These structural relations would be written as

$$\eta_1 = \beta_{12} \eta_2 + \gamma_{11} \xi_1 + \gamma_{12} \xi_2 + \zeta_1$$
$$\eta_2 = \beta_{21} \eta_1 + \gamma_{22} \xi_2 + \gamma_{23} \xi_3 + \zeta_2 \qquad [1.4]$$

In its general form the structural equations are written as

$$\boldsymbol{\eta} = \mathbf{B} \boldsymbol{\eta} + \boldsymbol{\Gamma} \boldsymbol{\xi} + \boldsymbol{\zeta} \qquad [1.5]$$

where η is a vector of observed dependent variables measured without error; ξ is a vector of observed independent variables measured without error; ζ is a vector of errors in equations; $\mathbf{B}$ is a matrix of coefficients relating the dependent variables to one another; and Γ is a matrix of coefficients relating the independent variables to the dependent variables. Special cases of equation 1.5 include multiple regression, path analysis, simultaneous equation systems, and panel analysis. This model is developed in Chapter 3.

The factor analytic and structural equation models are complementary. In the structural equation model the assumption that the variables are measured without error is often unrealistic, requiring the introduction of errors in variables or measurement error. Those using the factor model, in which errors in variables are of major concern, are often interested in making statements about the structural relationships among the unobserved factors. That is, there is a need for a structural equation model relating the factors. The result of the converging needs of those using structural equation models and factor models is the covariance structure model. The covariance structure model allows both errors in variables, as in the factor analytic model, and errors in equations, as in the structural equation model.

Figure 1.3 presents a simple example of the covariance structure model. The structural relationships in Figure 1.3 are identical to those in Figure 1.2, used to illustrate the structural equation model. The difference is that the structural relations in the covariance structure model are among latent variables, rather than observed variables. In the covariance structure model, latent variables are linked to observed variables in the same way as in the factor model. This is represented in Figure 1.3 by the lines linking the x's and y's in squares to the η's and ξ's in circles. The equations specifying these links are similar to those in Equation 1.1. For the dependent variables, the measurement model is

$$y_1 = \lambda_{11}^y \eta_1 + \epsilon_1 \qquad y_2 = \lambda_{21}^y \eta_1 + \epsilon_2$$

$$y_3 = \lambda_{32}^y \eta_2 + \epsilon_3 \qquad y_4 = \lambda_{42}^y \eta_2 + \epsilon_4$$

For the independent variables, the measurement model is

$$x_1 = \lambda_{11}^x \xi_1 + \delta_1 \qquad x_2 = \lambda_{21}^x \xi_1 + \delta_2 \qquad x_3 = \lambda_{32}^x \xi_2 + \delta_3$$

$$x_4 = \lambda_{42}^x \xi_2 + \delta_4 \qquad x_5 = \lambda_{53}^x \xi_3 + \delta_5 \qquad x_6 = \lambda_{63}^x \xi_3 + \delta_6$$

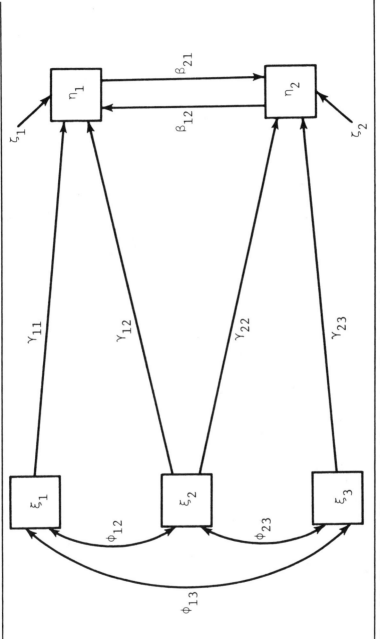

Figure 1.2 The Structural Component of the Covariance Structure Model

339

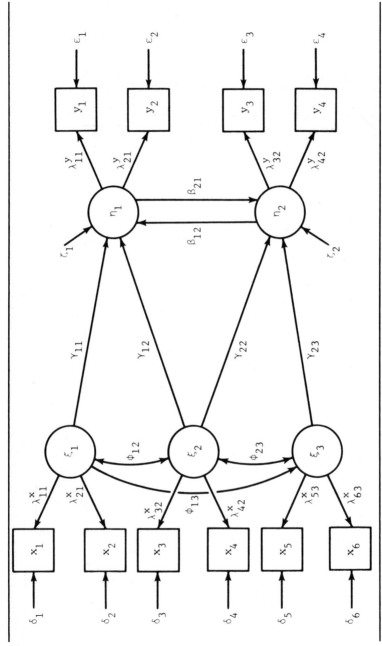

Figure 1.3 Combined Measurement Component and Structural Component of the Covariance Structure Model

In its general form, the covariance structure model consists of three equations. First, a structural equation model specifies the causal relationships among latent variables:

$$\boldsymbol{\eta} = \mathbf{B}\boldsymbol{\eta} + \boldsymbol{\Gamma}\boldsymbol{\xi} + \boldsymbol{\zeta} \qquad [1.6]$$

This equation has the same form as equation 1.5, the only difference being that $\boldsymbol{\eta}$ and $\boldsymbol{\xi}$ now contain latent variables rather than observed variables.

The second and third equations are a pair of measurement models formally similar to equation 1.2. In the first measurement model the observed x-variables are linked by the loading matrix $\boldsymbol{\Lambda}_x$ to the latent ξ-variables:

$$\mathbf{x} = \boldsymbol{\Lambda}_x \boldsymbol{\xi} + \boldsymbol{\delta} \qquad [1.7]$$

Errors in the measurement of $\mathbf{x}$ are contained in $\boldsymbol{\delta}$. In the second measurement model the observed y-variables are linked by the loading matrix $\boldsymbol{\Lambda}_y$ to the latent η-variables:

$$\mathbf{y} = \boldsymbol{\Lambda}_y \boldsymbol{\eta} + \boldsymbol{\epsilon} \qquad [1.8]$$

Errors in the measurement of $\mathbf{y}$ are contained in $\boldsymbol{\epsilon}$. The measurement equations 1.7 and 1.8, along with the structural equation 1.6, make up the covariance structure model that is developed in Chapter 4.

2. THE MEASUREMENT MODEL

The measurement component of the covariance structure model consists of a pair of confirmatory factor models formally identical to those developed in *CFA*. This chapter provides a formal specification of the two factor models and the assumptions linking them. The parameters of these models can be identified, estimated, tested, and interpreted in exactly the same way as the parameters of the single factor model presented in *CFA;* accordingly, these issues are not addressed here.

Specification of the Measurement Model

The covariance structure model has two sets of common factors. $\boldsymbol{\xi}$ contains s common factors that are related to q observed variables contained in **x**. $\boldsymbol{\eta}$ contains r common factors that are related to p observed variables contained in **y**. In the structural component of the covariance structure model the ξ's are unobserved exogenous variables, and the η's are unobserved endogenous variables. (These terms are defined in Chapter 3.) The observed variables and common factors are linked by a pair of factor equations:

$$\mathbf{x} = \boldsymbol{\Lambda}_x \boldsymbol{\xi} + \boldsymbol{\delta} \qquad [2.1]$$

$$\mathbf{y} = \boldsymbol{\Lambda}_y \boldsymbol{\eta} + \boldsymbol{\epsilon} \qquad [2.2]$$

$\boldsymbol{\Lambda}_x$ is a $(q \times s)$ matrix of the loadings of the x's on the ξ's, with the loading of x_i on ξ_j being designated as λ_{ij}^x. $\boldsymbol{\delta}$ is a $(q \times 1)$ vector of unique factors or errors in measurement that affect the x's. Similarly, $\boldsymbol{\Lambda}_y$ is a $(p \times r)$ matrix of loadings of the y's on the η's, with the loading of y_i on η_j being designated as λ_{ij}^y. And, $\boldsymbol{\epsilon}$ is a $(p \times 1)$ vector of unique factors that affect the y's. Each of the variables is assumed to be measured as a deviation from its mean:

$$E(\mathbf{x}) = E(\boldsymbol{\delta}) = 0 \qquad E(\boldsymbol{\xi}) = 0$$

$$E(\mathbf{y}) = E(\boldsymbol{\epsilon}) = 0 \qquad E(\boldsymbol{\eta}) = 0$$

Within each equation, the common factors and unique factors are assumed to be uncorrelated. Specifically it is assumed that

$$E(\boldsymbol{\xi}\boldsymbol{\delta}') = 0 \quad \text{or} \quad E(\boldsymbol{\delta}\boldsymbol{\xi}') = 0$$

$$E(\boldsymbol{\eta}\boldsymbol{\epsilon}') = 0 \quad \text{or} \quad E(\boldsymbol{\epsilon}\boldsymbol{\eta}') = 0$$

These and other assumptions are summarized in Table 2.1.

The variances and covariances of the ξ's are contained in the $(s \times s)$ covariance matrix $\boldsymbol{\Phi}$. The covariance matrix for the δ's is the $(q \times q)$, symmetric, and not necessarily diagonal, matrix $\boldsymbol{\Theta}_\delta$. The covariance matrix for the ϵ's is a similar $(p \times p)$ matrix $\boldsymbol{\Theta}_\epsilon$. The variances and covariances of the η's are contained in the $(r \times r)$ symmetric matrix $\text{COV}(\boldsymbol{\eta})$. This matrix is not given a unique letter (such as $\boldsymbol{\Phi}$ for the ξ's) since in the full covariance structure model it will be defined in terms of other parameters of the model. How this is done is described in Chapter 3 and need not concern us here.

Specification of the measurement portion of the covariance structure model involves imposing substantively motivated constraints on the

TABLE 2.1

**Summary of the Measurement Component of the
Covariance Structure Model**

Matrix	Dimension	Mean	Covariance	Dimension	Description
ξ	$(s \times 1)$	0	$\Phi = E(\xi\xi')$	$(s \times s)$	common exogenous factors
x	$(q \times 1)$	0	$\Sigma_{xx} = E(xx')$	$(q \times q)$	observed exogenous variables
Λ_x	$(q \times s)$	—	—	—	loadings of x on ξ
δ	$(q \times 1)$	0	$\Theta_\delta = E(\delta\delta')$	$(q \times q)$	unique factors for x
η	$(r \times 1)$	0	$COV(\eta) = E(\eta\eta')$	$(r \times r)$	common endogenous factors
y	$(p \times 1)$	0	$\Sigma_{yy} = E(yy')$	$(p \times p)$	observed endogenous variables
Λ_y	$(p \times r)$	—	—	—	loadings of y on η
ϵ	$(p \times 1)$	0	$\Theta_\epsilon = E(\epsilon\epsilon')$	$(p \times p)$	unique factors for y

Factor Equations:

$$x = \Lambda_x\xi + \delta \tag{2.1}$$

$$y = \Lambda_y\eta + \epsilon \tag{2.2}$$

Covariance Equation

$$\Sigma = \left[\begin{array}{c|c} \Lambda_y COV(\eta)\Lambda_y' + \Theta_\epsilon & \Lambda_y COV(\eta,\xi)\Lambda_x' \\ \hline \Lambda_x COV(\xi,\eta)\Lambda_y' & \Lambda_x\Phi\Lambda_x' + \Theta_\delta \end{array} \right] \tag{2.3}$$

Assumptions:

a. Variables are measured from their means: $E(x) = E(\delta) = 0$; $E(\xi) = 0$; $E(y) = E(\epsilon) = 0$; $E(\eta) = 0$.

b. Common and unique factors are uncorrelated: $E(\xi\delta') = 0$ or $E(\delta\xi') = 0$; $E(\eta\epsilon') = 0$ or $E(\epsilon\eta') = 0$; $E(\xi\epsilon') = 0$ or $E(\epsilon\xi') = 0$; $E(\eta\delta') = 0$ or $E(\delta\eta') = 0$.

c. Unique factors are uncorrelated across equations: $E(\delta\epsilon') = 0$ or $E(\epsilon\delta') = 0$.

parameter matrices: Λ_x, Λ_y, Φ, Θ_δ, and Θ_ϵ. These constraints can be either restrictions on parameters to equal fixed values and/or restrictions on sets of parameters to be equal.

At this point each of the factor models in equations 2.1 and 2.2 appears to be identical to the model described in *CFA*. Equation 2.1 is identical to the model in *CFA* if Λ_x is replaced by Λ; and equation 2.2 is identical if y, Λ_y, η, $COV(\eta)$, and ϵ are replaced by x, Λ, ξ, Φ, and δ. New assumptions are necessary, however, when the links between the two models are considered.

Relationships Between the Two Factor Models

While some of the variables are correlated across the two factor models, others are assumed to be uncorrelated. The observed x's and y's can be correlated. Their covariances are contained in the $(q \times p)$ matrix Σ_{xy}, whose $(i,j)^{th}$ element is the covariance between x_i and y_j. Similarly, the exogenous ξ-factors and endogenous η-factors can be correlated. Their covariances are contained in the $(s \times r)$ matrix $COV(\xi, \eta)$, or the $(r \times s)$ matrix $COV(\eta, \xi)$.

Just as the unique factors are assumed to be uncorrelated with the common factors in their own factor equation, they are assumed to be uncorrelated with the common factors in the other equation. Thus, it is assumed that

$$E(\xi\epsilon') = 0 \quad \text{or} \quad E(\epsilon\xi') = 0$$
$$E(\eta\delta') = 0 \quad \text{or} \quad E(\delta\eta') = 0$$

While the δ's can be correlated among themselves, and the ϵ's can be correlated among themselves, it is assumed that the δ's and ϵ's are uncorrelated. That is,

$$E(\delta\epsilon') = 0 \quad \text{or} \quad E(\epsilon\delta') = 0$$

Finally, it is assumed that the observed x's do not load on the latent η's, and that the observed y's do not load on the latent ξ's.

These ideas are illustrated in Figure 2.1. The circles represent latent variables, and the squares represent observed variables. Curved arrows linking two variables indicate that those variables are correlated; straight arrows indicate that the variable pointing affects the variable being pointed at. A heavy solid line separates portions of the model across which loadings or correlations cannot occur.

The Covariance Structure

Since the ξ's and η's are not observed, the parameters of the model must be estimated by means of the links between the variances and covariances of the observed variables and the parameters of the model. While estimation of the confirmatory factor model is not of concern to

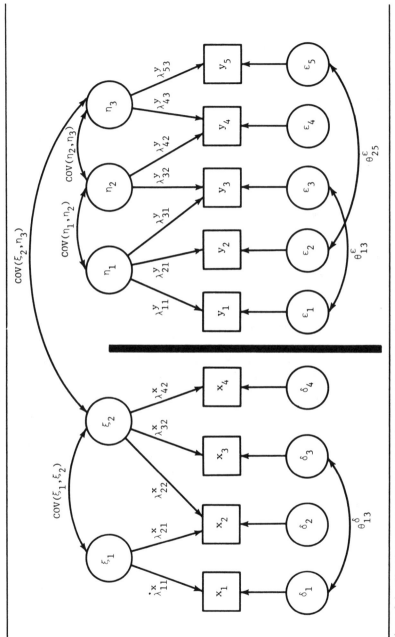

Figure 2.1 The Measurement Component of the Covariance Structure Model

345

us here (it has been fully considered in *CFA*), it is useful to consider the links between the observed variances and covariances and the parameters.

Let Σ be the population matrix of variances and covariances of the observed variables. This matrix is defined as

$$\Sigma = E\left[\begin{bmatrix} \mathbf{y} \\ \hline \mathbf{x} \end{bmatrix}\begin{bmatrix} \mathbf{y} \\ \hline \mathbf{x} \end{bmatrix}'\right] = \begin{bmatrix} E(\mathbf{y}\mathbf{y}') & E(\mathbf{y}\mathbf{x}') \\ \hline E(\mathbf{x}\mathbf{y}') & E(\mathbf{x}\mathbf{x}') \end{bmatrix}$$

Substituting the values for $\mathbf{x}$ and $\mathbf{y}$ contained in equations 2.1 and 2.2

$$\Sigma = \begin{bmatrix} E[(\Lambda_y\boldsymbol{\eta} + \boldsymbol{\epsilon})(\Lambda_y\boldsymbol{\eta} + \boldsymbol{\epsilon})'] & E[(\Lambda_y\boldsymbol{\eta} + \boldsymbol{\epsilon})(\Lambda_x\boldsymbol{\xi} + \boldsymbol{\delta})'] \\ \hline E[(\Lambda_x\boldsymbol{\xi} + \boldsymbol{\delta})(\Lambda_y\boldsymbol{\eta} + \boldsymbol{\epsilon})'] & E[(\Lambda_x\boldsymbol{\xi} + \boldsymbol{\delta})(\Lambda_x\boldsymbol{\xi} + \boldsymbol{\delta})'] \end{bmatrix}$$

After taking the transposes, making the necessary multiplications, taking expectations, and applying the assumptions about certain vectors of variables being uncorrelated, Σ can be written as

$$\Sigma = \begin{bmatrix} \Lambda_y\text{COV}(\boldsymbol{\eta})\Lambda_y' + \boldsymbol{\Theta}_\epsilon & \Lambda_y\text{COV}(\boldsymbol{\eta},\boldsymbol{\xi})\Lambda_x' \\ \hline \Lambda_x\text{COV}(\boldsymbol{\xi},\boldsymbol{\eta})\,\Lambda_y' & \Lambda_x\boldsymbol{\Phi}\Lambda_x' + \boldsymbol{\Theta}_\delta \end{bmatrix} \qquad [2.3]$$

The reader may want to work out the derivation of equation 2.3, although it is not essential for understanding the model. What is important to realize is that equation 2.3 decomposes the variances and covariances of the observed x's and y's into a function of the loading matrices Λ_x and Λ_y, the variances and covariances of the ξ's and η's, and the variances and covariances of the δ's and ϵ's. Constraints imposed on the parameter matrices structure the covariance matrix Σ. Estimation proceeds by finding estimates of the parameters that reproduce the sample variances and covariances of the observed variables according to equation 2.3 as closely as possible. Thus, equation 2.3 serves the same purpose as the covariance equation derived for the single confirmatory factor model in *CFA*.

Summary

This concludes our description of the measurement component of the covariance structure model. While the confirmatory factor model was developed in *CFA* as a powerful model in its own right, here it is used to relate observed variables to factors, with the intention of specifying a set of structural relations among these factors. How structural relations are specified is considered in the next chapter.

3. THE STRUCTURAL EQUATION MODEL

The second component of the covariance structure model is a structural equation model causally relating the latent variables that have been factored from observed variables through a measurement model. This chapter simplifies the covariance structure model by assuming that the latent variables are observed. This simplification facilitates understanding of the structural component of the covariance structure model and allows us to take advantage of the vast econometric literature on structural equation models for observed variables (in order of increasing difficulty, see Hanushek and Jackson, 1977; Wonnacott and Wonnacott, 1979; Theil, 1971). The issues of specification, identification, and interpretation developed in this chapter for observed variables are directly applicable to the structural equation model for latent variables in Chapter 4.

A second advantage of presenting the structural component without considering measurement error is that software developed for the covariance structure model is extremely useful for estimating structural equation models that incorporate equality constraints on structural parameters and/or the specification of zero covariances among some but not all of the errors in equations. Such constraints are increasingly common in social science applications, and particularly in panel models. Indeed, the most thorough treatment of panel models to date (Kessler and Greenberg, 1981) suggests that panel models be estimated with software for the covariance structure model, but it does not indicate how this is to be done. A secondary purpose of this chapter is to fill this gap in the literature on panel models.

The Mathematical Model

A structural equation model specifies the causal relationships among a set of variables. Those variables that are to be explained by the model are called *endogenous* variables. Endogenous variables are explained by specifying that they are causally dependent on other endogenous variables and/or what are called *exogenous* variables. Exogenous variables are determined outside of the model and, accordingly, are not explained by the model.

Let η be a $(r \times 1)$ vector of endogenous variables, and let ξ be a $(s \times 1)$ vector of exogenous variables. The model assumes that the variables are related by a system of linear structural equations.

$$\eta = \mathbf{B}\eta + \Gamma\xi + \zeta \qquad [3.1]$$

where $\mathbf{B}$ is a $(r \times r)$ matrix of coefficients relating the endogenous variables to one another; and Γ is a $(r \times s)$ matrix of coefficients relating the exogenous variables to the endogenous variables. ζ is a $(r \times 1)$ vector of errors in equations, indicating that the endogenous variables are not perfectly predicted by the structural equations.

Equation 3.1 is thought of as a *structural* equation, since it describes the assumed causal structure of the process being modeled. Restricting elements of $\mathbf{B}$ and Γ to equal zero indicates the absence of a causal relationship between the appropriate variables. Fixing the $(i,j)^{th}$ element of Γ to zero ($\gamma_{ij} = 0$) implies that the exogenous variable ξ_j does not have a causal effect on the endogenous variable η_i. Similarly, if the $(i,j)^{th}$ element of $\mathbf{B}$ is fixed to be zero ($\beta_{ij} = 0$), the endogenous variable η_i is assumed to be unaffected by η_j. The diagonal elements of $\mathbf{B}$ are assumed to equal zero, indicating that an endogenous variable does not cause itself.

Equation 3.1 can be rewritten by adding $-\mathbf{B}\eta$ to each side, resulting in $\eta - \mathbf{B}\eta = \Gamma\xi + \zeta$, or defining $\ddot{\mathbf{B}}$ as $(\mathbf{I} - \mathbf{B})$:

$$\ddot{\mathbf{B}}\eta = \Gamma\xi + \zeta \qquad [3.2]$$

While this form of the structural equation model is more common in the econometric literature, the form presented in equation 3.1 is slightly more convenient to interpret. A positive value in $\mathbf{B}$ indicates a positive relationship between two endogenous variables, whereas a positive value in $\ddot{\mathbf{B}}$ indicates a negative relationship. Since $\ddot{\mathbf{B}}$ is more convenient for stating a number of results, it is used as a shorthand notation for $(\mathbf{I} - \mathbf{B})$.

All variables are assumed to be measured as deviations from their means: $E(\eta) = E(\zeta) = 0$ and $E(\xi) = 0$. This does not affect the generality of the model, since the structural parameters contained in $\mathbf{B}$ and Γ are not affected by this assumption.

Just as common factors and unique factors are assumed to be uncorrelated in the factor model, the errors in equations and the exogenous variables are assumed to be uncorrelated in the structural equation model. That is, $E(\xi\zeta') = 0$, or equivalently, that $E(\zeta\xi') = 0$.

TABLE 3.1
Summary of the Structural Component of the
Covariance Structure Model

Matrix	Dimension	Mean	Covariance	Dimension	Description
η	$(r \times 1)$	0	$COV(\eta) = E(\eta\eta')$	$(r \times r)$	endogenous variables
ξ	$(s \times 1)$	0	$\Phi = E(\xi\xi')$	$(s \times s)$	exogenous variables
ζ	$(r \times 1)$	0	$\Psi = E(\zeta\zeta')$	$(r \times r)$	errors in equations
$\mathbf{B}$	$(r \times r)$	—	—	—	direct effects of η on η
$\ddot{\mathbf{B}}$	$(r \times r)$	—	—	—	defined as $(\mathbf{I} - \mathbf{B})$
Γ	$(r \times s)$	—	—	—	direct effects of ξ on η

Structural Equations:
$$\eta = \mathbf{B}\eta + \Gamma\xi + \zeta \qquad [3.1]$$
$$\ddot{\mathbf{B}}\eta = \Gamma\xi + \zeta \qquad [3.2]$$

Reduced Form Equation:
$$\eta = \ddot{\mathbf{B}}^{-1}\Gamma\xi + \ddot{\mathbf{B}}^{-1}\zeta \qquad [3.4]$$

Covariance Equation:
$$\Sigma = \left[\begin{array}{c|c} \ddot{\mathbf{B}}^{-1}(\Gamma\Phi\Gamma' + \Psi)\ddot{\mathbf{B}}^{-1} & \ddot{\mathbf{B}}^{-1}\Gamma\Phi \\ \hline \Phi\Gamma'\ddot{\mathbf{B}}^{-1} & \Phi \end{array} \right] \qquad [3.5]$$

Assumptions:

a. Variables are measured from their means: $E(\eta) = E(\zeta) = 0$; $E(\xi) = 0$.

b. Exogenous variables and errors in equations are uncorrelated: $E(\xi\zeta') = 0$ or $E(\zeta\xi') = 0$.

c. None of the structural equations is redundant: $\ddot{\mathbf{B}}^{-1} = (\mathbf{I} - \mathbf{B})^{-1}$ exists.

It is also assumed that $\ddot{\mathbf{B}} = (\mathbf{I} - \mathbf{B})$ is nonsingular (i.e., that $\ddot{\mathbf{B}}^{-1}$ exists). This assumption is not very restrictive, simply meaning that none of the equations in the model is redundant.

With these assumptions, summarized in Table 3.1, a number of covariance matrices can be defined. The covariance among the errors in equations, the ζ_i's, are contained in the symmetric matrix Ψ of dimension $(r \times r)$. Since the ζ_i's are assumed measured from zero (i.e., $E(\zeta_i) = 0$), Ψ can be defined as: $\Psi = E(\zeta\zeta')$. Values of Ψ are generally unknown, although off-diagonal elements can be restricted to zero to indicate that errors in equations are uncorrelated across two equations. The covariance matrix for the exogenous variables is defined as Φ, a $(s \times s)$ symmetric matrix. Since the exogenous variables are measured from their means, $\Phi = E(\xi\xi')$.

These ideas and the flexibility of the structural equation model can be illustrated by a series of examples.

Example 3.1: multiple regression. With one endogenous variable $(r = 1)$ and three exogenous variables $(s = 3)$, equation 3.1 is

$$[\eta_1] = [\underline{0}][\eta_1] + [\gamma_{11}\ \gamma_{12}\ \gamma_{13}]\begin{bmatrix} \xi_1 \\ \xi_2 \\ \xi_3 \end{bmatrix} + [\zeta_1]$$

or as it is more commonly written, $\eta_1 = \gamma_{11}\xi_1 + \gamma_{12}\xi_2 + \gamma_{13}\xi_3 + \zeta_1$. (Here and elsewhere, elements of parameter matrices are underlined if they have been constrained to equal the underlined value.) Φ contains the population variances and covariances for ξ_1, ξ_2, and ξ_3:

$$\Phi = \begin{bmatrix} VAR(\xi_1) & COV(\xi_1,\xi_2) & COV(\xi_1,\xi_3) \\ COV(\xi_2,\xi_1) & VAR(\xi_2) & COV(\xi_2,\xi_3) \\ COV(\xi_3,\xi_1) & COV(\xi_3,\xi_2) & VAR(\xi_3) \end{bmatrix} = \begin{bmatrix} \phi_{11} & \phi_{12} & \phi_{13} \\ \phi_{21} & \phi_{22} & \phi_{23} \\ \phi_{31} & \phi_{32} & \phi_{33} \end{bmatrix}$$

Ψ contains the variance of the only error in equation: $\Psi = [\psi_{11}]$. This is the simplest structural equation model, and it is equivalent to a single equation, multiple regression model. $//$ [1]

Example 3.2: a panel model. The complexity of Example 3.1 can be increased by considering a system of equations. This example, taken from Wheaton (1978), is a panel analysis of the sociogenesis of psychological disorder. The proposed model, presented in Figure 3.1, specifies the causal relationships among father's socioeconomic status (ξ_1), the respondent's socioeconomic status at three points in time (η_1, η_2, and η_4), and the number of symptoms of psychological disorder at two points in time (η_3 and η_5). In the original article there were two indicators of psychological disorder; in this example a single indicator, which is assumed to be measured without error, is used. The full model with both indicators is presented in Chapter 4.

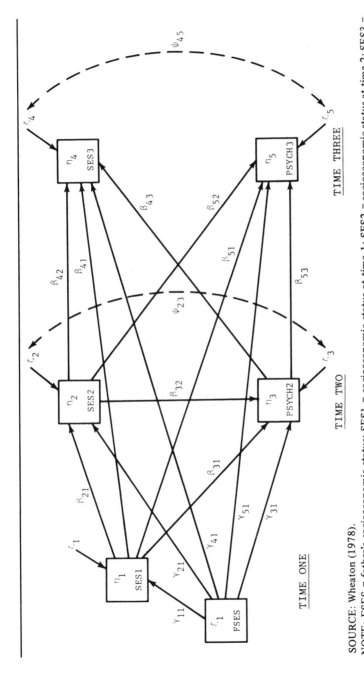

SOURCE: Wheaton (1978).

NOTE: FSES = father's socioeconomic status; SES1 = socioeconomic status at time 1; SES2 = socioeconomic status at time 2; SES3 = socioeconomic status at time 3; PSYCH2 = number of psychological sysmptoms at time 2; PSYCH3 = number of psychological symptoms at time 3.

Figure 3.1 Structural Equation Model for the Sociogenesis of Psychological Disorder

The structural equations for this model can be written as

$$
\begin{bmatrix} \eta_1 \\ \eta_2 \\ \eta_3 \\ \eta_4 \\ \eta_5 \end{bmatrix} = \begin{bmatrix} \underline{0} & \underline{0} & \underline{0} & \underline{0} & \underline{0} \\ \beta_{21} & \underline{0} & \underline{0} & \underline{0} & \underline{0} \\ \beta_{31} & \beta_{32} & \underline{0} & \underline{0} & \underline{0} \\ \beta_{41} & \beta_{42} & \beta_{43} & \underline{0} & \underline{0} \\ \beta_{51} & \beta_{52} & \beta_{53} & \underline{0} & \underline{0} \end{bmatrix} \begin{bmatrix} \eta_1 \\ \eta_2 \\ \eta_3 \\ \eta_4 \\ \eta_5 \end{bmatrix} + \begin{bmatrix} \gamma_{11} \\ \gamma_{21} \\ \gamma_{31} \\ \gamma_{41} \\ \gamma_{51} \end{bmatrix} \begin{bmatrix} \xi_1 \end{bmatrix} + \begin{bmatrix} \zeta_1 \\ \zeta_2 \\ \zeta_3 \\ \zeta_4 \\ \zeta_5 \end{bmatrix} \quad [3.3]
$$

Since there is only a single exogenous variable, $\Phi = [VAR(\xi_1)]$.

The covariances among the errors in equations are contained in Ψ. Two specifications of Ψ can be considered. In the first specification all errors in equations are assumed to be uncorrelated. That is, Ψ is restricted to be diagonal. A second, more realistic specification allows some of the errors in equations to be correlated. These correlated errors are indicated by the curved, dashed arrows connecting ζ_2 and ζ_3, and ζ_4 and ζ_5 in Figure 3.1. These covariances indicate that the errors in the equations predicting socioeconomic status (SES) and number of symptoms of psychological disorders at the same period of time are correlated. This might occur if the model were misspecified by the exclusion of variables that affect both SES and number of symptoms. The error caused by this misspecification would be picked up by ζ_2 and ζ_3 at time 2, and ζ_4 and ζ_5 at time 3; accordingly, these pairs of errors would be correlated. These constraints would be incorporated into Ψ as follows:

$$
\Psi = \begin{bmatrix} \psi_{11} & \underline{0} & \underline{0} & \underline{0} & \underline{0} \\ \underline{0} & \psi_{22} & \psi_{23} & \underline{0} & \underline{0} \\ \underline{0} & \psi_{32} & \psi_{33} & \underline{0} & \underline{0} \\ \underline{0} & \underline{0} & \underline{0} & \psi_{44} & \psi_{45} \\ \underline{0} & \underline{0} & \underline{0} & \psi_{54} & \psi_{55} \end{bmatrix}
$$

The importance of the decision on how to specify Ψ is illustrated in later sections on identification and estimation. //

Example 3.3: simultaneous causality. As a third example, consider the frequently referenced model from Duncan et al. (1971). In this model, illustrated in Figure 3.2, characteristics of a respondent and a

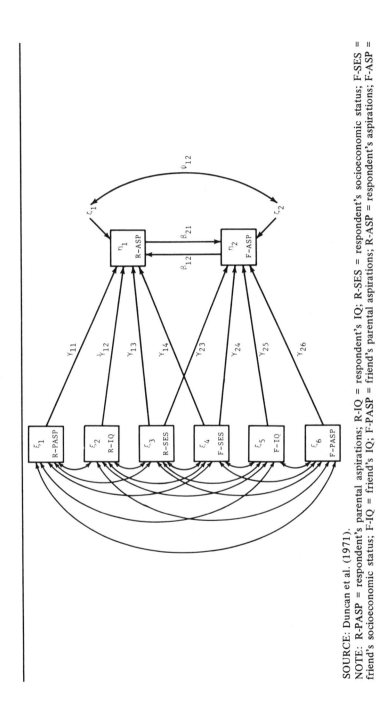

SOURCE: Duncan et al. (1971).

NOTE: R-PASP = respondent's parental aspirations; R-IQ = respondent's IQ; R-SES = respondent's socioeconomic status; F-SES = friend's socioeconomic status; F-IQ = friend's IQ; F-PASP = friend's parental aspirations; R-ASP = respondent's aspirations; F-ASP = friend's aspirations.

Figure 3.2 Structural Equation Model of Peer Influences on Aspirations

353

respondent's friend are used to predict the aspirations of the respondent and the respondent's friend. In the original model, two indicators of aspirations were used: occupational aspirations and educational aspirations. For the purposes of this chapter a single indicator, educational aspirations, is used. η_1 is the respondent's educational aspirations, and η_2 is the respondent's friend's educational aspirations. There are six exogenous variables. For the respondent, ξ_1 is a measure of the parents' aspirations for their child; ξ_2 is a measure of intelligence (hereafter referred to as IQ); and ξ_3 is a measure of SES. For the respondent's friend, ξ_6 is a measure of the parents' aspirations; ξ_5 is a measure of IQ; and ξ_4 is a measure of SES.

The structural equations for this model are

$$
\begin{bmatrix} \eta_1 \\ \eta_2 \end{bmatrix} = \begin{bmatrix} 0 & \beta_{12} \\ \beta_{21} & 0 \end{bmatrix} \begin{bmatrix} \eta_1 \\ \eta_2 \end{bmatrix} + \begin{bmatrix} \gamma_{11} & \gamma_{12} & \gamma_{13} & \gamma_{14} & 0 & 0 \\ 0 & 0 & \gamma_{23} & \gamma_{24} & \gamma_{25} & \gamma_{26} \end{bmatrix} \begin{bmatrix} \xi_1 \\ \xi_2 \\ \xi_3 \\ \xi_4 \\ \xi_5 \\ \xi_6 \end{bmatrix} + \begin{bmatrix} \zeta_1 \\ \zeta_2 \end{bmatrix}
$$

Thus, the respondent's aspirations (η_1) are assumed to be affected by the exogenous variables: his parents' aspirations (ξ_1), his IQ (ξ_2), his SES (ξ_3), and the SES of his friend (ξ_4) (i.e., $\gamma_{11} \neq 0$, $\gamma_{12} \neq 0$, $\gamma_{13} \neq 0$, and $\gamma_{14} \neq 0$; and $\gamma_{15} = \gamma_{16} = 0$). In the same way, the respondent's friend's aspirations (η_2) are assumed to be affected by his parents' aspirations (ξ_6), his IQ (ξ_5), his SES (ξ_4), and his friend's SES (ξ_3) (i.e., $\gamma_{23} \neq 0$, $\gamma_{24} \neq 0$, $\gamma_{25} \neq 0$, and $\gamma_{26} \neq 0$; and $\gamma_{21} = \gamma_{22} = 0$). Further, the respondents and friends are assumed to be mutually affected by one another's aspirations. Thus the respondent's aspirations (η_1) are affected by the respondent's friend's aspirations (η_2), and the respondent's friend's aspirations are affected by the respondent's aspirations (i.e., $\beta_{12} \neq 0$ and $\beta_{21} \neq 0$).

Finally, it is assumed that the errors in equations predicting respondent's aspirations are correlated with the errors in equations predicting the respondent's friend's aspirations:

$$
\boldsymbol{\Psi} = \begin{bmatrix} \psi_{11} & \psi_{12} \\ \psi_{21} & \psi_{22} \end{bmatrix}
$$

This might be caused by the exclusion of variables that jointly affect the respondent's and the friend's aspirations. //

The Covariance Structure

The covariances among the endogenous variables can be defined in terms of equation 3.1, the covariances among the exogenous variables (Φ), and the covariances among the errors in equations (Ψ). Since $\ddot{B}$ is assumed to be nonsingular, equation 3.2 can be multiplied by $\ddot{B}^{-1}$: $\ddot{B}^{-1}\ddot{B}\eta = \ddot{B}^{-1}\Gamma\xi + \ddot{B}^{-1}\zeta$, or more simply,

$$\eta = \ddot{B}^{-1}\Gamma\xi + \ddot{B}^{-1}\zeta \qquad [3.4]$$

Equation 3.4 is referred to as the *reduced form* of the structural equation model, since structural relationships are reduced to a set of equations in which the endogenous variables are functions only of the exogenous variables and the errors in equations.

Since it was assumed that $E(\eta) = 0$, the covariance matrix for η is equal to $E(\eta\eta')$. Using the reduced form equation 3.4 allows us to write

$$\begin{aligned}
COV(\eta) = E(\eta\eta') &= E[(\ddot{B}^{-1}\Gamma\xi + \ddot{B}^{-1}\zeta)(\ddot{B}^{-1}\Gamma\xi + \ddot{B}^{-1}\zeta)'] \\
&= E[(\ddot{B}^{-1}\Gamma\xi\xi'\Gamma'\ddot{B}^{-1'}) + (\ddot{B}^{-1}\Gamma\xi\zeta'\ddot{B}^{-1'}) + \\
&\quad (\ddot{B}^{-1}\zeta\xi'\Gamma'\ddot{B}^{-1'}) + (\ddot{B}^{-1}\zeta\zeta'\ddot{B}^{-1'})]
\end{aligned}$$

Distributing the expectation operator, making use of the assumption that $E(\xi\zeta') = 0$, and using the definitions of Φ and Ψ, it follows that

$$\begin{aligned}
COV(\eta) &= \ddot{B}^{-1}\Gamma\Phi\Gamma'\ddot{B}^{-1'} + \ddot{B}^{-1}\Psi\ddot{B}^{-1'} \\
&= \ddot{B}^{-1}(\Gamma\Phi\Gamma' + \Psi)\ddot{B}^{-1'}
\end{aligned}$$

Thus the covariances among the endogenous variables are defined in terms of the structural parameters Γ and $\ddot{B}$, and the covariances among the exogenous variables and among the errors in equations.

The covariances among the ξ's and η's are derived similarly. Since $E(\xi) = 0$ and $E(\eta) = 0$, $COV(\eta,\xi) = E(\eta\xi')$. Substituting the reduced form $\ddot{B}^{-1}\Gamma\xi + \ddot{B}^{-1}\zeta$ for η,

$$\begin{aligned}
COV(\eta,\xi) = E(\eta\xi') &= E[(\ddot{B}^{-1}\Gamma\xi + \ddot{B}^{-1}\zeta)\xi'] \\
&= E[\ddot{B}^{-1}\Gamma\xi\xi' + \ddot{B}^{-1}\zeta\xi'] \\
&= \ddot{B}^{-1}\Gamma\Phi
\end{aligned}$$

with the last equality following from the assumption that $E(\zeta\xi') = 0$ and the definition $E(\xi\xi') = \Phi$.

These results allow us to define the $(r+s \times r+s)$ covariance matrix Σ, containing the variances and covariances among the η's and ξ's:

$$\Sigma = \left[\begin{array}{c|c} \mathrm{COV}(\eta) & \mathrm{COV}(\eta,\xi) \\ \hline \mathrm{COV}(\xi,\eta) & \mathrm{COV}(\xi) \end{array}\right] = \left[\begin{array}{c|c} \ddot{\mathbf{B}}^{-1}(\Gamma\Phi\Gamma' + \Psi)\ddot{\mathbf{B}}^{-1} & \ddot{\mathbf{B}}^{-1}\Gamma\Phi \\ \hline \Phi\Gamma'\ddot{\mathbf{B}}^{-1} & \Phi \end{array}\right] \quad [3.5]$$

Σ has been defined in terms of the structural parameters in $\mathbf{B}$ and Γ, and the covariances contained in Φ and Ψ. Constraints imposed upon the structural parameters and upon the covariances restrict the values that Σ can assume. In practice Σ is unknown, but sample estimates of the covariances, contained in the matrix $\mathbf{S}$, are known. The process of estimation involves finding values of $\mathbf{B}$, Γ, Φ, and Ψ that produce a covariance matrix according to equation 3.5 that is as close as possible to the observed covariance matrix $\mathbf{S}$.

Types of Structural Equation Models

In the structural equation model procedures for proving identification and for estimating parameters depend on the forms of $\mathbf{B}$ and Ψ. Three forms of $\mathbf{B}$ need to be distinguished.

(1) $\mathbf{B}$ is a diagonal matrix, in which case endogenous variables are affected by exogenous variables, but not by endogenous variables.

(2) $\mathbf{B}$ is a triangular matrix, in which case endogenous variables can affect one another, but if η_j affects η_i, then η_i does not affect η_j.[2] That is, if $\beta_{ij} \neq 0$, then $\beta_{ji} = 0$.

(3) $\mathbf{B}$ has unrestricted elements above and below the diagonal. This allows any two endogenous variable to simultaneously affect one another. Thus, if η_j affects η_i, η_i can also affect η_j. If β_{ij} is not restricted to zero, β_{ji} may or may not be restricted to zero.

Two forms of Ψ are of concern.

(1) Ψ is diagonal. In this case, all of the errors in equations are uncorrelated. $\psi_{ij} = \psi_{ji} = 0$ for all $i \neq j$.

(2) Ψ is a symmetric, nondiagonal matrix. The errors in equation for at least two equations are correlated. That is, there is at least one $\psi_{ij} = \psi_{ji}$ that is not restricted to equal zero.

These forms of $\mathbf{B}$ and Ψ allow for six types of models.

Type 1. In the simplest case, both **B** and **Ψ** are restricted to be diagonal. For a single equation this corresponds to the multiple regression model. Example 3.1 above illustrates this case. If there is more than one equation, the information in one equation is of no use in identifying or estimating the parameters in the other equations. Each equation must be treated individually as a simple multiple regression.

Type 2. For this type of model no endogenous variable affects any other endogenous variable (i.e., **B** is diagonal), but the equations are related since the error in one equation is correlated with the error in another equation (i.e., an off-diagonal element of **Ψ** is not restricted to zero). When the exogenous variables in one equation are completely different from those in another equation, this corresponds to "seemingly unrelated regressions" (see Kmenta, 1971: 517-529).

Type 3. When **B** is triangular, an endogenous variable can affect another endogenous variable, but there is no simultaneous causality. If η_i affects η_j ($\beta_{ji} \neq 0$), η_j does not affect η_i ($\beta_{ij} = 0$). When this form of **B** is combined with a diagonal **Ψ**, the model is called recursive. The **B** matrix in Example 3.2 is triangular. In the first specification of **Ψ**, **Ψ** is assumed to be diagonal; hence the model is recursive.

Type 4. This case differs from the recursive model in that **Ψ** is not diagonal. As with the recursive model, **B** is assumed to be triangular. Models of this form commonly occur in panel models in which errors at the same time are correlated, or errors in equations for the same variable over time are correlated. In the second specifications of Model 3.2, **Ψ** is not diagonal and even though **B** is triangular, the model is not recursive.

Type 5. While models with simultaneous causality (i.e., **B** is not triangular or diagonal) are generally assumed to have errors correlated across equations (i.e., **Ψ** is not diagonal), this is not necessarily the case. If it can be justified that the errors in equations are uncorrelated, **Ψ** is diagonal regardless of the form of **B**. In some formulations of Example 3.3 this has been assumed.

Type 6. When simultaneous causality is present and errors in equations are correlated, Type 6 occurs. This model has been studied extensively by econometricians, and is referred to as a system of simultaneous equations, a nonrecursive model, an integrated structure, or a general interdependent system. Example 3.3 is an example of this type of model.

With these types of models in mind, it is possible to consider the issues of identification and estimation.

Identification

If a structural equation model is not identified, an infinite number of sets of parameters could generate the observed data. The researcher has no way to choose among the various solutions since each is equally valid or, if you wish, invalid. Identification can be obtained by imposing restrictions on **B**, **Γ**, and **Ψ**. Identification occurs if all but one set of parameters are excluded from consideration because they violate constraints imposed on the parameters being estimated.

The unrestricted structural equation model (i.e., no constraints on **B**, **Γ**, and **Ψ**) is unidentified. (See Wonnacott and Wonnacott [1979: 462] for a proof of this.) When **B** and **Ψ** have certain forms, the resulting models are always identified. Specifically, unrelated multiple regressions (Type 1), seemingly unrelated regressions (Type 2), and recursive equation systems (Type 3) are always identified. Models of Types 4 through 6 are unidentified unless sufficient additional restrictions are placed on **B**, **Γ**, and **Ψ**. Now let us turn to an examination of what types of restrictions are possible and how identification can be proven.

In simultaneous equation models (Type 6), identification is most often achieved by restricting selected elements of **B** and **Γ** to equal zero. If an element of **B** is restricted to zero, say β_{ij}, it means that the endogenous variable η_j does not affect the endogenous variable η_i. If an element of **Γ** is restricted to zero, say γ_{ij}, it means that exogenous variable ξ_j does not affect the endogenous variable η_i. Fisher (1966) has presented a powerful set of conditions for identification in terms of such exclusion restrictions. (See Wonnacott and Wonnacott [1979: 461-473] for a mathematically less demanding presentation of these conditions.)

The simplest condition to test is the *order condition*. It states that if an equation in a system of equations is identified, it must be true that the number of excluded variables in the equation is greater than or equal to the number of equations in the system minus one. Or in terms of constraints on **B** and **Γ**, the number of coefficients fixed to zero in a given row of **B** and **Γ** must be greater than or equal to the number of equations minus one. This is a necessary condition. If it is not true, the equation is not identified and cannot be estimated. If the condition is true, the model may or may not be identified. An example illustrates this condition.

Example 3.3: the order condition. The Duncan, Haller, and Portes model is a typical simultaneous equation system. The matrices of structural coefficients are

$$\mathbf{B} = \begin{bmatrix} \underline{0} & \beta_{12} \\ \beta_{21} & \underline{0} \end{bmatrix}$$

and

$$\mathbf{\Gamma} = \begin{bmatrix} \gamma_{11} & \gamma_{12} & \gamma_{13} & \gamma_{14} & \underline{0} & \underline{0} \\ \underline{0} & \underline{0} & \gamma_{23} & \gamma_{24} & \gamma_{25} & \gamma_{26} \end{bmatrix}$$

In row 1 of $\mathbf{\Gamma}$, there are two excluded variables: ξ_5 and ξ_6 are assumed not to affect η_1, as indicated by the constraints $\gamma_{15} = \gamma_{16} = 0$. Thus the number of excluded variables in the equation for η_1 is greater than the number of equations minus one: $2 > 1$, and the order condition for identification is satisfied. In the same way, two variables are excluded from the equation for η_2, and the necessary condition is also satisfied. //

A necessary and sufficient condition for identification is the *rank condition*. To state this condition, define $\ddot{\mathbf{B}}^{\#}$ as the matrix formed by excluding the row of $\ddot{\mathbf{B}}$ for the equation being considered, and deleting all columns for which there is not a zero in the excluded row. $\mathbf{\Gamma}^{\#}$ is defined by similar operations on $\mathbf{\Gamma}$. An equation is identified if and only if the rank of $[\ddot{\mathbf{B}}^{\#} | \mathbf{\Gamma}^{\#}]$, the matrix formed by joining $\ddot{\mathbf{B}}^{\#}$ and $\mathbf{\Gamma}^{\#}$, equals the number of equations minus one.[3] While this condition is often ignored in practice, this can be unwise. Even though the rank of $[\ddot{\mathbf{B}}^{\#} | \mathbf{\Gamma}^{\#}]$ cannot generally be known since the values of $\ddot{\mathbf{B}}$ and $\mathbf{\Gamma}$ are unknown (recall, they are to be estimated if the model is identified), it can sometimes be known that the rank is less than the number of equations minus one and, hence, that a given equation is not identified.

Example 3.3: the rank condition. To test the rank condition for the equation for η_1, first construct $\ddot{\mathbf{B}}^{\#}$ and $\mathbf{\Gamma}^{\#}$ by crossing out the appropriate elements of $\ddot{\mathbf{B}}$ and $\mathbf{\Gamma}$:

$$\ddot{\mathbf{B}}^{\#} = \begin{bmatrix} \cancel{1} & -\cancel{\beta_{12}} \\ -\cancel{\beta_{21}} & \cancel{1} \end{bmatrix}$$

and

$$\Gamma^{\#} = \begin{bmatrix} \gamma_{11} & \gamma_{12} & \gamma_{13} & \gamma_{14} & \underline{0} & \underline{0} \\ \underline{0} & \underline{0} & \gamma_{23} & \gamma_{24} & \gamma_{25} & \gamma_{26} \end{bmatrix}$$

Accordingly, $[\ddot{\mathbf{B}}^{\#} | \Gamma^{\#}]$ equals $[\gamma_{25}\ \gamma_{26}]$. The rank of $[\ddot{\mathbf{B}}^{\#} | \Gamma^{\#}]$ will equal one unless both γ_{25} and γ_{26} are exactly equal to zero in the population. While this cannot be known with certainly, it is unlikely, and we can reasonably conclude that the equation for η_1 is identified. The rank condition can be applied to the equation for η_2 in the same fashion. //

Example 3.2: the rank and order conditions. Wheaton's (1978) model (see Figure 3.1 and equation 3.3) is a typical panel model with errors in equations for the same time period being correlated. As described earlier, **B** is triangular, and if we assume that $\mathbf{\Psi}$ is diagonal, the model is recursive and, consequently, is identified. If $\mathbf{\Psi}$ is assumed to be symmetric but not diagonal, the model is not recursive even though **B** is triangular, and the model is not necessarily identified. To test for identification, the order condition can be applied:

Dependent Variable	Number of Excluded Variables	? $\geq$	Number of Equations Minus One
η_1	4	yes	4
η_2	3	no	4
η_3	2	no	4
η_4	1	no	4
η_5	1	no	4

The equations for η_2 through η_5 are not identified. To determine if the equation for η_1 is identified, the rank condition must be checked. First, consider the matrix $[\ddot{\mathbf{B}}^{\#} | \Gamma^{\#}]$, where crosses indicate elements to be deleted:

$$[\ddot{\mathbf{B}}^{\#} | \Gamma^{\#}] = \begin{bmatrix} 1 & \underline{0} & \underline{0} & \underline{0} & \underline{0} & \gamma_{11} \\ \beta_{21} & 1 & 0 & 0 & 0 & \gamma_{21} \\ \beta_{31} & \beta_{32} & 1 & \underline{0} & \underline{0} & \gamma_{31} \\ \beta_{41} & \beta_{42} & \beta_{43} & 1 & \underline{0} & \gamma_{41} \\ \beta_{51} & \beta_{52} & \beta_{53} & 0 & 1 & \gamma_{51} \end{bmatrix} = \begin{bmatrix} 1 & 0 & 0 & 0 \\ \beta_{32} & 1 & 0 & 0 \\ \beta_{42} & \beta_{43} & 1 & 0 \\ \beta_{52} & \beta_{53} & 0 & 1 \end{bmatrix}$$

The rank of $[\ddot{\mathbf{B}}^{\#} \mid \mathbf{\Gamma}^{\#}]$ is four; hence the equation for η_1 is identified without any restrictions on $\mathbf{\Psi}$. If restrictions are placed on $\mathbf{\Psi}$, the remaining equations may be identified, but the rank and order conditions cannot be used to determine it. //

In addition to exclusion restrictions, equality constraints (e.g., $\gamma_{23} = \gamma_{25}$), nonlinear restrictions, and restrictions on the covariances between errors in equations (e.g., $\Psi_{12} = \Psi_{21} = 0$) can also result in identification. When such restrictions are used, it is generally necessary to prove identification by solving the parameters of the model in terms of the variances and covariances of the observed variables, a necessary and sufficient condition for identification. An example of such a proof of identification is now given.

Example 3.2: identification. In the Wheaton model (see Figure 3.1), the assumption that $\mathbf{\Psi}$ is unrestricted is probably too harsh. Wheaton (1978) assumed that only the errors in equations predicting variables measured at the same point in time are correlated. The resulting $\mathbf{\Psi}$ is

$$
\mathbf{\Psi} = \begin{bmatrix} \psi_{11} & 0 & 0 & 0 & 0 \\ 0 & \psi_{22} & \psi_{23} & 0 & 0 \\ 0 & \psi_{32} & \psi_{33} & 0 & 0 \\ 0 & 0 & 0 & \psi_{44} & \psi_{45} \\ 0 & 0 & 0 & \psi_{54} & \psi_{55} \end{bmatrix}
$$

With these additional restrictions on $\mathbf{\Psi}$, the other equations in the model may be identified. To determine this, the parameters in $\mathbf{B}$, $\mathbf{\Gamma}$, and $\mathbf{\Psi}$ must be solved for in terms of the variances and covariances of the η's and ξ's.

The structural equations can be written as

$$\eta_1 = \gamma_{11}\xi_1 + \zeta_1 \tag{3.6}$$

$$\eta_2 = \beta_{21}\eta_1 + \gamma_{21}\xi_1 + \zeta_2 \tag{3.7}$$

$$\eta_3 = \beta_{31}\eta_1 + \beta_{32}\eta_2 + \gamma_{31}\xi_1 + \zeta_3 \tag{3.8}$$

$$\eta_4 = \beta_{41}\eta_1 + \beta_{42}\eta_2 + \beta_{43}\eta_3 + \gamma_{41}\xi_1 + \zeta_4 \tag{3.9}$$

$$\eta_5 = \beta_{51}\eta_1 + \beta_{52}\eta_2 + \beta_{53}\eta_3 + \gamma_{51}\xi_1 + \zeta_5 \tag{3.10}$$

We know from the rank and order conditions that equation 3.6, hence γ_{11}, is identified. Multiplying equation 3.6 by itself and taking expectations (recall that the variables are measured as deviations from zero, and hence the expectation of a product equals a variance or a covariance), results in

$$E(\eta_1\eta_1) = VAR(\eta_1) = \gamma_{11}{}^2 VAR(\xi_1) + 2\gamma_{11}COV(\xi_1,\zeta_1) + \psi_{11}$$
$$= \gamma_{11}{}^2 VAR(\xi_1) + \psi_{11}$$

Since γ_{11} is identified, $VAR(\xi_1)$ is known, and $COV(\xi_1,\zeta_1)$ is assumed to equal zero, ψ_{11} can be solved for and hence is identified.

Equation 3.7 can be treated similarly. First, multiply equation 3.7 by ξ_1 and take expectations:

$$E(\eta_2\xi_1) = COV(\eta_2,\xi_1) = \beta_{21}COV(\eta_1,\xi_1) + \gamma_{21}COV(\xi_1, \xi_1) + COV(\zeta_2, \xi_1)$$
$$= \beta_{21}COV(\eta_1,\xi_1) + \gamma_{21}COV(\xi_1,\xi_1)$$

since $COV(\zeta_2,\xi_1)$ equals zero by assumption. Next, multiply equation 3.7 by η_1 and take expectations:

$$E(\eta_2\eta_1) = COV(\eta_2,\eta_1) = \beta_{21}COV(\eta_1,\eta_1) + \gamma_{21}COV(\xi_1,\eta_1) + COV(\zeta_2,\eta_1)$$

$COV(\zeta_2,\eta_1)$ equals zero, which can be seen by multiplying Equation 3.6 by ζ_2, and taking expectations: $E(\eta_1\zeta_2) = \gamma_{11}E(\xi_1\zeta_2) + E(\zeta_1\zeta_2)$, which equals zero since $E(\xi_1\zeta_2)$ and $E(\zeta_1\zeta_2) = \psi_{12}$ are assumed to equal zero. Now there are two equations in two unknowns:

$$COV(\eta_2,\xi_1) = \beta_{21}COV(\eta_1,\xi_1) + \gamma_{21}COV(\xi_1,\xi_1)$$
$$COV(\eta_2,\eta_1) = \beta_{21}COV(\eta_1,\eta_1) + \gamma_{21}COV(\xi_1,\eta_1)$$

The parameters β_{21} and γ_{21} can be easily solved for and hence are identified.

ψ_{22} can be proved identified by multiplying equation 3.7 by itself and taking expectations:

$$COV(\eta_2,\eta_2) = \beta_{21}{}^2 COV(\eta_1,\eta_1) + \gamma_{21}{}^2 COV(\xi_1,\xi_1) + \psi_{22} +$$
$$2\beta_{21}\gamma_{21}COV(\eta_1,\xi_1) + 2\beta_{21}COV(\eta_1,\zeta_2) + 2\gamma_{21}COV(\xi_1,\zeta_2)$$

Since the covariances with ζ_2 are assumed to equal zero, and all other parameters in the equation except for ψ_{22} are either known or are identified, ψ_{22} can be solved for and hence is identified.

With the restrictions currently imposed, equation 3.8 is not identi-
fied. Multiplying equation 3.8 by ξ_1, η_1, and η_2 and taking expectations:

$$COV(\eta_3,\xi_1) = \beta_{31}COV(\eta_1,\xi_1) + \beta_{32}COV(\eta_2,\xi_1) + \\ \gamma_{31}COV(\xi_1,\xi_1) + COV(\zeta_3,\xi_1)$$

$$COV(\eta_3,\eta_1) = \beta_{31}COV(\eta_1,\eta_1) + \beta_{32}COV(\eta_2,\eta_1) + \\ \gamma_{31}COV(\xi_1,\eta_1) + COV(\zeta_3,\eta_1)$$

$$COV(\eta_3,\eta_2) = \beta_{31}COV(\eta_1,\eta_2) + \beta_{32}COV(\eta_2,\eta_2) + \\ \gamma_{31}COV(\xi_1,\eta_2) + COV(\zeta_3,\eta_2) \qquad [3.11]$$

While $COV(\zeta_3,\eta_1)$ and $COV(\zeta_3,\xi_1)$ equal zero, $COV(\zeta_3,\eta_2) = \psi_{23}$ does not.
Therefore, there are three equations in four unknowns (β_{31}, β_{32}, γ_{31}, and
ψ_{23}), which cannot be solved uniquely.

Attempts to find a fourth equation in order to solve for the four
unknowns cannot be successful, since each new equation introduces
additional unknowns. For example,

$$COV(\eta_3,\eta_3) = \beta_{31}{}^2COV(\eta_1,\eta_1) + \beta_{32}{}^2COV(\eta_2,\eta_2) + \gamma_{31}{}^2COV(\xi_1,\xi_1) + \\ \psi_{33}{}^2 + 2\beta_{31}\gamma_{31}COV(\eta_1,\xi_1) + 2\beta_{32}\gamma_{31}COV(\eta_2,\xi_1) + \\ 2\beta_{32}\beta_{31}COV(\eta_1,\eta_2) + 2\gamma_{31}COV(\xi_1,\zeta_3) + 2\beta_{31}COV(\eta_1,\zeta_3) + \\ 2\beta_{32}COV(\eta_2,\zeta_3)$$

While an additional equation has been added, so has the additional
unidentified parameter ψ_{33}. Three equations that cannot be solved for
four unknowns have been replaced by four equations that cannot be
solved for five unknowns. Attempts to find other equations with which
to solve for the parameters will be similarly thwarted by the introduction
of additional, unidentified parameters. Accordingly, the model with the
restrictions currently imposed is not identified, although equations 3.6
and 3.7 are identified.

Wheaton (1978) encountered the same unidentifiability of the structural component of the model he analyzed (even though he also had a
measurement model). The restrictions he imposed to identify the model
were that β_{32}, β_{41}, and β_{51} equal zero; that is, three of the causal paths
among the endogenous variables were assumed to be absent. With these
additional exclusion restrictions, the identification of the model can be
readily demonstrated.

Equation set 3.11 now contains three equations in three unknowns
that can be solved for. Proceeding in a similar fashion, the other
parameters in the model can also be shown to be identified. //

For an additional example of how models with constraints on **Ψ** can be proved to be identified, see Hanushek and Jackson (1977: 271-276).

Estimation

Once a structural equation model is known to be identified, estimation can proceed. If an attempt is made to estimate a model that is not identified, the estimates of the unidentified parameters are meaningless.

As with identification, the method of estimation depends on the form of the **B** and **Ψ** matrices. For unrelated multiple regression (Type 1), ordinary least squares is optimal. If **B** is diagonal, but **Ψ** is not (Type 2), the method of estimation depends on the exogenous variables. If the exogenous variables are identical in all equations, ordinary least squares provides unbiased and efficient estimates. If the equations do not share variables, the case of seemingly unrelated regressions, ordinary least squares is unbiased and consistent, but not efficient. Generalized least squares provides efficient estimates in this case.[4] For recursive models (Type 3) ordinary least squares provides consistent and efficient estimates. If the model does not include lagged endogenous variables, ordinary least squares is also unbiased. Simultaneous equation systems in which there are no constraints on **Ψ**, can be estimated by a variety of methods: two-stage least squares, instrumental variables, limited information maximum likelihood, full information maximum likelihood, and three-stage least squares (among others).

Each of the types of models just described and their methods of estimation have received extended discussion in the econometrics literature. See Hanushek and Jackson (1977) for a relatively simple introduction, Kmenta (1971) for a more thorough and demanding treatment, and Malinvaud (1970) for a very demanding treatment that approaches estimation in the manner closest to what is used for the covariance structure model. These models can be estimated with a variety of commonly available software packages. It is beyond the scope of this discussion to review these methods. Rather, the focus is on applications that cannot be easily incorporated into standard statistical packages and that have been relatively neglected in the econometrics literature. For example, if **Ψ** has some but not all off-diagonal elements restricted to zero or if equality constraints have been imposed (both of which occur commonly in panel models), most regression packages cannot provide the desired estimates. In such cases, the software developed for the covariance structure model provides the most convenient method of estimation.

Before discussing specific methods, a distinction between full information and limited information techniques—what are sometimes
referred to as single equation methods versus system methods—is necessary (see Hanushek and Jackson, 1977: 277-278). A limited information
technique estimates each equation separately without using information
on restrictions in other equations. Full information techniques estimate
the entire system of equations simultaneously and have the advantage
that the estimation of each parameter utilizes the information provided
by the entire system. Such methods are statistically more efficient. On
the other hand, full information techniques are limited by their advantages. Since the estimation of each parameter is dependent upon every
other parameter in the model, estimates of each parameter are affected
by misspecification in any equation of the model. Limited information
methods, while less efficient, estimate each equation separately; hence
estimation of one equation is not affected by misspecification in other
equations. Accordingly, when model specification is uncertain, limited
information methods are preferred.

Estimation using software for the covariance structure model can be
thought of as follows.[5] The researcher begins with the *sample* covariance
matrix S. Diagonal elements are variances of the observed variables,
and off-diagonal elements are covariances. If the data are standardized,
S contains the correlations among the observed variables. It is useful to
think of S as a partitioned matrix:

$$
S = \begin{bmatrix}
\begin{matrix} \text{Sample estimates} \\ \text{of covariances} \\ \text{among } \eta\text{'s} \end{matrix} & \begin{matrix} \text{Sample estimates} \\ \text{of covariances} \\ \text{between } \eta\text{'s \& } \xi\text{'s} \end{matrix} \\
\begin{matrix} \text{Sample estimates} \\ \text{of covariances} \\ \text{between } \xi\text{'s \& } \eta\text{'s} \end{matrix} & \begin{matrix} \text{Sample estimates} \\ \text{of covariances} \\ \text{among } \xi\text{'s} \end{matrix}
\end{bmatrix}
$$

An estimate of the *population* covariance matrix Σ is defined in terms of
estimates of $\ddot{B}$, Γ, Φ, and Ψ (see equation 3.5):

$$
\hat{\Sigma} = \begin{bmatrix} \widehat{COV}(\eta) & \widehat{COV}(\eta,\xi) \\ \widehat{COV}(\xi,\eta) & \widehat{COV}(\xi) \end{bmatrix} = \begin{bmatrix} \hat{\ddot{B}}^{-1}(\hat{\Gamma}\hat{\Phi}\hat{\Gamma}' + \hat{\Psi})\hat{\ddot{B}}^{-1} & \hat{\ddot{B}}^{-1}\hat{\Gamma}\hat{\Phi} \\ \hat{\Phi}\hat{\Gamma}'\hat{\ddot{B}}^{-1} & \hat{\Phi} \end{bmatrix}
$$

where the ^ indicates that the matrices contain estimates of population
parameters. These estimates must satisfy the constraints that have been

imposed on the model. Estimation involves finding values of $\hat{\ddot{\mathbf{B}}}$, $\hat{\boldsymbol{\Gamma}}$, $\hat{\boldsymbol{\Phi}}$, and $\hat{\boldsymbol{\Psi}}$ that generate an estimated covariance matrix $\hat{\boldsymbol{\Sigma}}$ that is as close as possible to the sample covariance matrix $\mathbf{S}$. This is done by considering all possible sets of matrices having the dimensions of the matrices $\ddot{\mathbf{B}}$, $\boldsymbol{\Gamma}$, $\boldsymbol{\Phi}$, and $\boldsymbol{\Psi}$. Many of these possible matrices must be excluded from consideration because they do not incorporate the constraints imposed on the parameters. Let $\ddot{\mathbf{B}}^*$, $\boldsymbol{\Gamma}^*$, $\boldsymbol{\Phi}^*$, and $\boldsymbol{\Psi}^*$ be any matrices that incorporate the imposed constraints. This set of matrices defines a matrix $\boldsymbol{\Sigma}^*$ according to the formula

$$\boldsymbol{\Sigma}^* = \left[\begin{array}{c|c} COV(\eta)^* & COV(\eta,\xi)^* \\ \hline COV(\xi,\eta)^* & COV(\xi)^* \end{array} \right] = \left[\begin{array}{c|c} \ddot{\mathbf{B}}^{*-1}(\boldsymbol{\Gamma}^*\boldsymbol{\Phi}^*\boldsymbol{\Gamma}^{*\prime} + \boldsymbol{\Psi}^*)\ddot{\mathbf{B}}^{*\prime-1} & \ddot{\mathbf{B}}^{*-1}\boldsymbol{\Gamma}^*\boldsymbol{\Phi}^* \\ \hline \boldsymbol{\Phi}^*\boldsymbol{\Gamma}^{*\prime}\ddot{\mathbf{B}}^{*\prime-1} & \boldsymbol{\Phi}^* \end{array} \right]$$

If $\boldsymbol{\Sigma}^*$ is "close" to $\mathbf{S}$, one might conclude that $\ddot{\mathbf{B}}^*$, $\boldsymbol{\Gamma}^*$, $\boldsymbol{\Phi}^*$, and $\boldsymbol{\Psi}^*$ are reasonable estimates of the population parameters. The problems of estimation are to measure how close $\boldsymbol{\Sigma}^*$ is to $\mathbf{S}$, and to find the values of $\ddot{\mathbf{B}}^*$, $\boldsymbol{\Gamma}^*$, $\boldsymbol{\Phi}^*$, and $\boldsymbol{\Psi}^*$ that produce the $\boldsymbol{\Sigma}^*$ that is as close as possible to $\mathbf{S}$.

A function that measures how close a given $\boldsymbol{\Sigma}^*$ is to the sample covariance matrix $\mathbf{S}$ is called a *fitting function*. A fitting function is designated as $F(\mathbf{S};\boldsymbol{\Sigma}^*)$, or to indicate that $\boldsymbol{\Sigma}^*$ is defined by $\mathbf{B}^*$, $\boldsymbol{\Gamma}^*$, $\boldsymbol{\Phi}^*$, and $\boldsymbol{\Psi}^*$, it may be written as $F(\mathbf{S};\mathbf{B}^*,\boldsymbol{\Gamma}^*,\boldsymbol{\Phi}^*,\boldsymbol{\Psi}^*)$. This function is defined over all possible $\mathbf{B}^*$, $\boldsymbol{\Gamma}^*$, $\boldsymbol{\Phi}^*$, and $\boldsymbol{\Psi}^*$ that satisfy the constraints on $\mathbf{B}$, $\boldsymbol{\Gamma}$, $\boldsymbol{\Phi}$, and $\boldsymbol{\Psi}$. Those values of $\mathbf{B}^*$, $\boldsymbol{\Gamma}^*$, $\boldsymbol{\Phi}^*$, and $\boldsymbol{\Psi}^*$ that minimize the fitting function for a given $\mathbf{S}$ are the sample estimates of the population parameters and are designated as $\hat{\mathbf{B}}$, $\hat{\boldsymbol{\Gamma}}$, $\hat{\boldsymbol{\Phi}}$, and $\hat{\boldsymbol{\Psi}}$.

Three fitting functions are commonly used in software for the covariance structure model. These correspond to unweighted least squares (ULS), generalized least squares (GLS), and maximum likelihood (ML).

The ULS estimators of $\mathbf{B}$, $\boldsymbol{\Gamma}$, $\boldsymbol{\Phi}$, and $\boldsymbol{\Psi}$ are those values that minimize the fitting function:

$$F_{ULS}(\mathbf{S};\boldsymbol{\Sigma}^*) = tr[(\mathbf{S} - \boldsymbol{\Sigma}^*)^2]$$

where "tr" is the trace operator indicating the sum of the diagonal elements of a matrix. The ULS estimator can be shown to be consistent without making any assumptions about the distribution of the observed variables (Bentler and Weeks, 1979). This means that for large samples, ULS is approximately unbiased. Not having to make distributional assumptions about the observed variables is an advantage, but it is offset by two limitations. First, there are no statistical tests associated with ULS estimation. Second, ULS estimators have a property known as *scale dependency,* a concept discussed in *CFA.*

The fitting function for GLS is more complex, with differences between **S** and $\mathbf{\Sigma}^*$ being weighted by elements of $\mathbf{S}^{-1}$ (see Jöreskog and Goldberger, 1972 for details). The GLS fitting function is

$$F_{GLS}(S;\Sigma^*) = tr[(S - \Sigma^*)S^{-1}]^2$$

The ML estimator minimizes the fitting function defined as

$$F_{ML}(S;\Sigma^*) = tr(\Sigma^{*-1}S) + [\log|\Sigma^*| - \log|S|] - (r + s)$$

where $\log|\Sigma^*|$ is the log of the determinant of $\mathbf{\Sigma}^*$. If $\boldsymbol{\xi}$ and $\boldsymbol{\eta}$ have a multivariate normal distribution, both GLS and ML have desirable asymptotic properties. The ML estimator is approximately unbiased, has as small a sampling variance as any other estimator, and is approximately normally distributed. This means that if the assumptions about the distribution of $\boldsymbol{\xi}$ and $\boldsymbol{\eta}$ hold, as the sample size gets larger, (1) the expected values of the sample estimates get closer and closer to the true population parameters; (2) the variance of the sampling distribution of the ML estimators becomes as small as possible with any estimator; and (3) the sampling distribution of the estimators becomes normal. In the covariance structure model, GLS is asymptotically equivalent to ML (Lee, 1977; Browne, 1974). Both methods of estimation are scale invariant and have desirable properties for statistical testing.

Note that these are asymptotic properties. Strictly speaking, they are justified only as the sample approaches an infinite size. An important practical question is, how large must a sample be in order to take advantage of the desirable asymptotic properties? Unfortunately, there is no definitive answer to this question, although Boomsma (1982) has obtained some results for the confirmatory factor model. (See *CFA* for details.) GLS and ML also require assumptions of normality, with GLS being justified under slightly less restrictive assumptions than ML (Browne, 1974). Unfortunately, very little is known about the effects of violations of the assumption of normality in our model.

Practical Considerations

In general, none of these estimators (ULS, GLS, and ML) has closed form solutions. The values that minimize the fitting functions must be found by numerically searching over possible values of **B**, **Γ**, **Φ**, and **Ψ**. Technical details on how the search is conducted need not concern us, although three practical problems are worth noting.

First, it is possible for search procedures to locate what is called a "local minimum." This is a value of the fitting function that appears to be the smallest possible when actually there are other smaller values. Such occurrences are thought to be rare (Jöreskog and Sörbom, 1981: I.31).

Second, the values of the parameters that minimize the fitting function may be outside the range of feasible values. For example, a variance may be estimated to be negative or a correlation to be greater than one. Such occurrences are thought to result from misspecified models or insufficiently large sample sizes. This issue is discussed in more detail in *CFA*.

Third, numerical searches can be costly in computer time. The time required for estimating a given model is based on (1) the number of independent elements in the covariance matrix for the observed variables, (2) the number of parameters to be estimated, and (3) how close the start values are to the actual values of the estimates. Software estimating the covariance structure model requires start values for each parameter that is to be estimated. Start values are guesses that the user supplies, which are used to compute the first Σ^*. The search proceeds by refining these initial guesses. The closer the start values, the easier it will be to find the final estimates. Choosing start values can be difficult, although the most recent version of LISREL (Jöreskog and Sörbom, 1981) has incorporated an algorithm for generating start values for most models.

The estimates obtained by ULS or GLS do not correspond to any commonly used methods of estimation for structural equation models and, hence, are not discussed further in this chapter. If assumptions of normality are made, the ML estimates correspond to full information maximum likelihood (FIML) estimates for structural equation models (see Theil, 1971: 524-525). If the assumptions of normality are not justified, full information maximum likelihood estimates are still justified since they are equivalent to the method of full information least generalized residual variance (see Jöreskog and Sörbom, 1981: III.53; Kmenta, 1971: 579). However, when assumptions of normality cannot be made, the statistical tests discussed below should be used with caution.

The most recent version of LISREL (Jöreskog and Sörbom, 1981) estimates start values. For structural equation models these initial estimates correspond to the well-known method of two-stage least squares

(Jöreskog and Sörbom, 1981: III.48), which provides limited information, consistent estimates of the parameters of the structural equation model.

Assessing Goodness of Fit

This section reviews the techniques for assessing goodness of fit that are available with software for the covariance structure model. A more detailed discussion is found in *CFA*. If a structural equation model is being studied which can be estimated with more traditional statistical packages (i.e., those without equality constraints or constraints on a Ψ that is not diagonal), additional methods of assessing the fit of a model can be employed. Extensive discussions of such techniques can be found in the econometric literature.

Examining values of the parameters. The first step is to consider the estimates of each individual parameter. Unreasonable values indicate that something is wrong with the model. The model may be misspecified, resulting in biased estimates. The model may not be identified, resulting in one of an infinite set of possible estimates. The sample may be so small that estimates are imprecise and asymptotic properties cannot be applied. The input data may be an inappropriate pairwise correlations or covariance matrix; or, the control cards for the program being used may be incorrectly coded.

Variances of the estimates. With GLS and ML the covariance matrix for the estimates is computed. With the variances of the estimates, z-tests of individual parameters can be performed to test the hypothesis that a parameter is equal to some fixed value. Such tests are identical to those generally employed in multiple regression. Recall that these tests are based on assumptions of normality and must be employed with caution if such assumptions are unrealistic.

Chi-square goodness-of-fit tests. A chi-square test can be computed with ML and GLS estimation to test the hypothesis H_0 that the observed covariance matrix was generated by the hypothesized model, against the alternative hypothesis H_1 that the covariance matrix is an unrestricted covariance matrix. Rejecting this hypothesis indicates that the model does not adequately reproduce the observed covariance matrix S. Degrees of freedom (df) for the chi-square test can be computed as follows:

df = the number of independent parameters under H_1 minus the number of independent parameters under H_0;

or more specifically,

> df = the number of independent elements in Σ minus the number of independent elements in **B**, **Γ**, **Φ**, and **Ψ**.

If a model is just-identified, the number of independent elements in Σ will equal the number of independent parameters in **B**, **Γ**, **Φ**, and **Ψ**, resulting in a chi-square of zero with zero degrees of freedom. Accordingly, the chi-square test will not be of value in assessing the fit of a just-identified model.[6]

Difference of chi-square tests. While F-tests are generally used in multiple regression to test simultaneous hypotheses (Wonnacott and Wonnacott, 1979: 184-186), a difference of chi-square test can be used for the same purpose when estimating regression models with programs for the covariance structure model. If model M_1 with X_1^2 and df_1 is nested in M_2 with X_2^2 and df_2, the hypothesis that the parameters restricted in M_1 but not in M_2 are equal to zero can be tested by the difference of chi-square test: $X^2 = X_1^2 - X_2^2$ with $df = df_1 - df_2$.

The coefficient of determination. In classical regression theory (see Wonnacott and Wonnacott, 1979: 180-181), the coefficient of determination is defined as the percentage of the variation in the dependent variable that is explained by the regression. The coefficient of determination for the equation predicting η_i can be defined as

$$R^2 = 1 - \frac{VAR(\zeta_i)}{VAR(\eta_i)}$$

where ζ_i is the error in the equation for η_i. Care should be used in applying the coefficient of determination to multiple equation systems, since what is accounted for as explained variation in η_i can include variation explained by errors in other equations.

As Example 3.2 will illustrate, it is possible to have a large R^2 and a chi-square that indicates an unacceptable level of fit. This corresponds to the situation in multiple regression where the R^2 is large, but a significant increase in the R^2 can be obtained if additional explanatory variables are included in the model. Equivalently, a significant improvement in fit can be obtained by relaxing constraints on parameters in the model.

Modification indices. If the fit of the model is not adequate, it is possible to improve the fit by adding additional parameters to the model. One approach to selecting which parameters to add is based on partial derivatives of the fitting function with respect to each of the parameters that have been fixed (Sörbom, 1975). The derivative indicates how rapidly the fitting function, and hence the chi-square, will decrease if the parameter is freed. Use of the derivative is limited since a parameter with a large derivative may have a fixed value very close to the value that would be estimated if that parameter were freed. If this were the case, the total improvement in fit would be small. Jöreskog and Sörbom (1981: I.42) have proposed a modification index that remedies the problem. The index for a given fixed parameter is equal to the expected decrease in the chi-square if that parameter were freed. It is suggested that only one parameter be relaxed at a time, since freeing one parameter may reduce or eliminate the improvement in fit possible by freeing a second parameter. The parameter to be relaxed at each step should have the largest modification index, and should make substantive sense to relax. (See *CFA* for more details.)

Interpreting Structural Coefficients

The structural coefficients in **B** and **Γ** can be interpreted as direct effects on the endogenous variables. β_{ij} indicates that a unit change in the endogenous variable η_j results in a change of β_{ij} units in η_i, all other variables being held constant. Similarly, γ_{ij} indicates that a unit change in the exogenous variable ξ_j results in a change in η_i of γ_{ij} units, holding all other variables constant. If the variables have been standardized, the interpretations are adjusted accordingly. A standard deviation change in η_j results in a β_{ij} standard deviation change in η_i, all other variables being held constant; a standard deviation change in ξ_j results in a γ_{ij} standard deviation change in η_i, all other variables being held constant.

These interpretations assume that all other variables are being held constant. In practice, however, a change in a given exogenous variable is likely to be associated with a change in more than a single other variable. Consider Example 3.3: γ_{13} indicates that a unit change in respondent's SES (ξ_3) results in a direct change of γ_{13} units in respondent's aspirations (η_1), assuming that a change in ξ_3 is not associated with a change in any other variables that can affect η_1. But in this model a change in ξ_3 is assumed to cause a change in η_2 (via the direct effect on γ_{23}), and a change in η_2 is assumed to affect η_1 (via the direct effect β_{12}). Thus, a change in ξ_3 has both a direct effect on η_1 and additional, indirect effects when the other variables are not assumed to be held constant. Accordingly, the total effect on η_1 of a change in ξ_3 must include at least the direct effect of ξ_3 on η_1 and the indirect effect of ξ_3 that operates through

η_2. This example illustrates that in interpreting effects in a structural equation model it is necessary to distinguish between direct, indirect, and total effects.[7]

In the model $\eta = B\eta + \Gamma\xi + \zeta$, the direct effects of η on η are contained in B, and the direct effects of ξ on η are contained in Γ. Total effects of ξ on η are obtained from the reduced form equation $\eta = (I - B)^{-1}\Gamma\xi + (I - B)^{-1}\zeta$. If Π is defined as $\Pi = (I - B)^{-1}\Gamma$, then π_{ij} indicates the total effect of a change in ξ_j on η_i. Total effects of η's on η's are more complex to derive since they must take into account the reciprocal effects among endogenous variables. In Example 3.3, a change in η_1 affects η_2 through β_{21}. The change in η_2 in turn affects η_1 through β_{12}, and so on. The resulting total effect of η on η is computed as $(I - B)^{-1} - I$. Indirect effects can be computed simply as the differences between total and direct effects. A detailed treatment of this topic and complete derivations can be found in Graff and Schmidt (1982), Fox (1980), and Jöreskog and Sörbom (1981).

To illustrate estimation and hypothesis testing in the structural equation model, Examples 3.2 and 3.3 are used. The reader is encouraged to replicate these examples using the data in the Appendix.

Example 3.3: estimation and hypothesis testing. In the form presented above, this model is a traditional simultaneous equation system that can be estimated by any of a number of methods of estimation. Table 3.2 presents estimates by the limited information methods of two-stage least squares (2SLS) and limited information maximum likelihood (LIML), and the full information methods of three-stage least squares (3SLS) and full information maximum likelihood (FIML). The first three methods were estimated using SAS's procedure SYSREG, and FIML was computed using LISREL V. While the full information estimates are most similar to each other and the limited information estimates are most similar to each other, estimates by all methods are very close.

Consider now the interpretation of the FIML coefficients in Table 3.2. The strongest direct effect on the respondent's educational aspirations (η_1) is the respondent's SES (ξ_3): A standard deviation increase in ξ_3 results in a direct increase of $0.277 (= \hat{\gamma}_{13})$ standard deviations in η_1, all other variables being held constant. This effect is statistically significant at the .001 level for a one-tailed test. The direct effect does not represent the total effect of ξ_3 on η_1, since a change in ξ_3 also affects η_2, which in turn affects η_1. The total effect is somewhat larger, equaling 0.296. The effects of ξ_1 and ξ_2 are also statistically significant, but slightly weaker.

TABLE 3.2
Alternative Methods of Estimation for Structural Equation
Model of Peer Influence on Aspirations (Model M_a)

Coefficient	2SLS Effect	t	LIML Effect	t	3SLS Effect	t	FIML Effect	z
β_{12}	0.158	1.39	0.158	1.37	0.157	1.38	0.157	1.38
γ_{11}	0.196	4.20	0.196	4.20	0.193	4.22	0.193	4.20
γ_{12}	0.252	4.86	0.252	4.86	0.254	4.97	0.254	5.00
γ_{13}	0.277	5.37	0.277	5.36	0.277	5.36	0.277	5.35
γ_{14}	0.050	0.83	0.050	0.83	0.050	0.83	0.050	0.83
β_{21}	0.240	1.90	0.240	1.90	0.238	1.89	0.239	1.91
γ_{23}	0.047	0.76	0.047	0.75	0.047	0.76	0.047	0.76
γ_{24}	0.254	5.33	0.254	5.33	0.250	5.27	0.251	5.21
γ_{25}	0.323	6.28	0.323	6.28	0.333	6.53	0.332	6.80
γ_{26}	0.201	4.58	0.201	4.58	0.189	4.40	0.189	4.32

NOTE: See Figure 3.2 or text for specific meanings of coefficients. All coefficients are standardized. 2SLS is two-stage least squares; LIML is limited information maximum likelihood; 3SLS is three-stage least squares; and FIML is full-information maximum likelihood. 2SLS, LIML, and 3SLS estimates were computed with the SAS procedure SYSREG. FIML estimates were computed with LISREL V.

Neither the direct effect of η_2 nor of ξ_4 is statistically significant. The overall fit of the model is statisfactory, with a chi-square of 1.88 with two degrees of freedom (prob = .39). See Table 3.3.

While the fit of M_a is satisfactory, it is instructive to consider whether the fit can be improved. In the equation for η_1, either the parameter γ_{15} or γ_{16} (but not both) could be freed and the resulting model would still be identified. Similarly, the parameter for γ_{21} or γ_{22} (but not both) could be freed. Since there is no substantive justification for including these effects, doing so is unjustified. Similarly, while additional exclusion constraints could be imposed (e.g., restricting γ_{14} to zero), there are theoretical reasons for including these variables.

The symmetry of the model suggests another approach. Each effect for the respondent corresponds to an effect for the respondent's friend. There is no reason to expect that corresponding effects for the friend and the respondent will be different. For example, the effect of the respondent's aspirations on the friend's aspirations should equal the effect of the

TABLE 3.3
FIML Estimates of Three Models for Peer Influences on
Aspirations (Models M_a, M_b, and M_c)

Coefficient	M_a Effect	z	M_b Effect	z	M_c Effect	z
β_{12}	0.157	1.38	0.194[a]	2.25	0.192[a]	2.24
γ_{11}	0.193	4.20	0.193	4.21	0.192[b]	6.01
γ_{12}	0.254	5.00	0.250	5.00	0.269[c]	8.13
γ_{13}	0.277	5.35	0.270	5.42	0.264[d]	7.40
γ_{14}	0.050	0.83	0.038	0.69	0.052[e]	1.20
β_{21}	0.239	1.91	0.194[a]	2.25	0.192[a]	2.24
γ_{23}	0.047	0.76	0.062	1.19	0.052[e]	1.20
γ_{24}	0.251	5.21	0.256	5.49	0.264[d]	7.40
γ_{25}	0.332	6.80	0.337	6.93	0.296[c]	8.13
γ_{26}	0.189	4.32	0.188	4.31	0.192[b]	6.01
Chi-square	1.88		2.12		4.28	
df	2		3		7	
prob	0.39		0.55		0.75	

NOTE: Roman letters indicate that coefficients are constrained to be equal. See Figure 3.2 or text for specific meanings of coefficients. All coefficients are standardized and estimated by FIML (full-information maximum likelihood). Estimates were computed with LISREL V.

friend's aspirations on the respondent's aspirations. This involves the constraint $\beta_{12} = \beta_{21}$ (see, for example, Jöreskog and Sörbom, 1981: III.88). This constraint is contained in model M_b of Table 3.3. The addition of this constraint adds one degree of freedom and increases the chi-square by 0.24. Assuming that a formal hypothesis test was appropriate (which it is not, given our exploratory search), the hypotheses H_0: $\beta_{12} = \beta_{21}$ could be tested with a difference of chi-square between the nested models M_a and M_b. The resulting chi-square of 0.24 with one degree of freedom indicates that the hypothesis cannot be rejected. The effect of imposing this constraint on β_{12} and β_{21} is as might be expected. The new estimates of $\beta_{12} = \beta_{21}$ are an "average" of those in model M_a, with an increase in their statistical significance.

In the same way, it can be argued that the effect of the respondent's SES on the respondent's aspirations would be equal to the effect of the friend's SES on the friend's aspirations; the effect of the respondent's IQ would equal the effect of the friend's IQ; the effect of the respondent's parents' aspirations would equal the corresponding effect for the friend; and the effect of the friend's SES on the respondent's aspirations would equal the effect of the respondent's SES on the friend. In terms of the coefficients, this suggests the constraints: $\gamma_{11} = \gamma_{26}$; $\gamma_{12} = \gamma_{25}$; $\gamma_{13} = \gamma_{24}$; and $\gamma_{14} = \gamma_{23}$. In model M_c in Table 3.3 these constraints have been added. The resulting model provides a significant improvement in fit, with a gain of four degrees of freedom and an increase in chi-square of 2.16 (prob = 0.75). Given the substantive motivation of the imposed constraints, it is reasonable to conclude that model M_c is the best-fitting model. / /

In this example the advantage of using the software for the covariance structure model is the ability to impose equality constraints. In Example 3.2 the advantage comes from allowing the estimation of a system of equations in which some but not all of the errors in equations are correlated.

Example 3.2: estimation and hypothesis testing. Table 3.4 contains the results of estimating three models for the sociogenesis of psychological disorder. The first model, M_a (in which it is assumed that $\beta_{32} = \beta_{41} = \beta_{51} = 0$), is the model that was shown to be identified earlier in this chapter. The substantive results obtained by estimating this model are similar to those obtained by Wheaton (1978: 394-395) with a more complex covariance structure model. There is high stability in socioeconomic status, as indicated by the large and statistically significant coefficients $\hat{\beta}_{21} = 0.877$ and $\hat{\beta}_{42} = 0.844$. The respondent's father's SES has a significant effect ($\hat{\gamma}_{11} = 0.294$) on the respondent's initial SES (η_1), that diminishes for later time periods. There is also significant stability in psychological disorder as reflected in the coefficient $\hat{\beta}_{53} = 0.495$. The earliest measure of the respondent's SES (η_1) has a statistically significant effect ($\hat{\beta}_{31} = -.010$) on the earlier measure of psychological disorder (η_3). No other effects of SES on psychological disorder are significant. Note that these coefficients are *not* standardized; hence it is misleading to compare magnitudes of coefficients. For additional discussion of these results, see Wheaton (1978).

The overall fit of M_a is poor, with a chi-square of 47.9 and two degrees of freedom. Each of the parameters in the model is included for theoret-

TABLE 3.4

FIML Estimates of Three Structural Equation Models for the
Sociogenesis of Psychological Disorders (Models M_a, M_b, and M_c)

Coefficient	M_a Effect	z	M_b Effect	z	M_c Effect	z
γ_{11}	0.294	6.52	0.294	6.52	0.294	6.52
β_{21}	0.877	44.10	0.861[a]	59.11	0.896[a]	69.45
γ_{21}	0.026	1.15	0.031	1.38	0.021	0.92
β_{31}	−.010	3.80	−.010	3.90	−.010	3.72
γ_{31}	−.002	0.76	−.002	0.73	−.002	0.78
β_{42}	0.844	40.01	0.861[a]	59.11	0.896[a]	69.45
β_{43}	−.057	0.18	−.035	0.11	0.018	0.06
γ_{41}	0.060	2.50	0.055	2.33	0.046	1.93
β_{52}	−.002	0.73	−.001	0.58	−.002	0.88
β_{53}	0.495	14.95	0.495	14.96	0.495	14.92
γ_{51}	−.003	1.34	−.003	1.38	−.003	1.31
ψ_{23}	1.69	2.68	1.69	2.68	1.72	2.72
ψ_{45}	2.37	4.28	2.37	4.28	2.35	4.41
ψ_{24}	−	−	−	−	−35.31	6. 1
Chi-square	47.95		49.31		1.58	
df	2		3		2	
prob	0.000		0.000		0.454	

NOTE: Roman letters indicate that coefficients are constrained to be equal. See Figure 3.1 or text for specific meanings of coefficients. All coefficients are unstandardized and estimated by FIML (full-information maximum likelihood). Estimates were computed with LISREL V.

ical reasons and hence should not be deleted. It might be reasonable to impose an equality restriction on the coefficients relating SES at an earlier time to SES at a later time: $\beta_{21} = \beta_{42}$.[8] This restriction is imposed in the model M_b, with a resulting chi-square of 49.3 with three degrees of freedom. Since M_b is nested in M_a, the hypothesis $H_0: \beta_{21} = \beta_{42}$ can be tested with a difference of chi-square test. The result is a chi-square of 1.36 with one degree of freedom; accordingly, the hypothesis cannot be rejected at the .10 level.

Since no other restrictions seem reasonable, the addition of parameters should be considered. The maximum modification index for M_b is equal to 39.1 for ψ_{24}, suggesting a very significant improvement in fit *if the model is identified.* The resulting model, labeled M_c in Table 3.4, is identified, and freeing ψ_{24} makes substantive sense. ψ_{24} is the covariance between the equation predicting SES at time 2 (η_2) and SES at time 3 (η_4), indicating that the error in equation prdicting SES at an earlier time is correlated with the error in equation at a later time. Such correlations of error terms are called serial correlation (see Kessler and Greenberg, 1981: 87) and can indicate that variables affecting both of the dependent variables in question have been excluded from the model. For example, educational attainment can be expected to affect SES (Blau and Duncan, 1967), yet it is not included in either the equations predicting SES at time 2 or SES at time 3. The expected result of this exclusion would be the serial correlation of ζ_2 and ζ_4. Estimating M_c results in a chi-square of 1.58 with two degrees of freedom, a very acceptable fit. The interpretations of the other parameters are unchanged. //

Summary

The structural equation model presented in this chapter is important in its own right. Its presentation in the context of the covariance structure model is justified in two respects. First, those who need a structural equation model without a corresponding measurement model will find that the software developed for the covariance structure model is useful for estimating nonstandard structural equation models. Second, to apply the covariance structure model it is necessary to construct a structural equation model among the latent variables. Such a model is formally identical to the model described in this chapter, the only difference being that the variables are latent rather than observed. How the measurement model of Chapter 2 and the structural equation model of this chapter can be merged is the topic of the next chapter.

4. THE COVARIANCE STRUCTURE MODEL

The factor model estimates latent variables from observed variables without regard for the structural relations among the latent variables. Yet it is often these structural relations that are of greatest theoretical interest. The structural equation model focuses on these structural relations, but must do so by assuming that all of the variables are measured without error. The very presence of the factor model as a statistical technique indicates that this assumption may be unjustified. The covariance structure model overcomes the complementary weaknesses and combines the complementary strengths of the factor analytic and the structural equation models by merging them into a single model that simultaneously estimates latent variables from observed variables and estimates the structural relations among the latent variables. Presenting the covariance structure model turns out to be a relatively simple task since most of the work has been completed in our presentations of the confirmatory factor model and the structural equation model. All that remains to be done is to add assumptions governing the links between the two components and to indicate how our results on identification, estimation, and hypothesis testing from earlier chapters can be applied to the covariance structure model.

The Mathematical Model

The structural component of the covariance structure model consists of a structural equation model that is formally equivalent to that considered in Chapter 3:

$$\eta = \mathbf{B}\eta + \mathbf{\Gamma}\xi + \zeta \qquad [4.1]$$

where η is a $(r \times 1)$ vector of *latent*, endogenous variables; ξ is a $(s \times 1)$ vector of *latent*, exogenous variables; and ζ is a $(r \times 1)$ vector of errors in equations. $\mathbf{B}$ is a $(r \times r)$ matrix of coefficients relating the endogenous variables to one another, and $\mathbf{\Gamma}$ is a $(r \times s)$ matrix of coefficients relating the exogenous variables to the endogenous variables. Equation 4.1 can be written alternatively as $\ddot{\mathbf{B}}\eta = \mathbf{\Gamma}\xi + \zeta$, where $\ddot{\mathbf{B}}$ is defined as $(\mathbf{I} - \mathbf{B})$.

The assumptions of Chapter 3 for the structural equation model still hold. First, the variables are measured as deviations from their means: $E(\eta) = E(\zeta) = 0$ and $E(\xi) = 0$. Second, there are no redundant equations: $(\mathbf{I} - \mathbf{B})^{-1} = \ddot{\mathbf{B}}^{-1}$ exists. Third, the errors in equations and the exogenous variables are uncorrelated: $E(\xi\zeta') = 0$, or equivalently, $E(\zeta\xi') = 0$. These assumptions and others related to the covariance structure model are summarized in Table 4.1.

The same definitions of covariances among variables also apply. The covariance matrix for the exogenous variables is: $\mathbf{\Phi} = E(\xi\xi')$. The covariance matrix for the errors in equations is a symmetric, not necessarily diagonal matrix: $\mathbf{\Psi} = E(\zeta\zeta')$. From Equation 4.1 and the assump-

TABLE 4.1
Summary of the Covariance Structure Model

Matrix	Dimension	Mean	Covariance	Dimension	Description
$\boldsymbol{\eta}$	$(r \times 1)$	0	$\text{COV}(\boldsymbol{\eta}) = E(\boldsymbol{\eta\eta'})$	$(r \times r)$	latent endogenous variables
$\boldsymbol{\xi}$	$(s \times 1)$	0	$\boldsymbol{\Phi} = E(\boldsymbol{\xi\xi'})$	$(s \times s)$	latent exogenous variables
$\boldsymbol{\zeta}$	$(r \times 1)$	0	$\boldsymbol{\Psi} = E(\boldsymbol{\zeta\zeta'})$	$(r \times r)$	errors in equations
$\mathbf{B}$	$(r \times r)$	—	—	—	direct effects of $\boldsymbol{\eta}$ on $\boldsymbol{\eta}$
$\ddot{\mathbf{B}}$	$(r \times r)$	—	—	—	defined as $(\mathbf{I} - \mathbf{B})$
$\boldsymbol{\Gamma}$	$(r \times s)$	—	—	—	direct effects of $\boldsymbol{\xi}$ on $\boldsymbol{\eta}$
$\mathbf{x}$	$(q \times 1)$	0	$\boldsymbol{\Sigma}_{xx} = E(\mathbf{xx'})$	$(q \times q)$	observed exogenous variables
$\boldsymbol{\Lambda}_x$	$(q \times s)$	—	—	—	loadings of $\mathbf{x}$ on $\boldsymbol{\xi}$
$\boldsymbol{\delta}$	$(q \times 1)$	0	$\boldsymbol{\Theta}_\delta = E(\boldsymbol{\delta\delta'})$	$(q \times q)$	unique factors for $\mathbf{x}$
$\mathbf{y}$	$(p \times 1)$	0	$\boldsymbol{\Sigma}_{yy} = E(\mathbf{yy'})$	$(p \times p)$	observed endogenous variables
$\boldsymbol{\Lambda}_y$	$(p \times r)$	—	—	—	loadings of $\mathbf{y}$ on $\boldsymbol{\eta}$
$\boldsymbol{\epsilon}$	$(p \times 1)$	0	$\boldsymbol{\Theta}_\epsilon = E(\boldsymbol{\epsilon\epsilon'})$	$(p \times p)$	unique factors for $\mathbf{y}$

Structural Equations:
$$\boldsymbol{\eta} = \mathbf{B}\boldsymbol{\eta} + \boldsymbol{\Gamma\xi} + \boldsymbol{\zeta} \tag{4.1}$$
$$\ddot{\mathbf{B}}\boldsymbol{\eta} = \boldsymbol{\Gamma\xi} + \boldsymbol{\zeta}$$

Factor Equations:
$$\mathbf{x} = \boldsymbol{\Lambda}_x\boldsymbol{\xi} + \boldsymbol{\delta} \tag{4.2}$$
$$\mathbf{y} = \boldsymbol{\Lambda}_y\boldsymbol{\eta} + \boldsymbol{\epsilon} \tag{4.3}$$

Covariance Equation:
$$\boldsymbol{\Sigma} = \left[\begin{array}{c|c} \boldsymbol{\Lambda}_y\ddot{\mathbf{B}}^{-1}(\boldsymbol{\Gamma\Phi\Gamma'} + \boldsymbol{\Psi})\ddot{\mathbf{B}}^{-1}\boldsymbol{\Lambda}_y' + \boldsymbol{\Theta}_\epsilon & \boldsymbol{\Lambda}_y\ddot{\mathbf{B}}^{-1}\boldsymbol{\Gamma\Phi\Lambda}_x' \\ \hline \boldsymbol{\Lambda}_x\boldsymbol{\Phi\Gamma'}\ddot{\mathbf{B}}^{-1}\boldsymbol{\Lambda}_y' & \boldsymbol{\Lambda}_x\boldsymbol{\Phi\Lambda}_x' + \boldsymbol{\Theta}_\delta \end{array} \right] \tag{4.4}$$

Assumptions:

a. Variables are measured from their means: $E(\boldsymbol{\eta}) = E(\boldsymbol{\zeta}) = 0$; $E(\boldsymbol{\xi}) = 0$; $E(\mathbf{x}) = E(\boldsymbol{\delta}) = 0$; $E(\mathbf{y}) = E(\boldsymbol{\epsilon}) = 0$.

b. Common and unique factors are uncorrelated: $E(\boldsymbol{\xi\delta'}) = 0$ or $E(\boldsymbol{\delta\xi'}) = 0$; $E(\boldsymbol{\eta\epsilon'}) = 0$ or $E(\boldsymbol{\epsilon\eta'}) = 0$; $E(\boldsymbol{\xi\epsilon'}) = 0$ or $E(\boldsymbol{\epsilon\xi'}) = 0$; $E(\boldsymbol{\eta\delta'}) = 0$ or $E(\boldsymbol{\delta\eta'}) = 0$.

c. Unique factors and errors in equations are uncorrelated across equations: $E(\boldsymbol{\delta\epsilon'}) = 0$ or $E(\boldsymbol{\epsilon\delta'}) = 0$; $E(\boldsymbol{\zeta\delta'}) = 0$ or $E(\boldsymbol{\delta\zeta'}) = 0$; $E(\boldsymbol{\zeta\epsilon'}) = 0$ or $E(\boldsymbol{\epsilon\zeta'}) = 0$.

d. Exogenous variables and errors in equations are uncorrelated: $E(\boldsymbol{\xi\zeta'}) = 0$ or $E(\boldsymbol{\zeta\xi'}) = 0$.

e. None of the structural equations is redundant: $\ddot{\mathbf{B}}^{-1} = (\mathbf{I} - \mathbf{B})^{-1}$ exits.

tions of the model, the covariance matrix for the endogenous variables is $COV(\eta) = E(\eta\eta') = \ddot{B}^{-1}(\Gamma\Phi\Gamma' + \Psi)\ddot{B}'^{-1}$ (as derived in Chapter 3).

Unlike the structural equation model considered in Chapter 3, η and ξ are not required to be observed variables, although some of them may be observed. Rather, η and ξ are related to the observed variables **x** and **y** by a pair of confirmatory factor models:

$$x = \Lambda_x\xi + \delta \qquad [4.2]$$

$$y = \Lambda_y\eta + \epsilon \qquad [4.3]$$

where **x** is a (q × 1) vector of *observed* exogenous variables and **y** is a (p × 1) vector of *observed* endogenous variables. Λ_x is a (q × s) matrix of loadings of the observed x-variables on the latent ξ-variables, and Λ_y is a (p × r) matrix of loadings of the observed y-variables on the latent η-variables. δ of dimension (q × 1) and ϵ of dimension (p × 1) are vectors of unique factors. Within each factor model, the unique factors may be correlated. That is, $COV(\delta) = E(\delta\delta') = \Theta_\delta$ and $COV(\epsilon) = E(\epsilon\epsilon') = \Theta_\epsilon$ are symmetric, but not necessarily diagonal. Note that equations 4.2 and 4.3 are identical to equations 2.1 and 2.2.

As with the factor models of Chapter 2, common factors are assumed to be uncorrelated with unique factors, both within equations—$E(\xi\delta') = 0$ or $E(\delta\xi') = 0$, and $E(\eta\epsilon') = 0$ or $E(\epsilon\eta') = 0$—and across equations—$E(\xi\epsilon') = 0$ or $E(\epsilon\xi') = 0$, and $E(\eta\delta') = 0$ or $E(\delta\eta') = 0$. Finally, it is assumed that the δ's, ϵ's, and ζ's are mutually uncorrelated: $E(\delta\epsilon') = 0$ or $E(\epsilon\delta') = 0$; $E(\delta\zeta') = 0$ or $E(\zeta\delta') = 0$; and $E(\epsilon\zeta') = 0$ or $E(\zeta\epsilon') = 0$.

The Covariance Structure

Since the variables are measured as deviations from their means, the covariance matrix for the observed variables can be defined as

$$\Sigma = E\left[\begin{bmatrix} y \\ \hline x \end{bmatrix}\begin{bmatrix} y \\ \hline x \end{bmatrix}'\right] = E\begin{bmatrix} yy' & yx' \\ \hline xy' & xx' \end{bmatrix}$$

where $\begin{bmatrix} y \\ x \end{bmatrix}$ is the (p+q × 1) vector formed by stacking **y** on top of **x**. Substituting equations 4.2 and 4.3 for **x** and **y** results in

$$\Sigma = E\begin{bmatrix} (\Lambda_y\eta + \epsilon)(\Lambda_y\eta + \epsilon)' & (\Lambda_y\eta + \epsilon)(\Lambda_x\xi + \delta)' \\ \hline (\Lambda_x\xi + \delta)(\Lambda_y\eta + \epsilon)' & (\Lambda_x\xi + \delta)(\Lambda_x\xi + \delta)' \end{bmatrix}$$

Upon multiplying,

$$\Sigma = E \left[\begin{array}{c|c} \begin{array}{c} \Lambda_y \eta\eta' \Lambda_y' + \epsilon\epsilon' \\ + \Lambda_y \eta\epsilon' + \epsilon\eta' \Lambda_y' \end{array} & \begin{array}{c} \Lambda_y \eta\xi' \Lambda_x' + \epsilon\delta' \\ + \Lambda_y \eta\delta' + \epsilon\xi' \Lambda_x' \end{array} \\ \hline \begin{array}{c} \Lambda_x \xi\eta' \Lambda_y' + \delta\epsilon' \\ + \Lambda_x \xi\epsilon' + \delta\eta' \Lambda_y' \end{array} & \begin{array}{c} \Lambda_x \xi\xi' \Lambda_x' + \delta\delta' \\ + \Lambda_x \xi\delta' + \delta\xi' \Lambda_x' \end{array} \end{array} \right]$$

By distributing the expectation operator, making use of the assumed zero covariances among the variables, and applying the definitions of the covariances among variables, the desired result is obtained:

$$\Sigma = \left[\begin{array}{c|c} \Lambda_y \ddot{B}^{-1}(\Gamma\Phi\Gamma' + \Psi)\ddot{B}^{-1}\Lambda_y' + \Theta_\epsilon & \Lambda_y \ddot{B}^{-1}\Gamma\Phi\Lambda_x' \\ \hline \Lambda_x \Phi\Gamma'\ddot{B}^{-1}\Lambda_y' & \Lambda_x \Phi\Lambda_x' + \Theta_\delta \end{array} \right] \qquad [4.4]$$

This rather imposing equation relates the variances and covariances of the observed variables to the parameters of the model. Assuming that the model is identified, estimation involves finding values for the eight parameter matrices that produce an estimate of Σ according to equation 4.4 that is as close as possible to the sample matrix S.

Special Cases of the Covariance Structure Model

Before discussing estimation and the preliminary issue of identification, it is informative to consider the confirmatory factor model and the structural equation model as special cases of the covariance structure model. Considering these models as special cases is not only useful for understanding the general model, it is also useful for understanding how software for the covariance structure model can be used to estimate other types of models.

The factor analytic model. Assume that $B = I$ (or $\ddot{B} = 0$), $\Gamma = 0$, $\Psi = 0$, $\Lambda_y = 0$, and $\Theta_\epsilon = 0$. These constraints reduce the structural component of the covariance structure model to $\zeta = 0$, with the ζ's having variances of zero. The measurement model for the y-variables is reduced to $y = \epsilon$, where the ϵ's must equal zero (since $E(\epsilon) = 0$ and $COV(\epsilon) = 0$). The measurement equation for the x's is identical to equation 2.1: $x = \Lambda_x\xi + \delta$. When the constraints are applied to the covariance equation 4.4, it reduces to $\Sigma = \Lambda_x\Phi\Lambda_x' + \Theta_\delta$, which is identical to the upper-left partition of equation 2.3.

Similarly, a factor model among the y-variables is obtained by restricting $\mathbf{B} = \mathbf{0}$ (or $\ddot{\mathbf{B}} = \mathbf{I}$), $\mathbf{\Gamma} = \mathbf{0}$, $\mathbf{\Lambda}_x = \mathbf{0}$, and $\mathbf{\Theta}_\epsilon = \mathbf{0}$. These constraints eliminate the measurement model for the x's. The structural equation is reduced to $\boldsymbol{\eta} = \boldsymbol{\zeta}$, with $\mathrm{COV}(\boldsymbol{\eta}) = \boldsymbol{\Psi}$. Thus, $\boldsymbol{\Psi}$ is equivalent to $\boldsymbol{\Phi}$ in the factor model for the x's. When the imposed constraints are applied to equation 4.4, the resulting covariance equation is $\boldsymbol{\Sigma} = \mathbf{\Lambda}_y \boldsymbol{\Psi} \mathbf{\Lambda}_y' + \mathbf{\Theta}_\epsilon$.

Structural equation model. The measurement model can be eliminated from the covariance structure model by equating the observed variables to the latent variables. This is accomplished by constraining the parameters $\mathbf{\Lambda}_x = \mathbf{I}$, $\mathbf{\Theta}_\delta = \mathbf{0}$, $\mathbf{\Lambda}_y = \mathbf{I}$, $\mathbf{\Theta}_\epsilon = \mathbf{0}$. Equations 4.2 and 4.3 are reduced to $\mathbf{x} = \boldsymbol{\xi}$ and $\mathbf{y} = \boldsymbol{\eta}$, indicating that the latent variables are exactly equal to the observed variables. Equation 4.1, which is equivalent to equation 3.1, is left unchanged. The covariance equation for the structural equation model (equation 3.5) is obtained from equation 4.4 by imposing the constraints $\mathbf{\Lambda}_x = \mathbf{I}$, $\mathbf{\Theta}_\delta = \mathbf{0}$, $\mathbf{\Lambda}_y = \mathbf{I}$, and $\mathbf{\Theta}_\epsilon = \mathbf{0}$. The special cases of the structural equation model considered in Chapter 3 can be obtained by imposing constraints on $\mathbf{B}$, $\mathbf{\Gamma}$, and $\boldsymbol{\Psi}$. Thus, the structural equation model is a special case of the covariance structure model, and can be estimated with software for the covariance structure model if the necessary constraints are imposed. (These special cases are not discussed further in this chapter.)

Examples

To illustrate specification, identification, estimation, and hypothesis testing, two examples that contain both measurement and structural components are used.

Example 4.1: a panel model with measurement error. This example combines the measurement model in Example 1 of *CFA* with the panel model in Example 3.2. It is roughly equivalent to the model analyzed by Wheaton (1978), although a number of changes have been made to simplify the presentation. Figure 4.1 diagrams the basic model.

There is one exogenous variable measuring father's SES (ξ_1), and endogenous variables corresponding to the respondent's SES at three points in time (η_1, η_2, and η_4) and the respondent's psychological dis-

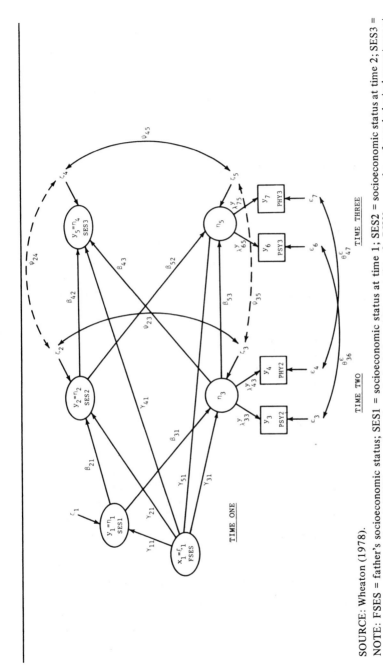

SOURCE: Wheaton (1978).

NOTE: FSES = father's socioeconomic status; SES1 = socioeconomic status at time 1; SES2 = socioeconomic status at time 2; SES3 = socioeconomic status at time 3; PSY2 = number of psychological symptoms at time 2; PSY3 = number of psychological symptoms at time 3; PHY2 = number of psychophysiological symptoms at time 2; PHY3 = number of psychophysiological symptoms at time 3.

Figure 4.1 A Covariance Structure Model for the Sociogenesis of Psychological Disorders

order at two points in time (η_3 and η_5). The structural model is identical to the final, identified version of Example 3.2:

$$
\begin{bmatrix} \eta_1 \\ \eta_2 \\ \eta_3 \\ \eta_4 \\ \eta_5 \end{bmatrix}
=
\begin{bmatrix}
0 & 0 & 0 & 0 & 0 \\
\beta_{21} & 0 & 0 & 0 & 0 \\
\beta_{31} & 0 & 0 & 0 & 0 \\
0 & \beta_{42} & \beta_{43} & 0 & 0 \\
0 & \beta_{52} & \beta_{53} & 0 & 0
\end{bmatrix}
\begin{bmatrix} \eta_1 \\ \eta_2 \\ \eta_3 \\ \eta_4 \\ \eta_5 \end{bmatrix}
+
\begin{bmatrix} \gamma_{11} \\ \gamma_{21} \\ \gamma_{31} \\ \gamma_{41} \\ \gamma_{51} \end{bmatrix}
\begin{bmatrix} \xi_1 \end{bmatrix}
+
\begin{bmatrix} \zeta_1 \\ \zeta_2 \\ \zeta_3 \\ \zeta_4 \\ \zeta_5 \end{bmatrix}
$$

Initially it is assumed that errors in equations are uncorrelated, except for errors predicting variables at the same time. Thus, the errors in the equations predicting SES at time two and psychological disorder at time two are correlated, and the errors in the equations predicting SES at time three and psychological disorder at time three are correlated. The resulting $\mathbf{\Psi}$ is

$$
\mathbf{\Psi} =
\begin{bmatrix}
\psi_{11} & 0 & 0 & 0 & 0 \\
0 & \psi_{22} & \psi_{23} & 0 & 0 \\
0 & \psi_{32} & \psi_{33} & 0 & 0 \\
0 & 0 & 0 & \psi_{44} & \psi_{45} \\
0 & 0 & 0 & \psi_{54} & \psi_{55}
\end{bmatrix}
$$

Unlike Example 3.2, a measurement model is used to link the observed variables to latent variables. Father's SES (ξ_1) is assumed to be measured without error, so that $x_1 = \xi_1$. In terms of the measurement equation 4.2, $\mathbf{\Lambda}_x$ is restricted to $\mathbf{I}$, and $\mathbf{\Theta}_\delta$ is restricted to $\mathbf{0}$: $\mathbf{x} = \mathbf{I}\boldsymbol{\xi} + \mathbf{0}$, or $\mathbf{x} = \boldsymbol{\xi}$. The measurement model for the y-variables is more complicated. The latent variables for the respondent's SES (η_1, η_2, and η_4) are assumed to be measured without error by y_1, y_2, and y_5. This involves the restrictions $\lambda_{11}^y = \lambda_{22}^y = \lambda_{54}^y = 1$ and $\theta_{11}^\epsilon = \theta_{22}^\epsilon = \theta_{55}^\epsilon = 0$. Each latent variable for psychological disorder is measured by two observed variables: the number of psychological symptoms and the number of psychophysiological symptoms. Thus, y_3 and y_4 load on η_3 with loadings λ_{33}^y and λ_{43}^y, and y_6 and y_7 load on η_5 with loadings λ_{65}^y and λ_{75}^y. The loadings λ_{33}^y and λ_{65}^y are fixed to one to set the metrics of η_3 and η_5, respectively (see Chapter 2 of CFA). Since $COV(\boldsymbol{\eta})$ is not a fundamental parameter (i.e., it is defined in terms of other parameter matrices), the metric of the η-variables can be set only by restricting the loadings in Λ_y. The resulting measurement equation for the y's is

$$
\begin{bmatrix}
y_1 \\
y_2 \\
y_3 \\
y_4 \\
y_5 \\
y_6 \\
y_7
\end{bmatrix}
=
\begin{bmatrix}
1 & 0 & 0 & 0 & 0 \\
0 & 1 & 0 & 0 & 0 \\
0 & 0 & 1 & 0 & 0 \\
0 & 0 & \lambda_{43}^y & 0 & 0 \\
0 & 0 & 0 & 1 & 0 \\
0 & 0 & 0 & 0 & 1 \\
0 & 0 & 0 & 0 & \lambda_{75}^y
\end{bmatrix}
\begin{bmatrix}
\eta_1 \\
\eta_2 \\
\eta_3 \\
\eta_4 \\
\eta_5
\end{bmatrix}
+
\begin{bmatrix}
0 \\
0 \\
\epsilon_3 \\
\epsilon_4 \\
0 \\
\epsilon_6 \\
\epsilon_7
\end{bmatrix}
$$

As was the case with Example 1 of *CFA*, it is assumed that errors in measurement for the same variables measured at different times are correlated. That is, $\theta_{36}^\epsilon \neq 0$ and $\theta_{47}^\epsilon \neq 0$. Since y_1, y_2, and y_5 are assumed to be measured without error, $\theta_{11}^\epsilon = \theta_{22}^\epsilon = \theta_{55}^\epsilon = 0$. The resulting covariance matrix is

$$
\Theta_\epsilon =
\begin{bmatrix}
0 & 0 & 0 & 0 & 0 & 0 & 0 \\
0 & 0 & 0 & 0 & 0 & 0 & 0 \\
0 & 0 & \theta_{33}^\epsilon & 0 & 0 & \theta_{36}^\epsilon & 0 \\
0 & 0 & 0 & \theta_{44}^\epsilon & 0 & 0 & \theta_{47}^\epsilon \\
0 & 0 & 0 & 0 & 0 & 0 & 0 \\
0 & 0 & \theta_{63}^\epsilon & 0 & 0 & \theta_{66}^\epsilon & 0 \\
0 & 0 & 0 & \theta_{74}^\epsilon & 0 & 0 & \theta_{77}^\epsilon
\end{bmatrix}
$$

The measurement model is represented in Figure 4.1 in two ways. When no measurement error is present, an observed and latent variable are both contained in the same oval. When measurement error is present, an observed variable is contained in a square linked by an arrow to a latent variable contained in a circle. //

Example 4.2: a nonrecursive model with measurement error. Our second example extends Example 3.3 by adding a measurement model for the endogenous variables, leaving the structural model unchanged. This model is diagrammed in Figure 4.2.

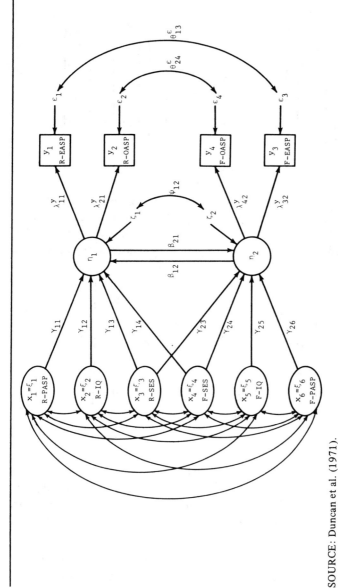

SOURCE: Duncan et al. (1971).

NOTE: R-PASP = respondent's parental aspirations; R-IQ = respondent's IQ; R-SES = respondent's socioeconomic status; F-SES = friend's socioeconomic status; F-IQ = friend's IQ; F-PASP = friend's parental aspirations; R-EASP = respondent's educational aspirations; R-OASP = resondent's occupational aspirations; F-OASP = friend's occupational aspirations.

Figure 4.2 A Covariance Structure Model of Peer Influences on Aspirations

The exogenous variables are assumed to be measured without error. That is, $\mathbf{x} = \boldsymbol{\xi}$, with the constraints $\boldsymbol{\Lambda}_x = \mathbf{I}$ and $\boldsymbol{\Theta}_\delta = \mathbf{0}$. Each of the endogenous variables has two indicators. η_1, the common factor for respondent's ambitions, is measured with y_1, the respondent's educational aspirations, and y_2, the respondent's occupational aspirations. Similarly, η_2, the common factor for the friend's ambition, is measured by y_3 and y_4. The measurement model for the η's is

$$\begin{bmatrix} y_1 \\ y_2 \\ y_3 \\ y_4 \end{bmatrix} = \begin{bmatrix} 1 & 0 \\ \lambda^y_{21} & 0 \\ 0 & 1 \\ 0 & \lambda^y_{42} \end{bmatrix} \begin{bmatrix} \eta_1 \\ \eta_2 \end{bmatrix} + \begin{bmatrix} \epsilon_1 \\ \epsilon_2 \\ \epsilon_3 \\ \epsilon_4 \end{bmatrix}$$

where λ^y_{11} and λ^y_{32} have been fixed to one to establish the metric of η_1 and η_2. Duncan et al. (1971) assumed that the measurement errors were correlated as indicated by the matrix

$$\boldsymbol{\Theta}_\epsilon = \begin{bmatrix} \theta^\epsilon_{11} & 0 & \theta^\epsilon_{13} & \theta^\epsilon_{14} \\ 0 & \theta^\epsilon_{22} & \theta^\epsilon_{23} & \theta^\epsilon_{24} \\ \theta^\epsilon_{31} & \theta^\epsilon_{32} & \theta^\epsilon_{33} & 0 \\ \theta^\epsilon_{41} & \theta^\epsilon_{42} & 0 & \theta^\epsilon_{44} \end{bmatrix}$$

θ^ϵ_{13} and θ^ϵ_{24} (and accordingly, θ^ϵ_{31} and θ^ϵ_{42}) indicate that the errors in the measurement of the respondent's and the friend's occupational aspirations are correlated, as are the errors in the measurement of the respondent's and friend's educational aspirations. Since similar errors in measuring occupational aspirations may have been made with both a respondent and his friend, these correlations are reasonable. θ^ϵ_{14} ($= \theta^\epsilon_{41}$) and θ^ϵ_{23} ($= \theta^\epsilon_{32}$) indicate that measures of friend's educational aspirations and respondent's occupational aspirations (and vice versa) are correlated. This seems unnecessary. If errors in the measurement of educational and occupational aspirations were correlated, it would be more reasonable to assume they were correlated in measures for the same person (i.e., θ^ϵ_{12} and θ^ϵ_{34}). Accordingly, θ^ϵ_{23} and θ^ϵ_{14} are constrained to zero in our analysis. //

Identification

As with the factor analytic and the structural equation models, identification must be demonstrated before estimation can proceed. Identification in the covariance structure model adds no new complications to our previous discussions. Difficulty is increased only because of the greater number of parameters that are often contained in covariance structure models.

A necessary condition for identification is that the number of independent parameters being estimated is less than or equal to the number of nonredundant elements of S, the sample matrix of covariances among observed variables. In counting the number of independent parameters, the symmetry of covariance matrices and imposed equality constraints must be taken into account. Thus, for example, if $\gamma_{11} = \gamma_{12} = \gamma_{13} = \gamma_{14}$ is an imposed constraint, the four parameters include only one independent parameter, since once the value of one parameter is known, the values of the others are also known. If, for example, ψ_{12} is a free parameter (since $\psi_{12} = \psi_{21}$ due to the symmetry of Ψ) ψ_{12} and ψ_{21} make up only one independent parameter. If t is the number of independent parameters in a covariance structure model, the necessary condition for identification is $t \leq \frac{1}{2}(p + q)(p + q + 1)$.

Unfortunately, no easily applicable sufficient, or necessary and sufficient, conditions for the full covariance structure model are available, although the conditions for the special cases considered earlier apply as appropriate. In general, identification must be proven by solving for the parameters of the model in terms of the variances and covariances of the observed variables. This is most easily achieved by first demonstrating that the parameters of the measurement model are identified, including the variances and covariances of the factors. Once covariances among the factors are known to be identified, the structural parameters can be identified by solving for them in terms of the covariances among the factors, rather than trying to solve them directly in terms of the covariances among the observed variables. This is sufficient for identification since, in identifying the measurement model, it was proven that the covariances among the factors could be solved for in terms of the covariances among the observed variables. Note that solving the structural parameters in terms of the variances and covariances among the factors is not sufficient for identification unless the variances and covariances among the factors have first been solved for in terms of the variances and covariances among the observed variables.

Proving that a model is identified can be quite difficult. Jöreskog and Sörbom (1978) argued that the computer can be used to determine if a model is identified. In computing maximum likelihood estimates of parameters, the information matrix is computed. (See Kmenta [1971: 174-186] for a discussion of the information matrix.) Roughly speaking, the information matrix corresponds to a matrix of variances and covariances of the parameter estimates. Jöreskog and Sörbom (1978: 11) stated

> If [the information matrix] is positive definite it is *almost certain* that the model is identified. On the other hand, if the information matrix is singular, the model is not identified [italics added].

The reader is warned that this is not a sufficient condition for identification. If the information matrix is positive definite, it is possible (even if unlikely) that the model is not identified and that the estimates of the parameters are arbitrary and meaningless. On the other hand, if identification has been "proven" by solving the parameters in terms of the variances and covariances of the observed variables, and the program indicates that the information matrix is *not* positive definite, an error in proving identification or in running the program may have been made. If the positive definiteness of the information matrix is used to "prove" that a model is identified (which is *not* recommended), a procedure suggested by Jöreskog (1978) should be implemented. If a model appears to be identified according to the information matrix, try several different sets of starting values as input to the maximum likelihood estimation program. If the resulting estimates are all equal, one can be more confident, albeit still uncertain, that the model is identified. Still, if one happens to estimate a model where the "almost certain" condition is satisfied, but the model is not identified, the resulting analyses are meaningless. The emphatic recommendation is: always prove that a model is identified by solving the model's parameters in terms of the variances and covariances of the observed variables.

Example 4.1: identification. The structural equations in this example are identical to those in Example 3.2 (compare Figures 3.1 and 4.1). The only difference is that the variables in the structural model in Example 3.2 are observed, whereas in this example some of them are latent. In Example 3.2 identification was proven by showing that each of the β's, γ's, and ψ's could be solved for in terms of the variances and covariances of the observed η's and ξ's. Since the structural equations are identical in this example, the same algebraic manipulations can be used to solve for each of the parameters in terms of the variances and covariances of the latent variables. If the variances and covariances for the latent variables are identified, then the structural component of this example is identified.

To identify the variances and covariances of the latent variables it must be shown that each can be solved for in terms of the variances and covariances of the observed variables. Since it is the measurement model that links the observed variables to the latent variables, we must begin with the measurement equations. These are

$$x_1 = \xi_1 \qquad\qquad y_1 = \eta_1 \qquad\qquad y_2 = \eta_2$$

$$y_3 = \eta_3 + \epsilon_3 \qquad y_4 = \lambda_{43}^y \eta_3 + \epsilon_4 \qquad y_5 = \eta_4$$

$$y_6 = \eta_5 + \epsilon_6 \qquad y_7 = \lambda_{75}^y \eta_5 + \epsilon_7$$

The covariances among the x's and y's can be computed by multiplying each pair of measurement equations, taking expectations, and making use of the assumptions that certain variables are uncorrelated. (To clearly indicate where covariances have been assumed to equal zero, such covariances are written with a line crossing them out.) The variances of the observed variables are

$$\sigma_{x_1 x_1} = \phi_{11}$$

$$\sigma_{y_1 y_1} = \text{VAR}(\eta_1)$$

$$\sigma_{y_2 y_2} = \text{VAR}(\eta_2)$$

$$\sigma_{y_3 y_3} = \text{VAR}(\eta_3) + \theta_{33}^\epsilon + 2\cancel{\text{COV}(\eta_3, \epsilon_3)}$$

$$\sigma_{y_4 y_4} = \lambda_{43}^{y\,2} \text{VAR}(\eta_3) + \theta_{44}^\epsilon + 2\lambda_{43}^y \cancel{\text{COV}(\eta_3, \epsilon_4)}$$

$$\sigma_{y_5 y_5} = \text{VAR}(\eta_4)$$

$$\sigma_{y_6 y_6} = \text{VAR}(\eta_5) + \theta_{66}^\epsilon + 2\cancel{\text{COV}(\eta_5, \epsilon_6)}$$

$$\sigma_{y_7 y_7} = \lambda_{75}^{y\,2} \text{VAR}(\eta_5) + \theta_{77}^\epsilon + 2\lambda_{75}^y \cancel{\text{COV}(\eta_5, \epsilon_7)}$$

The covariances among the observed variables are

$$\sigma_{x_1 y_1} = \text{COV}(\xi_1, \eta_1)$$

$$\sigma_{x_1 y_2} = \text{COV}(\xi_1, \eta_2)$$

$$\sigma_{x_1 y_3} = \text{COV}(\xi_1, \eta_3) + \cancel{\text{COV}(\xi_1, \epsilon_3)}$$

$$\sigma_{x_1y_4} = \lambda^y_{43} \, COV(\xi_1,\eta_3) + ~~COV(\xi_1,\epsilon_4)~~$$

$$\sigma_{x_1y_5} = COV(\xi_1,\eta_4)$$

$$\sigma_{x_1y_6} = COV(\xi_1,\eta_5) + ~~COV(\xi_1,\epsilon_6)~~$$

$$\sigma_{x_1y_7} = \lambda^y_{75} \, COV(\xi_1,\eta_5) + ~~COV(\xi_1,\epsilon_7)~~$$

$$\sigma_{y_1y_2} = COV(\eta_1,\eta_2)$$

$$\sigma_{y_1y_3} = COV(\eta_1,\eta_3) + ~~COV(\eta_1,\epsilon_3)~~$$

$$\sigma_{y_1y_4} = \lambda^y_{43} \, COV(\eta_1,\eta_3) + ~~COV(\eta_1,\epsilon_4)~~$$

$$\sigma_{y_1y_5} = COV(\eta_1,\eta_4)$$

$$\sigma_{y_1y_6} = COV(\eta_1,\eta_5) + ~~COV(\eta_1,\epsilon_6)~~$$

$$\sigma_{y_1y_7} = \lambda^y_{75} \, COV(\eta_1,\eta_5) + ~~COV(\eta_1,\epsilon_7)~~$$

$$\sigma_{y_2y_3} = COV(\eta_2,\eta_3) + ~~COV(\eta_2,\epsilon_3)~~$$

$$\sigma_{y_2y_4} = \lambda^y_{43} \, COV(\eta_2,\eta_3) + ~~COV(\eta_2,\epsilon_4)~~$$

$$\sigma_{y_2y_5} = COV(\eta_2,\eta_4)$$

$$\sigma_{y_2y_6} = COV(\eta_2,\eta_5) + ~~COV(\eta_2,\epsilon_6)~~$$

$$\sigma_{y_2y_7} = \lambda^y_{75} \, COV(\eta_2,\eta_5) + ~~COV(\eta_2,\epsilon_7)~~$$

$$\sigma_{y_3y_4} = \lambda^y_{43} \, VAR(\eta_3) + ~~\theta^\epsilon_{34}~~ + ~~COV(\eta_3,\epsilon_4)~~ + \lambda^y_{43} ~~COV(\eta_3,\epsilon_3)~~$$

$$\sigma_{y_3y_5} = COV(\eta_3,\eta_4) + ~~COV(\eta_4,\epsilon_3)~~$$

$$\sigma_{y_3y_6} = COV(\eta_3,\eta_5) + \theta^\epsilon_{36} + ~~COV(\eta_5,\epsilon_3)~~ + ~~COV(\eta_3,\epsilon_6)~~$$

$$\sigma_{y_3y_7} = \lambda^y_{75} \, COV(\eta_3,\eta_5) + ~~\theta^\epsilon_{37}~~ + ~~COV(\eta_3,\epsilon_7)~~ + \lambda^y_{75} ~~COV(\eta_5,\epsilon_3)~~$$

$$\sigma_{y_4y_5} = \lambda^y_{43} \, COV(\eta_3,\eta_4) + ~~COV(\eta_4,\epsilon_4)~~$$

$$\sigma_{y_4y_6} = \lambda^y_{43} \, COV(\eta_3,\eta_5) + ~~\theta^\epsilon_{46}~~ + \lambda^y_{43} ~~COV(\eta_3,\epsilon_6)~~ + ~~COV(\eta_5,\epsilon_4)~~$$

$$\sigma_{y_4y_7} = \lambda^y_{43} \lambda^y_{75} \, COV(\eta_3,\eta_5) + \theta^\epsilon_{47} + \lambda^y_{43} ~~COV(\eta_3,\epsilon_7)~~ + \lambda^y_{75} ~~COV(\eta_5,\epsilon_4)~~$$

$$\sigma_{y_5y_6} = COV(\eta_4,\eta_5) + ~~COV(\eta_4,\epsilon_6)~~$$

$$\sigma_{y_5y_7} = \lambda^y_{75} \, COV(\eta_4,\eta_5) + ~~COV(\eta_4,\epsilon_7)~~$$

$$\sigma_{y_6y_7} = \lambda^y_{75} \, VAR(\eta_5) + ~~\theta^\epsilon_{67}~~ + ~~COV(\eta_5,\epsilon_7)~~ + \lambda^y_{75} ~~COV(\eta_5,\epsilon_6)~~$$

While these equations may seem overwhelming, assumptions that errors and factors are uncorrelated, and that some pairs of errors are uncorrelated result in a significant simplification. When these simplifications are added to the equations (as indicated by the lines crossing out some terms), a number of parameters are easily proven identified since they are exactly equal to a covariance between observed variables. These are ϕ_{11}, $VAR(\eta_1)$, $VAR(\eta_2)$, $VAR(\eta_4)$, and all covariances between latent variables except for $COV(\eta_3,\eta_5)$.

The loadings are proven identified as follows:

$$\lambda^y_{43} = \sigma_{x1y4} \div \sigma_{x1y3}$$

$$\lambda^y_{75} = \sigma_{x1y7} \div \sigma_{x1y6}$$

Then using the fact that the loadings are identified, the remaining covariance between latent variables is proven identified:

$$COV(\eta_3,\eta_5) = \sigma_{y3y7} \div \lambda^y_{75}$$

Identifying the remaining parameters follows readily:

$$VAR(\eta_3) = \sigma_{y3y4} \div \lambda^y_{43}$$
$$\theta^\epsilon_{36} = \sigma_{y3y6} - COV(\eta_3,\eta_5)$$
$$\theta^\epsilon_{47} = \sigma_{y4y7} - \lambda^y_{43}\lambda^y_{75}COV(\eta_3,\eta_5)$$
$$VAR(\eta_5) = \sigma_{y6y7} \div \lambda^y_{75}$$
$$\theta^\epsilon_{33} = \sigma_{y3y3} - VAR(\eta_3)$$
$$\theta^\epsilon_{44} = \sigma_{y4y4} - \lambda^{y}_{43}{}^2 VAR(\eta_3)$$
$$\theta^\epsilon_{66} = \sigma_{y6y6} - VAR(\eta_5)$$
$$\theta^\epsilon_{77} = \sigma_{y7y7} - \lambda^{y}_{75}{}^2 VAR(\eta_5)$$

All parameters in the measurement model and all variances and covariances of the latent variables have been proven identified. Since the covariances between the latent variables are identified, the parameters of the structural model can be proved identified with exactly the same arguments as used in Example 3.2 of Chapter 3. //

Example 4.2: identification. As in the last example, the structural component of this model is identified if the variances and covariances of the latent variables are identified. The proof of this is identical to the proof of identification in Example 3.3. Since $x = \xi$, Φ is equal to the matrix of variances and covariances of the x's. Hence, Φ is identified. The measurement equations for the y's are

$$y_1 = \eta_1 + \epsilon_1 \qquad y_2 = \lambda^y_{21}\eta_1 + \epsilon_2$$

$$y_3 = \eta_2 + \epsilon_3 \qquad y_4 = \lambda^y_{42}\eta_2 + \epsilon_4$$

Since the ξ's are assumed to be uncorrelated with the ϵ's, the covariances between the η's and ϵ's are easily proven identified. For example, multiplying the equation for y_1 by $\xi_1 = x_1$ and taking expectations results in $E(y_1 x_1) = E(\eta_1 x_1) + E(\epsilon_1 x_1)$, or $\sigma_{y_1 x_1} = COV(\eta_1, x_1) = COV(\eta_1, \xi_1)$. The covariance equations for the y's are

$$\sigma_{y_1 y_1} = VAR(\eta_1) + \theta_{11}^{\epsilon} \qquad \sigma_{y_2 y_2} = \lambda_{21}^{y\,2} VAR(\eta_1) + \theta_{22}^{\epsilon}$$

$$\sigma_{y_3 y_3} = VAR(\eta_2) + \theta_{33}^{\epsilon} \qquad \sigma_{y_4 y_4} = \lambda_{42}^{y\,2} VAR(\eta_2) + \theta_{44}^{\epsilon}$$

$$\sigma_{y_1 y_2} = \lambda_{21}^{y} VAR(\eta_1) \qquad \sigma_{y_1 y_3} = COV(\eta_1, \eta_2) + \theta_{13}^{\epsilon}$$

$$\sigma_{y_1 y_4} = \lambda_{42}^{y} COV(\eta_1, \eta_2) \qquad \sigma_{y_2 y_3} = \lambda_{21}^{y} COV(\eta_1, \eta_2).$$

$$\sigma_{y_2 y_4} = \lambda_{21}^{y}\lambda_{42}^{y} COV(\eta_1, \eta_2) + \theta_{24}^{\epsilon} \qquad \sigma_{y_3 y_4} = \lambda_{42}^{y} VAR(\eta_2)$$

where assumed zero covariances have been left out of the equations. These ten equations contain eleven independent parameters; hence the equations cannot be solved for the parameters. If the measurement model for the y's was to be analyzed separately from the rest of the model, the model would not be identified. *But in the covariance structure model, identification of each parameter can use the information from the entire model.* In this case the covariance equations for y_2 and x_1, and y_4 and x_1 allow us to prove that the parameters for the measurement model for the y's are identified. The covariance equations are

$$\sigma_{y_2 x_1} = \lambda_{21}^{y} COV(\eta_1, \xi_1)$$

$$\sigma_{y_4 x_1} = \lambda_{42}^{y} COV(\eta_2, \xi_1)$$

Since $COV(\eta_1, \xi_1)$ and $COV(\eta_2, \xi_1)$ are identified, the two loadings can be solved for. Given that the loadings are identified, the variances of the η's are also identified:

$$VAR(\eta_1) = \sigma_{y_1 y_2} \div \lambda_{21}^{y}$$

$$VAR(\eta_2) = \sigma_{y_3 y_4} \div \lambda_{42}^{y}$$

This allows the identification of θ_{11}^{ϵ}, θ_{22}^{ϵ}, θ_{33}^{ϵ}, and θ_{44}^{ϵ}. The remaining parameters are proven identified as follows:

$$COV(\eta_1, \eta_2) = \sigma_{y_1 y_4} \div \lambda_{42}^{y}$$

$$\theta_{13}^{\epsilon} = \sigma_{y_1 y_3} - COV(\eta_1, \eta_2)$$

$$\theta_{24}^{\epsilon} = \sigma_{y_2 y_4} - \lambda_{21}^{y}\lambda_{42}^{y} COV(\eta_1, \eta_2)$$

Each parameter has been solved for in terms of the variances and covariances of the observed variables; hence the model is identified. Many of the parameters are overidentified, which the reader should attempt to verify by solving some of the parameters in different ways. //

Proving identification by solving for the parameters involves many steps, many parameters, and many places to make errors. To avoid such errors it is suggested that as a first step the measurement and structural equations of the model be written down with lower case Roman letters taking the place of the subscripted Greek parameters. This reduces the chances of incorrectly transcribing subscripts. Second, make a list of all of the covariance equations, using the Roman letters rather than the Greek. Third, make a list of all parameters that need to be identified. Fourth, make several copies of these lists, to be used in verifying your work. Fifth, as you prove that a parameter is identified, mark it as identified on the list of parameters and cross it out in each occurrence in the covariance equations. Proceed in this fashion until all parameters are proven identified. Sixth, wait a day and repeat step five without consulting your earlier proof. While this may seem to be a great deal of effort, remember that if an attempt is made to estimate a model that is not identified, all resulting analyses are meaningless.

Estimation

Once identification has been established, estimation can proceed. The covariance structure model can be estimated by any of the full-information methods discussed earlier: unweighted least squares (ULS), generalized least squares (GLS), and maximum likelihood (ML). Estimates are those values of the parameters that minimize the difference between the observed covariance matrix S and the predicted covariance matrix $\hat{\Sigma}$, where the definition of the difference between the two matrices is determined by the method of estimation. Estimating the covariance structure model adds no new difficulties to those discussed in *CFA*, the only difference being that the estimated covariance matrix is defined as follows (see equation 4.4):

$$\hat{\Sigma} = \left[\begin{array}{c|c} \hat{\Lambda}_y\hat{\bar{B}}^{-1}(\hat{\Gamma}\hat{\Phi}\hat{\Gamma}' + \hat{\Psi})\hat{\bar{B}}'^{-1}\hat{\Lambda}_y' + \hat{\Theta}_\epsilon & \hat{\Lambda}_y\hat{\bar{B}}^{-1}\hat{\Gamma}\hat{\Phi}\hat{\Lambda}_x' \\ \hline \hat{\Lambda}_x\hat{\Phi}\hat{\Gamma}'\hat{\bar{B}}'^{-1}\hat{\Lambda}_y' & \hat{\Lambda}_x\hat{\Phi}\hat{\Lambda}_x' + \hat{\Theta}_\delta \end{array} \right]$$

Without making any assumptions about the distribution of the observed variables, ULS can be shown to be consistent. The advantage of not requiring distributional assumptions is offset by ULS being scale dependent and not having any statistical tests associated with it. If the observed variables have a multivariate normal distribution, both GLS and ML have desirable asymptotic properties. ML is approximately unbiased, has as small a sampling variance as any other estimator, and is approximately normally distributed. GLS is asymptotically equivalent to ML. Greater detail on the properties of these estimators can be found in *CFA*.

Covariance structure models tend to have more parameters than factor analytic or structural equation models (although this is not necessarily so). This poses the practical problem that it may be expensive to compute the estimates. Each method of estimation proceeds iteratively, successively finding better and better estimates of the parameters. The first step in the iteration requires start values. The rate of convergence to the final estimates can be greatly speeded up if the start values are chosen accurately. A particularly useful feature of LISREL V is that start values are selected by the program for many types of models (Jöreskog and Sörbom, 1981: I.32).

Assessment of Fit

No additional techniques are required to assess the fit of the covariance structure model. Accordingly, this section only reviews the techniques presented in earlier chapters and in *CFA*.

Examining values of the parameters. The parameters from the measurement component of the model can be examined and interpreted in exactly the same way as the parameters of the factor analytic model. Similarly, the parameters in the structural component of the covariance structure model can be interpreted as in the structural equation model. Negative variances, correlations greater than one, and unreasonably large parameter estimates all signal that something is wrong. Possible problems are misspecification, a pairwise covariance matrix, an unidentified or nearly unidentified model, and/or faulty control cards for the software being used.

The signs of parameters should be carefully examined. Some programs refer to our $\mathbf{B}$ as "BETA," while others refer to our $\ddot{\mathbf{B}}$ as "BETA." It is important to realize which definition is being used. If equality constraints are being imposed on parameters from two different matrices, the "equal" parameters may be forced to have opposite signs. For example, in using LISREL V the constraint that β_{ij} (not $\ddot{\beta}_{ij}$) equals γ_{mn}, results in the imposed equality: $\beta_{ij} = -\gamma_{mn}$. Unless the estimates are examined with care, it is easy to miss such problems.

Variances and covariances of the parameters. The variances of the parameter estimates can be computed with GLS and ML estimation. Under assumptions of the normality of the observed variables, the parameter estimates are asymptotically normally distributed, allowing z-tests of hypotheses that individual parameters are equal to some constant. From the covariances between estimates it is possible to compute correlations between estimates. Large correlations indicate that it is difficult to distinguish between the two parameters. This is the problem of empirical underidentification discussed in *CFA*.

Chi-square goodness-of-fit tests. Under the assumptions of normality, ML and GLS estimation provide a chi-square test of the proposed model against the alternative model that Σ is unconstrained. Large values of the chi-square relative to degrees of freedom indicate that the model does not provide an adequate fit of the data. Degrees of freedom for the chi-square test are df $= \frac{1}{2}(p + q)(p + q + 1) - t$, where t is the number of independent parameters being estimated.

A difference of chi-square test can be used to compare nested models. If M_1 can be obtained from M_2 by constraining one or more of the parameters in M_2, M_1 is said to be nested in M_2. If M_1 with X_1^2 and df_1 is nested in M_2 with X_2^2 and df_2, for large samples $X^2 = X_1^2 - X_2^2$ is distributed as chi-square with df $= df_1 - df_2$. Large values of the chi-square relative to the degrees of freedom indicates that the additional constraints imposed in the restricted model M_1 should be rejected.

Effects of sample size on hypothesis testing. Hypothesis testing with either the chi-square test or the z-test is affected by the size of the sample being analysed.[9] Superficially the effects of sample size on tests with the chi-square statistic appear to be contradictory to the effects of sample size on z-tests of individual parameters. For example, as sample size gets larger, it is more likely that a given model will be rejected as inadequate to reproduce the observed covariance matrix (i.e., the probability level gets larger). At the same time, the statistical significance of individual parameters tends to increase (i.e., the probability level gets smaller). These results are, however, perfectly reasonable.

With larger sample sizes sampling variability decreases. Differences between two samples are likely to be smaller due to the larger sample size. Since there is less sampling variability, a given lack of fit is more likely due to the null hypothesis being false (e.g., a parameter is not equal to the hypothesized value) than to sampling variability (e.g., a parameter is not equal to the hypothesized value due to peculiarities of a particular sample). Consequently, as sample size increases, smaller and smaller differences between the estimated value of a parameter and hypothesized value become significant.

A similar result holds for the chi-square test. One way of viewing the chi-square test is as a simultaneous test of the differences between the observed and predicted covariances among observed variables. As sample size increases, smaller and smaller differences between observed and predicted covariances become statistically significant, in the same way that smaller and smaller differences between estimated values of individual parameters and hypothesized values of those parameters become statistically significant.

As a consequence, in very large samples almost any model with positive degrees of freedom is likely to be rejected as providing a statistically unacceptable fit. This is true even when the rejected model is what Bentler and Bonett (1980: 591) call "minimally false." Their idea of a minimally false model refers to a model that is rejected on the basis of a chi-square test when the differences between the elements of the observed covariance matrix S and the covariance matrix predicted by the model $\hat{\Sigma}$ are trivial. They conclude that even though a better model might be able to explain these deviations, the original model might explain all that is of substantive importance. Jöreskog and Sörbom (1981: I.38-39) put the same idea somewhat differently, indicating that the statistical problem is not one of testing a particular hypothesis, but of determining whether a model provides an adequate fit of the data.

The precise relationship between test statistics and sample size is very simple. For ML and GLS estimation, the chi-square statistic is computed as $(N - 1) \Delta$, where N is the sample size and Δ is a quantity that depends on the covariance matrix for the observed variables but not the sample size. For example, assume that two samples are fit to the same model. Sample 1 has N_1 observations and sample 2 has N_2 observations. Assume that both samples have exactly the same covariance matrix for the observed variables. Since Δ is not a function of sample size, Δ would be the same for both samples. The chi-squares would differ, however, due to the differences in sample size. Specifically, $X_1^2 = (N_1 - 1)\Delta$ and $X_2^2 = (N_2 - 1)\Delta$. The relationship between the two chi-squares would be

$$X_2^2 = X_1^2 \frac{N_2 - 1}{N_1 - 1}$$

A similar relationship exists between sample size and the magnitude of the z-statistic. Consider any specific parameter, call it ω. The variance of the sampling distribution of $\hat{\omega}$ is equal to $[\Delta/(N-1)]$, where Δ is a value that does not depend on the sample size. Once again, assume that two samples are fit to the same model. Sample 1 has N_1 observations and sample 2 has N_2 observations. Assume that both samples had exactly the same covariance matrix for the observed variables. Since Δ is not a function of sample size, Δ would be the same for the analysis of both samples. The variances of the sampling distribution would differ, however, due to the differences in sample size. Specifically, $\hat{\sigma}_1^2 = \Delta/(N_1-1)$ and $\hat{\sigma}_2^2 = \Delta/(N_2-1)$. The relationship between the two variances would be

$$\hat{\sigma}_2^2 = \hat{\sigma}_1^2 \frac{N_1 - 1}{N_2 - 1}$$

The formula for the z-statistic is $z = (\hat{\omega} - \omega^*)/\hat{\sigma}$, where ω^* is a constant that ω is hypothesized to equal. Since $\hat{\omega}$ and ω^* are not affected by changes in the sample size, the effect of changes in sample size on the z-statistic is

$$z_2 = z_1 \sqrt{\frac{N_2 - 1}{N_1 - 1}}$$

where z_1 is the z-statistic for the sample of size N_1, and z_2 is the z-statistic for the sample of size N_2.

Modification indices. If a model does not fit adequately, a specification search can be conducted. Parameters can be dropped from the model if they are not significantly different from zero. Alternatively, parameters can be added to the model. By relaxing the parameter with the maximum value of the modification index (defined in Chapter 3 and *CFA*), the greatest improvement in fit is obtained. In specification searches several points should be kept in mind. First, all models considered must be proven identified. Second, the chosen model cannot be formally tested with a z-test or a chi-square test. Since the model was selected by the data, it cannot be tested with the same data. Third, the search should be guided by substantive considerations. Even if the model initially suggested by substantive theory is rejected, there are generally some parameters that are definitely required on the basis of past research, and some parameters that make no sense to include (e.g., in a panel model letting variables at time 2 affect variables at time 1). These parameters should not be dropped or added, respectively, to improve the fit of the model.

Derivative parameters. It is sometimes useful to compute additional parameters derived from those estimated for the model. Correlations among the latent variables can be computed from the covariances that have been estimated. For example, the correlation between ξ_i and ξ_j can be computed as $\rho_{ij} = \phi_{ij} \div \sqrt{\phi_{ii}\phi_{jj}}$, where the ϕ's are elements of Φ. To evaluate multiple indicators of latent variables, reliabilities can be computed. (See *CFA* for details on the computation and interpretation of reliabilities.) Within the structural component of the model, the coefficient of determination can be computed for each equation. In the equation predicting η_i, the coefficient of determination is equal to $R^2 = (s_{ii} - \hat{\psi}_{ii})/s_{ii}$. Our discussion of the coefficient of determination in Chapter 3 applies here as well. Any of the parameters considered in our earlier discussion of the factor model and the structural equation model can be applied directly to the more general covariance structure model.

These techniques are now illustrated with our two examples.

Example 4.1: estimation and hypothesis testing. Table 4.2 contains the results from the ML estimation of six models for the sociogenesis of psychological disorder. Model M_d corresponds most closely to the model estimated by Wheaton (1978).[10] Models M_a, M_b, and M_c are substantively unrealistic, but are useful for illustrating a number of points in hypothesis testing and model specification. Models M_e and M_f extend Wheaton's model by incorporating serially correlated errors.

Model M_a assumes that all errors in equations are uncorrelated, that all errors in variables are uncorrelated, and that no parameters are constrained to be equal. The fit of this model is poor, with a chi-square of 142.6 and 13 degrees of freedom. Model M_b adds two sets of substantively reasonable equality constraints (1) $\beta_{21} = \beta_{42}$, indicating that the stability of SES is constant over time; and (2) $\lambda_{43}^y = \lambda_{75}^y$, indicating that the loadings on the psychophysiological symptoms subscale are equal at both points in time. Imposing these constraints frees two degrees of freedom and increases the chi-square by 4.84. This allows a test of the joint hypothesis H_0: $\beta_{21} = \beta_{42}$ and $\lambda_{43}^y = \lambda_{75}^y$ in M_a. The appropriate test statistic is $X^2 = X_b^2 - X_a^2 = 4.84$ with df $= df_b - df_a = 2$ degrees of freedom. The hypothesis cannot be rejected at the .05 level.

TABLE 4.2
FIML Estimates of Six Covariance Structure Models for the
Sociogenesis of Psychological Disorder (Models M_a to M_f)

Parameter	M_a	M_b	M_c	M_d	M_e	M_f
γ_{11}	0.294***	0.294***	0.294***	0.294***	0.294***	0.294***
β_{21}	0.877***	0.862[a]***	0.861[a]***	0.860[a]***	0.894[a]***	0.893[a]***
γ_{21}	0.026	0.031*	0.031*	0.031*	0.021	0.021
β_{31}	-.010***	-.010***	-.010***	-.008***	-.008***	-.006***
γ_{31}	-.002	-.002	-.002	0.000	-.000	-.000
β_{42}	0.844***	0.862[a]***	0.861[a]***	0.860[a]***	0.894[a]***	0.893[a]***
β_{43}	0.052	0.160	-.002	-1.495***	-.846**	-.916*
γ_{41}	0.061***	0.056***	0.055***	0.053***	0.044**	0.045***
β_{52}	-.000	0.000	-.000	0.000	-.000	0.001
β_{53}	0.601***	0.661***	0.619***	0.672***	0.649***	0.949***
γ_{51}	-.002	-.002	-.002	-.000	-.000	0.000
COR(ζ_3, ζ_2)	–	–	–	0.293***	0.269***	0.243***
COR(ζ_4, ζ_2)	–	–	–	–	-.276***	-.268***
COR(ζ_5, ζ_3)	–	–	–	–	–	-.389**
COR(ζ_5, ζ_4)	–	–	–	0.186***	0.181***	0.122***
λ_{43}^y	0.211***	0.244[b]***	0.268[b]***	0.485[b]***	0.443[b]***	0.503[b]***
λ_{75}^y	0.271***	0.244[b]***	0.268[b]***	0.485[b]***	0.443[b]***	0.503[b]***
REL(η_3, y_3)	0.823	0.746	0.676	0.367	0.408	0.361
REL(η_3, y_4)	0.250	0.304	0.331	0.588	0.546	0.625
REL(η_5, y_6)	0.740	0.792	0.729	0.413	0.446	0.392
REL(η_5, y_7)	0.407	0.355	0.394	0.730	0.657	0.749
COR(ϵ_3, ϵ_6)	–	–	0.278	0.465***	0.457***	0.469***
COR(ϵ_4, ϵ_7)	–	–	0.140	-.364**	-.200	-.386**
Chi-square	142.65	147.49	131.00	89.84	45.37	40.79
df	13	15	13	11	10	9
prob	0.00	0.00	0.00	0.00	0.00	0.00

NOTE: Roman letters indicate that coefficients are constrained to be equal. * indicates significance at .10 (.20) level for one-(two-)tailed test; ** at .05 (.10) level for one-(two-)tailed test; *** at .025 (.050) level for one-(two-)tailed test. See Figure 4.1 or text for specific meanings of coefficients. All coefficients are unstandardized and estimated by FIML (full-information maximum likelihood). Estimates were computed with LISREL V.

M_c relaxes θ^ϵ_{36} and θ^ϵ_{47}, the covariances between errors in the same measures at two points in time. The motivation for relaxing these parameters is that if, for example, the psychological symptoms subscale contained measurement error at time 2 (y_3), it is possible that similar sources of measurement error are present at time 3 (y_6). That is, $\theta^\epsilon_{36} \neq 0$; similarly, for psychological symptions (y_4 and y_7), $\theta^\epsilon_{47} \neq 0$. Freeing these parameters uses two degrees of freedom and decreases the chi-square by 16.5. Thus the hypothesis H_0: $\theta^\epsilon_{36} = \theta^\epsilon_{47} = 0$ can be rejected at any conventional level of significance.

Models M_a and M_c each use the same number of parameters to reproduce the covariance matrix, with M_c being more successful, as indicated by the smaller chi-square. Whether this difference of 11.7 in the chi-square is statistically significant cannot be formally tested, since M_a and M_c are not nested. However, given the substantively more realistic characteristics of M_c, it would be the preferable model.

M_d adds same-time correlated errors in equations to M_c. Freeing ψ_{23} and ψ_{45} results in a significant improvement in fit, with a change in chi-square of 41.2 and a loss of two degrees of freedom. While the overall fit of the model is still not statistically acceptable ($X^2 = 89.8$ with $df = 11$), it is comparable to the fit obtained by Wheaton for a similar model.

Model M_d does not provide an acceptable fit, even though it is the model suggested by theory. The maximum modification index for M_d is for the coefficient ψ_{24}, with a value of 36.6. ψ_{24} corresponds to a serial correlation between the equations predicting SES at time 2 and SES at time 3. Its presence is reasonable given that it is likely that the model has excluded other variables that are important for explaining SES. M_e frees this covariance, reducing the chi-square by 44.5 with a loss of one degree of freedom, a significant improvement in fit. M_f extends this reasoning by adding a serial correlation between the two equations predicting psychological disorders. While the improvement in fit is not as large, it is significant at the .05 level.

Model M_f still does not provide a statistically adequate fit with a chi-square of 40.8 and nine degrees of freedom. The maximum modification index in M_f is 17.37 for θ^ϵ_{26}. However, since the variance of ϵ_6 is constrained to equal zero, it makes no sense to free the covariance between ϵ_6 and ϵ_2. This illustrates the point that in using the modification index it must be kept in mind that there is no gain if the fit of a model is improved by adding meaningless parameters.

The results of greatest interest are contained in the structural portion of the model. They are nearly identical to those obtained in the structural equation model of Chapter 3 (see M_b in Table 3.4), with one important difference. The path from psychological disorder at time 2 to SES at time 3 is statistically significant in M_d, while it isn't significant in the earlier structural equation model or in Wheaton's (1978: 396) original article. Substantively this path is important, indicating what Wheaton called a social selection effect—"a retardation in status attainment between [time 2] and [time 3] attributable to disorder" (Wheaton, 1978: 392). This type of effect is in contrast to social causation effects as indicated by the path from SES at time 1 to psychological disorder at time 2. The analysis here finds evidence of both social causation (as indicated by the structural parameter β_{31}) and social selection (as indicated by the structural parameter β_{43}), whereas Wheaton found only an effect of social causation.

The reader should not take the differences between these findings and those of Wheaton as a critique of the original analysis. In adapting Wheaton's model for the present purposes, a number of simplifying assumptions were made. While these simplifications are ones that a researcher might impose in order to model the sociogenesis of psychological disorder, they are nonetheless simplifications. The fact that a substantive difference is found reflects a cost of the great power of the covariance structure model. Because of the complexity of the model, many decisions in the specification of a model have to be made that are not dictated by substantive considerations. These decisions can affect the substantive conclusions drawn from the model. Because of full-information estimation, making changes in one part of the model can affect results in a seemingly quite different part of the model. For example, in moving from M_c to M_d, the social selection effect (β_{43}) changed from being statistically nonsignificant to being significant. Also, as shown with M_e and M_f, the introduction of other reasonable parameters can affect other parameters in the model.

The most useful information in the measurement component of the model is the reliabilities of the various measures. In models M_a through M_c the measures of psychological symptoms (y_3 and y_6) are the most reliable. However, in M_d the measures of psychophysiological symptoms (y_4 and y_7) are the most reliable. Further, in moving from M_c to M_d, the covariances in errors in measurement become statistically significant. //

Example 4.2: estimation and hypothesis testing. The second example extends Example 3.3 by adding two indicators for each of the endogenous variables (compare Figures 3.2 and 4.2). In Chapter 3 it was argued that, given the symmetry between the effects for the respondent and the respondent's friend, corresponding parameters should be constrained to be equal. For example, the effect of the respondent's IQ on the respondent's ambitions (γ_{12}) should equal the effect of the friend's IQ on the friend's ambitions (γ_{25}). Similarly, the loading of the respondent's occupational aspirations (y_2) on the respondent's ambitions (η_1) should equal the loading of the friend's occupational aspirations (y_4) on the friend's ambitions (η_2). That is, $\lambda_{21}^y = \lambda_{42}^y$. The resulting model is estimated in Table 4.3 and is referred to as M_a. The overall fit of the model is quite good, with a chi-square of 30.6 with 24 degrees of freedom (prob = 0.17).

The results from the structural component of the model are essentially the same as those obtained in Example 3.3. Any changes are due to the new dependent variables, which are now latent variables based on two measures of aspirations. For both respondents and friends, measures of educational aspirations are more reliable indicators of ambition than are measures of occupational aspirations.

Educational aspirations are measured for both friends and respondents. Given that the same measure is used twice, it is possible that errors in measurement are correlated—that is, $\theta_{13}^\epsilon \neq 0$. Similarly, errors in the measurement of occupational aspirations might be correlated: $\theta_{24}^\epsilon \neq 0$. Model M_b incorporates this change. Freeing two parameters, thus giving up two degrees of freedom, results in a change in the chi-square of 14.5, a very significant improvement in fit. The values of the other parameters in the model are not appreciably different from those in M_a, and the overall fit of the model is improved with a chi-square of 16.1 with 22 degrees of freedom (prob = 0.81). //

Summary

The covariance structure model is complex, and our treatment of it has been all too brief. It is easy to lose sight of its potential in the complexities of the mathematical development. Perhaps the best way to master the model is to study and reproduce substantive applications of the model. The following books and articles are recommended for this purpose: Alwin and Jackson (1982), Bagozzi (1981), Bielby et al. (1977), Bynner (1981), Dalton (1982), Jöreskog (1974, 1978), Judd and Milburn (1980), Kenny (1979), Kessler and Greenberg (1981), Krehbiel and

TABLE 4.3
FIML Estimates of Two Covariance Structure Models for Peer
Influences on Aspirations (Models M_a and M_b)

Parameter	M_a	M_b
β_{12}	$0.202^{a}***$	$0.201^{a}***$
γ_{11}	$0.166^{b}***$	$0.170^{b}***$
γ_{12}	$0.307^{c}***$	$0.310^{c}***$
γ_{13}	$0.233^{d}***$	$0.235^{d}***$
γ_{14}	$0.071^{e}***$	$0.074^{e}***$
β_{21}	$0.202^{a}***$	$0.201^{a}***$
γ_{23}	$0.071^{e}**$	$0.074^{e}***$
γ_{24}	$0.233^{d}***$	$0.235^{d}***$
γ_{25}	$0.307^{c}***$	$0.310^{c}***$
γ_{26}	$0.166^{b}***$	$0.170^{b}***$
COR (ζ_1, ζ_2)	$-.065$	$-.162$
λ^y_{21}	$0.936^{f}***$	$0.908^{f}***$
λ^y_{42}	$0.936^{f}***$	$0.908^{f}***$
REL(η_1, y_1)	0.450	0.475
REL(η_1, y_2)	0.394	0.392
REL(η_2, y_3)	0.464	0.490
REL(η_2, y_4)	0.406	0.403
COR(ϵ_2, ϵ_4)	–	$0.267***$
COR(ϵ_1, ϵ_3)	–	0.065
Chi-square	30.63	16.10
df	24	22
prob	0.17	0.81

NOTE: Roman letters indicate that coefficients are constrained to be equal. * indicates significance at .10 (.20) level for one-(two-)tailed test; ** at .05 (.10) level for one-(two-)tailed-test; *** at .025 (.050) level for one-(two-)tailed test. See Figure 4.2 or text for specific meanings of coefficients. All coefficients are unstandardized and estimated by FIML (full-information maximum likelihood). Estimates were computed with LISREL V.

Niemi (1982), Long (1981), Sullivan and Feldman (1979), and Wheaton et al. (1977). The manuals for LISREL IV and LISREL V also contain a number of useful applications (Jöreskog and Sörbom, 1978, 1981).

5. CONCLUSION

Factor models, regression and correlation models, multiple indicator models, and second-order factor models, among others, can each be incorporated into the common framework of the covariance structure model. Yet, even with the power and flexibility of the covariance structure model, a number of limitations remain in the form of the model that we have presented. No provision has been made for comparing models across groups. For ML and GLS, all observed variables are assumed to be normally distributed, even though in practice dichotomous and ordinal variables are common. All models are assumed to be linear, and all constraints are either exclusion constraints or simple equality constraints. A number of researchers are working to extend the model along these lines. These include P. Bentler, K. Jöreskog, R. McDonald, B. Múthen, D. Sörbom, and D. Weeks. Advances are being published regularly in such journals as *Psychometrika, Multivariate Behavioral Research, British Journal of Statistical and Mathematical Psychology,* and *Econometrica.* While a detailed presentation of these important advances is beyond the scope of this monograph, a brief overview may help the reader to pursue them further.

Group comparisons. Fundamental research questions often involve testing for the presence of group differences. Does the effect of variable x on variable y differ for males and females? Are there differences between treatment and control groups? Extensions of the covariance structure model to deal with group comparisons have been made primarily by K. Jöreskog and D. Sörbom and are incorporated in LISREL IV and LISREL V (Jöreskog and Sörbom, 1978, 1981), although models by Bentler and Weeks (1979) and McDonald (1980) can also incorporate group differences. Analysis essentially involves simultaneously estimating covariance structure models for each group and comparing the effects of various constraints across groups. Applications of this approach include Sörbom (1982) and Magidson (1977).

Analysis of discrete data. For estimation by ML or GLS, variables are assumed to be approximately normal. If data are highly nonnormal, ULS estimation is suggested. If the variables are dichotomous or ordinal, and they can be assumed to reflect unobserved variables that are continuous, then polychoric, tetrachoric, and polyserial correlations (see Guilford and Fruchter, 1978) can be used as input for estimation by ULS. Jöreskog and Sörbom (1981: chap. IV) have demonstrated the application of this approach using LISREL V.

More complex structures and constraints. Earlier it was noted that in the most general case the covariance structure model can be considered as a model that explains covariances among observed variables as *any* function of a set of parameters (assuming the resulting model is identified). Such an extremely general model has been discussed by McDonald (1978) and Jöreskog (1978), although for practical purposes such general formulations cannot be applied. Somewhat less general models that have important practical applications have been developed by Bentler (Bentler, 1976; Bentler and Weeks, 1979) and McDonald (1980). The most important advantages are their ability to include a wider variety of constraints on parameters and to incorporate more complex measurement models.

Software for the covariance structure model. Each of these enhancements of the covariance structure model, as well as the basic covariance structure model, requires sophisticated software. Indeed, each breakthrough in the development of the covariance structure model has required a corresponding breakthrough in statistical software. Thus it is appropriate to conclude with a brief discussion of the programs that are available.

The first program developed for the covariance structure model was LISREL, written by K. G. Joreskog and M. van Thillo (1972) while at Educational Testing Service (ETS). The first version of this program is limited by a cumbersome set of control cards and the inability to compute standard errors. Its greatest advantages were being the first program available and being distributed without charge from ETS (although it is no longer available). A second version of LISREL, known as LISREL II, included the calculation of standard errors. The reader is warned that some copies of this version contain serious errors. The most recent version of LISREL, LISREL V, is distributed by

International Educational Services (1525 East 53rd Street, Suite 829, Chicago, IL 60615). It has the advantages of a simple control language for setting up many types of models, computation of ULS and ML estimates, estimation of standard errors, computation of modification index, the ability to compute start values, and features that allow group comparisons and analysis of ordinal data.

MILS is a program developed by Ronald Schoenberg at the National Institute of Mental Health and can be obtained free of charge by writing to R. Schoenberg (National Institutes of Health, Building 31, Room 4C11, Bethesda, MD 20205). This program computes standard errors, GLS and ML estimates, allows group comparisons, and extends the covariance structure model to include some multiplicative models. The greatest limitations of this program are that control cards are more difficult to code, initial start values are not computed, and some useful statistics are not conputed (e.g., the modification index). It has the advantage of computing statistics to assess the stability of the solution and standard errors of the indirect effects.

EQS is a program developed by Peter Bentler. This program includes many of the features of LISREL V, including the ability to do group comparisons, the calculation of initial start values, and ULS and ML estimation. In addition, EQS allows more complex constraints, computes GLS estimates, and estimates the more general covariance structure model presented by Bentler and Weeks (1979).

COSAN is a program developed by R. McDonald and described in McDonald (1980). In some respects this appears to be the most general of the available programs, allowing the users to write FORTRAN subroutines to estimate nonstandard models.

Given the complexity of the covariance structure model and the programs used to estimate it, it is extremely easy to incorrectly set up the control cards for the program being used. Not only does this result in incorrect estimates (the incorrectness of which may be difficult to detect), but it can be expensive. Experience suggests that correct models are far cheaper to estimate than incorrect models. Until a user is familiar with a package, it is important to reestimate models that have been published in the literature to ensure an adequate understanding of the program being used. The examples given above can be used for this purpose; necessary data are given in the Appendix.

APPENDIX: COVARIANCE/CORRELATION MATRICES FOR EXAMPLES

TABLE A

Correlations and Standard Deviations from Wheaton, Hennepin Sample (N = 603)

Variables	FSES	SES1	SES2	SES3	PSY2	PHY2	PSY3	PHY3
FSES	1.000							
SES1	0.257	1.000						
SES2	0.248	0.882	1.000					
SES3	0.264	0.827	0.863	1.000				
PSY2	-.072	-.166	-.096	-.089	1.000			
PHY2	-.038	-.104	-.016	-.030	0.454	1.000		
PSY3	-.092	-.120	-.088	-.006	0.526	0.247	1.000	
PHY3	-.013	-.139	-.011	-.005	0.377	0.309	0.549	1.000
S.D.	19.98	22.82	22.85	22.69	1.45	0.555	1.38	0.503

SOURCE: Blair Wheaton, "Sociogenesis of Psychological Disorder," *American Sociological Review* Vol. 43, pp. 383-403 (Table 2). Copyright ©1978 by American Sociological Association. Reprinted by permission.

VARIABLE IDENTIFICATIONS (followed by labels in Examples 3.2 and 4.1, respectively):

FSES: Father's socioeconomic status (ξ_1, x_1)
SES1: Socioeconomic status time 1 (η_1, y_1)
SES2: Socioeconomic status time 2 (η_2, y_2)
SES3: Socioeconomic status time 3 (η_4, y_5)
PSY2: Psychological disorders time 2 (η_3, y_3)
PHY2: Psychophysiological disorders time 2 (none, y_4)
PSY3: Psychological disorders time 3 (η_5, y_6)
PHY3: Psychophysiological disorders time 3 (none, y_7)

TABLE B
Data from Duncan, Haller, and Portes (N = 329)

Variables	R-IQ	R-PASP	R-SES	R-OASP	R-EASP	F-IQ	F-PASP	F-SES	F-OASP	F-EASP
R-IQ	1.0000									
R-PASP	0.1839	1.0000								
R-SES	0.2220	0.0489	1.0000							
R-OASP	0.4105	0.2137	0.3240	1.0000						
R-EASP	0.4043	0.2742	0.4047	0.6247	1.0000					
F-IQ	0.3355	0.0782	0.2302	0.2995	0.2863	1.0000				
F-PASP	0.1021	0.1147	0.0931	0.0760	0.0702	0.2087	1.0000			
F-SES	0.1861	0.0186	0.2707	0.2930	0.2407	0.2950	-.0438	1.0000		
F-OASP	0.2598	0.0839	0.2786	0.4216	0.3275	0.5007	0.1988	0.3607	1.0000	
F-EASP	0.2903	0.1124	0.3054	0.3269	0.3669	0.5191	0.2784	0.4105	0.6404	1.0000

SOURCE: O. D. Duncan, A. O. Haller, and A. Portes, "Peer Influences on Aspirations: A Reinterpretation," *American Journal of Sociology*, Vol. 74, pp. 119-137 (Table 1). Copyright © 1968 by The University of Chicago. Reprinted by permission of University of Chicago Press.

VARIABLE IDENTIFICATIONS (followed by labels in Examples 3.3 and 4.2 respectively):

R-IQ: Respondent's IQ (ξ_2 , x_2)

R-PASP: Respondent's parental aspirations (ξ_1 , x_1)

R-SES: Respondent's socioeconomic status (ξ_3 , x_3)

R-OASP: Respondent's occupational aspirations (none, y_2)

R-EASP: Respondent's educational aspirations (η_1 , y_1)

F-IQ: Friend's IQ (ξ_5 , x_5)

F-PASP: Friend's parental aspirations (ξ_6 , x_6)

F-SES: Friend's socioeconomic status (ξ_4 , x_4)

F-OASP: Friend's occupational aspirations (none, y_4)

F-EASP: Friend's educational aspirations (η_2 , y_3)

NOTES

1. The symbol "//" will be used to designate the end of an example.

2. More precisely, this condition means that **B** can be reduced to a triangular matrix by a suitable ordering of the equations.

3. The rank of a $(r \times c)$ matrix **X** is the size of the largest nonsingular submatrix of **X**. For example, the rank of

$$X = \begin{bmatrix} 1 & 2 \\ 3 & 4 \end{bmatrix}$$

is two since **X** is invertible; the rank of

$$X = \begin{bmatrix} 1 & 2 & 1 \\ 3 & 4 & 3 \\ 1 & 1 & 1 \end{bmatrix}$$

is two since **X** is not invertible, but

$$\begin{bmatrix} 1 & 2 \\ 3 & 4 \end{bmatrix}$$

is a (2×2) submatrix of X and is invertible.

4. Generalized least squares in this context refers to the single equation method of estimation sometimes referred to as Aitken's least squares.

5. This approach to estimation is different from that commonly found in the econometric literature. The ULS and GLS estimators do not correspond to any commonly found in that literature. ML corresponds to full information maximum likelihood. Malinvaud's (1970) approach to estimation is most similar to that presented here.

6. To say that a just-identified model has zero degrees of freedom is not to say that if a model has zero degrees of freedom it is just-identified. Unidentified models can have zero degrees of freedom.

7. For a more detailed treatment of direct, indirect, and total effects in causal modeling, see Wonnacott and Wonnacott (1981: 194-207), Alwin and Hauser (1975), and Duncan (1975).

8. While equality constraints are often justified in panel models, it may be unrealistic in this case. The Hennepin region was experiencing industrialization over the period from time 2 to time 3, but it was not from time 1 to time 2. Consequently, the stability of SES may have changed. I thank B. Wheaton for pointing this out. For purposes of illustration, however, it is useful to consider this constraint.

9. These results are not peculiar to the covariance structure model. They apply generally to problems of statistical inference.

10. Our specification differs from Wheaton's in two major respects. First, Wheaton assumes imperfect measurement of SES, while we assume perfect measurement. Second, we have assumed that the stability of SES over time is constant, while Wheaton did not (see Note 7). These modifications have been made for pedagogical reasons, rather than substantive reasons. The reader is encouraged to examine the original article (Wheaton, 1978).

REFERENCES

ALWIN, D. F. and R. M. HAUSER (1975) "The decomposition of effects in path analysis." American Sociological Review 40: 37-47.

ALWIN, D. F. and D. J. JACKSON (1982) "The statistical analysis of Kohn's measures of parental values," pp. 197-223 in H. Wold and K. Jöreskog (eds.) Systems Under Indirect Observation. New York: Elsevier North-Holland.

BAGOZZI, R. P. (1981) "An examination of the validity of two models of attitude." Multivariate Behavioral Research 16: 323-359.

BENTLER, P. M. (1980) "Multivariate analysis with latent variables: causal modeling." Annual Review of Psychology 31: 419-456.

————— (1976) "Multistructure statistical model applied to factor analysis." Multivariate Behavioral Research 11: 3-25.

————— D. G. BONETT (1980) "Significance tests and goodness-of-fit in the analysis of covariance structures." Psychological Bulletin 88: 588-606.

BENTLER, P. M. and D. G. WEEKS (1979) "Interrelations among models for the analysis of moment structures." Multivariate Behavioral Research 14: 169-185.

BIELBY, W. T., R. M. HAUSER and D. L. FEATHERMAN (1977) "Response errors of nonblack males in models of the stratification process." Journal of the American Statistical Association 72: 723-735.

BLAU, P. and O. D. DUNCAN (1967) American Occupational Structure. New York: John Wiley.

BOCK, R. D. and R. E. BARGMANN (1966) "Analysis of covariance structures." Psychometrika 31: 507-534.

BOOMSMA, A. (1982) "The robustness of LISREL against small sample sizes in factor analysis models," pp. 149-173 in H. Wold and K. Jöreskog (eds.) Systems Under Indirect Observation. New York: Elsevier North-Holland.

BROWNE, M. W. (1974) "Generalized least-squares estimators in the analysis of covariance structures." South African Statistical Journal 8: 1-24.

BYNNER, J. (1981) "Use of LISREL in the solution to a higher-order factor problem in a study of adolescent self-images." Quality and Quantity 15: 523-540.

DALTON, R. J. (1982) "The pathways of parental socialization." American Politics Quarterly 10: 139-157.

DUNCAN, O. D. (1975) Introduction to Structural Equation Models. New York: Academic.

————— A. O. HALLER, and A. PORTES (1971) "Peer influences on aspirations: a reinterpretation," pp. 219-244 in H. M. Blalock, Jr. (ed.) Causal Models in the Social Sciences. Chicago: Aldine.

FISHER, F. M. (1966) The Identification Problem in Econometrics. New York: McGraw-Hill.

FOX, J. (1980) "Effect analysis in structural equation models." Sociological Methods and Research 9: 3-28.

GOLDBERGER, A. S. (1971) "Econometrics and psychometrics: a survey of communalities." Psychometrika 36: 83-107.

————— O. D. DUNCAN (1973) Structural Equation Models in the Social Sciences. New York: Seminar.

GRAFF, J. and P. SCHMIDT (1982) "A general model for decomposition of effects," pp. 197-223 in H. Wold and K. Jöreskog (eds.) Systems Under Indirect Observation. New York: Elsevier North-Holland.

412

GUILFORD, J. P. and B. FRUCHTER (1978) Fundamental Statistics in Psychology and Education. New York: McGraw-Hill.

HANUSHEK, E. A. and J. E. JACKSON (1977) Statistical Methods for Social Scientists. New York: Academic.

JÖRESKOG, K. G. (1978) "Statistical analysis of covariance and correlation matrices." Psychometrika 43: 443-477.

——— (1974) "Analyzing psychological data by structural analysis of covariance matrices," pp. 1-54 in R. C. Atkinson et al. (eds.) Contemporary Developments in Mathematical Psychology, vol. 2. San Francisco: Freeman.

——— (1973) "A general method for estimating a linear structural equation system," pp. 85-112 in A. S. Goldberger and O. D. Duncan (eds.) Structural Equation Models in the Social Sciences. New York: Seminar.

——— A. S. GOLDBERGER (1972) "Factor analysis by generalized least squares." Psychometrika 37: 243-260.

JÖRESKOG, K. G. and D. SÖRBOM (1981) LISREL V. User's Guide. Chicago: National Educational Resources.

——— (1978) LISREL IV. User's Guide. Chicago: National Educational Resources.

——— (1976) LISREL III: Estimation of Linear Structural Equation Systems by Maximum Likelihood Methods. User's Guide. Chicago: International Educational Services.

JÖRESKOG, K. G. and M. van THILLO (1973) LISREL: A General Computer Program for Estimating a Linear Structural Equation System Involving Multiple Indicators of Unmeasured Variables. Research report 73-5. Department of Statistics, Uppsala University, Uppsala Sweden.

——— M. van Thillo (1972) LISREL: A General Computer Program for Estimating a Linear Structural Equation System Involving Multiple Indicators of Unmeasured Variables. Princeton, NJ: Educational Testing Service.

JUDD, C. M. and M. A. MILBURN (1980) "The structure of attitude systems in the general public." American Sociological Review 45: 627-643.

KENNY, D. A. (1979) Correlation and Causality. New York: John Wiley.

KEESLING, W. (1972) "Maximum likelihood approaches to causal flow analysis." Ph.D. dissertation University of Chicago.

KESSLER, R. C. and D. F. GREENBERG (1981) Linear Panel Analysis. New York: Academic.

KMENTA, J. (1971) Elements of Econometrics. New York: Macmillan.

KREHBIEL, K. and R. G. NIEMI (1982) "A new specification and test of the structuring principle." Paper delivered at the annual meeting of the American Political Science Association.

LEE, S. Y. (1977) "Some algorithms for covariance structure analysis." Ph.D. dissertation. University of California, Los Angeles.

LONG, J. S. (1981) "Estimation and hypothesis testing in linear models containing measurement error," pp. 209-256 in P. V. Marsden (ed.) Linear Models in Social Research. Beverly Hills, CA: Sage.

McDONALD, R. P. (1980) "A simple comprehensive model for the analysis of covariance structures: some remarks on applications." British Journal of Mathematical and Statistical Psychology 33: 161-183.

McDONALD, R. P. (1978) "A simple comprehensive model for the analysis of covariance structures." British Journal of Mathematical and Statistical Psychology 31: 59-72.

MAGIDSON, J. (1977) "Toward a causal model approach for adjusting for preexisting differences in the nonequivalent control group situation: general alternative to ANCOVA. Evaluation Quarterly 1: 399-419.

MALINVAUD, E. (1970) Statistical Methods of Econometrics. New York: Elsevier North-Holland.

SCHOENBERG, R. (1982) MILS: A Computer Program to Estimate the Parameters of Multiple Indicator Linear Structural Models. Bethesda, MD: National Institutes of Health.

SÖRBOM, D. (1982) "Structural equation models with structured means," pp. 183-195 in H. Wold and K. Jöreskog (eds.) Systems under Indirect Observation. New York: Elsevier North-Holland.

——— (1975) "Detection of correlated errors in longitudinal data." British Journal of Mathematical and Statistical Psychology 28: 138-151.

SULLIVAN, J. L. and S. FELDMAN (1979) Multiple Indicators. Beverly Hills, CA: Sage.

THEIL, H. (1971) Principles of Econometrics. New York: John Wiley.

WHEATON, B. (1978) "The sociogenesis of psychological disorder." American Sociological Review 43: 383-403.

——— B. MÚTHEN, D. ALWIN, and G. SUMMERS (1977) "Assessing reliability and stability in panel models," pp. 84-136 in D. R. Heise (ed.) Sociological Methodology, 1977. San Francisco: Jossey-Bass.

WILEY, D. E. (1973) "The identification problem for structural equation models with unmeasured variables," pp. 69-83 in A. S. Goldberger and O. D. Duncan (eds.) Structural Equation Models in the Social Sciences. New York: Seminar.

WONNACOTT, R. J. and T. H. WONNACOTT (1979) Econometrics. New York: John Wiley.

WONNACOTT, R. H. and R. J. WONNACOTT (1981) Regression: A Second Course in Statistics. New York: John Wiley.

Additional References

BENTLER, Peter M. (1989) EQS:Structural Equations Program Manual. Los Angeles: BMDP Software.

BOLLEN, Kenneth A. (1989) Structural Equations with Latent Variables. New York: John Wiley.

JÖRESKOG, Karl G., and D. SÖRBOM (1988) LISREL 7: A Guide to the Program and Applications. Chicago: SPSS, Inc.

INDEX

Adjusted correlation matrix:
definition of, 69, 150
Alpha factoring, 42, 63, 79, 81, 94-95,
121, 144
definition of, 69, 150
Anderson-Rubin criterion, 137
Assumption of factorial causation, 114
Assumption of parsimony, 114

Bartlett method, 137
Binormamin, 107
Biquartimax, 104
Biquartimin criterion, 106
definition of, 69, 151
BMD, 1, 5, 54, 56, 57, 65, 146
BMDP, 332
*British Journal of Mathematical and
Statistical Psychology,* 65, 146, 405

Canonical correlation analysis, 159, 230,
243
use of principal components in, 235-
237
Cattell's scree criterion, 190, 197
Causal analysis, 15
Characteristic roots, 168
Coefficient of determination, 14, 399
Cluster:
definition of, 228
Cluster analysis:
use of principal components in, 225,
228-229
COFAMM, 65, 128
Common factor, 79
definition of, 70, 151, 251
Common factor model:
variants in, 89-95
Common factors, 262, 335, 348
structural relations among, 255-257
Common part:
definition of, 70, 151
Communality, 89, 96, 206

definition of, 69, 151
Conference on Structural Equation
Models, 334
Confirmatory factor analysis, 3, 45, 79,
80, 117, 121, 123-128, 138, 145,
209-210, 247-328, 334
and measurement component of covariance structure model, 340, 346
comparing factor structures, 127-128
computer programs for, 128
definition of, 70, 151
introduction to, 114-128
one-group/population, 123-127
types of, 123
versus exploratory factor analysis,
251-255, 262
Confirmatory factor model, 254, 276,
331, 333, 378
advantage of over exploratory factor
model, 319-320
assessment of fit in, 301-319
basic components of, 258
crucial component of, 295
estimation of, 296-301
fitting functions used in, 297-300
flexibility of, 320
formal specification of, 265-269
identification in, 274-295
limitations of, 257, 321
multimethod-multitrait model, 269-273
software to estimate, 322-323
specification of, 258-274
summary of, 265
Correlation:
definition of, 70, 151
Correlation coefficient, 10
Correlation matrix, 42, 118, 143, 144,
158, 319
Correlation models, 405
Correspondence analysis, 239-242
application of for social scientists, 240
goal of, 239

COSAN, 407
Covariance:
  definition of, 70, 151
Covariance equation, 274
Covariance matrix, 42, 118, 123, 124,
  143, 144, 302, 319
  data collection/preparation of, 41-42
Covariance structure, 273-274, 344-346,
  355-356, 380-381
  derivation of from factor structure, 17-
  26
  uncertainties inherent to deriving factors from, 32-37
Covariance structure analysis, 45, 128,
  331, 333
  definition of, 70, 151
  See also LISREL model
Covariance structure model, 255, 256,
  329-413
  assessment of fit of, 395-403
  combined measurement component
    and structural component of, 340
  computer software for estimating,
    332, 365-366
  equations of, 341
  estimation of, 394-395
  identification in, 388-394
  mathematical model of, 378-380
  matrix equations of, 322-323
  measurement component of, 336, 345,
    346
  measurement model of, 341-347
  relationships between the two factor
    models in, 344
  software for, 406-407
  special cases of, 383-387
  specification of the measurement
    model of, 341-344
  structural component of, 339
  summary of, 379
  summary of measurement component
    of, 343
  summary of structural component of,
    349
  See also LISREL model
Covariance structure model software:
  assessing goodness of fit with, 369-
  371
  fitting functions used in, 366-367

Covariation:
  definition of, 70, 151
Covarimin, 106
  bias of, 107
  definition of, 70, 151
Cronbach's alpha, 131

Data matrix, 41
  entity mode of, 41
  variable mode of, 41
DATATEXT, 1
Determinant:
  definition of, 70, 151
Direct oblimin:
  definition of, 70, 151
Discriminant analysis, 159, 236
  use of principal components in, 230-
  231

Econometrica, 405
Econometrics, 331, 334
Educational and Psychological Measure-
  ment, 65, 146
Educational Testing Service, 334, 406
Efficient statistical estimation principle,
  92
Eigenequation, 85-87
Eigenvalue, 145, 168
  definition of, 70, 151
Eigenvalue criterion, 43, 110, 111-112.
  See also Kaiser criterion
Eigenvector, 168
  definition of, 70, 152
Empirical underidentification, 302, 303
EQS, 407
Equimax, 102, 104
  definition of, 70, 152
Error component:
  definition of, 71, 152
Error-free data:
  definition of, 70, 152
Expectation:
  definition of, 71, 152
Exploratory factor analysis, 3, 76, 79, 80,
  94, 114, 117, 121, 124, 125, 126,
  209, 249, 301, 309, 316
  definition of, 71, 152
  limitations of, 252
  steps in applying to actual data, 40, 78

versus confirmatory factor analysis,
251-255, 262
Exploratory factor model, 253, 260, 276,
280
identification in, 275

Factor analysis:
and accommodation of measurement
errors, 62-63
application of to error-free data, 45-53
as statistical technique, 50
computer programs to perform, 1, 5,
54-58, 65, 102
description of, 3-4, 251
distinguishing characteristic of, 16
doing, 4-5
factor loadings in, 15
fundamental concepts of, 6-16
fundamental postulates of, 37-40
introduction to, 1-74
level of measurement required for, 141
logical foundations of, 6-40
main objective of, 32, 207
major steps in actual, 40-45
practical issues and, 75-155
statistical methods of, 75-155
uses for, 4
Factor analysis problems, 32-37
competing causal structures, 35-37
one covariance structure/different factor loadings, 32
one covariance structure/varying number of factors, 32-35, 38
rotation, 32, 35
Factor analysis solutions:
obtaining, 40-65
obtaining through computer programs,
54-58
Factor analytic model, 381-382, 388,
395, 399
as measurement model, 335
degree of empirical confirmation for,
114-117, 120-121
number of empirical constraints implied by, 117-121
See also Factor models
Factor-based scales, 138-140
Factor extraction:
definition of, 71, 152

Factorial complexity:
definition of, 71, 152
Factorial determination:
definition of, 71, 152
Factoring methods, 62, 63
Factor loading:
definition of, 71, 152
unequal, 132-134
Factor models, 405
and covariance structures, 17-40
oblique, 22-26, 42
one-common, 47, 48
one-common with many variables, 17-
18
one-common with random measurement errors, 63
orthogonal, 19-21, 42
path model for five-variable, two-common, 19, 23
path model for multi-variable, one-
common, 17
path model for oblique two, 25
path model for six-variable, two
oblique, 46, 77
path model for two-common, 21
path model for two-variable, one-
common, 7, 8
two-common, 19-21, 22-26, 47, 48-
50, 95
Factor pattern matrix, 20, 101
definition of, 71, 152
Factor rotation, 213-214
Factors, 251
definition of, 9, 71, 152
extraction of initial, 42-43, 80-97
minor, 64
Factor scale construction, 44-45, 80, 128-
141
methods for, 128
reasons for, 128
Factor scales:
indeterminacy of, 129-134
reliability of, 129-132
univocal, 136
use of, 44-45
Factor score:
definition of, 71, 152
Factor structure matrix, 20
definition of, 71, 152

FORTRAN, 407
F-tests, 370

Generalized least squares (GLS), 298-
300, 302, 303, 304, 310, 317, 366,
367, 368, 369, 394, 395, 396, 397,
405, 406, 407
GIGO model, 252
Goodness of fit tests, Chi-square, 208,
301, 303-305, 307, 308, 309, 369-
370, 396, 397, 398
Gramian:
definition of, 71, 152
Graphic rotation procedure, 98-99

Identification, 274, 276-282, 347
conditions for, 282-289
covariance structure and, 277-281
estimation and, 274-276
of the confirmatory factor model, 274-
295
testing as necessary condition for, 282-
285
Image analysis, 95-97, 144
Imaging factoring, 42, 62, 81, 121
definition of, 71, 153
Indeterminancy, degree of, 131
Influential observations, 228
definition of, 225
International Educational Services, 407
Interpretability and invariance, criterion
of, 110, 113
Interpretation, 347

Jolliffe's criterion, 190, 197, 221

Kaiser's criterion, 43, 58, 64, 123, 172,
190, 197, 208
definition of, 71, 153
See also Eigenvalue criterion

Latent roots, 195, 239
Latent variable equation systems, 331.
See also LISREL model
Latent vectors, 168, 195, 239
Least-squares solution, 42, 79, 81, 83, 89-
90, 91, 93, 94, 110, 111
definition of, 72, 153
Linear combination:

definition of, 71, 153
Linear discriminant function analysis,
159, 230, 243
Linear structural relations model, 331.
See also LISREL model
Linear system:
definition of, 72, 153
LISREL (computer software), 250, 301,
322, 331, 334, 368, 372, 395, 405,
406, 407
manuals for, 405
LISREL model, 65, 255, 321, 334
applications of, 334
confirmatory factor analysis as preface to, 247-328
covariance structure model as introduction to, 329-413
Little Jiffy, 65

Mark IV, 65
Mathematical models, 335-341
Matrix, rank of, 28
Matrix algebra, 157, 249, 262
Maximum likelihood (ML), 209, 298,
299-300, 302, 303, 304, 310, 313,
317, 366, 367, 368, 369, 394, 395,
396, 397, 399, 405, 406, 407
Maximum likelihood procedure, 42, 43,
47, 79, 81, 94, 110, 111, 117, 120,
137, 144, 145, 210
definition of, 72, 153
solutions based on, 91-94
Maximum likelihood solution scales, 95
Measurement models, 257
Method factors, 306
MILS, 250, 322, 407
Minimum residuals method (Minres), 90,
297
Moments structure model, 331. See also
LISREL model
Monte Carlo experiments, 110, 113
definition of, 72, 153
Multicollinearity, 243
definition of, 215
Multicollinearity problems, 159, 209,
216, 242, 303
Multimethod-multitrait (MMMT) mod-
els, 257, 269, 270, 273, 306, 307
Multiple common factors, 136-138

Multiple indicator models, 257, 334, 405
Multiple regression analysis, 242, 338
Multivariate analysis procedures, 209
Multivariate Behavioral Research, 405

National Institute of Mental Health, 407
Nested models, 305-307
Normed variables, 10. *See also* Standardized variables
Number of factors problem, 109-113
    rules applied in addressing, 110-113

Oblimax:
    definition of, 72, 153
Oblimin, 106
    definition of, 72, 153
    solutions based on factor pattern with, 107-108
Oblique factors:
    definition of, 72, 153
Oblique rotation, 51, 79, 100
    definition of, 72, 153
    Direct Oblimin and, 44, 51
    factor loadings in, 106
    methods of, 105-108, 108
Orthogonal factors:
    definition of, 72, 153
Orthogonal rotation, 51, 79, 97, 101, 106, 198
    definition of, 72, 153
    methods of, 102-105
    OSIRIS, 1, 5, 54, 56, 57, 65, 146
    Varimax and, 44, 51, 52, 58, 199
Outlying observations, 226, 227, 228
    definition of, 225

Panel analysis, 338
Panel models, 334, 360
Path analysis, 338
Path coefficients, 15
Pearson's correlation coefficient. *See also* Product-moment correlation coefficient
Polychoric correlation, 321, 406
Polyserial correlation, 321, 406
Postulate:
    definition of, 37
    of factorial causation, 37, 39, 72, 154
    of parsimony, 38, 39, 73, 154

Principal axis factoring, 63, 89, 90, 91
    definition of, 72, 153
Principal components:
    decomposition of the variables and, 192-193
    decomposition properties of, 192-195
    definition of, 72, 154
    geometrical properties of, 173-192
    of patterned correlation matrices, 195-198
    other techniques related to, 237-242
    regression on, 215-216
    rotation of, 198-200
    spectral decomposition of correlation/covariance matrix and, 193-195, 242
    statistical independence of, 216
    use of in canonical correlation analysis, 235-237
    use of in cluster analysis, 225, 228-229, 242
    use of in discriminant analysis, 230-231
    use of to detect outlying and influential observations, 225-228, 242
    use of to select subset of variables, 200-204, 242
    uses of in regression analysis, 215-224
    See also Principal components analysis
Principal components analysis, 42, 79, 81, 82-85, 89, 157-245
    advantage of, 225
    basic concepts of, 165-173
    components scores, 140-141
    computer programs for, 184, 191
    description of, 157
    goal of, 157, 159, 171, 178
    iterative, 207-208
    parsimony and, 158
    principle use of, 171
    use of with other multivariate analysis procedures, 230-237, 242
    versus canonical correlation analysis, 159
    versus discriminant analysis, 159
    versus factor analysis, 87-89, 159, 205-214
    See also Principal components
Principal components regression, 216-219

420

Principal coordinate analysis, 237-239
  goals of, 239
Product-moment correlation coefficient,
  10. *See also* Pearson's correlation
  coefficient
PROMAX, 58
Promax oblique rotation, 108
Psychometrics, 331
Psychometric sampling, 121
Psychometrika, 65, 146, 405

Quartimax, 102, 103, 104, 106
  definition of, 73, 154
Quartimin, 106
  bias of, 107
  definition of, 73, 154

Random measurement error, 63
Rank of a matrix:
  definition of, 73, 154
Rank theorem, 30, 38-39, 59, 81, 117
  restricted use of, 31
Real data analysis:
  complications in, 58-64
Reference axes, 100-101
  definition of, 73, 154
  solutions based on, 105-107
Regression analysis, 15, 209
  uses of principal components in, 215-
  224
Regression models, 405
Reliability, degree of expected, 131
Reliability coefficient, 120
Residual-mean-square, 120
Root-staring criterion, 113
Rotation, 53
  approaches to, 98
  methods of, 44, 97-109
  of principal components, 198-200
  to a target matrix, 108-109
  to a terminal solution, 43-44
Rotation, problem of, 32, 39

Sampling adequacy:
  and empirical confirmation, 121-123
Sampling variability, 58-60, 134-136
  Bartlett's criterion, 135-136
  least squares criterion, 135
  regression method, 134-135

SAS, 1, 5, 54, 56, 57, 65, 146, 184, 332,
  372
Scale dependency, 297-298, 367
Scale indeterminancy, 289
  and setting a metric, 289-295
  identification and, 292-295
Scatterplots, 174
Scree graph, 172
Scree-test, 110, 112-113
  definition of, 73, 154
Second-order factor models, 334, 405
Selection bias, 60-62
Significance tests, 110-111, 112, 117,
  124, 144, 145
Simple structure, 99-100
  definition of, 73, 154
Simultaneous equation models:
  identification in, 275
Simultaneous equation systems, 334, 338
Spearman-Brown formula for reliability,
  131
Specification, 347
Specification searches, 308-317
  estimation and hypothesis testing, 310-
  317
Specific component:
  definition of, 73, 154
Spectral decomposition theorem, 217,
  239
SPSS, 1, 5, 54-56, 57, 65, 146, 184, 332
Standardization, 317-319
  of latent variables, 317
  of observed variables, 317
Standardized regression coefficients, 15
Standardized variables, 10. *See also*
  Normed variables
Statistical significance tests, 43
Structural equation model, 321, 331, 334,
  378, 382, 388, 395, 399
  as component of covariance structure
  model, 347-377
  estimation methods of, 372-377
  estimation of, 364-367
  flexibility of, 350
  full information maximum likelihood
  method of, 364, 365, 368, 372
  identification in, 358-364
  instrumental variables estimation
  method of, 364

interpreting structural coefficients of, 371-377
limited information maximum likelihood estimation method of, 364, 365, 372
mathematical model of, 347-355
multiple regression and, 350
panel model and, 350, 352
reduced form of, 355
simultaneous causality and, 352, 354-355
testing identification in, 361-364
testing order condition of, 358-359
testing rank and order conditions of, 360-361
testing rank condition of, 359-360
three-stage least squares estimation method of, 364, 372
two-stage least squares estimation method of, 364, 368-369, 372
types of, 356-357
use of in behavioral sciences, 337
use of in social sciences; 337
Structural equation model type 5, 357, 358
Structural equation model type 4, 357, 358
Structural equation model type 1, 357, 358
ordinary least squares estimation of, 364
Structural equation model type 6, 357, 358
Structural equation model type 3, 357, 358
ordinary least squares estimation of, 364
Structural equation model type 2, 357, 358
method of estimation of, 364
Substantive importance, criterion of, 110, 112
major disadvantage of, 112
SYSTAT, 191

Target matrix:
definition of, 73, 154
rotation to, 108-109
Tetrachoric correlation, 321, 406
Trait factors, 306

Unique component:
definition of, 73, 155
Unique factor:
definition of, 73, 155, 251-252
Unique factors, 262, 335, 348
Unweighted least squares (ULS), 297, 298, 300, 302, 310, 317, 366, 367, 368, 394, 395, 406, 407

Variables:
anti-image of, 95, 96
communality of, 15
definition of, 9
degree of factorial determination of, 18
endogenous, 347
exogenous, 347, 348, 350
factorial complexity of, 18
image of, 95
latent, 251, 334, 338, 347, 377
linear combinations of, 11-15
observed, 333, 334, 338, 347, 377
properties of, 9
types of, 10
uniqueness component of, 15
unobserved, 333, 334
Variance:
definition of, 73, 154
Variation:
definition of, 73, 154
Varimax, 102, 103, 104, 106, 213, 214
definition of, 73, 155
Vectors, 168

Wechsler Adult Intelligence Scale (WAIS), 158

Z-test, 308, 369, 396, 398

ABOUT THE EDITOR

MICHAEL S. LEWIS-BECK, Professor of Political Science at the University of Iowa, received his Ph.D. from the University of Michigan. Currently, in addition to editing the Sage monograph series *Quantitative Applications in the Social Sciences (QASS),* he is editor of the *American Journal of Political Science.* He has authored or coauthored numerous books and articles, including *Applied Regression: An Introduction, New Tools for Social Scientists: Advances and Applications in Research Methods, Economics and Elections: The Major Western Democracies,* and *Forecasting Elections.* In addition to his work at the University of Iowa, he has taught quantitative methods courses at the Inter-University Consortium for Political and Social Research (ICPSR) Summer Program at the University of Michigan and The European Consortium for Political Research (ECPR) Summer Program at the University of Essex. Also, he has held visiting appointments at the Catholic University in Lima, Peru, and the University of Paris I (Sorbonne) in France.

ABOUT THE AUTHORS

GEORGE H. DUNTEMAN is currently Chief Scientist at the Research Triangle Institute, where he is actively involved in applied research, primarily in the social and behavioral sciences. He has previously held research appointments at the Educational Testing Service and the U.S. Army Research Institute. He has also held assistant and associate professorships at the University of Rochester and the University of Florida, respectively. During the 1987-1988 academic year he was a Visiting Professor of Management in the Babcock School of Management at Wake Forest University where he taught the MBA core course in quantitative methods. Dr. Dunteman received his Ph.D. from Louisiana State University in industrial/organizational psychology with a minor in industrial engineering. He also has an M.S. degree from Iowa State University with a major in industrial psychology and a minor in statistics. His B.A. degree from St. Lawrence University is in sociology. He is currently on the editorial board of *Educational and Psychological Measurement* and had published widely in professional journals. He previously authored two books for Sage—*Introduction to Linear Models* (1984) and its companion volume, *Introduction to Multivariate Analysis* (1984).

JAE-ON KIM is Professor of Sociology and the director of the Center for Asian and Pacific Studies at the University of Iowa. He received his Ph.D. from the University of California, Berkeley. He specializes in political sociology, social inequality, quantitative methods, and East Asian societies. He has published articles in such journals as *American Journal of Sociology, American Political Science Review, American Sociological Review,* and *Social Forces,* and his books include *Equality and Political Participation: A Seven Nation Comparison* (1978), coauthored with Verba and Nie. His current projects are: (1) a comparative study of values of the three East Asian Societies—China, Japan, and Korea; (2) a study of natural experiments in party formation and electoral rules; (3) a joint project to establish general social survey for East Asian Societies; (4) a monograph on sensitivity analysis that deals with problems of imperfect data and incomplete theories in social science research.

J. SCOTT LONG is Professor and Chair of Sociology at Indiana University. His publications, focusing on issues of scientific productivity and academic careers, have appeared in *American Sociological Review, Social Studies of Science,* and *Sociological Methods and Research,* among others.

CHARLES W. MUELLER, Professor of Sociology at the University of Iowa, received his undergraduate education at Iowa State University and his Ph.D. from the University of Wisconsin, Madison. He has published articles on social stratification and quantitative methods in such journals as *American Sociological Review, Sociological Methods and Research,* and *Work and Occupations.* He is currently involved in research on organizational turnover and employee commitment and satisfaction.